JURISDICTIONAL ACCUMULATION

The majority of European early modern empires – the Castilian, French, Dutch, and English/British – developed practices of jurisdictional accumulation, distinguished by the three categories of extensions, transports, and transplants of authority. This book is concerned with various diplomatic and colonial agents which enabled the transports and transplants of sovereign authority. Through historical analyses of ambassadors and consuls in the Mediterranean based on primary and secondary material, and on the empires' Atlantic imperial expansions and conquests, the book makes a major analytical contribution to historical sociology. As an interdisciplinary exercise in conceptual innovation based on a Political Marxist framework and its concept of social property relations, the book goes beyond common binaries in both conventional and critical histories. The new concept of jurisdictional accumulation brings ambassadors, consuls, merchants, and lawyers out of the shadows of empire and onto the main stage of the construction of early modern international relations and international law.

MAÏA PAL is Senior Lecturer in International Relations, Department of Social Sciences, Oxford Brookes University.

JURISDICTIONAL ACCUMULATION

An Early Modern History of Law, Empires, and Capital

MAÏA PAL
Oxford Brookes University

CAMBRIDGE
UNIVERSITY PRESS

CAMBRIDGE
UNIVERSITY PRESS

University Printing House, Cambridge CB2 8BS, United Kingdom

One Liberty Plaza, 20th Floor, New York, NY 10006, USA

477 Williamstown Road, Port Melbourne, VIC 3207, Australia

314–321, 3rd Floor, Plot 3, Splendor Forum, Jasola District Centre, New Delhi – 110025, India

79 Anson Road, #06–04/06, Singapore 079906

Cambridge University Press is part of the University of Cambridge.

It furthers the University's mission by disseminating knowledge in the pursuit of education, learning, and research at the highest international levels of excellence.

www.cambridge.org
Information on this title: www.cambridge.org/9781108497206
DOI: 10.1017/9781108684538

First published 2021

A catalogue record for this publication is available from the British Library.

ISBN 978-1-108-49720-6 Hardback

To the renegades that keep the law moving

Une once de jurisdiction vaut plus qu'une livre d'or

(An ounce of jurisdiction is worth more than a pound of gold)
motto of a fifteenth-century jurist from Visé, a town at the Flanders–Wallonia crossroads (in de Schepper, 2007: 187)

CONTENTS

ACKNOWLEDGEMENTS

History matters in the face of today's list of crises, especially when it consists in attempts to break temporal and spatial categories, and to resist the persistent myth of capitalism's inevitability. For this task, the dialectical method of historical materialism rejects historical starting points that separate a so-called materialism of the present from a so-called idealism of the past. Instead, this project assumes the impossibility of drawing clear lines between past and present, materialism and idealism, and targets histories of capitalism that structurally reproduce these separations, as well as those which fall into the opposite trap of combining any past with any present.

Still, theoretical answers do not always cut through the social historian's anxieties generated by her inevitable distancing from contemporary problems. Thankfully, if long-scale historical projects have become rarer in an academic market hungry for quick fixes and trendy soundbites, they remain particularly worth cherishing as they provide opportunities for the researcher to be materially grounded by the large number of people that she meets, shares with, learns from, riles against, and which all deserve acknowledging here. Many names will be missing below since I began working on this project over twelve years ago, and I hope all those I cannot thank here will nevertheless know that I am grateful to them, especially the community of students and staff at the University of Sussex from 2007 to 2013 while this project emerged as a doctoral thesis. From this community, a special thank you to Benno Teschke and Beate Jahn for the standard of scholarship they inspired and their supervisory attention to detail, as well as to Tarik Kochi and Susan Marks as astute and generous examiners.

Thanks to my Oxford Brookes University students, especially on the 'Law, Empires, and Revolutions' module, whose questions helped me make the long jump from doctoral thesis to book typescript. Thanks to friends and colleagues Doerthe Rosenow, Chris Hesketh, Tina Managhan, Victoria Browne, Ingrid Medby, Dana Mills, Lucy Ford,

Stephen Hurt, Gary Browning, and Abbey Halcli. Special thanks to Molly Cochran for always providing such astute advice and support and whose mentorship I am so grateful for. I also want to thank the department for granting me research leave to finish the typescript.

In France, many thanks to Jörg Ulbert for his time and expertise on consuls, and to Sylvie Drago and Patrick Boulanger at the Archives de la Chambre de Commerce et d'Industrie de Marseille. Thanks to the movement of the Gilets Jaunes – Les Rudistes, Joëlle, Nine, Karine, Michelle, Jean-Marc, Manu, Tristan – for giving me hope and teaching me new tricks, both essential to finishing the project during the autumn–winter of 2018–2019.

I was lucky to present parts of this work to various audiences over the years, and most recently at the Centre for Critical International Law at the University of Kent, the Socialist Theory and Movements seminar at the University of Glasgow, the Centre for Advanced International Theory at the University of Sussex, and the Diplomacy in the Early Modern Period Network at the University of Oxford.

Thanks to all the comrades along the way, during the London 'Historical Materialism' conferences, and especially the HM editorial board for your friendship and time off for the book. Special thanks to the Political Marxism research group at the University of Sussex – especially Sam Knafo, Julian Germann, Kamran Matin, Javi Moreno Zacarés, Pedro Dutra Salgado, and especially Benno Teschke for the continued support and suggestions. Thanks to the broader Marxist and critical community for answering my questions and challenging me with your own – Charlie Post, David McNally, Spencer Dimmock, Neil Davidson (RIP), Grietje Baars, Pepjin Brandon, Mike Zmolek, Steve Miller, Jessica Evans, Rob Knox, Tor Krever, Alex Anievas, Rose Parfitt, Luis Eslava, Illan Rua Wall, Eric Loefflad, Ntina Tzouvala, Umut Öszu, Dan Margolies, Will Hanley, and crucially Heide Gerstenberger and Richard Drayton for their particularly stimulating suggestions. I also want to thank Iver Neumann and Halvard Leira, as well as Erica Heinsen-Roach for their generosity in answering my obscure queries.

At Cambridge University Press, a big thank you to Tom Randall and Claire Sissen, to the anonymous reviewers, and especially to copy-editor Martin Barr for his excellent work in difficult circumstances and help in making the production process a human one. In Oxford, thank you to Eddie Keene and Hamish Scott for their suggestions, generosity, and for sparking my burgeoning passion for social aspects of early modern diplomacy. Claire Vergerio: thank you for providing intellectual and moral support and helping me strategically navigate through Oxford's libraries and coffee shops. Samentha Goethals, Miriyam Aouragh, Arthur Duhé, Nancy Lindisfarne, João Henrique Roriz, Geraldine Delestienne: thank you for being particularly inspiring renegades.

Finally, infinite thanks to my extended families in the UK, USA, and France – coucou Héloïse ! – for always being there in spite of my absences. Thanks to my parents Marie-José Sat, Vincent Pal, and Peter Vollhardt, for all the privileges, love, and support that made this project possible. Jérémie Judek, merci pour tous les moments de joie et d'amour, et pour me rappeler de prendre le temps du temps.

Introduction

Jurisdiction, Empires, and Capital: Stories of Accumulation

In the Eastern and Southern ports of the early modern Mediterranean – in Algiers, Tunis, Tangier, Tripoli in Libya, and on the Levantine shores of the Ottoman Empire – foreign merchants and sailors were forbidden to frequent the ale houses of the port in which they disembarked. In exchange, they were allowed 'national' ale houses, a nation in this case referring to the local community or colony of merchants and residents belonging to a particular country and present in a foreign port or trading city. These ale houses were privileges attached to each nation's consulate, which consisted in an office run by a consul as the representative, judge, and solicitor for the nation's trading and residential affairs.

The stories, disputes, and negotiations that must have been conducted within the confines of these ale houses – between merchants, captains, factors, and sailors from Marseille, London, Copenhagen, Amsterdam, Malta, Venice, Livorno, and other major trading cities – remain today elusive. This is a pity, since they would undoubtedly help us to better understand early modern empires and the legal mechanisms developed to secure and expand trading interests on the North African and Levantine coast.

If the specific role of foreign ale houses in the early modern Mediterranean is not the subject of this book, this example illustrates the types of spaces and institutions that this book is concerned with. These spaces or institutions could be considered, albeit anachronistically, as extraterritorial; or perhaps as 'preparing men's minds to accept [the] extraordinary fiction' of extraterritorial sovereignty (Mattingly, 1955: 242). In other words, this book is concerned with how certain jurisdictional actors in certain spaces and institutions shaped key political principles and mechanisms of early modern legal orders, principles and mechanisms that remain present or resonate in our contemporary order.

Yet when referring to such spaces, Mattingly emphasises the role of embassy chapels in Northern European cities such as London, Paris, and Amsterdam, as the first 'little islands of alien sovereignty' (1955: 244).

These little islands enabled by embassy chapels became essential staging posts for the emergence of permanent ambassadorial practices and territorially defined states. Thus, Mattingly's account of extraterritoriality became highly influential in the discipline of International Relations (IR) for explaining the emergence of modern territorial sovereignty (Ruggie, 1993).[1]

In contrast, this study explores a range of other spaces in different institutional and geographical settings, such as the ports of the Mediterranean and the colonies of the Americas. These characterised the jurisdictional complexities of diplomatic and economic relations between leading European empires and contest the dominant focus on embassy chapels as marking the invention of extraterritoriality and considered necessary to the emergence of territorial sovereignty.

Consular establishments are some of these particularly neglected spaces in international historiography. Ports and consulates were frequented by individuals of a much lower social order, status, and function than ambassadors and with a less direct relation to the historically fetishised institution of the modern state. The neglect of consuls also relates to the lack of consideration of socio-economic factors in grand diplomatic and international relations narratives. This historiographical lacuna is nevertheless surprising, since if any place were to be significant for illustrating extraterritorial fictions, the ports of the Mediterranean with consular representatives – as well as most ports subject to colonial and imperial expansion – may be more obvious candidates than embassy chapels in a few cities in Northern Europe mostly witness to confessional struggles.

These ports were characterised by multiple overlapping and conflicting jurisdictional arrangements involving a wide range of commercial, political, religious, linguistic, cultural, and judicial encounters. A range of professions frequented consulate ports and, in some cases, needed authorisations to do so – merchants obviously, but also priests and other ecclesiastics, artisans such as bakers, hairdressers, servants, tailors, cooks, clerks, surgeons. The variety of these migrants indicates the broader

[1] The discipline of International Relations will be referred to as 'IR', whereas the expression 'international relations' will be retained to refer to the ensemble of social relations that cross the boundaries of sovereign or otherwise independent political entities and social groupings. As is broadly accepted from its wide usage, the meaning of the term 'international' in this expression has gone beyond the actual historical limits of its components (i.e. it is not limited to relations between nation states, *stricto sensu*, but equates instead to transhistorical terms such as 'intersocietal' or 'trans-societal').

social impact these mixed jurisdictional spaces had on the everyday lives and mobility of local populations as well as on people in their home destinations.

If the comparison between consular ale houses and embassy chapels remains anecdotal, and perhaps amusing, it nevertheless points to a key question about the relation between ambassadorial and consular spaces. How did ambassadors and consuls differently relate to the royal, commercial, and imperial elites and institutions they depended upon and were used to enhance and enrich? Answering this question reveals something new about the history of extraterritoriality and early modern empires. Exploring the relations between European ambassadors and consuls, and other jurisdictional actors used for imperial expansion, opens a window into the world of jurisdictional accumulation, a world with a much wider range of early modern jurisdictional spaces and actors. These spaces and actors have been unduly neglected as factors of large-scale social change.

Specifically, jurisdictional accumulation is a conceptual device that reveals how certain actors of imperial expansion were extending, transporting, and transplanting the authority of their sovereign, while also, when possible, improving their own social status. Jurisdictional accumulation thus refers to both the accumulation of claims, rights, titles and functions, and the accumulation of revenue from those legal requests and privileges. It emphasises the difficulties in dissociating – for these actors and during this period – the accumulation of property, jurisdiction, and wealth.

This analysis helps to overcome some of the puzzles and problems of periodising early modern extraterritoriality by emphasising jurisdiction instead of territoriality or sovereignty as major drivers of early modern social change, as argued in conventional narratives following classic scholars such as Mattingly. Jurisdictional accumulation captures a new narrative on the 'social property relations' of early modern empires and capital, notably through the social origins and legal means of settlement, negotiation, and trade of various sub-sovereign diplomatic and imperial actors.

The following introduces the problem of early modern extraterritoriality, followed by the context, argument, and methods used for tackling this problem. Before closing with an outline of the book's chapters, this introductory one defines the project's three main axes: law, empires, and capital. In particular, it discusses why we need to separately conceptualise law in terms of jurisdiction, why we need another book on early modern

European empires, and why we need to include capital from a Marxist perspective in a historical sociology of international law.

The Problem of Early Modern Extraterritoriality

Generally, extraterritoriality is understood as a form or practice of jurisdiction associated with the assertion of authority beyond the territorial limits of that authority. History has produced many cases and types of extraterritorial jurisdiction. Some historians trace a common thread from ancient treaties in the Mediterranean basin to early modern capitulations in the Ottoman Empire, and to European, American, and Russian extraterritorial courts in late-nineteenth-century Middle East, Asia, and Africa.

In the twentieth century, and most affirmatively since the 1980s, extraterritoriality has reappeared as part of a transnational regulatory boom mostly driven by acts and disputes emerging from the foreign application of United States (US) law and thus characteristic of US hegemony (Raustiala, 2009; Ryngaert, 2015; Putnam, 2016). However, it is also a practice developed by various other states and organisations. Considered a legal principle used in juridical arguments, as well as a geopolitical device or practice (Haskell, 2019), extraterritoriality affects legal domains of commercial law or antitrust, intellectual property, investment, anti-corruption, criminal or environmental law, as well as human rights. It raises issues concerning the responsibility of states under international law and creates various types of disputes in the legal and diplomatic realms.

This latest rise of extraterritorial arguments and practices has encouraged legal historians to look at the various appearances of this concept in international history. Legal histories of extraterritoriality have largely focused upon its various manifestations in the 'semi-sovereign' states and colonies of the late-nineteenth century, where it was used by the Great Powers – France, Britain, Germany, the United States, Russia – as a powerful tool of imperial domination through the establishment of extraterritorial courts and unequal treaties. The nineteenth century witnessed the emergence and widespread usage of the term 'extraterritoriality', also known as 'exterritoriality' in this period, leading to the most substantial, global, and structuring manifestations and effects of this practice.[2]

[2] For a recent collection of historical studies on extraterritoriality, see Margolies *et al.* (2019).

This book contrasts with this focus on nineteenth-century extraterritoriality by expanding on the few exceptions that have studied its early modern wider effects, and contesting the conventional narrative offered by diplomatic history. According to the latter, early modern extraterritoriality has mostly been associated with the emergence of ambassadorial privileges roughly from the sixteenth century onwards. This highlights a crucial neglect in histories of international law and international relations concerning the role of consular jurisdiction and other jurisdictional practices of the early modern world. This neglect questions the role attributed to the shift from personal to territorial concepts of sovereignty, considered central to the construction of the European qua international legal order through the evolving practices of ambassadorial immunity in Northern Europe. In effect, a wider set of often maritime and more 'private' practices of extraterritoriality and jurisdictional extensions of authority, in Southern Europe and across the Atlantic, have been excluded or left to the margins of international history.

Exploring extraterritoriality from a historical sociology perspective allows us to retrieve these practices and also ask the question of continuity and rupture in long-term perspectives of international legal orders. To what extent do the different forms of extraterritoriality (e.g. consular jurisdiction, treaties, settlements, ambassadorial privileges, courts) differ in their use by geopolitical actors? Who are the actors that drive these processes in different historical periods? And, finally, what do these processes tell us about the standard drivers of international change in the early modern period, such as states, monarchies, cities, ports, empires, and their dynastic, military, and commercial elites?

Context and Argument

To guide us through these questions, the stars have recently aligned for an in-depth and secondary study of early modern imperial and jurisdictional history. In the last few decades, social sciences scholarship has significantly turned its attention to the topic of early modern imperial expansion. Some would even call it the 'golden age' for studies of empires (Lachmann, 2018: 1127). Simultaneously, after being mostly inactive during the second half of the twentieth century, the field of international legal history has been significantly prolific in the last two decades. Many recent contributions reflect a broad interdisciplinarity in the social sciences in terms of method, theoretical concepts, and geographical focus.

There is also an increasingly undisputed consensus to revisit the near exclusive focus on territorial states as key drivers of international legal change, which has led to an increase of legal histories of early modern and modern empires. This turn is finally influencing the IR discipline (Pitts, 2018; Wallenius, 2019), which aside from a few exceptions (Ruggie, 1993; Keene, 2002; Cutler, 2003; Raustiala, 2009), remained limited in its understanding and incorporation of legal history.

This book is inspired by various counter-narratives to the classic rise of the European qua international legal order, as well as by a revival of Marxist historical sociology and of critical histories and theories of international law. It focuses on the study of European imperial practices by taking up the challenge of revealing one of the underlying modes of expansion that drove Europeans into a world they legally colonised and exploited.

This mode or set of practices is innovatively called 'jurisdictional accumulation', a new concept developed by this project, which distinguishes the following narrative from the classic story of European expansion by revealing the practices of a neglected set of sub-sovereign actors and processes in the history of international relations and international law. These consist of, for the most part, ambassadors, consuls, lawyers, parliamentarians, magistrates, theologians, certain clergy, and merchants. Their practices are set in the context of their social origins – and class – and their role in shaping new legal institutions and mechanisms of imperial ordering and expansion.

The key argument of the book is, most simply, that the majority of European early modern empires – the Castilian, French, Dutch, and English/British – are best characterised as developing practices of jurisdictional accumulation. These practices are distinguished by the three categories of extensions, transports, and transplants of authority, and this book is mostly concerned with various diplomatic and colonial agents which enabled the transports and transplants of their sovereign's authority. Through these historical analyses, the book consists in two major analytical contributions for the field of historical sociology. The first is an interdisciplinary exercise in conceptual innovation; the second, a mix of methodological angles. These intertwined contributions enable us to go beyond common binaries (structure–agency, internal–external, specificity–similarity, territory–sovereignty) in both conventional and critical histories of international relations and international law.

IR theory has assumed that early modern jurisdictional complexity naturally led to Westphalian modernity – and how the post-Westphalian period of so-called absolute sovereign territoriality and state formation emerged to resolve the overly personal forms and jurisdictional overlaps of early modern polities. Instead, jurisdictional accumulation emphasises the constitutive, *sui generis*, and self-sustaining character of early modern modes of jurisdictional expansion. It therefore breaks up the historical link between jurisdiction and sovereignty accepted by conventional IR theory as a given or natural cause of the origin of territoriality.

In sum, jurisdictional accumulation is a device that breaks apart the linear and Eurocentric histories of territorial sovereignty that continue to dominate IR, by revealing the extent to which the early modern world was 'up for grabs' and the myriad legal ways imperial actors 'grabbed' it.

A crucial implication of dislodging the role of states and territorial sovereignty as key drivers of social change in the early modern period is the focus on empires. In addition, the focus on jurisdictional accumulation shows how the period's multiple jurisdictional claims reflect each empire's specific social property relations. These contested structures arise from struggles in their respective local contexts, as well as from struggles arising from the attempts to conquer and contain foreign and indigenous social property relations. Thus, social property relations are at the basis of this study, and inform the typology of jurisdictional accumulation in various ways.

Extensions of authority concern all empires and refer to the legal incorporation of land (and the people living on that land) that is contiguous or internal to the expanding authority. Extensions include the colonial expansion of England into the British Isles, the attempts at unification of Iberia's fragmented kingdoms or *reinos*, the various laws and collaborations pursued by the French monarchy to centralise and expand royal authority, and the struggles of the Dutch provinces to emerge as a confederation recognised by other European powers.

These cases of extension are discussed in Chapter 3 focused on social property relations, but the category of extensions remains secondary to the main focus of this project which is the distinction between transports and transplants of authority. These consist in the diplomatic and colonial practices of expansion that were deployed beyond the internal and immediate frontier zones and borders of each empire, and which therefore presented each empire with specific difficulties and opportunities related to jurisdictional incorporation and more innovative extraterritorial strategies.

Transplants of authority consist in conquests of people and territory, by a sovereign and its representatives, through the creation and development of jurisdictional institutions that organically develop (as hybrid social property relations) in their colonial setting. These practices rely on the attribution of jurisdictional subjectivities to indigenous groups and to their use of judicial institutions, based on a broad meaning of jurisdiction or *dominium* as ownership *and* rule over both people and territory. The classic case of transplanting authority is illustrated by the Castilian Empire in the 'New World'.

In contrast, the French, Dutch, and English empires are mostly characterised by *transports* of authority, that is the outsourcing of the sovereign authority to conquer, own, and trade over land and resources. This outsourcing is mostly driven by commercial interests and by chartered companies and settlers. It refers to a restricted conception of *dominium* focused on ownership or property – rather than rule – for which the subjugation of people through jurisdictional incorporation is not the primary means and aim of colonisation.

These distinctions are analytical generalisations and therefore have important exceptions and nuances. Specifically, they overlap across empires when trying to distinguish between their use of diplomatic actors. The aristocratisation of French ambassadors (largely copied by Castile) and the French monarchy's development of a unique consular model (relentlessly used to control and regulate most effectively its agents in the Mediterranean) are better understood as *transplants* of authority. French consuls had wide jurisdictional functions and were direct representatives of the king. They were political and economic actors, which shaped French mercantilism in the Mediterranean as a jurisdictional mode of production. They created organic colonies and transplanted the authority of their sovereign in ways that also escaped the jurisdiction of their sovereign and created their own zones of influence. Moreover, their neglect in histories of diplomacy and international law contributed to the separation of political and economic spheres, as well as to the shaping of Christian and non-Christian legal zones of exclusion.

However, the deployment of ambassadors and consuls by the English and Dutch empires is better understood instead as *transports* of authority. Although these actors played important roles, they were less jurisdictionally autonomous, and played different functions for their sovereigns and provinces than French consuls and ambassadors, as is seen through the role of trading companies in their appointment and regulation, in these actors' distinct social origins (less aristocratic and emerging from gentry and merchant class), and through each case's social property relations shaping those functions according to specific limitations and motivations.

If social property relations are considered analytically primary and help to explain the specificities of each case, they do not reveal a logic of causality that can explain similar outcomes. For example, although the French, English, and Dutch are analysed as being characterised by transports of authority in terms of their strategies for colonial jurisdictional accumulation, they each had different social property relations that eventually led to this outcome. Moreover, the French case is the most complex in this typology because it is characterised as transplanting authority through its diplomatic actors in the Mediterranean and transporting its authority through companies and settlers in North America. The point here is not to provide a theory of jurisdictional accumulation, with a clear pattern of causes and outcomes, but to reveal different paths and transitions, entanglements, and encounters based on a methodological choice for understanding different movements of jurisdictional expansion according to the method of outward internalism.

Simply qualifying the early modern age as jurisdictional is already widely accepted and present in the historical literature. However, the contribution of this project is first to analytically situate and develop this concept of jurisdiction as a *constitutive* and independent factor, rather than as an adjective or addendum to existing institutions and actors; and, second, to focus on *practices* rather than ideas of jurisdictional accumulation. Most literature on the history of international law has focused on doctrine and fails to satisfactorily link social, geopolitical, and doctrinal factors. Instead, this study only refers to doctrine when it is relevant to these practices or if it concerns specific jurisdictional debates. For example, in the case of the role of the Iberian kingdoms in the history of international law, doctrine arguably played a more important role for practice than in other cases and is therefore an unavoidable part of this story.

The book's central argument has thus two major implications. On the one hand, mapping 'the jurisdictional' onto the existing typology of modes (i.e. feudalism, mercantilism, absolutism, capitalism, but also more specific types such as the dynastic, agrarian, or theological) is an additional way to understand the complex processes that shape early modern inter- and trans-societal relations (i.e. between and across various polities and jurisdictional borders). In other words, the argument brings specificity and complexity to the early modern period. On the other hand, it helps to better understand a key similarity between

European empires and regimes of social property relations overlapping between different modes, without claiming strict causal and linear links between these modes, and in particular between mercantilist, jurisdictional, and capitalist accumulation. The aim is to raise the question of this distinct set of practices as a significant characteristic of early modern imperial expansion, list some of the key practices of jurisdictional accumulation, and give a general introductory picture of its contribution to histories of international law and international relations.

In other words, the key analytical payoff of the argument is to incorporate these empires' internal specificities without completely losing sight of external similarities that enable a wider picture of the period's fundamental transformations. This avoids the vague and inadequate notions of the 'international' and the 'global' to describe the early modern period and establishes jurisdiction and accumulation as inescapable but contextualised and constitutive terms for early modern imperialism.

Methods

The research involves a mix of primary and secondary research methods developed in the context of a historical sociology approach. This implies a comparative framework and the search for historical patterns and ruptures drawn from a sample of in-depth cases. These are set in a long-term and large-scale narrative of the development of extraterritoriality focused on sub-sovereign actors grounded in each empire's key sets of contested social property relations.

The book thus defends an analytically driven approach to international history without losing sight of the diverse, diffuse, specific, and unintended conditions of social relations. This analysis is open-ended and theoretically inquisitive rather than definitive and targeted at one specific disciplinary audience or theoretical debate. It is primarily drawn from historical materialism but also acknowledges the need for more methodological positioning and questioning of the Marxist approach to historical sociology. It draws from critical histories of international law and from new histories of empire and diplomacy to enrich this approach.

The different research methods applied in this book consist, first, in a review of secondary sources on the emergence and role of extraterritoriality in the history of modern international relations and international law. This analysis – introduced in Chapter 1 and developed in the substantial Chapters 3–7 – reveals an early modern international history of actors competing and collaborating for jurisdictional authority, that is rights, titles, and functions, as well as sovereigns competing and collaborating for the determination of overlapping or separate orders and domains of jurisdictional activity. These practices can be distinguished as transplants, transports, and extensions of authority. This typology helps to compare a set of criss-crossing similarities and differences that characterise different strategies emanating from Castile, the Dutch Republic, England, and France.

Second, the book builds a conceptual framework to compare these multifaceted practices of extraterritoriality across the four cases. Jurisdictional accumulation is proposed as a concept building on international legal histories but grounded in a historical materialist approach based on the concept of contested social property relations. This conceptual framework is especially important since the political economy of both extraterritoriality and diplomatic actors has been largely ignored.

Third, the book engages in a selective examination of primary sources to test a key argument emerging from the secondary comparative analysis, that is the contrast between the aristocratisation of French ambassadors and the deployment of a unique consular model as two strategies of French jurisdictional accumulation. The cases of ambassadors and consuls are at the heart of the book's research problem (i.e. the role of extraterritoriality in shaping territorial sovereignty and its specific diplomatic context). These cases are thus investigated more thoroughly than other practices of jurisdictional accumulation, and the questions posed in this case were: how do consular and ambassadorial strategies of expansion relate and what type of jurisdictional accumulation can they be identified as?

This research was conducted in the archives of the Chambre de Commerce et d'Industrie de Marseille (CCIM), which contain rich and underexplored resources for early modern Mediterranean diplomatic and maritime history. The primary research (discussed in Chapter 5) looks at a selection of correspondence and memoranda between royal authorities, the Chambre de Commerce de Marseille (CCM) – as it was called in the seventeenth century – and French merchants in the Mediterranean. The selection is concerned with the French embassy in Istanbul from the mid- to late- seventeenth century, and more specifically with the issue of the replacement of the ambassador with a consul or resident in the 1660s.[3] This unique but illustrative case reveals the potential of comparing

[3] French archival sources and much of the secondary literature uses Constantinople to designate the city of Istanbul post-1453. However, since Ottomans already used the name

ambassadorial and consular practices as contested yet intertwined jurisdictional forms of accumulation. Specifically, it shows how Colbert and the CCM were both keen to maintain Mediterranean diplomacy as consular rather than ambassadorial, and points to the development of contrasting yet complementary strategies of diplomatic deployment in Northern and Southern Europe as transplants rather than transports of authority.

Aside from this specific foray into primary material, the book's general reliance on secondary research inevitably runs into various limitations. The first concerns the four empires chosen for this project, and which are discussed only in terms of their Mediterranean, Southern, and Northern American contexts.[4] The Mediterranean is an area of focus particularly justified by the terms of the enquiry, that is achieving a better understanding of extraterritoriality in the early modern period. This area of English Empire remains understudied, as is the case for the role of the Dutch in the region. If the French Empire's history in the Mediterranean benefits from a wider scholarship, albeit less from an anglophone perspective, this book contributes to this history by comparing the French jurisdictional approach to that of the English, Dutch, and Iberian empires.

Another important limitation concerns the analysis of the Dutch case, which consequently emerges as more peripheral in the overall project. This peripheral status does not necessarily reflect its comparative

Istanbul in the early modern period, it is more historically accurate to use this term, even though it was not officially and internationally recognised until the twentieth century.

4 A number of early modern empires are not dealt with in this study, such as most importantly the Portuguese, Chinese, Japanese, Persian, and Mughal empires. The Ottoman Empire is also only referred to in the context of the European empires under scrutiny. This is justified by the initial aim of this study in addressing the classic narrative of diplomacy, international law, and international relations based on the European cases, and the absence or relative lack of information about diplomatic institutions in these other cases (e.g. the Ottoman Empire did not establish permanent consuls or ambassadors until the late eighteenth–nineteenth centuries, in spite of hosting Europeans from the seventeenth century). The Eurocentric consequences of this choice are discussed in more detail in Chapter 2. However, considering this study also develops a methodology for analysing the jurisdictional nature of early modern empires, it also remains open to whether further projects might find the framework of jurisdictional accumulation relevant for these other contexts, as it remains committed to being based on each case's social property relations. Their exclusion is also justified by a lack of sources and texts on which a secondary analysis such as the following could satisfactorily rest. Moreover, this book limits itself to colonies in the Mediterranean, North and South America, for reasons of clarity, coherence, and availability of secondary sources.

historical importance, even in terms of jurisdictional practices. The major risk is to accentuate already existing problematic assumptions due to the neglect of this case in historiography. However, for now, analysis of this case will have to remain limited because of the relative lack of research regarding the Dutch Empire's sociolegal history, the complexity and diversity of its various provinces, and the vast disagreements on how to categorise and explain its unique structure, emergence, and rapid success and decline. Therefore, the propositions for the Dutch Republic remain more modest and focus on existing debates regarding the transition to capitalism and the jurisdictional impact of the provinces' social property relations. However, the discussion contributes a neglected jurisdictional angle that provides useful starting points for further studies.

The contrast of England's agrarian, diplomatic, and imperial history is important, but this study is not one of English exceptionalism. In various ways, each case has its own specificities. Neither is the analysis constructed by the chronological and sequential rise and fall of the Iberian, French, Dutch, and British empires, as has been characteristic of historiography for most of the twentieth century.[5] Instead, revealing jurisdictional accumulation requires the interweaving of imperial expansion, jurisdictional politics, and capital, as axes that have not been simultaneously systematised into a coherent and diachronic framework. This is the book's major methodological challenge and contribution. It implies focusing on the similarities and differences between these polities' jurisdictional strategies without assuming a teleological path dependency governed by the search for causal links or the origins of capitalism or modernity. In other words, it defends a processual–agentic rather than consequentialist approach to history. The approach is reflected in the book's structure, as the historical narrative is conducted by its analytical and agentic angles, each chapter discussing every empire both in turn and simultaneously according to analytical patterns and ruptures so as to resist the methodological nationalism that remains dominant in mainstream and critical histories.

In sum, the present study of extraterritoriality provides an alternative genealogy of the transitions between international legal orders. It puts the spotlight on actors and processes at the political and historiographical margins of international law and international relations. Historicising

[5] Classic examples include: Bull & Watson, 1984; Grewe, 2000; Schmitt, 2003.

extraterritoriality shows how merchants, as well as members of lower orders of the nobility and rising gentry, and even in some cases commoners, were at the forefront of early modern European imperial expansion through the processes of jurisdictional accumulation. These individuals mainly consisted of lawyers, jurists, theologians, priests, merchants, magistrates, ambassadors, envoys, consuls, sailors, and varyingly obscure types of adventurers.

Specifically, the strategies characterising early modern European empires – and used by imperial agents to extend their jurisdictional reach, as individuals or for those they represent – provide concrete and varied examples of the specificity of mercantile and dynastic elites, as well as the role of lower-order social groups in international relations and international law. For example, we find empires developing new types of diplomatic actors, collaborating with regional elites, negotiating treaties with Mediterranean rulers, allowing and controlling colonial elites in the 'New World' through complex legal mechanisms, or negotiating jurisdictional arrangements with indigenous populations.

Tracing the differences between these strategies enriches the concepts of accumulation usually found in historical sociology (primitive, geopolitical, commercial, capitalist) to understand the big social and political changes of the early modern period. Moreover, it situates these strategies in the Atlantic and the Mediterranean as particular sites where European empires had to develop alternative practices to compete and secure trading and political interests. They did so in the face of, on the one hand, a more powerful and jurisdictionally challenging trading partner, the Ottoman Empire; and, on the other, a different set of challenges and opportunities for colonisation and settlement cross-Atlantic. This alternative genealogy puts the spotlight on the Mediterranean as a particularly important space for jurisdictional accumulation and jurisdictional conflicts between early modern empires. This region has tended to be neglected in recent international history, in comparison to the emphasis on the Atlantic and Pacific as sites of early modern accumulation, dispossession, and legal ordering.

Definitions

Some key terms – the project's guiding axes – need to be defined. First, concerning the legal axis, the central contribution is the need to differentiate jurisdiction from law as a set of practices that deserves more sustained and independent historical and conceptual analysis.

Jurisdiction today is generally understood in its technical dimensions as the de facto right to exercise justice, the 'ordering of legal authority', leading most legal literature on extraterritorial jurisdiction to be concerned with conflicts of laws and jurisdictions (Dorsett & McVeigh, 2012: 4–6). However, even from a technical and dispute- or case-based approach, jurisdiction points to the de facto, practical, and constitutive dimension of the law which should concern historical sociology as the study of social change.[6]

In effect, jurisdiction remains mostly ignored in historical sociologies in IR and not deemed worthy of more in-depth, systematic, or reflective analysis. It has been accepted for some time now that IR scholars need to become better historians, by either engaging more with primary sources or with a wider range of secondary sources. Yet the narrative of the universal standard of sovereign statehood is still claimed by most of the conventional literature to have arisen with the 1648 treaties of Westphalia and to have gradually been established worldwide by the nineteenth century. The continuing importance of Westphalia as a benchmark for the history of the modern state in spite of the many critiques of such a use since the late 1980s shows that the early modern – and hence the jurisdictional – has always been present in the classic narratives of the history of international relations and international law. However, the 'early modern' has remained just that (i.e. a prelude to modern territorial and state-based political institutions and principles, which has not been sufficiently understood *sui generis*).

A growing and critical 'jurisdictional' literature has emerged from scholars such as Rush (1997), Ford (1999), Goodrich (2008), Orford (2009), Benton (2010), Tomlins (2010), Dorsett and McVeigh (2012), and Pahuja (2013). Some of these scholars have lamented the lack of 'a theory of jurisdiction' (Ford, 1999: 922)[7] while others have elaborated on the various historical manifestations of jurisdiction and its role in state formation, empire, and colonisation. This project situates itself somewhere in between Ford's theory of jurisdiction and Pahuja's illustrative use of jurisdiction as 'orientation' and as 'jurisdictional thinking'

[6] In international human rights law, jurisdiction is defined as the 'actual exercise of control and authority by a state' (Milanovic, 2011: 8) and as '*de facto* political and legal authority; that is to say, practical political and legal authority that is not yet legitimate or justified' (Besson, 2012: 864).

[7] Ford's theory of jurisdiction is based on its definition as 'a relationship between the government and individuals, mediated by space' (1999: 904).

(2013: 69). It provides a framework that takes as a starting point the transformative, contested, and layered definition of jurisdiction, as well as the focus on jurisdiction's declarative and pre-constitutive role in relation to law and to sovereignty (Dorsett & McVeigh, 2012).

This book provides different examples of actors and institutions concerned with the legal ordering of authority – in the technical sense – yet it also explores a more critical sense of jurisdiction, which 'actively works to produce something' (Dorsett & McVeigh, 2012: 6), and which reverses the technical definition according to which 'jurisdiction is an exercise of sovereignty' (Pahuja, 2013: 69); instead, it is as, if not more, important to account for how 'sovereignty is a practice of jurisdiction' (Pahuja, 2013: 70) since jurisdiction is 'the practice of pronouncing the law', and thus a declaration of its 'existence' and of 'the authority to speak in the name of the law' (Dorsett & McVeigh, 2012: 4). A critical approach to jurisdiction is thus concerned with the de facto, prelegal phase of the enunciation of rules and laws and its potential for understanding the role of law in contributing to the social construction of major principles of international relations and international law.

This critical approach is fundamental in highlighting the ways in which non-critical approaches have stripped jurisdiction of its historicity, and of its potentially constitutive force, leaving it bare and neutralising its potential as a material factor of social change in historiography, as 'timeless, natural and indeed inevitable' (Ford, 1999: 929). This manifests itself in narratives of early modern Europe widely considered as the classic period or golden age of jurisdictional encounters and conflicts. However, it is used there in a descriptive sense to denote the elusive and overlapping boundaries of the early modern period. It is not explored as a determining agency or structure – and as pattern or rupture – and the term is not considered to significantly shift in meaning spatially or temporally.

Instead, this book revisits the potential of a spatiotemporally differentiated narrative of jurisdiction as well as its analytical potential to explain the messier imbrication of law, politics, and economics in processes of early modern imperial ordering. Westphalian narratives are contested by focusing on the endurance of the jurisdictional mode of expansion present up until the nineteenth century and fundamental to a different interpretation of the dynastic politics shaping the Westphalian era.

It is crucial to separate early modern jurisdictional practices from sovereign and territorial practices so as to qualify these terms according to early modern actors rather than according to their modern equivalents or to the consequentialist history of modern sovereignty and capitalism. Presentism remains a problem in legal and international relations history.

> Western legal histories are frequently presented as simple tales. The stories told have, from the perspective of the present, a sense of Whiggish inevitability as they move across time towards us and our more familiar forms. To avoid complication, such accounts highlight and often exaggerate the importance of the laws that have become dominant over time. They neglect both a wide variety of other laws and normative orders.
>
> (Donlan & Heirbaut, 2015: 9)

This project thereby contributes to highlighting the actors, practices, and orders that may not have become dominant over time. If it relies on notions of jurisdiction as constitutive of power relations, these are *potentially and not necessarily* driving the construction of 'material legal forms of sovereign, state and territory' (Dorsett & McVeigh, 2012: 5). In other words, it is crucial to ensure that this constitutive function of jurisdiction remains a potentiality determined by historical specificities. Jurisdictional practices are thus grounded in the set of contested social property relations specific to each empire under discussion.

Second, regarding the imperial axis, contemporary IR and international legal historians – in the context of the rising influence of postcolonial, decolonial, and anti-Eurocentric approaches – are increasingly exploring new ways to understand European and non-European history. However, beyond current methodological debates regarding types of Eurocentrism – and discussed in Chapter 2 – the study of the expansion of legal orders and mechanisms has been particularly problematic or difficult to provincialise or decentre. Since the authority of common and civil law systems remains mostly undisputed, their conquest of major parts of the world has been met with much less controversy than other aspects of European imperial expansion. For example, it is common for contemporary historians of the British Empire to express how the rule of law was a gift to the world, the jewel in the crown of British imperialism, an exception that redeems the enterprise. The law thus retains key functions in today's various revisionist and nostalgic exhibitions of why we should retain the glorious and forget the bloody past.[8] Similarly, for historians of the French Empire, the potential

[8] Interestingly, if the law is invoked as an argument against popular discontent targeting the continued glorification of those responsible for enslaving, killing, and subjugating in the

primacy and exception of French legal codes and constitutional system over absolutist monarchies, enlightening the world since 1789, is understood as a universal good that all should be naturally proud of and celebrate.

An important objective of this study is therefore to contribute to scholarship that focuses on early modern empires and their practices of expansion, competition, plunder, and exploitation. It does so by reconnecting *legal*, *imperial*, and *diplomatic* history to the *socio-economic* histories of European empires. The intellectual, military, and religious histories of European empires remain obviously crucial, and the point is not to ignore these. However, they have been vastly favoured in historiography to the detriment of the relations between the domains focused on here.

The book's third major axis – capital – emphasises its historical materialist approach. Capital is thus understood in the Marxist sense of contested social relations between various actors and institutions that structure the access to, and possibilities for the accumulation of, resources necessary for social reproduction. These structures are identified as 'social property relations' and are used as the analytical starting point for this study.

Most simply, historical materialism consists in a method that seeks 'to encompass historical specificity, as well as human agency, while recognizing within it the logic of modes of production' (Wood, 1995: 59). This method questions how early modern empires sought to establish their authority by expanding through law and the search for wealth, and in some cases, through newly emerging capitalist social relations – or, in Wood's terms, through specific legal, commercial, and capitalist agency and modes of production.

The choice of the term 'accumulation' inevitably refers to other Marxist concepts of accumulation and thus to the large-scale expansion and reproduction of resources. The aim is therefore to distinguish as well as connect jurisdictional accumulation to other processes characterising this period and which have been used to understand the early modern

name of empire, it is mostly in terms of the so-called illegality of the protests, especially of those in Bristol in June 2020 when the statue of local slaver Edward Colston was thrown in the river during Black Lives Matter demonstrations. Rather than using the law as an argument for why empire was overall beneficial, and thus reconnecting the legal system with its colonial and imperial past, focusing on the law and the legality of protests seems to have been a safer strategy for those keen to protect and maintain these symbols of empire.

history of international law, such as primitive accumulation (Neocleous, 2012) or geopolitical accumulation (Teschke, 2003). However, jurisdictional accumulation in this project refers mostly to the accumulation of rights, functions, and titles. Revenue or wealth acquired from jurisdictional accumulation remains difficult to ascertain and dissociate from other sources of revenue, such as commercial capital. Providing even only a very general assessment of this revenue is beyond the scope of this study and requires a separate research project. Nevertheless, it is certain that consuls, corsairs, chartered companies, settlers, etc. extracted significant revenue from the jurisdictional privileges they acquired, though they also had significant costs, which they often tried to claim back from their sovereigns through the legal privileges they had acquired or thought they deserved – hence the book's focus on jurisdictional accumulation as primarily the search to accumulate those functions, rights, and titles as means to achieve property and sovereignty.

This focus is also justified by the way in which early modernity, when seen through the lens of jurisdictional accumulation, is not primarily deployed to better explain the rise of modernity and the origins of – or transitions to – capitalism. This concept is first of all put forward to better understand the historical phase during which Europe expanded its control on an increasingly global scale and to highlight its specificities.

The difficulty here lies in accounting for the shifting meaning and practices of 'capital' in a period of conflicting and overlapping modes of production and expansion. In effect, the question of the transition to capitalism cannot be ignored, even if it is not the primary research problem here, since these modes of expansion inevitably coexisted and in some cases overlapped such as in English/British America.

Moreover, a significant focus in the vast literature on the early modern period has been on defining it as mercantilist. Recent debates on the transition to capitalism have focused on the issue of whether mercantilism is a structurally necessary and sufficient mode of expansion or accumulation for the transition to capitalism, nationally and globally. This issue also remains contested in Marx's work, who oscillated on this point depending on the periods and left the question open in his unfinished manuscripts. This book proposes to shift the terrain of the debate towards providing a more nuanced picture of these modes and by adding the notion of jurisdictional accumulation to question the homogeneous use of the term 'mercantilism' when identifying early modern strategies and actors.

Marxist historiography has also ignored the significance of the concept of jurisdiction, and in response it is used here to emphasise the importance of maritime and mercantile spaces for the development of (geo) political class dynamics and reproduction. The presence of these various modes for the development of specific practices such as ambassadorial representation and the role of jurisdictional actors is illustrated by the neglected role of maritime consuls, at the crossroads of mercantile and geopolitical expansion.

When approached from this angle, capital is understood widely, and the book plays with the notion of jurisdiction as a form of capital, as the motto used as epigraph denotes. This implies there are different types of capital determined by contested social property relations. These shape the diverging social origins of leading European imperial actors, such as ambassadors and consuls, and the social implications of contending diplomatic and expansionist strategies. This understanding of capital avoids falling prey to a structural concept of capitalism that can ultimately only provide an approach of *a*historical materialism to understand the important geopolitical, economic, and legal transitions of the early modern period.

Thus, if this book draws on a Marxist conceptual framework, it is not written primarily as a defence and exposition of Marxism in IR and international law. The primary drive is historical and concerned with legal ruptures and patterns. Nevertheless, the book does defend the ways in which historical materialism provides original and necessary questions to explore early modern jurisdictions that would not be generated by using an alternative conceptual matrix or theoretical framework, such as a Weberian, constructivist, or postcolonial approach to historical sociology.

Chapter Outlines

Chapters 1 and 2 expand on these definitional, theoretical, and methodological problems. Chapter 1 problematises the classic history of diplomacy in relation to extraterritoriality and presents the key debates in IR and international law to which this study contributes. This chapter further shows that classic diplomatic history's focus on embassies and Grotius to historicise extraterritoriality has contributed to the Westphalian imaginaries that remain dominant and maintain linear trajectories of the shift from personal to territorial concepts of sovereignty. If a range of new studies are also contesting this approach and account of early modern jurisdiction, they nevertheless remain limited in terms of not fundamentally questioning the link between extraterritorial and territorial sovereignty based on the analysis of ambassadorial immunity and the shift from the personal – the ambassador – to the territorial – the embassy. These limitations call for new approaches to this history.

Chapter 2 discusses historical sociology as the framework adopted to develop a new approach to early modern jurisdictions. The project aims to enrich diplomatic history's institutional and cultural paradigm through a more productive engagement with new legal histories of extraterritoriality and historical materialist approaches. Debates regarding Eurocentrism and how to conceptualise imperial agency in historical sociology are discussed, and an outward methodological internalism is proposed as required by the research problem posed in Chapter 1, namely the problem of narrow and linear sources of the means of imperial expansions of authority such as ambassadorial immunities. To frame this methodology, the commodity form theory of law is discussed as a powerful but overly structural approach to processes of expansion that conflates mercantilism and capitalism. In response, the methodology is framed instead by Political Marxism, as a more agency-based and historicist approach to international history, which relies on the concept of social property relations.

Chapter 3 begins the substantial empirical analysis by focusing on the social property relations – class and legal institutions – of each case under examination. It builds on social histories of these cases, broadly but not exclusively from the Political Marxist tradition, by engaging with (international) legal history. This chapter lays the groundwork for the following chapters in terms of presenting the major institutions, actors, and jurisdictional disputes that are necessary to build the following contributions to diplomatic and legal history. The analysis of social property relations in Chapter 3 provides some bases to understand the local specificities of the Castilian kingdom and its American colonies, emphasising the broader Iberian fragmented assemblage and the role of theologians in the particular politico-religious form of empire linked to principles of morality and law. In France, the focus is on the reign of Louis XIV and his ministers in trying to contain the various jurisdictional regimes and conceptions of space, as well as its legal actors and orders. The debate on the role of England's social property relations is discussed in relation to the role of the common law and of enclosures in primitive accumulation and the transition to capitalism. Finally, the section on the

Dutch Republic also highlights the problem of transition and the specific jurisdictional context of its confederation, as well as the role of merchants and magistrates in shaping its politics. Although it is not the main focus of this chapter, it implicitly describes practices that could be considered as extensions rather than transports or transplants of authority.

Both Chapters 4 and 5 contribute to rejecting simplistic linear accounts of the gradual modernising of the diplomatic profession, which is claimed to provide the basis for a modern system of international relations and accompanies Westphalian narratives of the international order and of extraterritoriality. The chapters map key changes and geographical patterns in the social origins and composition of early modern diplomatic and jurisdictional actors. They question how these diplomatic actors might map onto the typology of jurisdictional accumulation adopted in this study, and what neglected aspects of their history it may reveal.

Chapter 4 links analyses of social property relations to scholarship on the social origins of the diplomatic corps and the aristocratisation of ambassadors from the late seventeenth century. It presents the debates in diplomatic theory and history regarding the social origins or functions of actors regarded as necessary or ideal to fulfil diplomatic duties. The chapter argues that the aristocratisation of ambassadors led by France and Castile – and later Spain – can be understood as a jurisdictional strategy of collaboration between noble classes and sovereigns to sustain an 'old regime' Europe. Moreover, the chapter proposes to separate the cases of Castile and France, leading this trend, from those of England/Britain and the Dutch Republic, which used diplomats and the importance of their social origins and functions according to different criteria leading to different extraterritorial strategies. Thus, the typology of jurisdictional accumulation can be used to contrast French and Castilian strategies of ambassadorial recruitment as transplants of authority, with English and Dutch counterpart strategies as transports. Transplants mark the former's more embodied and organic reliance on the prestige of the person of the ambassador, whereas the latter favoured the potential utility and political requirements of their more merchant-based imperial agents in shaping the social diversity of their ambassadorial corps, and therefore can be identified through the more functional concept of transports.

Chapter 5's study of the practices of Dutch, French, and English consuls in the Mediterranean is at the heart of the book's argument for jurisdictional accumulation since it illustrates key relations of jurisdictional collaboration and conflict between sovereigns, merchants, trading companies, and regional institutions. It discusses what was expected of consuls and the range of their jurisdictional functions, the policies and strategies developed such as the restrictive regulations increasingly put in place for the French service and its unique model of salaried and commissioned consuls, as well as the different practices found in Christian and non-Christian parts of the Mediterranean. Through a selection of archive material regarding events in the French embassy in Istanbul from the 1660s to 1680s, the analysis reveals a more interdependent relation between ambassadors and consuls in shaping so-called extraterritorial and jurisdictional spaces in the early modern period. Incorporating these challenges – based on class differences or social origins – formulates new research questions regarding the role of consular diplomacy, its connection to the aristocratisation of ambassadorial diplomacy, and the development of different forms of early modern mercantilism. For similar reasons to those raised in the conclusion of the preceding chapter, the analysis of consuls concludes that French consular practices are better categorised as transplants of authority, in contrast to the less jurisdictionally autonomous role of English and Dutch consular attempts to transport their sovereign's authority.

These conditions pave the way for discussing colonial practices of jurisdictional accumulation in Chapter 6. These consist, in the Iberian case, of the *requerimiento*, *encomiendas*, *audiencias*, and the various jurisdictional opportunities provided by the above institutions and practices, leading to jurisdictional competition and subjectivities in colonial New Spain. The open question of Castile's mercantilism is also discussed in relation to its governance and administrative structures and commercial–legal institutions. These practices are considered *transplants* of authority because they create organic and autonomous institutions that remain hybrids linked to the royal authority at the centre of the empire, and rely on the jurisdictional incorporation of both settlers and Native American subjectivities. In other words, Castilian practices of imperial expansion transplant Castilian authority and are primarily concerned with authority over people, which provides both jurisdictional opportunities of contestation and subjugation. A different set of practices of jurisdictional accumulation are then presented relating to the French, Dutch, and English/British empires. These mostly relate to trading and chartered companies and settlements primarily concerned with authority over land and resources, a process for which the inhabitants of the colonised land need to be excluded rather than jurisdictionally incorporated. The more commercial, indirect, and outsourced practices of these empires are discussed through the debates on mercantilism and the practices of corsairing, which produced conditions for jurisdictional accumulation as *transports* of authority, that is focused on the use of intermediaries and a jurisdictional distancing between the imperial centres and their colonies.

Chapter 7 concludes the book by discussing in more detail the conceptual and historiographical implications of the analysis of consuls in Chapter 5 and of the jurisdictional practices of accumulation in Chapter 6. Exploring different meanings of jurisdiction for the doctrine of the law of nations by Castilian theologians and for England's famous *Calvin's Case* – both focused on cross-Atlantic colonisation – reveals the importance of the difference between transplants and transports of authority as shaped by different notions of *dominium*. In effect, transplants of authority refer to notions of *dominium* that incorporate both ownership of things and people *and* rule or judicial authority over things and people. In contrast, transports of authority refer to a more restricted notion of *dominium* focused on the ownership of things, or what some might identify as private property. Finally, in the Mediterranean, jurisdictional accumulation reveals how early modern consuls, as the most significant and neglected of jurisdictional actors, were shaping key legal fictions (political/economic and Christian/non-Christian) that were maintained in the later-nineteenth-century's construction of modern international law, and which contributed to excluding peoples from the standards of civilisation. Thus, the book concludes with these remarks aimed at opening debates on the significance and potential future of the concept of jurisdictional accumulation. If nothing else, this concept will have contributed to the growing scholarship on the shared histories of international relations and international law. Echoing Christopher Hill's wise advice to fellow historians, it also hopes to contribute to this generation's need to rewrite its history as it relives different aspects of its predecessors' experiences; namely, the recurring lives of empire and accumulation.

1

Early Modern Extraterritoriality

Amid the general focus on the late-nineteenth century in international legal history,[1] and the focus on ambassadorial immunity in IR history, some scholars have favoured a transhistorical approach to extraterritoriality. This traces the practice since ancient times and defines extraterritoriality as a fundamental social relation between different groups of human beings:

> Foreigners were barbarous in the eyes of early men. Early man stood in great fear of the magic of strangers. He resorted to a variety of ceremonies in order to protect himself against the devilish power of the stranger. But in the course of time the natives were convinced that this attitude of strict exclusiveness could not be permanently maintained. As soon as they failed to find in their own association the satisfaction of their desires and the supply of their wants, they were compelled to go beyond it and enter into relations of some sort with the surrounding world. The alien, therefore, was incapable of amenability to the same jurisdiction to which the natives were subjected. For this reason we find that in the ancient world foreigners were either subjected to their own laws and customs or were placed under a special jurisdiction. It is in these relations and under these conditions that we find the earliest traces of extraterritoriality.
>
> (Kassan, 1935: 240)

Its sweeping and universalist assumptions grate on contemporary sensibilities and are challenged by anthropological studies, yet the main argument captures the lost importance of jurisdiction as a significant sociological process. Specifically, the quote exemplifies the basis to a broad transhistorical approach to extraterritoriality that resituates the term as a simple relation of otherness – 'a special jurisdiction' – and avoids the problems encountered by diplomatic historians such as Buckley trying to find extraterritoriality's 'exact date of practical origin'

[1] For key studies of nineteenth-century extraterritoriality, see Scully, 2001; Horowitz, 2004; Kayaoglu, 2010; Cassel, 2012; Ruskola, 2013; Özsu, 2014.

(1966: 350). Moreover, this transhistorical sense departs quite significantly from the classic use of the term, which remains attached, either as a cause or outcome, to the Westphalian emergence of the modern sovereign states system.

Closer to this conventional state-centric account, we find a more historically limited and politically defined sense that uses extraterritoriality to denote the simple extension of authority and privileges to persons located outside the limits of that authority. It refers to the shifting types of consuls and representatives, or messengers, found throughout recorded history and maintains a diplomatic conception of extraterritoriality, albeit a temporally broad one (Liu, 1925; Numelin, 1950; Leira & Neumann, 2008, 2012; Coller, 2011; Stein, 2012; Tait Slys, 2014).

Although these studies explicitly or implicitly acknowledge that in premodernity, 'the very concept of extraterritoriality made little sense, as no clear concept of territorial sovereignty existed at that time' (Leira & Neumann, 2012: 162), they nevertheless choose to use the term to understand the continuities between institutions such as the Greek *proxenia* in the sixth century BC, or the Roman consul or peregrine in the third century BC, as 'precursors to later instances of extraterritorial jurisdiction associated with consuls' (Leira & Neumann, 2012: 162). Similarly, although Tait Slys focuses on the evolution of extraterritorial consular jurisdiction in the nineteenth-century Ottoman and Chinese empires, she refers to ancient Greece and premodern consular history to find links with previous extraterritorial arrangements (2014: 13–14). However, she is careful to note the differences between premodern and modern applications of extraterritorial jurisdiction, recalling sociological aspects of the passage by Kassan:

> Early instances of consular jurisdiction seem to have been the result of mutual concessions of hospitality – underscored by an idea of the immiscibility of the alien in one's religious and civic community – rather than the outcome of an explicit policy of legal imperialism. Because an orthodox doctrine of the strict territoriality of laws did not exist, the ancient and medieval societal attitude towards the coexistence of a multiplicity of legal systems on a single territory appears to have been broader and more tolerant than contemporary doctrines on the attribution of jurisdiction. The fact that consular relations were, in the past, largely the prerogative of private parties or trading companies is another considerable difference between prior conceptions and those of the present.
>
> (Tait Slys, 2014: 15)

In spite of their attention to non-European cases and their adoption of a transhistorical use of extraterritoriality, Leira and Neumann (2008: 3) also discuss Wicquefort's 1681 analysis of consuls as merchants with no 'extraterritorial rights', thus using the term 'extraterritorial' in a more limited sense of ambassadorial immunity. Numelin also adopts a transhistorical approach defined by diplomatic privileges, when he notes the presence of 'extraterritorial rights and other diplomatic privileges' in the Amphictyonic Councils of the Hellenic world of the fourth and fifth centuries BC and interchangeably uses the terms 'exterritorial or diplomatic privileges' (1950: 310). This leaves open the question of why and how this term becomes defined as diplomatic privileges and of the potential issues this may create. This is the present chapter's central question.

Another type of transhistorical sense can also be found beyond the confines of legal and diplomatic history, such as in the work of literary critic Enzo Traverso, for whom 'a figure of extraterritoriality' signifies 'exile' and a 'stranger' (2016: 11). 'Political exiles' and 'internal emigrants' in early-twentieth-century Parisian Bohemia 'were in search of an "extraterritorial" space that would provide refuge from political oppression and from generally accepted behavior and moral conventions' (2016: 125). This more subjective or affective political and sociological sense is also found in a collection of essays on 'extraterritorialities' by authors from a very wide range of disciplines and professions with the aim of not respecting disciplinary boundaries and established legal–political truth claims about the concept (Amir & Sela, 2016).

Thus, extraterritoriality is not simply a technical legal word used by legal professionals and diplomats. These other meanings and interpretations add to the confusions as well as to the potential richness surrounding its wider extra-academic use. In other words, extraterritoriality has an 'X' factor, a *je ne sais quoi* that disturbs and fascinates, that transcends the meaning of its own term of territoriality, and which also signifies its potentially significant role in driving or shaping social change beyond the practice of diplomatic privileges. It raises the uncomfortable notions of aliens, strangeness, and atopia, which the practice of modern bordering need as much as they combat, contain, and exclude them.

If the present work is more concerned with the legal–political truth claims made concerning extraterritorial jurisdiction, and specifically with the historical narratives used to sustain those claims, the spilling over of the term outside these strict and often elitist academic boundaries shows the need to address the historical imaginaries built by those disciplines and boundaries. Ultimately, the aim is to further open them to other, more public, and aesthetic imaginaries. Conceptions of power, borders, and territoriality remain continuously disputed, on physical terrains as well as on the bodies occupying them. Whether as exceptions and privileges of immunity to sustain the emerging form of the territorial state, or as a sense of exile and political refuge in times of total despair, extraterritoriality conveys a sense of the impossibility of a politically, economically, and legally fixed and closed space. It is one of the main conditions of possibility for a world made of borders and is therefore necessarily a part of any revolutionary or radical attempt to contest and change the negative effects of that world on solidarity and hospitality.

Section 1.1 introduces some general points concerning the history of principles and practices of early modern extraterritoriality and the challenge of consuls so as to set up the task of the chapter, that is explaining the wider spectrum of European extraterritorial practices). Section 1.2 presents the central tenets of classic diplomatic history, followed by Section 1.3 looking at its relationship to the disciplines of IR and international law. Section 1.4 presents in more detail the reductive role of Grotius, ambassadors, and embassy chapels in the classic diplomatic history's narrative of early modern extraterritoriality, before concluding on the need to open up a broader or stretched approach to early modern extraterritoriality that proposes to distinguish between extensions, transports, and transplants of authority.

1.1 The Neglect of Early Modern Extraterritoriality and the Challenge of Consuls

Early modern extraterritoriality has been generally ignored by IR and international legal history. In IR and the diplomatic history it relies on, extraterritoriality refers to the main institutions enabling the rise of permanent diplomacy, namely resident embassies and ambassadors' privileges of independence and immunity. These institutions are in turn considered cornerstones of the emergence of the modern sovereign state and its international order. This classic narrative has dominated diplomatic historiography since the early-twentieth century. In spite of major advances in critical IR and historical sociology since the 1980s, the classic narrative of diplomatic history remains a cornerstone of the discipline's mainstream theories.

Some exceptions to this neglect have nevertheless recently emerged. In IR, Thomson (1994) wrote a landmark study on extraterritorial forms of violence in the early modern period. However, this work remains embedded in a neo-Weberian approach that posits the development of the European states system as linear, progressive, and universal from the sixteenth century onwards, and therefore runs counter to the methodological aims of this study. Most other exceptions are found in the work of legal historians of empire concerned with the early modern period and who focused their understanding of extraterritoriality on how it affected individuals outside the confines of state or royal diplomatic institutions. In effect, this history has focused on England and *Calvin's Case* as an essential source of debate and legal argument regarding conflicts of jurisdiction and principles for the application of sovereign rights.[2] It is also considered the first decision over the divided nature of extraterritorial extensions of sovereignty and jurisdiction shaping the English and later British Empire, highlighting the jurisdictional difference between the king and the common-law's authority (Fitzmaurice, 2003; Bilder, 2004; Hulsebosch, 2005; Macmillan, 2006; De Luca, 2008; Tomlins, 2010; Brett, 2017). *Calvin's Case* directly concerned Scottish subjects, but was also used to justify transports of authority, and extinctions of authority, on Native Americans and their lands. This case is further discussed in Chapter 7.

More pertinently, Miles analyses extraterritoriality as a general principle and practice, 'a control mechanism' which could mean both a privilege and a 'symbol of shame' (2019: 88) and which is observed across the early modern period as a means of uneven and messy empire-building used by chartered companies such as the VOC, EIC, and Levant Company. She therefore adopts a methodologically more open approach to de-reifying the state and ambassadors as main extraterritorial actors and introduces the types of consular and mercantile practices further discussed in this book.

In spite of these exceptions and of the recent revival of scholarship in international legal history, early modern extraterritoriality has remained a neglected area of study.[3] A large-scale single-issue study of this topic remains wanting. Conventional literature that does happen to cover the topic narrows the origin of the legal concept and device of extraterritoriality to the diplomatic privilege of immunity and to the development of embassies – and more specifically to embassy chapels – in capitals and courts of sixteenth- and seventeenth-century mainland Europe (Mattingly, 1955). Accordingly, the principle of extraterritoriality was theorised in Grotius's 1625 *De Juri Belli ac Pacis*, who considered it a

[2] *Calvin's Case* 7 Coke Report 1a, 77 English Reports, 377, 1608.

[3] For accounts of this turn, see Hueck, 2001; Koskenniemi, 2004, 2011, 2016; Duve, 2014; Dhondt, 2016.

fiction similar to that of sovereignty (i.e. sovereignty that is '*quasi extra territorium*' (Adair, 1929: 5–6). IR scholars, and especially influential texts by Ruggie (1983, 1993), have adopted Mattingly's analysis of the invention of extraterritoriality through embassy chapels as a necessary counterpoint to the emergence of 'absolute sovereignty' in early modern Europe, leading to states 'tolerating within themselves little islands of alien sovereignty' (1955: 244). For Ruggie, this 'unbundled territoriality' (1993: 165) or 'principle of extraterritoriality' is the 'first specifically modern invention of diplomacy' (1983: 279) and thus a characteristic of the states system which has survived the early modern period and continues to complicate theories of IR and contemporary processes of globalisation and capitalism. Mattingly's focus on embassy chapels has therefore shaped IR theory on extraterritoriality.

Because of this focus on representation and immunity, consuls have been gradually excluded or sidelined from the history of modern extraterritoriality, because they did not necessarily have the credentials to represent a sovereign, and therefore were not considered worthy of the same immunity and privileges. They were therefore only rarely considered to be fully or even half-fledged diplomatic actors in the sense attributed to ambassadors. They therefore have not been considered as important to understand the origins and development of early modern and modern extraterritoriality, in spite of their primary role in the early modern capitulations and in previous treaties in the Mediterranean.[4]

From approximately the fifteenth and sixteenth centuries, European consuls in the Mediterranean had a variety of well-established jurisdictional tasks and prerogatives, a central one being the implementation of the capitulations (France in 1536 (debated), 1565, 1632, and 1672; England in 1580; Dutch in 1612). Capitulations were a 'class of instruments known generally to the early Ottomans as *ahdnameler* ('pledges', or, more literally, 'letters of promise') and to non-Muslim sovereigns as 'capitulations' (from *capitula*, for the 'chapters' into which they were typically divided)' (Öszu, 2012: 431). They were also known as *imtíyāzāt* in Ottoman Turkish (Trivellato, 2009: 115). They are generally considered diplomatic agreements, shifting according to Western or Ottoman perspectives and interpretations from unilateral to bilateral treaties between European sovereigns and the Ottoman Empire. Until the eighteenth century, they mainly consisted of unilateral privileges

[4] See Chapters 5 and 7 for more details on this process of historiographical neglect.

accorded to European merchants for trading in Ottoman territory such as exemptions from head taxes, lower customs duties, as well as the exercise of the freedom of religious worship, arbitration over commercial and civil disputes between members of their nation, and criminal jurisdiction and protection over members of their nation such as the privilege to be tried in their home jurisdictions (Trivellato, 2009: 115).[5] The Ottoman considered them as 'imperial decrees – unilaterally granted and unilaterally revocable pledges to non-Muslim sovereigns with which political alliances or trading partnerships had been struck' (Öszu, 2012: 431).

However, during the seventeenth century, the balance started to shift more prominently towards European powers. For example, the capitulation of 1672 agreed with France 'established commercial advantages and the French Crown's extraterritorial authority' (Takeda, 2011: 40), by allowing its merchants a 3 per cent – rather than 5 – customs duty on the value of import and export commodities (a privilege also detained by the English) as well as further concessions in the following decade, which placed France as the leading power in the region (Trivellato, 2009: 115).

European – and especially non-European – consuls have been largely ignored in diplomatic historiography and in 'national histories of foreign affairs', unfairly turning them into diplomatic 'sidekicks' (Leira & Neumann, 2008: 3–4), in spite of their presence as mercantile, juridical, and diplomatic agents in the Western Mediterranean from the twelfth and thirteenth centuries:

> According to Ulbert (2006: 12), the first such usage of the term hails from the year 1117 AD. Practice predated theory. The colonies of foreigners in Constantinople, under the principle of the personality of laws, had some sort of autonomy and their own special magistrates from at least the ninth and tenth centuries. Subsequently, Italian port cities made treaties both with the Byzantine Empire and the Moslem rulers of the Eastern Mediterranean, treaties that allowed the city states to appoint individual compatriots to hold commercial jurisdiction over the colony of expatriates in the receiving polities. From the twelfth century onwards, these magistrates were known as consuls, a title imported from the Western Mediterranean. Similarly, in the thirteenth century, the Khipchak Khanate, better known as the Golden Horde, allowed for the appointment of Genovese consuls in settlements along the Northern coast of the Black Sea. Whereas the sending polities usually elected the first consuls, as the

[5] For an analysis of administrative and merchant institutions associated to early modern nations, see Fernandez Chavez & Gamero Rojas (2017).

> colonies of expatriates grew they would tend to elect their own consuls, as was the common practice in the Western Mediterranean. The European consuls of the Eastern Mediterranean were gradually granted both criminal and civil jurisdiction over their compatriots, and ultimately jurisdiction also in cases where their compatriots were involved in regular civil and criminal cases in the receiving polity. In the final centuries of the Ottoman Empire consuls became *virtually independent of local authorities.*
>
> (Leira & Neumann, 2012: 163; my emphasis)

In sum, the term extraterritoriality is used either very loosely or very narrowly. It denotes, in the first loose sense, jurisdictional extensions and transports of authority throughout recorded history, *or*, in the second narrower sense, ambassadorial immunity emerging in Northern European cities in the sixteenth and seventeenth centuries.

Neither of these positions is satisfactory. Instead, retrieving a wider spectrum of extraterritorial practices and social relations, which nevertheless respects the context and specificities of actors in certain historical patterns and transitions, is therefore the book's central challenge.

Responding to this challenge could take two directions: one concerned with non-European practices, and the other concerned with European practices. The first direction would be to address the ways in which the history of premodern forms of extraterritoriality and of the actors associated with this practice remains empirically and methodologically Eurocentric. The existence of complex notions of internal, external, and trans-societal forms of jurisdiction and consular-type institutions – in other words, the exchange of personal privileges, exemptions, and trading representatives – existed outside of Europe well before it emerged in the Mediterranean basin, for example in India, China, and along the Eurasian trade system (Numelin, 1950; Zourek, 1957; Banaji, 2011). According to Leira and Neumann (2012: 163), 'the practice of granting internal jurisdiction to groups of foreign merchants can be dated in Asian sources at least from the eighth century and onwards', and 'the office of *wakil al-tujjar*, in existence at least since the twelfth century, was quite similar to the consular office as it developed in the Western Mediterranean, with the holder recognised as leaders of the communities of traders by the local polities'.

However, this book is not concerned with extra-European forms of jurisdiction. This direction is a crucial one to develop, but the following argues that another direction is also fundamental to take. If some historians have focused on what has distinguished Europeans' approach to jurisdictional innovations by looking at the establishment of permanent consulates in the Mediterranean, most grand diplomatic narratives have been even more reductive by focusing on ambassadorial privileges of immunity and territorial embassy chapels in mainland, and mostly Northern, Europe.

For now, this project is therefore concerned with the more complex forms of extraterritoriality in and around Europe, in an attempt to at least dislodge Eurocentrism methodologically, if not empirically. It maintains that such a focus is a necessary step in the construction of anti-Eurocentric histories, and contributes to methodologically disturbing the Eurocentric narrative, in spite of the study's empirical Eurocentrism. In other words, dislodging the methodological Eurocentrism of extraterritoriality also implies questioning and opening up the narrative of its narrow definition inside Europe.

The next chapter discusses these questions of empirical and methodological Eurocentrism in more detail and in relation to existing debates in historical sociology. First, the following presents the narrative adopted by twentieth-century historians which has led to a strict definition of extraterritoriality exclusively linked to ambassadorial immunity as the central focus of critique for this study.

1.2 Classic Diplomatic History, IR, and International Law

The historiography of international relations, international law, and diplomacy are closely related fields that have largely influenced each other since the disciplines' institutional beginnings in the late-nineteenth and early-twentieth centuries. IL became a profession in the late-nineteenth century, notably with the creation of the International Law Association and l'Institut de Droit International in the 1870s (Neff, 2006: 40). The conventional story sees IR gradually following as a discipline in its own right in the early-twentieth century.[6] However, both disciplines were still very interlinked. Emerging IR scholars were generally trained as lawyers, and international law constituted the most tangible and direct

[6] British scholars from the University of Aberystwyth awarded the first Chair in International Politics in 1919, but universities in London, Geneva, and Chicago quickly followed during the 1920s. See Sylvest (2005) for a detailed account and Vitalis (2005) for a critique of this narrative that focuses on the racial and imperialist origins of the discipline developing simultaneously in the United States through key journals such as the *Journal of Race Development*, later named *Foreign Affairs*.

manifestation of thinking about how to remedy the diversity and clash of political entities. In their early days as professions, the interconnection between IR and international law was grounded in the progressive promises of an international rule of law leading to experiments in international institutional design, consisting in a series of congresses, conferences, and conventions during the nineteenth century, where diplomats played a central role and emerged as a fully established profession.[7]

Thus, diplomacy has been the traditional area of interest for scholars of international history up to the late-twentieth century. For Dhondt (2016), it still represents the most significant source of primary and archival material in terms of quantity and availability, and produces original contributions to the field of legal history. In effect, relations between diplomats and between diplomats and their sovereigns, during the signing of major treaties and at major congresses and conferences, have constituted the main source of knowledge for explaining the emergence of modern states and international orders. The importance of the treaties of Westphalia is a key example for this focus, which has led to historical scholarship in the discipline of IR being dominated by the search for the origins and development of state institutions, the influence of intellectual history on those institutions, and the tracing of links between leading diplomats and the classical legal theory canon.

The tradition most influential in this endeavour has been the English School in IR. Since its early contributions (Wight, 1977; Bull & Watson, 1984), the European states system's birth was dated to 1648. The treaties of Westphalia set the scene for European society to become an international society of states through various processes of expansion during the nineteenth century. Defined by its Grotian legalistic influence and via media position between liberal and realist IR theory (Little, 2000), the

[7] The initial rise of mostly private and non-political arrangements set standards for the Postal Union, telegraph, and railway services, thereby interlocking the development of rules with the expansion of (European) international society. Consequently, dominant positivist theories, seeing 'laws as commands issuing from a sovereign person or body' (Shaw, 2008: 29), had to transfer this reasoning to the international scene 'and immediately came face to face with the reality of a lack of supreme authority' (29). This move left international law scholars with the enduring problem of the sources of international legal obligation: how could international law, as the common will of sovereign states, be binding and superior to the will of individual states? The failure to resolve this issue weakened the positivists and strengthened the claims of the early liberal internationalists, as it implied thinking 'the essence of law as beyond juridical description' (Shaw, 2008: 30). This problem has also been referred to as the Austinian challenge.

English School is logically attractive to international lawyers and has greatly influenced their narrative of Westphalia. However, this narrative has since been authoritatively contested in IR.

Yet one wonders how many more critical studies it will take to dislodge the dominance of Westphalian modernity as a historical marker for understanding the early modern world. In spite of the debate having become redundant, the problem persists (de Carvalho, Leira, & Hobson, 2011; Schmidt, 2011; Pitts, 2017). What has been called the Westphalian 'imaginary' (Osiander, 2001: 251) implies either literally harking back to 1648 as the gateway date to modernity or taking the assumption of the Westphalian system as a widely accepted marker, however imprecise. Both are used to mark the most significant shift to modern conceptions of territoriality. One of the most elaborate attempts to historicise extraterritoriality since early modernity posits the following concerning Westphalia:

> territoriality did not arise suddenly with the Treaty of Westphalia. The set of agreements and understandings encompassed by the phrase Westphalian nonetheless flagged an important if imprecise shift in world history . . . Westphalia has thus become a useful marker for a new political order within Europe, an order that eventually spread throughout the globe.
>
> (Raustiala, 2009: 11, emphasis added)

Although IR has produced since the 1990s many destructive analyses of the Westphalian mythical edifice (e.g. Krasner, 1993; Osiander, 2001; Teschke, 2003), it remains a heavily encased benchmark in the non-historically inclined areas of the discipline and in most of its pedagogical material, as well as in other disciplines in the social sciences which uncritically reproduce this myth.[8] The treaties of Westphalia did not usher in the dawn of abstract territoriality, as is generally claimed but instead maintained a period of personal relations of power – what Teschke (2003) calls geopolitical accumulation – in a complex patchwork of imperial and princely sovereignties and quasi-sovereignties until the early-nineteenth century and the final breakdown of the Holy Roman Empire. Koskenniemi (2016) has also expanded the critique of enduring state centrism and the Westphalian fetish in international law studies, which he finds present even in the postcolonial histories that have emerged in the recent international legal history turn.

[8] See Beaulac (2004) for a post-structuralist critique of the Westphalian discourse in international law.

Nevertheless, since the late-twentieth century, international history has seen significant shifts in the methods and topics adopted by scholars influenced by the waves of Marxist, postmodern, and postcolonial theories in the social sciences, and more specifically the emergence of critical legal studies, new approaches to international law, Third World approaches to international law, and in IR, the big 'Third Debate' (Lapid, 1989), which opened up the discipline's small epistemological box to a plethora of post-positivist or interpretivist and critical approaches and topics. Thus, we see the development in IR of, for example, feminist approaches, international political economy, critical security studies, and historical sociology, as distinct theoretical and methodological areas in which scholars can specialise and go beyond the traditional association of IR with diplomatic relations, and the institutionally narrow and Eurocentric narrative of the emergence of international society this association produced.

Some scholars of the new diplomatic history turn also reject the classic Westphalian narrative. As Windler comments following contributions in the volume by Sowerby and Hennings (2017), and also Niels May's work, the Peace of Westphalia does not appear 'as a particularly relevant epochal boundary' (Windler, 2017a: 261). Using this 'watershed moment … ignores disputes relating to the status within the *Ständegesellshaft*' which were as relevant as disputes over sovereignty (2017a: 261–262). For these authors at the forefront of the new diplomatic history current, the importance of Westphalia 'in the longue durée' is 'paled by the structural changes around 1800' (2017a: 262).

The classic way in which historians have characterised extraterritoriality in the early modern period is to define it in stricter political and legal terms as a transport of authority, and more specifically, as the shift from a personal to a territorial transport of authority. This simplified matters for the purpose of clarity but with consequences that have been over time erased or forgotten. In other words, for most of the early modern period, sovereigns and suzerains, kings and princes, cities and companies used ambassadors or messengers to carry out tasks of representation, information, and negotiation (Bély, 2007: 3). Individuals were chosen to bear the official titles of ambassador, envoy, messenger, resident, consul, agent, etc.[9] and were in principle protected because they

[9] The hierarchy and terminology of these ranks and occupations vary greatly across time and space, with extraordinary ambassadors being the most illustrious role from late Middle Ages, followed by permanent ambassadors and an increasing variety of officials

were thought to *personally* carry with them the laws of the homeland or of the person they were instructed to represent. This practice was justified legally by the concept of personal law and reached back into notions of Roman law and various medieval texts. Towards the end of the early modern period, so from the late-seventeenth–eighteenth centuries, the shift to a *territorial* transport of authority is argued to be marked by the emergence of permanent embassies as fixed spaces where ambassadors and their entourage could claim immunity. Their protection was therefore guaranteed by the transport of sovereign authority to that embassy as a territorial space, and to the ambassador by his status and function as being in charge of the embassy.

Thus, the classic diplomatic literature associates extraterritoriality with the emergence of both permanent embassies in the fifteenth and sixteenth centuries, and ambassadorial immunity in the sixteenth century.[10] In spite of some exceptions discussed above, this narrative has been very influential in IR, notably through the work of the English School.[11]

For Bull, a landmark IR historian, the 'legal recognition of the extraterritoriality of ambassadors by foreign services in the period of Louis XIV' is the most important stage of the mid–late seventeenth century in the institutionalisation of modern diplomatic relations (1977: 160).[12] However, very few historians of diplomacy or international relations engage at length, directly or exclusively, with the issue of extraterritoriality. Indirect or passing references remain set in the context of the European shaping of the profession of modern diplomacy and mostly in relation to the development of the modern state. In effect, the history of modern diplomacy has been central to the classic narrative of

working with them, as embassies and consulates developed throughout the subsequent centuries. The literature distinguishes generally between ambassadors (extraordinary and resident) at the top and a variety of agents at the lower levels. For a detailed analysis of titles since the early Middle Ages, see Moeglin and Pequignot (2017: 345–359) and Poumarède (2007).

10 For classic early modern diplomatic histories, see Numelin, 1950; Mattingly, 1955; Carter, 1966; Anderson, 1993; Davis-Cross, 2007. For histories of ambassadorial immunity, see Adair, 1929 and Frey & Frey, 1999.

11 For classic texts in IR building on diplomatic history sources as bases for the English School approach, see Butterfield, & Wight, 1966; Bull, 1977; Wight, 1977; Watson, 1982; Bull and Watson, 1984; Keene, 2002; Buzan & Lawson, 2015. Some of these will be discussed in more detail in the next chapter.

12 Other stages are 'the emergence of resident embassies in Italy in the fifteenth century, spreading throughout Europe as a whole in the sixteenth' and 'emergence of the diplomatic corps in the eighteenth century' (Bull, 1977: 160).

European *qua* modern *qua* international state formation. Accordingly, the European march to modernity was driven by the slow establishment of ambassadorial privileges over more or less three hundred years, from the Venetians' first permanent embassies with other Italian city states in the early to mid-fifteenth century, to their generalisation across Europe by the mid-eighteenth century.

When international historians do mention extraterritoriality, studies are invariably based on Adair's 1929 work on early modern ambassadorial immunities entitled *The Exterritoriality of Ambassadors in the Sixteenth and Seventeenth Centuries*. This text has been the classic reference point for questions of early modern immunity and diplomatic historians' understanding of extraterritoriality for nearly a hundred years, and there are significant reasons for this longevity.[13] However, in spite of its strengths, Adair's work remains limited to a narrow conception of the various instances of early modern transports of authority, and particularly in terms of the actors used as main and only recipients and practitioners of this phenomenon, that is early modern ambassadors. The other significant limitation is caused by his reference to Grotius and both are discussed below.

1.3 Grotius, Ambassadors, and Embassy Chapels

Adair emphasises that extraterritoriality emerged as a practice based on personal law and was only later discussed by legal theorists and regulated by law in the seventeenth century.[14] Thus, the 'idea' of extraterritoriality

[13] For Mattingly (1955: 257), Adair 'is not only a thorough treatment of its subject making conscientious use of concrete historical instances to illuminate the writings of the jurists, but a good general introduction to the later Renaissance literature about the international law of diplomacy'. Lachs's (1965: 116–140) chapter on 'exterritoriality' heavily leans on Adair's focus on Grotius and ambassadorial immunity. For Anderson (1993: 295), Adair 'remains the standard work on an important topic'. For Dover and Scott (2015: 693), 'the standard work remains E. R. Adair'. Raustiala (2009: 9–13) relies heavily on Adair and Mattingly for his understanding of late medieval and early modern forms of personal law and ambassadorial privilege. Extraterritoriality is analysed as an 'outgrowth of Westphalian territoriality' (Raustiala, 2009: 13) emerging from the rise of European embassies and the Westphalian 'system' of territorial sovereignty. Frey and Frey (1999: 196) also lean on Adair's conception of the shift from personal to territorial law. Leading French diplomatic historians Bély (2007: 191, 319) and Poumarède (2007: 14) also rely on Adair.

[14] This point is emphasised in three reviews by Grafton Wilson (1930), Stowell, (1930), Ronalds (1930) and can therefore be considered to have been well received and transmitted by historiography.

can be traced back to the recognition of the 'personal immunity of an ambassador and the sacredness of his functions', based on contractual Roman law, and on medieval legal texts including the rights of ambassadors such as Castile's *Siete Partidas* (Adair, 1929: 6).

Adair's reference to Hugo Grotius as coining the term *'quasi extra territorium'* is critical in shaping his narrow understanding of early modern extraterritoriality. The term Adair refers to – *'fictione simile constituerentur quasi extra territorium'* – belongs to a passage in book 2, chapter 18, section 4, paragraph 5 of *De Jure Belli ac Pacis* (1625).[15]

> an Exception should be made in Favour of Embassadors, who, as they are, by a Sort of Fiction, taken for the very Persons whom they represent . . . so may they *by the same kind of Fiction be imagined to be out of the Territories* of the *Potentate*, to whom they are sent. Hence it is, that they are not subject to the Laws of the Country, where they reside.
>
> (Grotius, 2005: 912, emphasis added)[16]

Grotius is still labelled as the first legal theorist to recognise this practice (Frey & Frey, 1999: 186) and give it a particular definition in relation to 'the Territories of the Potentate'. If Frey and Frey (1999: 186) remain somewhat careful by briefly asserting that Grotius's idea of extraterritoriality should not be conflated with how it later evolved, and that his approach to ambassadorial privilege was 'neither new nor remarkable' (Frey & Frey, 1999: 187), they nevertheless acknowledge his founding role and clarify that 'Grotius began with the idea of immunity and from that deduced the concept of extraterritoriality' (187), showing how his legacy has narrowed the concept of extraterritoriality to ambassadorial privilege. Most problematically, their account of the contemporaneous

[15] Adair (1929: 5–6) cites the 1646 edition of Grotius's *De Jure Belli ac Pacis*.

[16] The 2005 edition is the edition and translation most referred to today. The various translations of this passage diverge slightly and show different versions of how to define territories and sovereigns, with the 2005 edition referring more carefully to the 'Territories of the Potentate', thus the territories belonging to the sovereign, rather than simply the arguably anachronistic terms of 'countries' or 'state' in older translations: 'Ambassadors as if by a kind of fiction are considered to represent those who sent them . . . In consequences, *by a similar fiction, ambassadors were held to be outside of the limits of the country* to which they were accredited. For this reason they are not subject to the municipal law of the *state* within which they are living' (Grotius, 1925, emphasis added). Moreover, the similar 1901 translation by A. C. Campbell refers to a 'kind of fiction' according to which ambassadors represent those who sent them, while another fiction ensures that they are considered 'outside of the limits of the country to which they were accredited' (quoted by Frey & Frey, 1999: 186).

success and widely read reception of Grotius – based on Nussbaum's (1954) work – has now been seriously challenged by authors such as van Ittersum (2006). Napolitano also develops Grotius's legacy but gives it more nuance by emphasising a concept of 'spatial fiction of immunity', which applies 'Grotius's characterization of ambassadorial immunity as a "double fiction" to the built environment' (2012: 197). This argument retrieves the link Grotius makes between the personal and territorial conceptions of sovereignty in the passages quoted above, as territorial ambassadorial immunity is a fiction constructed *similarly* to the fiction of personal ambassadorial representation. By being linked, these conceptions serve 'both to represent sovereignty but also to embody it' (Napolitano, 2012: 197).

However, they nevertheless play an essential role in limiting conceptions of early modern extraterritoriality to (1) the practice of ambassadors, who were a minority among a large and socially complex variety of diplomatic and jurisdictional actors and (2) the relation between personal and territorial sovereignty as a 'double fiction', binding these two phenomena to each other, excluding any others, and anchoring them in a very limited set of mostly French diplomatic practices.

A similar analysis to Adair is found in Holdsworth's classic history of the English law, where the 'prevalence of permanent embassies in the sixteenth century made it necessary to go beyond the vague' approach to ambassadorial immunity current in the Middle Ages (1945: 40).[17] Holdsworth refers to a quote from Nys for his understanding of 'exterritoriality', who describes, in line with interpretations of Grotius, two fictions, one being the sovereign's personal representation, and the other being the 'exterritoriality' of the ambassador. These fictions led, according to Nys (1894: 341), to 'exaggerations' of privileges, which can be justified in light of the local 'disorders' or 'capricious despots' they were confronted with.[18] Furthermore, Mattingly also places a lot of the responsibility on Grotius, whose arguments including 'complete diplomatic exterritoriality' 'finally prevailed', whether they were 'a stroke of legal genius or merely an evidence of the anarchy into which Western

[17] 'It was only gradually that the extent of [the ambassador's] immunity from the process and jurisdiction of that country's courts was defined by the help of ideas, first, that he represents the person of his sovereign, and secondly that, by a legal fiction, he, his dwelling-place, and his suite, are regarded as being outside the territory of the state to which they are accredited.'

[18] Holdsworth (1945: 40)

society was falling' (1955: 240). In other words, what matters for these scholars is that Grotius's views prevailed, regardless of their context.

Scholars following Adair have thus largely adopted his approach to Grotius and to extraterritoriality. Mattingly writes that the 'modern formulation', 'doctrine', or 'theory' of extraterritoriality is said to emerge over the eighteenth century marking the shift from a personal to a territorial conception of sovereignty. This is also followed by the more recent authorities on the history of diplomatic immunities (Frey & Frey, 1999: 196). Similarly, for Napolitano, 'the most fundamental transformation of sixteenth-century diplomacy was the establishment of the residential embassy in capital cities throughout Europe', where 'the immunities previously associated with the diplomat himself took on built form, representing a shift from a personal to a territorial model of embassy' (Napolitano, 2012: 60–61). Another version by Buckley recalls the legacy of 'personal law' from the 'earliest times', 'carried' by the ambassador, and how the 'early idea [of extraterritoriality] developed, theoretically, over the centuries' so 'that by the sixteenth century the theory, or fiction, of extraterritoriality had come to stay' (1966: 350–351).

Adair's argument implies a unilinear view of the transport of authority between key political and legal actors. This linearity is expressed by the shift from an *idea* of a transport of authority attached to the person of the diplomat – who is representing the sovereign – to a *doctrine* of a transport of authority attached to the territory of the embassy – which is representing the kingdom or state. In other words, the modern doctrine of extraterritoriality, according to this classic approach to diplomatic history, is the result of the shift from the diplomat (the personal) to the embassy (the territorial).

The practice at the heart of this shift from ideas to doctrine is that of the emergence of embassy chapels. They are considered to have played a significant role not only as spaces of religious dissent, but also as '[p]robably the largest single factor in preparing men's minds to accept [the] extraordinary fiction' of exterritorial sovereignty (Mattingly, 1955: 242), as already noted in the introductory chapter. Frey and Frey (1999: 160) follow Mattingly on this point, and they also remain slightly cautious by adding that the embassy chapel was 'probably' more important than any other issue in preparing men for extraterritoriality. It seems surprising that the importance of the role of embassy chapels has not been further explored and remains a probability, especially considering how leading IR scholars have referred to them in their analysis of modern territoriality (Ruggie, 1993). One author that looks a little closer at these institutions is Kaplan (2002), who argues that embassy chapels follow the emerging practice of semi-permanent representatives to foreign courts initiated by the Renaissance Italian city states in the 1520s.[19] However, this work largely reproduces analyses by Adair and Mattingly. In the seventeenth century, capital cities in England and the Dutch Republic were at the forefront of tolerating the largest number of embassy chapels. Moreover, they were also the first to legislate extraterritoriality in terms of ambassadorial immunity, by the Dutch in 1651 and by England in 1709 (Kaplan, 2002: 344).[20]

Before embassy chapels became accepted and regulated in the late-seventeenth and eighteenth centuries, diplomatic immunities 'did not extend to violations of the host country's fundamental laws' such as heresy (Kaplan, 2002: 343). Therefore, providing ambassadors with the possibility to practise outwardly a 'heretic' faith in their chapel was highly controversial, and constituted an opportunity for rulers to enact conflicts with their rivals, forge alliances, and stir up religious strife. Embassy chapels thus represent one of the crucial means through which territorialisation occurred in Western Europe and illustrate the social conflicts at the origins of the modern doctrine of extraterritoriality. They disturbed the less controversial idea of the personal transport of authority that prevailed beforehand as a principle of ambassadorial immunity.

There is no doubt that controversial embassy chapels and the evolution of diplomatic immunities were interlinked and provided an important context for shaping the practice of dividing sovereignties and their attendant privileges according to new arguments and logics of expansion (Frey & Frey, 1999: 177–185). Yet, as noted above, there are already a number of significant challenges to this type of general narrative from outside the field of diplomatic history. Even inside it, Dover and Scott (2015: 665) acknowledge the problematic 'tidiness and linearity' of the trajectories in Mattingly's work and in the studies they have influenced regarding embassy chapels. Tallon (2017: 21) contests the cliché of early modern French politics as driven by '*raison d'état*'. Moreover, Leira and

[19] In the 1550s, embassy chapels were operating in London and other cities. They grew in number from 1600, and increased further following the negotiations of the Thirty Years War. By the 1680s, most 'national' capitals tolerated them, as well as Vienna (imperial capital) and self-governing states (e.g. Venice). London counted eight or nine, The Hague counted seven, Paris four, and the Dutch sponsored twelve in various capitals. They were also found in various capitals of the Holy Roman Empire (Kaplan 2002: 343).

[20] However, embassy chapels were first only tolerated in France and England, even though their presence augmented in the Dutch Republic during the seventeenth century (Mattingly, 1955: 243).

Neumann (2012: 165), in their discussion of consular diplomacy, show that the 'move from the principle of the personality of the law ... to territorial law associated with the sovereign state was gradual and uneven'.

A number of recent studies have emphasised a broader conception of early modern diplomacy. The field of new diplomatic history has expanded its use of sources, exploring broader aspects of the function and consequences of diplomacy, and considering a larger variety of actors qualifying as diplomats.[21] This has led to studies of the individual lives of diplomats – and of the wider social and geographical implications of their functions – emphasising the cultural, religious, aesthetic, and linguistic aspects of early modern and nineteenth-century politics.[22] This new literature is a welcome addition to the narrower repertoire of the classic diplomatic studies, even though, as Carrió-Invernizzi remarks, diplomatic history was particularly resistant to these interdisciplinary changes, 'doing so even later than political history or the history of international relations' (2014: 603). Carrió-Invernizzi speaks of 'a cultural turn or cultural peak' (2014: 608).

For example, Napolitano (2012: 209) uses Nussdorfer's expression of a 'web of jurisdictions' to qualify the functioning basis of France's somewhat pioneering Roman embassy. This embassy is singled out for its development of new diplomatic strategies of territorialisation using visual, architectural and symbolic means to assert Louis XIV's authority, mixing personal and territorial forms of sovereignty. Napolitano uses this case to illustrate Louis XIV's role in shaping new conceptions of extraterritoriality. Although her work is anchored in the tradition set up by Adair and Mattingly linking extraterritoriality to ambassadorial immunity, she is also careful to note the broader aspects of this practice. She

21 Although the term 'diplomat', as we understand it today, only appears in the late-eighteenth century, the occupation of diplomacy refers here more broadly to the early modern use of envoys, messengers, representatives, consuls, nuncios, legates, that is ambassadors of various statuses and designations placed on missions by their sovereign, prince, or other jurisdictional entity they might represent – such as the pope, a lord, a city, or a company (on issues with the term diplomacy, see Bély, 2007: 23, 133, 583, 645).

22 For recent new approaches to the history of diplomacy on the early modern period, see Bély, 1990 and 2007; Frigo, 2000; Scott, 2007; Schweizer & Schumann, 2008; Watkins, 2008; Hampton, 2009; Adams & Cox, 2011; Jacobsen, 2011; Sowerby & Hennings, 2017; Fedele, 2017. For a short general overview of recent developments in early modern diplomatic history, see Dover & Scott, 2015. For earlier attempts, see Duroselle, 1953; Renouvin, 1954; Craig, 1979. For an analysis of the evolution of the classic diplomatic history and its revisions in the twentieth century as new diplomatic history, see Carrió-Invernizzi (2014). As an example of the cultural turn, see Jacobsen (2011: 2), for whom 'diplomats were important conduits for transfer of luxury goods and cultural influences back to England' and 'active agents of cultural borrowing'.

therefore complicates the Adair line by arguing that the 'pursuit and defense of extraterritoriality varied from city to city and depended heavily on the diplomatic relations between powers and the governing practices of individual sovereigns' (Napolitano, 2012: 68).

Thus, rather than the linearity and tidiness of the classic diplomatic history narrative, where there is a more or less straight link between the emergence of ambassadorial immunity – protected by regular and territorially fixed embassies – and the establishment of territorial sovereignty as the constitutional principle of modern states, the notion of a 'web of jurisdictions' is proposed in addition to local conditions of interpretations and applications of how authority was transported and represented (e.g. 'from city to city').

Napolitano's work provides an account of jurisdictional complexity and of the variety of political representations of sovereignty and privilege among a myriad of early modern actors. This disturbs the simple picture and pioneering role of embassy chapels, and chimes with studies more broadly in the social sciences on early modern empires and jurisdictional pluralism. However, it still contributes to a methodologically narrow history of extraterritoriality, excluding consuls and practices of jurisdictional accumulation that did not concentrate on the territorial space of European embassies.

1.4 Conclusion: A New Approach to Extraterritoriality?

In light of these issues, it is necessary to ask whether the term 'extraterritoriality' is appropriate for the early modern period. What other terminology and framework could be used? Both 'diplomacy' and 'extraterritoriality' are modern terms (eighteenth and nineteenth century respectively) used for early modern times. Although there is a tacit agreement that the term 'extraterritoriality' does not come into practice or existence until the nineteenth century, many historians find it acceptable to use it for the early modern period. For example, '[w]hile he does not use the term "extraterritorial" Ayrault's concept is fundamentally the same insofar as the ambassador carries with him the laws of his homeland' (Napolitano, 2012: 59).[23] However, this further shows the limited

[23] Pierre Ayrault was a sixteenth-century French jurist and humanist (1516–1601). For an in-depth study of his contribution to the relation between early modern diplomatic practice and the construction of international legal orders, see Fedele (2016).

conception of extraterritoriality as a transport of personal law retained by scholars such as Napolitano.

There are valid reasons for keeping the term extraterritoriality and giving it a transhistorical abstract sense, as authors such as Kassan and Tait Slys have done. For one, there is an emerging historical scholarship interested in the concept and using the term, such as scholars identified in the new diplomatic history and historical international law turns since the 1990s. Extraterritoriality and other jurisdictional arrangements are being given increasing attention, and asking to give the term away might be counterproductive, even though it is historically inaccurate and anachronistic for the early modern period and implies a path dependency to modern territoriality.

However, rather than replacing the term with another descriptive alternative, it is more helpful to rethink the methodology and conceptual framework with which to look for instances of early modern extraterritoriality. This would help to explain the importance of these various instances for other major events of European and colonial history as well as for shifts to modernity. In other words, it is not the use of the term extraterritoriality that is problematic per se, but the implications and in particular the exclusions and erasures its use has been accompanied by. Crucially, what needs to be avoided is the lack of systematic reflection involved in the major narratives including the link from extraterritoriality – as ambassadorial privilege – to territorial sovereignty.

In fine, a new approach to extraterritoriality is necessary according to two objectives. First, a new approach should widen the spectrum while taking note of empires' specificities, and this project proposes to use the notions of extensions, transports, and transplants of authorities to do so. These emerge from the practices discussed in the following chapters and are more representative of jurisdictional practices of imperial expansion.

Extensions refer to assertions of authority in spaces contiguous or considered retroactively as internal to the kingdom or republic in question and therefore consist in geographical or physical extensions of territory in the most literal sense. Examples are the voluntary, coerced, or negotiated integrations of otherwise autonomous regions and provinces in Iberia, the Dutch Republic, and France, or the case of England's colonial expansion in the British Isles. Extensions are considered mostly in Chapter 3 when discussing processes of state formation. These relate less to imperial expansion so are therefore less of a focus in this project for defining jurisdictional accumulation.

Transports and transplants of authority, however, are the main focus of Chapters 4–7. Transplants (which are found in specific legal history debates as well as in histories of empire)[24] are used here to distinguish practices of jurisdictional accumulation that are more driven by sovereigns and their advisers than third parties and have organic and socially wide intentions and consequences on the land, people, and resources targeted and usually colonised. Authority is not only transported but transplanted and therefore takes on a life of its own. Transplants are mostly used in the case of Iberian expansion but it also makes sense to qualify French diplomatic strategies that set them apart from their counterparts, in both ambassadorial and consular contexts, since distinctive strategies were developed (aristocratisation and consular regulation) which led to significant new processes of diplomatic and jurisdictional politics with enduring consequences for the functioning of diplomacy.

Transports refer to the more indirect, outsourced, and commercially driven practices of jurisdictional accumulation led by the Dutch, French, and English colonial practices. Although their outcomes can be as, if not more, destructive and devastating than transplants, their intentions and means are characterised by a jurisdictional distancing between the sovereign, settlers, and those colonised, often through the quasi-sovereignty of a third party (chartered company, settler, merchant), and by a focus on territory rather than people. Chapter 7 also reflects on these distinctions in terms of doctrinal and case-based examples that point to how transplants referred to broader conceptions of jurisdiction – or *dominium* – encapsulating both ownership and rule, while transports of authority tended to favour a more restricted definition focused on ownership of things such as land and resources.

The second objective of a new approach to extraterritoriality needs to account for problems of Eurocentrism and of linear chronologies of modernity so as to go beyond the narrow territorial concepts of sovereignty and jurisdiction. To explain the theoretical and methodological context of this framework, the following chapter discusses the contribution of international historical sociology and the specific debates regarding Eurocentrism and modernity relevant to the role of extraterritoriality in the early modern period. It uses and also questions a Political Marxist and international historical sociology approach, which can

[24] For the use of the concept of 'transplants' for early modern empires, see Tomlins (2010).

integrate the above typology of jurisdictional accumulation as extensions, transports, and transplants, and which is deployed in subsequent chapters to discuss the social origins of diplomats and the evolution of the occupation as it faced the structural changes of agrarian capitalism, absolutism, and mercantilism. This means a more critical and sociological look at the ambassadorial basis of the so-called modern doctrine of extraterritoriality and the class dynamics inherent in this practice.

2

Historical Sociology, Marxism, and Law

Historical sociology is a broad interdisciplinary framework for the study of international relations which has known a certain revival since the 1990s. It consists in a particular approach to comparative analysis that looks for general patterns of causation and development while integrating particular moments of change, transition, and disruption. It does not prescribe a definitive or exclusive set of methods or even a set of fixed theoretical assumptions for how to research the organisation of world politics, its units of analysis, or how the world should be governed. It can be adopted from a descriptive or a normative standpoint, and it has brought together scholars from a variety of theoretical positions.

Historical sociology is therefore a loose and open framework, focused on large-scale and long-term comparative studies of social structures and change. This makes it particularly useful to an analysis of the historical construction of early modern law, empires, and capital which needs to engage with various disciplines and schools of thought in the social sciences. In the present study, historical sociology is used to develop an alternative social history of early modern extraterritoriality. To present this approach, the following chapter is divided into two parts, so as to make sense of how this history is influenced: first, by critical histories of international relations and international law (Part 1); second, how it is shaped conceptually by Political Marxism and by Marxist approaches to law such as the commodity form theory (Part 2).

The previous chapter established the key puzzles in the definitions of early modern extraterritoriality. It presented the classic diplomatic history literature and its influence on the discipline of IR, and problematised this account in terms of its narrow focus on ambassadors in Northern Europe, their embassies, and embassy chapels. It concluded by discussing why a new approach to the subject is necessary according to two objectives. First, the approach needs a definition of extraterritoriality which accounts for legal agency and the differences between extensions, transports, and transplants of authorities. Second, it needs to account for problems of Eurocentrism and of linear chronologies of modernity so as to go beyond the narrow and territorially defined concepts of sovereignty and jurisdiction.

In brief, this consists primarily in a methodological choice – a 'stretched' yet not transhistorical definition of extraterritoriality – privileging the need for an interdisciplinary and comparative rather than exhaustive historical approach.[1] However, it also needs to account for historical specificity. Historical sociology claims to be able to account for continuity and rupture, structure and agency, and to do so it relies on different research methods that bring different disciplines and theoretical positions into dialogue. Specifically, the methods adopted in this book contribute to recent efforts in historical sociology to counter mainstream IR approaches to international history, which rely on static and fixed concepts and on the reification of internal and external spheres leading to the problem of methodological nationalism (Go & Lawson, 2017: 3–4).

Thus, jurisdictional accumulation, in a first instance provides an angle and narrative about European early modernity that goes beyond static and fixed concepts of (extra)territoriality. In a second instance, it reveals layers of legal and political agency that contest the nationally determined internal and external borders of European expansion. The book is therefore structured by chapters each comparing a specific set of practices across four leading European empires discussed simultaneously rather than by chapters divided geographically or nationally and dealing with each empire separately. The structure adopted follows the basic elements of jurisdictional accumulation as a methodological conceptual matrix, that is the social property relations that ground the practices of extensions, transports, and transplants of authority (Chapter 3); key examples of diplomatic agents engaging in different types of jurisdictional accumulation (Chapters 4 and 5); and finally the colonial practices of transports and transplants followed by key implications for historiography (Chapters 6 and 7).

In Part 1 of this chapter, the discussion defends a cautious and problem-driven position of outward 'methodological internalism' for the study of extraterritoriality. This position is also an opportunity to engage with contemporary debates in IR theory and international historical sociology from a legal perspective. This implies a focus on European contexts and the outward processes of jurisdictional accumulation that

[1] For an application of the term 'stretched' in social sciences and Marxism, see Knox (2016a).

European actors explored as forms of class reproduction and exploitation. However, it rejects the claim that such an approach is a Eurocentric dead end.

Section 2.1 discusses general problems in historical sociology such as Eurocentrism, followed in Section 2.2 by the argument for a negative and outward methodological internalism as the method developed in response to these debates, and finally how this method is influenced by the contribution of critical histories of international law and empire.

Part 2 of this chapter is concerned with the contribution of Marxist approaches to law. The chapter goes into the book's critique of the commodity form theory of law in more depth, through its use of a Political Marxist approach. The chapter concludes by discussing the rationale and potential implications of the concept of jurisdictional accumulation as a basis to the following chapters.

PART 1 HISTORICAL SOCIOLOGY AND THE PROBLEM OF EUROCENTRISM

2.1 Foundations

Historical sociology is a large-scale and comparative interdisciplinary tradition that is concerned with societal developments, their causes, and their consequences, and with identifying points and patterns of rupture, transition, and continuity. It queries the development of history and sociology in the twentieth century as separate academic endeavours and considers that this separation has been to the detriment of attempts to understand social and institutional relations. Historical sociology defends – albeit with significant variance depending on the theoretical origins of its protagonists – the study of the past as a means to understand and shape the present. In Christopher Hill's famous words:

> history has to be rewritten in every generation, because although the past does not change the present does; each generation asks new questions of the past, and finds new areas of sympathy as it re-lives different aspects of the experiences of its predecessors.
>
> (1991: 15)

In IR terms, this translates to 'a critical approach which refuses to treat the present as an autonomous entity outside of history, but insists on embedding it within a specific socio-temporal bloc' (Hobson, 2002: 13). The origins of historical sociology are usually ascribed to the nineteenth and twentieth centuries and most characteristically to the later works of Karl Marx and more explicitly to Max Weber (1949) and C. Wright Mills (1959) as the first major social critics of capitalist modernity concerned with the implications of large-scale social sciences' analyses. This first wave comes to an end in the early-twentieth century before a revival emerges in the 1970s first from largely neo-Weberian scholars concerned with the lack of historical and comparative analysis in history, sociology, and political science (Moore, 1967; Skocpol, 1979, 1984; Aron, 1986; Mann, 1986; Tilly, 1990), and second from a neo-Marxist approach Anderson, 1974; Brenner, 1977; Hobsbawm, 1994; Wallerstein, 1997).[2] Both these currents shaped the contributions by IR scholars which became significant to the discipline from the 1990s onwards. Calls for a 'second wave' of Weberian and Marxist historical sociology (Hobson, 1998) contested the ahistoricism, presentism, and Eurocentrism of realism and neorealism in IR, and suggested historical sociology as a way to 'provide new ways of theorising and explaining the emergence and development of the modern international system/society in its multiple dimensions' (Hobson, 2002: 20).[3]

The most recent debates suggest a periodisation of either 'waves' (Hobson *et al.*, 2010) or 'competing centres of gravity' (Teschke, 2014) that cover work by IR scholars from a range of perspectives – English School, constructivist, postcolonial, Political Marxist, neo-Gramscian, world-systems theory, post-Marxist, open-Marxist, and studies based on the theory of uneven and combined development (U&CD). In spite of major differences, these scholars would tend to agree that historical sociology is not about studying contemporary events, nor is it concerned with short-term intervals or history as exceptional cases disconnected from longer-term social directions. Historical sociology can take a diachronic or a synchronic angle as long as this is pursued in a comparative set of cases. Moreover, the critical or third-wave approaches to historical sociology explore international or global history and contemporary problems as conceptually interwoven (i.e. from relational and (self) reflexive perspectives). This approach is justified on the account that IR theories are problematically dominated by illusory, fixed, and/or imprecise temporalities – or myths and benchmark dates.[4] Critical historical

[2] For a review of these waves, see Smith (1991) and Lapointe & Dufour (2012).

[3] See the debate in Hobson (1998) and the edited volume by Hobson & Hobden (2002).

[4] For various critiques of the usual benchmark dates used in IR, see Teschke (2003), de Carvalho *et al.*, (2011), and Buzan & Lawson (2014).

sociology is therefore premised on the argument that historiography in IR is not an antiquarian exercise and is necessarily determined by other methodological, epistemological, and political considerations. This chimes with parallel efforts across the discipline to revisit the conventional narratives of the discipline's emergence as driven by racial and imperial interests (Jahn, 2000; Vitalis, 2015). Historical sociology proposes to develop alternatives to the vertical and reductive conceptual frameworks that have shaped the discipline in the twentieth century, such as the levels of analysis triad – the individual, the state, and the international system – or binaries such as 'the West' versus 'the rest'.[5]

IR scholarship has produced landmark works, which have pushed for specific historical arguments as much as theoretical debates. Recent contributions have tended to focus on identifying the fundamental changes of the modern international system. Buzan and Lawson (2015) have most vocally emphasised the importance of the nineteenth century in establishing the seemingly irreversible foundations of the modern order as 'the great transformation'. They do so according to a 'composite approach' that defends the simultaneous and interconnected analysis of 'multiple beginnings'. Their project has been met with a number of objections and critical engagements (Cooper, 2017) that reveal the diversity of theoretical standpoints shaping the discipline.[6] A related area of historical sociology in IR discusses how to historicise modernity and capitalism beyond the European modern state and the Eurocentrism this unit of analysis – inter alia – reproduces. In response, one of the main tasks of critical scholarship in the early-twenty-first century has been to question the Eurocentric construction of IR and argue for a focus on non-Western history so as to begin the task of decolonising the discipline (Grovogui, 2009; Bhambra, 2010; Sabaratnam, 2011; Hobson, 2012; Gulsah Capan, 2017).

In spite of this recent call, the present study reproduces what could be called a geographical, historical, or empirical Eurocentrism by focusing on four leading European empires and their role in shaping practices of international law. This is a conscious choice that is nevertheless informed by postcolonial critiques and by the debates about how best to conceptualise and tackle Eurocentrism in IR and beyond. The most significant part of the 'decentring and provincialising Europe' agenda so as to 'decolonise' IR undoubtedly consists in studying the development of

[5] For a more detailed discussion of historical sociology in IR, see Pal (forthcoming).

[6] See the symposium 'Theory, History, and the Global Transformation' in the volume 8, Issue 3 (2016) of *International Theory*.

international law and international relations as these occur – or are affected by actors – outside Europe, whether these extra-European actors play a central role in shaping world politics or not. However, Eurocentrism is not solely or even, one might argue, primarily defined by a geographical, empirical, or historical focus. In other words, studies looking, or originating from, outside Europe can fail to actually dislodge the methodological and normative implications of Eurocentrism (Bhambra, 2007; Go, 2013; Bilgin, 2016: 495; Go & Lawson, 2017: 8). If driven by geographical or empirical criteria alone, anti-Eurocentrism merely situated outside Europe can reinforce 'methodological Eurocentrism'. In other words, merely studying other contexts than the European one does not make a study anti-Eurocentric, and vice versa. Moreover, it is important to emphasise the goal of anti-Eurocentrism, rather than non-Eurocentrism, as the latter implies an illusory state that cannot be achieved in an academic context that remains structurally and institutionally Eurocentric. This also means, crucially, that Eurocentrism is a methodological and epistemological problem that should be of concern to any approach and research topic in IR (Bilgin, 2016: 497).

Various notions of Eurocentrism have been conflated and debated in the recent plethora of anti-Eurocentric arguments. For some, this leads to a certain abuse of the term (Kuru, 2016: 352). Kuru distinguishes simply but clearly between an ideological Eurocentrism and a historical Eurocentrism, which is another way of emphasising the importance of research methods and frame to the study of geographical context. Bilgin (2016: 494) differentiates between an 'erroneous' Eurocentrism linked to specific historical assumptions that mistakenly place Europe as 'playing central roles in shaping world politics', and a Eurocentric 'consciousness' which enables the former and has also been identified as a 'deep' Eurocentrism (Reus-Smit, 2016). Critiques of the anti-Eurocentric literature are not new. Wallerstein (1997) and Wood (2001) issued warnings that contributed to some difficult debates between Marxist and postcolonial approaches to the topic. This critique has been reiterated recently by Duzgun (2018a) who has highlighted the problem of 'methodological presentism' in anti-Eurocentric literature leading to the creation of problematic 'new spatial hierarchies' in order to fulfil strict criteria of non-Eurocentrism. These hierarchies rewrite or erase the historical and anti-ideological Eurocentrism that has characterised the development of certain institutions and which is therefore unavoidable for certain research projects.

At the other end of the critical IR spectrum on Eurocentrism, Hobson and Sajed (2017) argue that, bar a very few exceptions, critical IR (including Marxist, postcolonial, and poststructuralist scholarship) is guilty of Eurofetishism in its various failed attempts to be fully anti-Eurocentric.[7] Most simply, the central dilemma of critical IR consists in how to provide a conceptual framework that can account for, on the one hand, the exploitative and dominating role of Europe and the West in world politics, and, on the other, forms of power, agency, and structure inside and outside Europe that can resist or be autonomous from the former.

Linked to this dilemma are two crucial questions. First, if knowledge production was shaped by Western imperialism and other forms of Western domination, how should we in the West produce knowledge that can counter the relations of inequality reproduced by this heritage? And, second, how do we temporally and spatially understand and explain the exploitative and dominating role of Europe and the West? This second question is the one this book is most concerned with, although the former remains essential to develop adequate methods for the latter. Hobson and Sajed's critique and proposals ambitiously – and controversially – offer preliminary answers to these questions by providing a theoretical definition of non-Western agency, further discussed below. Less controversially, however, by identifying a widespread 'critical-Eurocentrism' (2017: 22), they argue that anti-Eurocentrism should be justified methodologically (i.e. not by geographical, historical, or empirical criteria of analysis but by theoretical and conceptual choices).

These choices imply challenging the myths of the linear, homogeneous, and singular, universal, and progressive development of European institutions, and require the study of the evolution of legal, political, and economic institutions *in* as much as *outside* Europe. It also means being able to incorporate analyses that reveal in some cases the central role played by European institutions, without this creating or reproducing a methodological standard that mistakenly erases non-Western agency. What this book aims to show is that the framework of jurisdictional accumulation can help to answer the second question raised above with this cautionary remark at the forefront of its approach.

[7] Eurofetishism 'occurs when the analyst reifies or fetishizes the West as having absolute power and agency such that it obscures or elides the co-constitutive social relations between Western and non-Western agents', thus eternalizing and naturalizing 'the "all-powerful West"' (Hobson & Sajed, 2017: 7)

How can one revisit the legal expansion of early modern European empires – and account for their role in shaping modern international law and international relations – without reproducing a standard narrative of the territorial sovereign state or of extraterritoriality that becomes methodologically Eurocentric, and without contributing to a Eurocentric 'consciousness'?

In other words, the book aims to revisit Europe while speaking to methodological and normative problems of Eurocentrism in IR and international law. The difficult question is whether jurisdictional accumulation can deliver on methodologically challenging the myths of the linear, homogeneous, and singular, universal, and progressive development of European institutions. To do so according to Hobson and Sajed's 'fully relational ontology', the following sections and chapters would need to show whether this concept accounts for 'the co-constitutive, hybrid, polymorphous, and interstitial properties' that shape Western and non-Western agency (2017: 5, 9). Unfortunately, or not, it cannot claim to fulfil all of these properties, primarily because this study questions the theoretical approach that underlies this definition and gives it analytical primacy over historical specificities.

First, jurisdictional accumulation cannot accept the 'Western' adjective for the early modern period in the apparently modern sense it is used by Hobson and Sajed. More importantly, it cannot claim to *fully* account for non-Western agency in a transhistorical sense implied by their 'fully relational ontology'. Nevertheless, jurisdictional accumulation contributes to arguments about the construction of the cross-Atlantic and Western/Eastern Mediterranean by imperial and consular agents who helped to shape the definitions of jurisdiction and the distinctions between ownership and rule, between political and economic spheres, and between Christian and non-Christian jurisdictional spaces. Jurisdictional accumulation aims to contribute to the understanding of European expansion while providing a multilinear, collaborative, entangled, and exploitative development of early modern extraterritorial jurisdiction in Europe and at its emerging Mediterranean and Atlantic borders. Especially in the case of the Castilian empire, it provides a specifically hybrid and organic account of transplants of authority through an analysis of both metropolitan and colonial social property relations.[8] The term 'interstitial' is also helpful as a criterion for

[8] The turn to 'entangled histories' was developed from the French '*histoire croisée*' (Werner and Zimmermann, 2006) as a response to the externalism and objectivism of comparative

characterising jurisdiction, often operating at the interstices of personal and sovereign authority, although it is not a term significantly developed in this project. However, if, for Hobson and Sajed, Western and non-Western agency are exclusively co-constitutive, their project of a 'fully relational ontology' becomes a *sine qua non* to all historical sociology. Historically, that is a major claim that would need further justification and cannot be assumed, according to the research undertaken here, to apply to all practices of jurisdictional accumulation. Many of these, encapsulated by the term of transports of authority, were intentionally established by sovereigns as more indirect, outsourced, and therefore less – if even at all – co-constitutive between 'Western' and 'non-Western' agency. In sum, I can only leave it to the readers to judge for themselves whether these properties are sufficient for their own understanding of Eurocentrism and anti-Eurocentrism. To help with this task, the following goes deeper into the way in which jurisdictional accumulation is deployed in this project.

2.2 Against a Theory of 'the International' and for a Negative and Outward Methodological Internalism

The specific challenge that concerns us here in the area of critical historical sociology relates to how certain large-scale social phenomena such as capitalism, mercantilism, or the modernity of certain institutions such as diplomacy, should be attributed to European actors and institutions. A central question in Marxist historical sociology, and one particularly relevant to this study, is whether situating the transition to capitalism in seventeenth-century England is not only empirically or historically Eurocentric, but also methodologically or ideologicallfy Eurocentric. Although the transition or Brenner debate started in the 1980s (Aston & Philpin, 1985) and was historically and geographically limited to early modern England and Europe, it still continues today as it

history. It is a multidimensional and plural approach that focuses on 'processes of transfer, between societies, nations or civilizations, and its consequences' (Elliott, 2012: 182). The concept of entanglements is present in global historical sociology (Go & Lawson, 2017), in legal history (Duve, 2014; Donlan & Heirbaut, 2015), and in imperial history (Cañizares-Esguerra, 2018). In many ways, and following Elliott, this turn is indeed old wine in new bottles, and it fails to fully acknowledge its theoretical and methodological implications. However, the explicit conceptualisation of 'processes of transfer' marks a positive step away from methodological nationalism and is given more analytical weight in this study through the tripartite typology of jurisdictional accumulation.

encapsulates the methodological problems raised by the anti-Eurocentric literature in terms of the sequence of causal analysis (i.e. whether we should begin with a theory of the international or with a historical research problem).[9]

2.2.1 Methodological Humility and Epistemological Choices

The first step to consider is Anievas and Nişancioğlu (2015), Anievas and Matin (2016), and Rosenberg's (2016b) critiques of internalist positions to the transition debate. They argue that 'methodological internalism' has helped to generate in classical historical sociology (or in its first and second waves) the problem of Eurocentrism. They identify methodological internalism with 'the assumption that the character of a society's development is determined by its internal structures and agents' (Anievas & Matin, 2016: 5). At the same time, they argue that the task of theorising 'the international' has thwarted the development of a more influential historical sociology tradition among the US-led political science qua IR mainstream (Rosenberg, 2006, 2016a). The lack of a 'systematic theoretical apparatus capable of incorporating the coexistence and interaction of multiple societies as a distinct sphere of developmental dynamics and social causality' (Anievas & Matin, 2016: 4) is stopping scholars – who may be empirically anti-Eurocentric by involving the agency of non-Western actors and institutions in their work – from being methodologically anti-Eurocentric. In other words, non-Western agency can only be dissociated from the Eurocentric agenda and participate in the IR discipline as an autonomous agent if it is theorised through a systemic apparatus such as U&CD 'through which we can decentre or provincialise Europe as the privileged or sole author of history' (Anievas & Nişancioğlu, 2015: 276). In effect, this theory is considered by Hobson and Sajed (2017: 8) as one of the exceptions in critical IR which can account for non-Western agency in the broad and interconnected sense they identify.

U&CD or any other theory that begins from a universal conception of multiplicity, interconnectedness, and unequal development – as distinct from the messiness of historical and geographical contingency and unintended outcomes – is very appealing if it could provide a methodological basis for agency in its most plural, encompassing and open sense

[9] See Part 2 of this chapter for a fuller exposition of the Brenner debate.

possible. Unfortunately, such a theory is only possible in a world devoid of history. Reversely, internalism should also not determine a priori or universally the approach of historical sociology, and the type of internalism U&CD proponents describe is indeed reductive. However, the internalism they describe does not correspond to the social property relations approach developed by Brenner and his followers.[10]

In other words, the theory that fixes once and for all the Eurofetish is a mirage. This does not mean that attempts to pursue it do not bring about new and necessary analyses of the West and non-West in shaping world politics. Yet, following arguments by Knafo (2010, 2017), attaining a methodological position that erases academia's biases and solves its methodological problems remains a task for which we do not have the tools yet. Thus, we need to 'cut our losses' (Knafo, 2017) since we cannot achieve a theory that can be equivalent and total for every aspect and encounter of social relations.

Consequently, historical sociology should be methodologically problem-driven (i.e. it should maintain the primacy of specific historical arguments and research problems). Theoretical solutions to larger social and methodological problems (e.g. U&CD as solution to the Eurocentrism – and hence racism – in IR) hide the complexity and myriad social and cultural causes of those problems. Reclaiming the methodological for historical sociology means, as a first step in the sequence of causality driving research, to find ways to maintain 'the coexistence and interaction' – not on the ontological level between 'multiple societies' – but on the epistemological and hermeneutic level. This means finding ways to maintain 'the coexistence and interaction' between the disciplines' conceptualising of practices and actors on the one hand, and how practices and actors are affected or determined by disciplines on the other hand. In other words, this study defends the

[10] See Cammack's (2017) review of Anievas and Nişancioğlu (2015). See Pal (2018) for a review and critique of their concepts of internalism. The authors conflate two definitions of internalism, one being the 'ontological absence of non-European societies in histories of capitalism and modernity' where 'the internal' refers to Europe; and the second being the methodological '"inside-out" model of social causality' where development is 'endogenous and self-propelling', in which Europe (or England) is considered 'core' and 'prime mover' and can also be implied to be morally and culturally superior (Anievas & Nişancioğlu, 2015: 4–5)' (Pal, 2018: 105). In addition, the second methodological definition of internalism has two variants or causal logics that are also conflated: the 'domestic analogy' and 'the singular to the plural' logic. The authors fail to differentiate between these so as to more accurately assess the approaches under critique, and especially Political Marxism.

dialectics and praxis of social relations – that is, the relations between totality and agency, and between theory and practice – as the primary methodological and theoretical starting points for historical sociology.[11] If 'the philosophy of praxis postulates the immanent unity of material and ideological conditions in an historical process of becoming' (Cutler, 2008: 216), this process must be multidimensional and not assume that the immanent unity produces or implies a universal theory of agency, but instead postulate how their different manifestations, interpretations, and positions are consistent with their immanent unity.

Ignoring social relations of power – or class struggles – between actors involved in knowledge production and those involved in the practices 'to-be-known' flies in the face of understanding not only social sciences' epistemologies but also how capitalism functions today. In other words, critical scholarship must take seriously the implications of a century of positivist and behavioural social science that remains dominated by the policy-driven metric of quantitative data and impact measurement. This knowledge economy and rise of immaterial labour in some contexts – discussed by continental Marxists (Lazzarato, Lordon) as well as post-structural, postcolonial, decolonial, and self-reflexive IR (Mignolo, De Lissovoy) – has shown that the way in which we (in the Western academy) theorise is not a neutral, apolitical, or ahistorical endeavour. Therefore, any attempt to posit a theory of multiple social coexistence is conditioned by the power relations in which those thinking that coexistence have been able to evolve. The fact that social sciences and international theory are written in certain contexts by certain people – predominantly white, Western or European, male, from privileged backgrounds, and academically secured and stamped – relativises the objective relation to historical development they wish to capture, in spite of their efforts to minimise and atone for their privilege. Critical scholars cannot escape or avoid this context. Fully avoiding this bias, which I elsewhere referred to as a hermeneutic disjuncture (Pal, 2018), as well as the dynamics of class and other social hierarchies in academic knowledge production are – for now and the foreseeable future – unavoidable.[12] However, it does raise a responsibility of methodological humility

[11] These concepts are further developed in Part 2.

[12] For a discussion of how to shape a critical pedagogy for IR, see Odysseos and Pal (2017). See Pal (forthcoming) for a further discussion on how to develop a methodological and pedagogical approach to historical sociology in IR.

and thus of dialectical/praxis-driven choice in how to navigate historical sociology.

2.2.2 *Revisiting Internalism*

The second step to understand the approach in this book explores the position of a *negative* and *outward* 'methodological internalism'. A *negative* methodological internalism implies that the internalism adopted is – following from the first step discussed above – secondary to the historical research problems pursued and for which a form of internalism may appear as most appropriate. An *outward* form of internalism pushes conventional definitions of the term outside its territorial and static confines. A conventional definition of internalism refers to 'analytical narratives and causal explanations that are confined to dynamics within a particular territory' (Go & Lawson, 2017: 4).

In contrast, an outward internalism determined by the research question of early modern extraterritorial jurisdiction refers to analytical narratives and causal explanations that *begin* from dynamics within particular *spaces*. In other words, it opens the 'territory' box to concepts of authority, multiple forms of sovereignty, and, crucially, to jurisdiction, as other ways of bordering power and means of class exploitation. Moreover, an outward internalism assumes that the 'internal structures and agents' (Anievas & Matin, 2016: 5) of a social context can be as determining as their external structures.[13]

In sum, the internalism explored throughout this study is secondary to – or dependent on – the research problem, and this research problem (Northern–Eurocentric and territorial definitions of extraterritorial authority reduced to ambassadorial privileges) necessitates an examination of European extraterritorial practices that emerged within and were

[13] For the sake of the argument, I follow these authors' use of 'internal' and 'external' structures of agents. However, it remains unclear how exactly to differentiate between these structures. Does internal mean personal and individual, that is determined and concerned with the personal characteristics of – or potential advantages to – an agent? Whereas external would refer to social, impersonal, and institutional structures independent from the actions, abilities, or characteristics of individuals? If so, this leaves open the question of the interaction, overlap, or uncertainty between these extremes of the agency–structure debate. In other words, this distinction errs dangerously towards a positivist problem-solving approach to the debate rather than a dialectical co-constitutive standpoint. These questions will be further questioned in Part 2 when discussing Political Marxism.

extended, transported, and transplanted throughout and beyond Europe. In other words, the research problem requires an inside-out analytical narrative and causal logic of explanation.

In addition, the argument can be pushed to more general contexts and definitions of internalism. To more accurately make sense of social and geopolitical relations in the early modern period, it is necessary to differentiate the causal logics of methodological internalism identified as lacking in the analysis of Anievas and Nişancioğlu (2015) (i.e. the 'domestic analogy' and 'the singular to the plural'). These refer to distinct social processes in the early modern period before they get subsumed in the nineteenth-century capitalist global political economy. By then, the state form becomes the standard political and legal unit according to which other political and legal forms become colonised, silenced, or erased.

In effect, let us assume that the 'domestic analogy' implies that the European state form (State A) imposes itself as the standard for a political entity (Colony B) and another political entity (Colony C). We can illustrate this colonial logic as: A to B and A to C. In contrast, the 'singular to plural' logic implies that the European state form (State A) imposes itself and is more or less equally applied as the homogeneous standard for a group of political entities or even for 'the rest' of the world. We can illustrate this logic as: A to (B + C). Both logics (assuming for the sake of the argument that they both occur since they are both found across classic historical sociology texts) may utilise different means and invoke different justifications for colonisation (religious, civilisational, etc.) but they become equivalent processes in terms of their outcome in a late-nineteenth-century world where the international legal order has posited the universal standard of the state form and European imperialism more or less imposes itself homogeneously and in concert. This is exemplified in the Hague and Berlin conferences, or the 'Scramble for Africa' and other 'Eurafrica' projects that helped or at least wished to produce this similar outcome. In other words, in the context of a global capitalist political economy, the different logics of state extraterritoriality or legal imperialism (as extensions, transports, or transplants of authority) lead to or are driven by the same outcome, the imposition of the modern territorial state form.

However, in the early modern period, jurisdictional international relations and different imperial practices lead to *different* outcomes. Therefore more emphasis needs to be placed on the differences between their internal causal logics of accumulation and state formation because these differences did not lead to the common outcome one finds in the late-nineteenth and early-twentieth centuries. In other words, the logics of 'domestic analogy' and 'singular to plural' are too reductive and do not serve the same useful purpose as they do in the later period emphasising the unique process of the imposition of the standard state form. Instead, early modern practices involve a wider variety of actors and institutions that negotiate, for themselves and for their sovereigns, practices of accepted social interaction leading to state formation and various forms of accumulation. The forms of authority that are extended, transported, and transplanted vary from empires, dynastic sovereigns, composite monarchs, republics, cities, even chartered companies. Moreover, French, English, Dutch, or Iberian actors reproducing their sovereign's jurisdictional practices in the Mediterranean and in the Americas, and therefore expanding the sovereign or city's power, differed significantly – in their character, occupations, objectives, means at their disposal – from each other and from their counterparts posted in other parts of the world. Homogenising the internalism from which the conditions of international formal reproduction originate – before being mediated by interaction and external conditions, to adopt this clumsy and reductive vocabulary – fails to acknowledge the specificities of the early modern pre-capitalist and capitalist world. Worse, it leads to erroneously homogenising extraterritorial practices.

Two further elements justify the use of the term 'internalism' in spite of its negative baggage. First, a major aim of this study is to argue for the construction of international legal orders and the constitutive role of jurisdictional struggles as locally specific and often personally driven contests. Second, the starting point for this enquiry has been Europe, and a significant part of the sources for that enquiry rely on the concept of social property relations, which has been negatively and reductively identified as internalist by its critics. The project therefore aims to open this question of how to identify different forms of internalism, and to clarify how its use can be justified.

Jurisdictional accumulation justifies using internalism to refer to processes of development where the logic of causality is 'outward' (Pal, 2018: 111). This does not mean that jurisdictional accumulation is necessarily spatially restricted to Europe or European actors. However, in the cases studied, it is historically shaped by them and their attempts to differentiate themselves, especially in the Mediterranean, from those they considered non-European or simply other by being non-Christian.

Through this revisited narrative of the contested practices and new actors of extraterritorial jurisdiction – that is, through jurisdictional accumulation – this study, in spite of its internalism, contributes to anti-Eurocentric efforts in historical sociology and IR because it revisits the standard narratives of the construction of early modern legal orders and aims to methodologically dislodge them. Specifically, it breaks apart the classic shift from the personal to the territorial in diplomatic histories reproducing the Westphalian imaginary, and integrates relations between colonial and metropolitan social property relations to define different types of jurisdictional accumulation.

However, beyond these methodological abstract statements and the general historical claims about the jurisdictional diversity and multiplicity of the early modern world, one needs to further show why extraterritorial jurisdiction needs to be studied from the inside-out or as an outward movement. This will be one of the key tasks of the subsequent empirical chapters, which show the role of social property relations in revealing differences between contiguous extensions of authority (Chapter 3), while providing a basis from which to understand differences between transplants and transports of authority (Chapters 4–7).

To conclude: internalism should not be used as an a priori charge or accusation against a historical approach. An internalist method is not necessarily Eurocentric. Attributing theoretically narrow definitions of internalism to historical analyses does not suffice to dislodge their merits. Having established the central tenets of the book's use of historical sociology, the following discusses another significant source for exploring extraterritorial jurisdiction, namely, the historiography of empires in international legal history. These sources are crucial for building the framework of jurisdictional accumulation, as well as broadening the application of historical sociology and Marxism in IR and in international legal theory, discussed in Part 2.

2.3 Imperial and International Legal History

2.3.1 Classic Histories of International Law

Grewe's (2000) magisterial work, influenced by Schmitt (2003), is considered as the classic reference point for histories of international law. Another key text is the recent work by Neff (2014) which adopts a broader and different angle of periodisation but retains the same doctrinal focus and sequencing for the early modern period from the neo-scholastics to Grotius, Westphalia, and other key markers of modern territorial sovereignty. However, Grewe remains the 'most widely read English-language general history of the field today' (Koskenniemi, 2017a: 3) and is used in key critical works such as Miéville (2005) and Baars (2019: 78).[14] Although empirically rich, these analyses have various methodological and empirical problems, some of which are discussed in the following as relevant to the concepts developed in this project.

Grewe and Schmitt's political realist narratives reach further than nineteenth-century imperialism by emphasising the state-led power politics that in their view ultimately determine the movement of history. Looking at early modern concepts of the political, they also ideologically question the formation of the liberal state and its legal institutions. Grewe's *The Epochs of International Law* (2000) is based on separate hegemonic or imperial moments to periodise the history of international law. He also analyses shifts from notions of *ius gentium* to *ius inter gentes* and *ius publicum europaeum* to account for the early modern periods, incorporating classical theorists and political developments.

Many legal historians accept Grewe's division of the early modern period into these three successive frameworks of intersocietal rules and customs. The late medieval *jus gentium* (fifteenth–sixteenth centuries) refers mostly to the right of natural partnership and communication. It implied the notion of a 'universal' realm (*res publica christiana*), where Christians could enjoy and be accountable to the same rights and duties.

The shift to *jus inter gentes* (sixteenth–seventeenth centuries) marks the turn to more independent state-like entities, and implies the emergence of concerted agreements and treaties 'between' nations as to the laws of war, trade, and communication. *Jus inter gentes* develops more subjective rights for international actors, the concept of *rayas* (divisions of the world), and the concept of *terra nullius* (i.e. vacant space crucial to early modern colonisations and their doctrinal justifications).

The *jus publicum europaeum* (seventeenth–eighteenth centuries) is also referred to as the *droit public de l'Europe*. It consists in a more technically, professionally, and spatially demarcated framework for

[14] Although Nussbaum's piece (1954) is more often quoted in Anglo-American textbooks of international law, it is of significantly less depth and richness than Grewe's. However, the English translation of Grewe (2000) is altering this, making the work gradually more present albeit with the cautions required by its Schmittian influence and apologism of Hitler's Germany (Koskenniemi, 2000; Miéville, 2005: 155; Armstrong *et al.*, 2007: 67; Teschke, 2011a, 2011b). A less recent but still useful classic of the anglophone history of international law is Butler and Maccoby (1928).

European relations. Experts are trained to write territorial treaties, the demand for which significantly augments, and scholars become employed to analyse the rights that such treaties and overseas expansion create: notably, the development of *terra nullius* as the right to use non-occupied and/or non-cultivated land, the right to punish those transgressing the law of nature, dynastic rights of succession, and amity lines (replacing the *rayas* of the previous era).

However, in parallel to these longer-term categories, the early modern period comprised overlapping international legal orders and sources, such as merchant law (*lex mercatoria*), maritime law, natural law (*jus naturalis*), *jus communis*, canon law, Roman civil law, and feudal law (Berman, 1983). Because of the parcellised and multi-jurisdictional nature of early modern sovereignties, these orders and codes overlapped and were 'stacked', following Péquignot and Belissa's term '*l'empilement des normes*' (2016: 311). The personalised, territorially unfixed forms of sovereignty, along with the lack of centralised government, confirmed the fluidity and interdependence of continental legal doctrine and practices. This contests the notion of law and politics as separable domains, and challenges some of the distinctions and narratives of Grewe and Schmitt's work.

Grewe sustains a state-centric, power-politics conception of international relations, where international law reflects rather than conditions reality. This is unfolded through a long-haul account of the history of modern international law, from the crystallisation of the Holy Roman Empire and the papacy during the ninth century, up until the end of the twentieth century. In each epoch, international law was fashioned by a distinctive hegemonic power or system of power, that is Spain, France, Britain, and America. Here at least, the birth of the modern international legal order is understood as a longer and more complex historical process in the spirit, if not the letter, of historical sociology. However, since international rules and norms are elaborated and/or transformed under the pressure of national ideologies and prerogatives, international law remains a formal and restricted legal structure translating the vagaries of international politics.

Grewe's account is a rich and often reliable historical source, but his focus on the political power of each hegemon, that is Spain, France, and England as determining the course of modern international law is problematic. This chronological series results in each power being defined in relation to its failure or progress over the other. As such it focuses on the similarities between each state so as to construct a more homogeneous and linear account of the history of international law, which hides the social property relations that constituted the formation of each state, and the colonial social property relations that shaped the agency of imperial actors. Specifically, it ignores the social struggles that are played out in determining the hegemony of each state, and the implications of these social relations for how we conceive of international law and politics. Crucially, this account omits a central similarity between these empires, which is here referred to by practices of jurisdictional accumulation, as processes that reflect strategies of expansion of authority as transplants, transports, and extensions.

2.3.2 The Turn in International Legal History

The turn in critical international legal history since the 1990s has greatly contributed to critiques of the above classic literature. A significant problem is the way in which classic studies integrate the abundant work of classical legal and political thinkers to the dominantly 'nineteenth century-centric' narrative of the rise of modern international society (Lesaffer, 2002, 2017: 103). This has resulted in multiple anthologies of classical legal thought rather than historical sociologies of jurisdictional and jurisprudential developments. That is to say, the succession of mostly Vitoria, Suàrez, Gentili, Grotius, Pufendorf, and Vattel is written in a continuum where each author is linked to his peers in an attempt to find the running thread of progress from primitive to developed, medieval to modern, naturalist to positivist. This creates a classical ontology that results in legitimising modern discipline while also generating problematic debates (Jahn, 2000, 2006).

In response, histories of early modern imperialism have grown by being more critical of these standard narratives and by focusing more on contextual intellectual history and international political thought (Pagden, 1987; Bartelson, 1995; Tuck, 1999; Armitage, 2000; Koskenniemi, 2001; Keene, 2002; Fitzmaurice, 2003; MacMillan, 2006; Brett, 2011; Dupuy & Chetail, 2013; Moyn & Sartori, 2015; Armitage & Pitts, 2016; Pitts, 2017; Kadelbach *et al.*, 2017).[15]

[15] Another trend has also emerged focusing on economic and institutional history such as the work of Douglas North and Steven Pinker (for an introductory review, see Calafat & Monnet, 2017), but this literature has been less influential for international legal history and is therefore not engaged with in this project.

This doctrinal focus has been very rich and increasingly focuses on problems of reception and contextualism (Keene, 2017; Vergerio, 2018). However, this richness has been 'to the detriment of legal practice' (Lesaffer, 2017: 103). Nevertheless, new work is emerging that is explicitly calling for a focus on global practices of legal ordering and of the specificities of colonial legal territoriality (Hébié, 2015; Wallenius, 2019). The present project also leaves the doctrinal literature aside to focus on more influential histories of international law in terms of practices, and in terms of their potential to enrich historical sociology in IR.

The field of international legal history has included large-scale comparative histories (e.g. Alexandrowicz, 1967; Anghie, 1999; Koskenniemi, 2001; Benton, 2002, 2010) and has developed the links between the growth of empires and international law (Benton, 2006; Benton & Ross, 2013; Belmessous, 2015; Benton *et al.*, 2017; Koskenniemi *et al.*, 2017).[16] If this critical historiography focuses on colonial practices to explain shifts in doctrine, and specifically its arguments on the construction of modern sovereignty through the interdependent distinction between coloniser and colonised (Simpson, 2004; Anghie, 2005; Bowden, 2005; Cavallar, 2008; Kayaoglu, 2010), it broadly understands the effects of imperialism and colonisation outside Europe as constitutive of European expansion and modern sovereignty. This literature therefore plays a significant role for the anti-Eurocentric agenda and for a transition towards a more practice-informed focus on doctrine.

Nevertheless, historians of international law and empire remain shy in front of the private and commercial dimensions of this history. They have focused more on sovereignty than property (Koskenniemi, 2016), neglecting how 'expansion took place through private operators, colonial or trading companies, and by way of private contract and the exercise of the right of private property' (Koskenniemi, 2017a: 10).[17] This project therefore speaks to some of this neglect, not by focusing on private

[16] Anghie's work is the result of scholarship in the 1960s and 1970s with Third World scholars such as R. P. Anand or Judge T. O. Elias. One Western and notable example is C. H. Alexandrowicz (1967) (Chimni, 2008: 500). A new collection puts forward Alexandrowicz's path-breaking work in shifting the European gaze, notably towards the East (Armitage & Pitts, 2016). More radical and Marxist scholars such as Chimni also recognise themselves under the acronym of TWAIL (Third World approaches to international law). For a recent analysis, see Eslava (2019).

[17] For some notable exceptions, see Cutler (2003), Neocleous (2012), Cavanagh (2014, 2017), Koskenniemi (2013, 2017b), Garcia-Salmones (2017), Kochi (2017), and Baars (2019).

property per se, but on social property relations more generally, and on jurisdiction as a process neither public nor private but generating and transferring authority in a myriad of ways for a variety of actors. Bringing together these practices under the banner of the concept of jurisdictional accumulation enables to further the analysis of early modern empires in the history of international relations while accounting for the 'hybridised' approach called for by critical international legal historians (Koskenniemi, 2016).

Moreover, international legal history still lacks in theoretical and methodological debates in comparison to those discussed above in IR. The legal field has been very rich in empirical studies, yet it has lacked in theoretical and methodological statements that go beyond the positivism of the early comparatists or that fully account for the critical pluralism that is often implicitly adopted in recent studies. Although interest and scholarship on the history of international law has significantly increased, problems of methodology, of definition of explicit research problems remain, alongside the recourse to chronologies of 'great thinkers' as a silent answer to those questions without sufficiently tackling the methodological problems and decisions such histories require (Vergerio, 2019). These methodological lacunae are starting to shift with the debate between Orford (2017) and Benton (2019) regarding criteria of historical validity, Tomlins's (2016) critique of micro-contextualism in pluralist legal histories, and d'Aspremont's (2019) plea for a more radical disciplinary imagination and interventionist history writing that develops a whole range of 'new' 'markers, periodization, and causal sequencing' (110–115) so as to remedy the problems of the 'historical turn'. In response to this wide indictment and plea, and to the significant burden placed on what is to be considered 'new', this project might seem disappointing as it undoubtedly engages and reproduces 'old' markers, periodisation, and causal sequencing, and contributes to what d'Aspremont identifies as the impossibility of critical historiography of international law. However, the project nevertheless provides new conceptual ground to shift some of these methods of historical writing and emphasises the methodological humility and care required when engaging on such projects, perhaps a necessary step before turning 'a blind eye' to the old and imagining the new (113).[18]

[18] There are two significant fields of legal history that this project does not fully engage with. First, the legal transplants literature in legal history (Ewald, 1995; Watson, 1995; Legrand, 1997; Halperin, 2009) is a theory about legal change and a method that is based on more

To conclude on Part 1, the jurisdictional aspect of early modern history is thus widely accepted by international legal historians, but it is rarely questioned or discussed in any conceptual depth. Moreover, these historical studies tend to focus on specific cases and lack a comparative sociological approach. If Marxist approaches respond to this missing angle with a more long-term and systemic or structural starting point, existing studies fail to account for the jurisdictional and diplomatic diversities of the early modern period (Cutler, 2001; Miéville, 2005). Nevertheless, this chapter argues that they can provide a broader methodological framework necessary for this study, on the condition that they integrate the empirical richness of the preceding body of work and reflect more on concepts such as jurisdiction to broaden the Marxist vocabulary of political and legal practices.

PART 2 MARXISM AND LAW

Part 1 dealt with the first objective emerging from the previous chapter, that is engaging with and responding to problems of Eurocentrism and modernity raised by histories of extraterritoriality. Part 2 tackles the second objective: the need for a stretched definition of extraterritoriality which accounts for the differences between extensions, transports, and transplants of sovereign authorities. In other words, this project needs a framework that accounts for legal agency in a broader context of competing processes of accumulation and modes of production.

In response, the following argues that historical materialism – or, in short, Marxism – provides a totalising yet agential conceptual framework that can account for these jurisdictional struggles in the context of the development of capitalism, international law, and the modern state system. However, different Marxist approaches produce different narratives of this development, and for this project, Political Marxism provides

traditional approaches to comparative history that tend to be methodologically nationalist. Their particular definition of 'transplants' is not the one adopted in this project. Second, there is a rich treaty and settler colonial literature (Ford, 2010; Belmessous, 2012, 2015) which looks at the more technical aspects of treaty negotiation and imposition between empires, settlers, and indigenous groups. This literature remains in many respects beyond the purview of this study but will be referred to in terms of settlement practices in Chapter 6 and has overall significantly contributed to legal pluralism and to the better understanding of jurisdiction and legal imperialism. See Meguro (2019) for an alternative definition of transplants in international legal history a better historical and methodological basis than the influential commodity form theory of law.

As a lone voice in international law explicitly developing the contours of a Marxist historical sociology, Cutler argues that such an approach entails retrieving the 'mechanisms by which laws become internalised in the consciousness of people'; only then might we

> begin to theorise law as an effective agent in history ... This involves developing a constitutive theory of international law in which the law is understood as operating in a dialectical movement between legal theory and the practices of actors.
>
> (2002: 197–198)

Here the links between the theoretical and practical, the micro and macro, internal and external, or individual and structural levels of social interaction are explicitly combined and encapsulated in the 'dialectics and praxis' of international law and international relations (Cutler, 2002).[19] Exploring mechanisms by which people internalise laws recalls Mattingly's search for the events and processes that 'shaped men's minds to the fiction of extraterritoriality'. Yet the quote is a helpful albeit abstract reminder that this search should incorporate methodological conditions of dialectics and praxis (i.e. the interdependent relations between totality and agency on the one hand, and theory and practice on the other).

Cutler's theoretical work is a good introduction to understanding the relationship between international relations and international law. It paves the way for a dialogue between the two leading approaches to the history of law and capitalism, namely the commodity form theory of law and the tradition of Political Marxism. This dialogue generates a fruitful and necessary debate, yet one not sufficiently engaged with. It cannot be done full justice here, yet the discussion concludes that the two approaches to law and capitalism reproduce a more general distinction between two approaches to history in Marxist scholarship, a consequentialist approach – in the commodity form theory – and a 'processual–agentic' approach – for Political Marxism (Teschke, 2017). For our present purposes, the discussion extracts the three following theoretical and historical foundations.

[19] For a more recent and contemporary-driven attempt to develop historical sociology in international law, see Cutler & Gill (2015).

First, Marxism provides, on a most fundamental conceptual level, a totalising yet agency-based approach. This means it is relational and concerned primarily with the social relations shaping and shaped by large-scale phenomena such as modes of production or geopolitical orders. It is therefore broad enough to accommodate a larger panoply of manifestations of extraterritoriality. This dialectical foundation is shared by both Political Marxism and the commodity form theory of law.

Second, on a more theoretical level, Marxism provides a critical and emancipatory dimension to the study of international relations and international law. Its praxis contests the Eurocentric linear and progressive narrative of European qua international society, as well as the unequal relations of class, race, and gender in knowledge production. However, Marxist approaches differ in their counter-narratives to the development of capitalism, modernity, and international law. Consequentialist theories of the international identify the emergence of capitalism as a multicausal phenomenon originating in multiple sites and found in the logic of the commodity form theory of law focused on external similarities and the individual to states analogy. In contrast, Political Marxism provides a focus on agency through class struggle as well as a sharper and more specific conception of the emergence of capitalism that gives space to other processes of accumulation and modes of production in explaining the development of international law and modernity.

Third, and more historically, both approaches make significant contributions to incorporating law into a Marxist framework and narrative. However, Political Marxism opens up more space for a political economy of jurisdictional struggles as both transitional and non-transitional to capitalism. These provide the possibility for social change through the more interstitial, ambiguous, and unintended space of jurisdiction, essential to the different manifestations of extraterritoriality. Political Marxism also provides the concept of social property relations, which enables a focus on jurisdictional spaces as characterised by quasi-public actors (lawyers, consuls, ecclesiastics) belonging to aspiring classes (merchants, gentry, lower nobility, lower clergy). Thus, legal agency or legal social relations emerge as a manifestation of class struggle that affects the concurring modes of production of the early modern period: mercantilism in continental Europe and capitalism in England, and, more arguably, in the Dutch Republic.

In sum, Political Marxism provides a more historically nuanced and less structurally determined focus than the commodity form theory of law, by emphasising legal agency and jurisdiction through relations between class struggles and modes of production. Its central concept of social property relations will be used throughout this project. However, the project will also be an opportunity to enrich and further debates inside Political Marxism – and Marxism more generally – in favour of a historicist and methodological turn that emphasises the agency of legal actors in major social changes of the classic period of European transitions from feudalism.

The following sets out the more general foundations and steps in shaping Marxism and law, before looking more closely at Cutler's work on transnational merchant law and the legitimacy crisis, followed by the commodity form theory of law, its critique from a Political Marxist angle, and finally how these approaches help to define the method of historical sociology adopted for this project and encapsulated in the concept of jurisdictional accumulation.

2.4 Foundations

Since the late 1990s, there has been an increasing amount of Marxist scholarship addressing issues on international law.[20] For an earlier generation of scholars (e.g. Fine *et al.*, 1979; Fryer *et al.*, 1981; Sugarman, 1983), the task was to address a crude reading of Marx on law that took the base–superstructure distinction as a starting point.[21] They acknowledged the lack of theorising of law in Marx's writings and the consequent danger of 'easy generalization and accompanying avoidance of history' (Corrigan & Sayer, 1981: 22). In response, they developed less functionalist definitions of law influenced by E. P. Thompson's critique of structural Marxists (1978). Aided by the end of the Cold War, scholars started reinterpreting the Soviet legal theorist Evgeny Pashukanis (1978),

20 For example, Cutler, 1997; Marks, 1997; Chimni, 1999; Miéville, 2005; Bowring, 2008; Knox, 2009, 2010; Bachand & Lapointe, 2010; Neocleous, 2012; Schwöbel-Patel, 2012; Cutler & Gill, 2015; Brabazon, 2016; Knox, 2016a; Brophy, 2017; O'Connell, 2017; Reynolds, 2017; Krever, 2018; O'Connell, 2018; Rasulov, 2018; Baars, 2019; Özsu, 2019; Parfitt, 2019; Taylor, 2019; Tzouvala, forthcoming. See Marks (2008) for an edited volume on Marxism in international law. See Knox (2016b, 2018) for a review and bibliography of the field. See O'Connell and Özsu (forthcoming) for the first major handbook on Marxism and law.

21 For example: 'The totality of these relations of production constitutes the economic structure of society, the real foundation on which arises a legal and political superstructure and to which correspond definite forms of social consciousness' (Marx, 1971: 20).

while becoming more and more critical of the post-1990s' appetite for international justice. Although scholars in the 1980s were dismissive of Pashukanis's formalism (e.g. Fryer *et al.*, 1981; Warrington, 1983), Miéville's (2005) interpretation has resurrected his commodity form theory for the world of critical international law. This has come in parallel to the development of Marxist-inspired Third World approaches to international law (TWAIL) and their focus on the role of Western imperialism in constructing what became universal legal principles and institutions and the need to rewrite this history from a Third World perspective including non-Western agency (e.g. Chimni, 1999; Gathii, 2000; Eslava, 2019).

A historical materialist approach starts from the premise that law needs to be understood as process, not as a thing-in-itself (Marks, 2007: 203). Law is manifested *in* and *as* social relations that continuously structure the manifold of human relationships. If this claim is in line with a more general move in mainstream legal theory since the New Haven School (McDougall & Lasswell, 1996), historical materialism in addition implies a holistic, structural, and 'totalising' conception of law.

> Where international law is concerned, the concept of totality highlights the need for a complex kind of analysis that connects international legal norms with the wider processes through which their interpretation is shaped and enabled. It urges us to approach things relationally, rather than in isolation, and to pay attention to the larger social forces that create the conditions in which international legal ideas and concepts emerge, develop and get deployed.
>
> (Marks, 2008: 15)

In effect, international law's totalising condition is a priori assimilated to the expansion of modern sovereignty and capitalism. Marxist critiques argue that international law maintains relations of dependence between states and other international legal actors. It does so by providing institutional standards and frameworks for state intervention, diplomacy, and trade that enshrine dominant class interests. These power relations hide behind a discourse of progressive and egalitarian principles, which translates into a faith in international law as a means for social justice and underlies public debates and various 'humanitarian' practices. Therefore, Marxists are by definition sceptical of liberal paradigms and the practices of intervention they justify.

However, the way in which this scepticism is converted into the theory and practice of international law remains a terrain of debate. Miéville's often-quoted radical conclusion gave one of the positions in this debate a clear formulation:

> The attempt to replace war and inequality with law is not merely utopian – it is precisely self-defeating. A world structured around international law cannot but be one of imperialist violence. The chaotic and bloody world around us *is the rule of law*.
>
> (2005: 319)

Yet this conclusion is strongly theoretical and leaves practitioners, activists, and everyday commentators in the dark as to how to navigate fighting for and achieving rights as one of the few ways to secure small victories in the legal battles against abuses committed by states or corporations. Marxists remain divided, if not mystified by what we could call a 'liberal dilemma'. If Knox (2010) shows that this problem revolves around a lack of engagement with the distinction between strategy and tactics, he argues that lawyers should adopt a position of 'principled opportunism' so as to navigate the dilemmas and contradictions of short-term emancipatory struggles for rights.

The following discussion suggests that Marxist legal theory also suffers from the poorly addressed tension between structure and agency. Of course, Marxist scholarship has gone through different waves of addressing this problem, which in more practical political terms, boils down to the split between reformist and revolutionary socialists. Nevertheless, this problem persists and is accentuated by the sophistication of international legal processes and their growing interdependence with contemporary international relations.

An important element of Marxist theory remains its emancipatory potential and ability to incorporate, in its conceptual framework of analysis, the possibility of change and agency as much as structural determination. This concern will frame the following analysis, not in terms of the future of capitalism and law, but in terms of mercantilism, the emergence of capitalism, and the relation of these modes of production to the development of international law and extraterritorial jurisdiction. Cutler's critique of mainstream approaches and her historical analysis of early modern private international law is a useful starting point.

2.5 Transnational Merchant Law and the Legitimacy Crisis

Cutler (1999, 2003) develops a conceptually wide historical materialism 'as a philosophy of praxis and as a method of critical analysis' (2008:

202), focused on contemporary developments in transnational economic law. Through this she raises the issue of the rise of private authority in international relations and international law, identifying a fundamental 'legitimacy crisis'. Mainstream theories are inadequate in explaining the current relationship between international law and international relations, she argues, since they obscure the 'real' configurations of power through their narrow conception of states as the only 'legitimate' actors. Cutler shows how power configurations today have gone beyond the distinction between public and private spheres. Transnational corporations and other dominant actors have managed to increase their participation in decision-making over international affairs and specifically, over the rules and behaviour of their businesses. However, they have done so by acquiring de facto significance while remaining *de jure* insignificant.

> Public definitions of authority and law block the association of politics with private activity and actors, while state-centric and territorial theories of rule confine political activity to the state and create impediments to recognizing the political nature of private international trade law.
>
> (Cutler, 2003: 60)

Accordingly, a currently entrenched mercatocracy has caused a disjuncture between theory and practice at the root of international law's legitimacy crisis.[22] 'The law has ceased to constitute, mirror and, in some cases, to discipline its "subject", the state and state practice. The "subject" has in fact, been reconfigured in the legally "invisible" form of the transnational corporation' (2001: 147). International law's legitimacy crisis lies in the 'problem of the subject', that is the question of who has, or can have, legal personality, which places extraterritorial disputes at the centre of this research problem. However, Cutler focuses on the disciplinary context and concludes that the inconsistencies between liberal democracy and 'the new private authority over international affairs' (1999) are a consequence of the dichotomy between on the one hand the normative and theoretical structure of liberalism, and on the other the state-centric unit rigidity of realism.

[22] This corresponds to the rise of a new law merchant (transnational economic law, law of private international trade, and international business law) since the nineteenth century. This involves the renewed preference for private arbitration over adjudication, where privatised processes of dispute resolution are replacing dispute settlement by national judicial authorities in areas such as securities, antitrust, competition law, regulations, and consumer protection.

Cutler's use of dichotomies is helpful in terms of highlighting how these have come to structure the development of international law and international relations into public and private spheres, whether for property rights ('bundles of rights' and 'ownership of things') (2002); jurisdictional or legal–political orders (national and international, public and private); or for IR theory (liberalism and realism). This approach also helps in understanding how these dichotomies have brought international law to a crisis of legitimacy, while also limiting the emancipatory and socially wider potential of law by narrowly framing the terms of capitalist competition between the two forces of fragmentation and centralisation.

However, the gains in terms of a historically broader and simplified picture of the rise of private international law, contributing theoretically to contemporary issues, come at a cost from the point of view of the history of extraterritoriality. Her work provides a significant part of the story necessary to this project, and is a lone forerunner in terms of linking late medieval and early modern mercantile practices back to the construction of private and public realms of modern legitimacy (an achievement she has not been sufficiently recognised for). Cutler fulfils powerfully the task of a historical sociology and Marxist approach that is historically grounded yet turned towards the present. Moreover, Cutler's focus on mercantile and 'private' legal mechanisms provides an important aspect of the early modern history of extraterritoriality, arising out of growing trade relations between competing empires and the need to regulate these relations (mainly with the Ottoman Empire, but also China and North Africa).

Despite these insights, this project needs to look further for the potential of a Marxist framework of analysis. Cutler's commitment to understanding the rise of private authority and the legitimacy crisis forces her to ignore the wider political manifestations of merchants through jurisdictional practices such as consular agency. Since our aim here is to challenge the neglected role of extraterritoriality in the construction of modern international relations and international law, conventionally seen through the narrow picture of Northern European ambassadorial privileges, this implies exploring the politics of extraterritoriality as well as its various economic, religious, and cultural manifestations. Reversely, the history of extraterritorial jurisdiction cannot be reserved to the development of the law merchant. If extraterritoriality did develop from the increasing presence of merchants and the development of trade in the Mediterranean basin and then further east, the development of consular jurisdiction and the treatment of foreigners was not limited to the regulation of trade. It was as much, if not more in some cases, concerned with policing and adjudicating all aspects of the life of foreigners in port cities.

In other words, the history of extraterritoriality does not strictly follow that of the law merchant (and specifically, does not fully corroborate the argument on the autonomy of the merchant order). It might have contributed to it to a certain extent, but this history, as will be shown in subsequent chapters, reveals a broader set of legal strategies and relations between sovereigns and their various representatives. Merchant and non-merchant actors displayed different patterns of property relations based on personal and feudal, or absolutist and local/regional institutions with jurisdictional power. These legal strategies display patterns that reproduce semi-feudal, mercantilist, and absolutist forms of sovereignty and jurisdiction, and do not necessarily anticipate capitalist processes such as those of land improvement and the rights and conceptions of property that accompanied this specifically capitalist strategy of exploitation. Thus, Cutler's framework of analysis is not historically adequate for an analysis of extraterritoriality or more accurately, of jurisdictional accumulation.

Finally, Cutler's work adopts more explicitly the model of the commodity form theory of law, albeit with an emancipatory outlook (2002: 251; 2008: 202; 2014). This leads us to consider more thoroughly Miéville's commodity form theory of international law.

2.6 From Pashukanis to Miéville

The commodity form theory of law starts from the basis that the exchange of commodities requires a form of ownership of the commodity exchanged, and a recognition of such ownership by both parties involved. These parties – individuals – become abstract owners of commodities. In other words, commodity exchange requires private property, which in turn generates the legal personality of individuals. From this relation, law is developed as a body of regulations to ensure the terms of the exchange. In the same way as commodities are bearers of value,[23]

[23] It is a physical relation between physical things. As against this, the commodity-form, and the value-relation of the products of labour within which it appears, have absolutely no connection with the physical nature of the

legal subjects are bearers of rights. This means the legal relation, in parallel to the commodity relation, exists at the level of circulation as opposed to production; more specifically, the sphere of production is irrelevant to the *emergence* of the legal subject. 'Relations of production must be analysed to make sense of the particular class relations under capitalism, but the *legal* relations remain an expression of the relations of circulation' (Miéville, 2005: 93). Thus, the increase and global expansion of trade (i.e. commodity relations) from the sixteenth century onwards resulted in the gradual generalisation of a particular legal form. If historically content-specific, this legal form is in its most basic 'embryonic' sense, the assumption of private property and legal personality for the exchange of goods.

To apply this theory to international law, a second premise is attached to the above: '[s]overeign states coexist and are counterposed to one another in exactly the same way as are individual property owners with equal rights' (Pashukanis, in Knox, 2009: 416). The analogy between individuals and states assumes that states are formally equal sovereigns in the same way as individuals are abstracted as equal owners of commodities. However, Pashukanis's theory of the state argues that the development of public authority is *contingent* on the legal form.

> Pashukanis's claims that (proto-)international law historically predates domestic law have nothing to do with any putative ontological primacy of the international sphere: it is, rather, because law is thrown up by and necessary to a systematic commodity–exchange relationship, and it was between organised but disparate groups without superordinate authorities rather than between individuals that such relationships sprang up.
>
> (Miéville, 2005: 131).

commodity and the material relations arising out of this. It is nothing but the definite social relation between men themselves which assumes here, for them, the fantastic form of a relation between things. In order, therefore, to find an analogy we must take flight into the misty realm of religion. There the products of the human brain appear as autonomous figures endowed with a life of their own, which enter into relations both with each other and with the human race. So it is in the world of commodities with the products of men's hands. I call this the fetishism which attaches itself to the products of labour as soon as they are produced as commodities, and is therefore inseparable from the production of commodities.

(Marx, 1976: 165)

This enables Miéville to clarify the difference between the 'legal form' and 'law', where domestic law and international law are understood as two 'moments' of the legal form:

> what we might call *proto*-international law, the legal form regulating relationships between organised social groups, predates capitalism and the bourgeois state. Only when the bourgeois state becomes the central subject of those relations can we with full justification call them international law: that is when the 'international' is born. But *the form of the relations* already existed ... Thus the state is central to the *development* of law, domestic and international, but not to the legal form itself.
>
> (2005: 132)

Thus, two conditions are essential for the transition from 'intersocietal' legal relations (proto-international law) to international law: the emergence of the bourgeois state as standard political unit of international relations and the universalisation of commodity exchange, as the economic and military means of reproduction of the bourgeois state form. Capitalism can only be fully grasped once these two conditions come into play. The phenomenon that captures at the same time the emergence of the bourgeois state and the expansion of trade is mercantilism, as an 'economic–political strategy for state-building'. This argument constitutes the backbone of the commodity form theory of international law and is used to justify a definition of capitalism based on commodity exchange.[24] This definition implies that:

> the seventeenth century's political forms were transitional to capitalism. It should be borne in mind, though, that whether or not Europe in the seventeenth century and even eighteenth century *is* deemed so transitional, it is undeniable that this mercantilist era saw the massive expansion of international trade, central to the structure of the most powerful European states. It is during this period that the *categories concomitant on that trade* – the legal forms – begin to universalise. This was the birth of true international law. As trade became global, and definitional to sovereign states, the international order *could not but become* an international legal order.
>
> (2005: 200, added emphasis)

[24] 'The analysis of mercantilism as central to the transition to capitalism is not simply an addendum to the commodity-form analysis of international law: it is constructed on exactly that theory's dialectical formulations about the nature of commodity exchange' (Miéville, 2005: 224).

> Even more than the epoch of the absolutist state this is the epoch of the *mercantilist* state – it is in the very fabric of the most powerful sovereign states of this age that they are international, maritime and mercantilist. Mercantilism (and its laws) was crucial for the consolidation of the sovereign state – absolutist or otherwise – and a transition to a capitalist world economy.
>
> (2005: 203)

Thus, if the commodity form theory of law accounts for the continuity of history (the legal form remains while law as content changes), it also determines the transition to capitalism. Seventeenth-century mercantilism, as sociopolitical content, drove the change from a mercantilist to a global capitalist political economy, and this change was manifested in the development of maritime and merchant law.

As a final point to this presentation, Miéville claims as a contribution to Pashukanis, that the commodity relation necessarily implies coercion.[25] International trade demanded the protection and constant drive of militarily competing European imperialisms. As a market, international trade also generated legalisation. These two outcomes enshrined early modern polities, however unequal politically, in a system of equal exchange and coercive violence. International law (as a legal system without superordinate authority) became the necessary structure of capitalist international relations with colonialism and imperialism as inevitable corollaries.

For Miéville, Pashukanis provides an explanation for the tenacity of the problem of the source of international legal obligation. Since the legal form emerges in commodity exchange irrespective of a superordinate authority (the 'contingency' of the state), mercantilism assures that this process also occurs and crystallises at the international level. In other words, the problem of the source of international legal obligation (or the Austinian challenge) is not a problem, but a condition of international relations. However, this also means *all international social relations* are trapped in the ambiguity or indeterminacy characterising international law (Koskenniemi, 2005). It follows that analytically isolating legal

[25] 'Violence – coercion – is at the heart of the commodity form. For a commodity meaningfully to be "mine-not-yours" – which is, after all, central to the fact that it is a commodity that will be exchanged – some forceful capabilities must be implied. If there were nothing to defend its "mine-ness", there would be nothing to stop it becoming "yours". Coercion is implicit' (Miéville, 2008: 113). Thus, deviation, sanctions, and violence are inherent to international norms rather than external pathological manifestations.

relations ignores these conditions and reproduces the illusion that the problem of the source of international legal obligation is merely an obstacle that international law will in time overcome:

> The problem *is* actually intractable. In the commodity-form theory, law is simultaneously a form inhering between two free, abstract individuals *and* a necessary subjection to coercion. For this reason, there *is no* neat solution. It is not the legal theory which is paradoxical, but the relations that it represents.
>
> (Miéville, 2005: 149)

In sum, international law and international relations are wedded by imperialism, as the capitalist driver of mercantilism and military coercion, to a life of mutual indeterminacy. Capitalist social relations based on the commodity form are paradoxical because they produce freedom and subjection, and legal theory (and the lack of international legal theory) represents this dilemma. But to what extent can this theoretical structure historically account for extraterritoriality and other legal strategies of early modern expansion?

2.7 A Historical and Theoretical Critique of the Commodity Form Theory

The commodity form theory of international law is a major contribution as it provides a theoretical framework explaining the inevitable failure of contemporary international law to fulfil its missions because of its structural connection to the capitalist mode of production. It incorporates the transition to capitalism into the history of juridical expansion – and vice versa – and provides a theory that appears to solve the problem of why law and capitalism appear to have separate yet inevitable and natural histories. In this theory, the legal form pre-dating capitalism becomes obsolete through the specific configuration of capitalist political and legal content. Moreover, it provides an analysis putting mercantilism at the centre of the transition to capitalist international law and international relations, as a central explanatory process intrinsic to their development.

However, this theory fails to account for pre- and non-capitalist legal agency or for legal relations occurring during the process of transition as autonomous from or contesting processes of capitalist transition. The theory is based on a structurally predetermined and consequentialist – or 'structural-functionalist' – approach to the emergence of capitalism. It reproduces the mode of international theorising defended by some critical IR scholars in Part 1 of this chapter and which were rejected, first for lacking the hermeneutic or epistemological distance or praxis considered necessary for historical sociology, and second for overly focusing on external dynamics.

The first problem to discuss is historical, and concerns the conflation between mercantilism and capitalism. If some recent Marxist studies of international law have raised issues with historical aspects of Miéville's analysis, such as the overdetermining focus on war and coercion (Knox, 2009; Taylor, 2019: 58), the concept of global class (Baars, 2019: 20–21) or the ambiguities over what constitutes 'domestic law' and how the transition between 'inter-polity' and 'international' law occurs (Baars, 2019: 20), these studies do not let these considerations affect his main theoretical arguments. The second problem this section thus tackles is theoretical and relates to the structural consequences of an approach focused on external similarities or in Miéville's terms, 'shared characteristics' between early modern states.

2.7.1 The Question of Mercantilism

Miéville holds back from defining mercantilism, which is astonishing considering its centrality to his thesis. Ultimately, his definition is broad and multilayered. The term is used interchangeably as an economic system, a state policy, a set of doctrines, a form of political relations, the ensemble of maritime and merchant law, and even as an adjective for sixteenth-century 'adventuring' or colonialism (2005: 229). He moves from a cryptic and circular formulation in the introduction – 'mercantilism can best be understood as a form transitional to capitalism . . . The economic in the political of mercantilism is the flipside of the political in the economic – the commodity – in international law' (2005: 7) – to chapter five, where we get a sense of 'mercantilist state-building' as a legal phenomenon through an analysis of the Navigation Acts, the East India Companies, and the debates over the freedom of the seas (2005: 204–214).

Less clearly, 'just as mercantilism is distinct from but directly related to capitalism, so earlier colonialism is distinct but related to general and to "new" imperialism' (2005: 230). However, in his chapter six, mercantilism is defined as a dominant system and 'economic–political strategy for state-building' and can be dated from 1600 to 1776 (230). Another important difference is that between English mercantilism (East India Company and Navigation Acts) and the French variant (or Colbertism).

Thus, in sum, mercantilism refers to 'European state-consolidation' (2005: 233), maintaining a 'minimal' international legal order, the *droit public de l'Europe*. As it ignored colonies' legal identity, this system became untenable from the late-eighteenth century.

Since Miéville leans on Grewe, it is useful to first point out what is problematic in Grewe's account. Mercantilism is conventionally defined as the overseas counterpart of the European balance of power. If in Europe 'States fought over people and territories', overseas 'they fought over trade, navigation and the colonial fortunes' they competed over (Grewe, 2000: 295). Mercantilism generated the formation of the 'legal institutions serving colonial expansion and political and economic methods of colonial policy' (Grewe, 2000: 296). It is associated with Colbertism, nationalism, colonial monopolies, effective control of trade and maritime police (instead of exclusive and sovereign rights over the oceans), and trading companies. Mercantilism's particularity was the way in which states negotiated with traders, a strategy not deployed on their European territories.

However, if Grewe's conception of Westphalian Europe ignores the dynastic and personal nature of attempts to produce public international law, his conception of mercantilism should be resisted too as it gives a false sense of a clear dividing line for strategies inside and outside Europe.[26] Moreover, discussions of mercantilism also suffer from the arbitrary division between the metropolitan and colonial spheres as internal and external. Instead, merchants operated transnationally and from port to port, and the institutions required by the various jurisdictional configurations of European monarchies to negotiate, protect, and deter merchant networks produced various manifestations of mercantilism that transcend dichotomies and principles of modern geopolitics.

A broader definition of mercantilism emphasises 'private ownership and accumulation of state-sponsored titles to wealth for the mutual benefit of king and privileged traders and manufacturers' (Teschke, 2003: 209). The Europe vs. overseas distinction is therefore set aside, and the connections between these two spheres of expansion are

[26] Instead, the argument of this book is that strategies both inside and outside Europe were jurisdictional, and that using this European and extra-European line of demarcation is unhelpful. As we see in subsequent chapters, it is more useful to show how sovereigns increasingly *extended* and assembled their jurisdictional authority over contiguous and fragmented regions and *transported* or *transplanted* their jurisdictional authority to people and territories already governed by other rulers, contending empires, or considered available for conquest and colonisation.

potentially left open. Moreover, venality and the collaboration between the ruling classes, characteristic of so-called French absolutism and which played an important part in strengthening mercantilist policies, can be considered as 'accumulation of state-sponsored titles to wealth'. In this approach mercantilism can be interpreted as the worldwide extension of absolutist Europe, that is 'a geographical strategy of extending the accumulating reach of premodern states, not a qualitative change in the logic of world order' (Teschke, 2003: 204). Accordingly, mercantilism is broadly understood as a pre-capitalist process based on the internal and external accumulation of surplus by political means (i.e. coercion of direct producers or of unequal exchange) (2003: 210), which on its own was not a sufficient factor to develop capitalist social property relations.

These political and coercive aspects also partly explain for Miéville (2005: 203) the assumption between (international) law and mercantilism and are therefore emphasised as a critique of the Political Marxist account of the transition to capitalism. In *Capital* (Marx, 1959: vol. I, 323–337), Marx distinguishes between merchant capital and industrial capital and argues that if mercantilism is a historical premise to the development of capitalist production, it remains merely an 'agent', 'incapable by itself of promoting and explaining the transition from one mode of production to another' (1959: 327). However, as shown by Banaji (2017, 2019), who argues for a coherent history of capitalism associating merchant and industrial capital, a different view can also be based on some of Marx's comments in *Capital* (vol. III) and on analyses of early modern merchant capital as 'direct control of production', for example putting out systems, international money markets, plantation businesses ('colonial trades'), and the produce trades (e.g. through the semi-public prerogatives of trading companies such as the VOC or EIC).

Miéville's conception of mercantilism can be associated to Banaji's and to other critiques of the Political Marxist's approach such as Anievas and Nişancioğlu (2015), Ince (2018), and Brandon (2011). In contrast, Political Marxism maintains the distinction between two types of capital shaping the seventeenth century. On the one hand, Political Marxism focuses on capital derived from market dependence and imperatives (shift in social property relations over productivity of labour occurring in agrarian capitalism and changing England into an enclosed and waged-labour economy which later became industrial capital and shaped the leading British Empire of the nineteenth century). On the other hand, Political Marxism acknowledges pockets of merchant capital and wage labour found across the early modern period but considers these were not sufficient to alter the broader structures of personal, feudal, or absolutist/mercantilist modes of political and economic exploitation.

In other words, the political and coercive aspects of mercantilism emphasised in Teschke's definition remain more important for determining surplus than the economic networks of merchants and the occasional occurrence of capitalist relations of production maintained by those networks. Nevertheless, Teschke's definition is too broad and does not allow for the *specificities* of early modern practices of accumulation of surplus by political and jurisdictional means. In other words, the definition does not disaggregate the 'accumulation of state-sponsored titles to wealth' into various jurisdictional rights, functions and more direct titles acquired for wealth such as the acquisition of venal offices. Moreover, mercantilism should be disaggregated in the early modern period beyond the French and English divide so as to account for other national specificities – and especially the competing forms of mercantilism in the Mediterranean between the English, Dutch, and French as shown through an analysis of their consular services – but also those determined by the distinction between extensions, transports, and transplants of authority.

In sum, jurisdictional accumulation, through the practices and actors discussed in subsequent chapters, reveals different aspects of mercantilism that specify this broad category of political surplus. One of the questions generated by this concept, and which have to be left to future projects, is whether the presence of pockets of merchant capital involving direct control of production and wage labour, or the proto-industrialism of many commercial cities, can be more fruitfully identified as jurisdictional accumulation, and what specifically are the jurisdictionally determined elements of these mercantile and manufacturing practices.

2.7.2 'Shared Characteristics' and the Individual–State Analogy

Miéville's account cannot avoid an overarching structure that bundles together and predetermines the causes of jurisdictional expansion and extraterritoriality. His narrative does not account for the differing legal strategies of expansion in constructing early modern forms of sovereignty, in European and non-European polities. Crucially, this missing history cannot simply be added to his narrative. The commodity form theory of law itself is put into question by the need to account for historical specificity and contingency and is limited by its method based on the search for states and legal actors' external similarities. Similarly to

Anievas and Nişancioğlu (2015), what exactly this 'external' condition entails remains unclear. The commodity form theory therefore fundamentally clashes with a position of methodological internalism discussed in Part 1 and necessary for a focus on legal agency and various processes of political, commercial, cultural, religious, and ideological expansions of authority.

For Miéville, if the legal form pre-dates capitalism, the emergence of a 'world market' is the moment of the international legal form, whether one considers mercantilism to be transitional to capitalism – as he does – or not (2005: 201). This is because the universalisation of the legal form occurs 'at the level of the value form', that is circulation, not production (2005: 201). However, this only holds if one accepts the primacy of form analysis and more generally the analysis of political economy from the premise of categories as forms of social relations. By contesting the theorisation of private property and commodity exchange as homogeneous and founding abstractions, the debate on the role of mercantilism as transitional becomes essential at both levels of form and content (i.e. theoretically and historically). If so, the transition does matter to the universalisation of the legal form and Miéville's theory can be challenged historically. In effect, it excludes a priori the possibility of colonial and mercantile practices that universalised feudal, absolutist, or mercantilist (i.e. as non-capitalist) configurations of state power and property relations. The critique is thus twofold: theoretically, commodity form theory does not allow for the possibility of historical specificity and contingency, and historically, this condition is confounded by a revisionist history that emphasises the heterogeneity of state formation and extraterritorial practices shaping seventeenth-century mercantilism.

Baars (2019: 20) also acknowledges this problem when asserting that there is a lack of specificity in Miéville's concepts of domestic and international law. If 'one did not predate the other', they argue for an approach that emphasises 'the common root and form of domestic and international law' (20). Moreover, they also specify the need to focus on 'collectivities' as the types of legal subjects present during 'the transitional period' (20). These comments show the need to further historicise the implications of the commodity form theory through closer studies of specific actors and events in the history of international law and international relations, which Baars does through the actor of the corporation.[27]

[27] For a further analysis of Baars (2019), see Pal (forthcoming).

Yet, since Miéville sees these practices to be irrelevant to the validity of the commodity form theory, his defence is to focus on states' 'external similarities'. He compares the historical work of Teschke (2003) and Grewe (2000) by noting indeed that Teschke assesses the specificities of European states, whereas Grewe looks at their similarities:

> for the historian of international law, the focus on these states' internal dynamics to point out their differences leaves relatively unexplored their external dynamics, in which certain shared characteristics between absolutist and non-absolutist states are visible. From this perspective, though care must be exercised, it is possible to make generalisations about the various state forms ranging from the 'high' absolutism of the French model even to the English non-absolutist model . . . There were of course unique political forms in each country. But one risks obscuring as much as illuminating in focusing so carefully on the specifics of a state form internally that the shared changes in European states in general goes unnoticed.
>
> (Miéville, 2005: 202–203)

In spite of the care taken, Miéville is led to apply, by focusing on states' external dynamics, anachronistic and abstract conditions of the capitalist legal form of the state to heterogeneously constituted societies (i.e. geopolitical spaces in which capitalism was absent).[28] In other words, Miéville's focus on shared characteristics or external dynamics adopts a logic of causality that is based on the domestic or individual-state analogy, taken from Pashukanis's analogy between individuals as owners of commodities and the bourgeois state form. Pashukanis develops the concept of the bourgeois state form in a short but groundbreaking essay (in Miéville, 2005: 321–335). He equates the rise of institutions such as administration, bureaucracy, trade, and other emerging bourgeois professions with that of international lawyers, their institutions, and ideas.

First, and most generally, this claim brushes over fundamental differences in state formation essential to the development of international

[28] Aside from the debate about what constitutes capitalist relations of production (wage labour, market dependency, separation from the means of production), which were also not all together present in these spaces, the first important element missing is a fixed, territorial, or otherwise bounded state, not determined by personal or dynastic relations of power or social property relations. In the seventeenth century, the various political actors of the Holy Roman Empire and of Iberia and France were struggling to define the conceptual and geographical frontiers of their sovereignty (e.g. Teschke, 2003; Lacher, 2006; from a different theoretical perspective, see Bartelson, 1995). This also applies to those in the Mediterranean under direct or mediated Ottoman rule (Duzgun, 2018b).

relations and international law. After Westphalia, the so-called *droit public de l'Europe* consisted mainly of diplomacy and burgeoning foreign policy. This order was conducted by aristocrats and the military in defence of dynastic interests and of a European 'public' identity in name or in form that crystallised the 'private' family interests of European monarchs *against* a rising bourgeois (and revolutionary) class (Belissa, 1998; Teschke, 2003; Scott, 2007; Keene, 2013). This was an important struggle, which marked the initial development of public international law and diplomacy as separate and antagonistic strategies to the rise of capitalism. This is further accentuated by the research below according to which the aristocratisation of diplomacy, alongside practices of consular agency, established competing processes of jurisdictional accumulation and reproduced political, economic, and legal privileges mostly independent from capitalist social property relations, but crucial to shaping different forms of mercantilism. Through the aristocratisation of ambassadors, the French ruling class was able to maintain and assert itself alongside the dynastic interests it shared with other European sovereignties.

Thus, Pashukanis's concept and its application by Miéville omits important conceptual, geopolitical, and class divergences in the development of domestic public law and public international law. The construction of modern international legal forms cannot be reduced to the generalisation of the bourgeois state form, based on commodity exchange and a reified notion of private property, especially if one is searching for transitional specificities of processes of accumulation at the level of agents tasked with the legal expansion of personal sovereignty.

Second, an analysis based on external similarities particularly obscures the history of the origins of extraterritoriality. Specifically, it does not allow us to account for how these extensions, transports, or transplants of authority were the product of common law, merchant law, feudal personal law (such as 'the man carries with him the law of his own land'), or other legal sources, and whether these had any role in shaping mercantilism and other political forms of state expansion and imperialism. These expansions generated the malleability of legal content or legal relations to the universalisation of the commodity form necessary to capitalism. In other words, commodity exchange cannot explain all forms of imperial legal practices. On the contrary, it is made more complex and diverse by those practices.

In most cases, nineteenth-century extraterritoriality was a transformative process for non-European states, which resulted in the expansion or reproduction of the imperial state's form as a bourgeois capitalist state in the sense described by Miéville, as discussed in Part 1. Here the universalisation of the commodity form theory is less problematic. However, the early modern period was characterised by jurisdictional struggles and spaces and by different imperial practices. This situation produced different outcomes of imposed political and class exploitation, or of divisions of jurisdiction and sovereignty calling for the distinction between extensions, transports, and transplants. The logic of domestic or individual–state analogy – leading to the equivalent outcome of the state form necessary to global capitalism – is inapplicable to the early modern period characterised by varying outcomes of extraterritoriality and jurisdictional accumulation.

Moreover, juridical expansion is characterised by the manifestation of the social struggles *actually constructing* the 'shared characteristics' Miéville uses as an analytical basis. Focusing on states' external similarities assumes the success or unimportance of legal strategies of expansion, neither of which are satisfactory assessments. Focusing on external similarities applies to a system whose transformation is complete, not to a transitional period, for example how should one understand 'external similarities' when faced with *personal* sovereignty and other uncertain, ad hoc, feudal and absolutist forms of diplomatic and political representation? As Marks (2007: 207) notes, Miéville's 'sharp line ... between international law's inside and its outside does not seem to do justice to his own characterization of international law as a part of political processes'. Thus, the theoretical move of extending the legal form that inheres between individual owners of commodities to the state form clashes with a conception of international law characterised by the interconnection of political processes and the potential of legal agency as transformative.

In effect, the commodity form theory of international law is not sufficient for framing a historical sociology of extraterritoriality and jurisdictional accumulation in the early modern period. To develop this work, we need a theoretically more open and sociologically richer historical materialist approach that can explain the various relations between differentially developing states, their geopolitical conflicts and wars, and other legal institutions across early modern Europe, its imperial fringes, and its colonies. The following section examines Political Marxism, which is expressly concerned with the internally specific historiography of (international) social relations, and which makes space for how 'economic, political, legal, cultural, and ideological relations and institutions' configure modes of production and class exploitation (Lafrance & Post, 2019b: 23).

2.8 Political Marxism and Jurisdictional Agency

2.8.1 Foundations

The following retraces the development of Political Marxism and its focus on specificity and agency, as an answer to the critiques made against Miéville's commodity form theory of law. Political Marxism was a label attributed in the 1980s by historian Guy Bois to the work of social and political historians Robert Brenner and Ellen Wood. The 'Brenner debate' on the transition to capitalism has known various iterations since the original collection in Aston and Philpin (1985).[29] Political Marxism is rooted in Robert Brenner's (1976, 1977) historical work on early modern Europe and on the transition from feudalism to capitalism. The approach develops Marx's mature work in *Capital* and the *Grundrisse* rather than his earlier work on the transition, leading some to identify it as *Capital*-centric Marxism (Post, 2015).

The main argument, later extended by Wood (1981, 1995), Comninel (1987, 2000), and Dimmock (2014), asserts that capitalism originated in England as a result of specific social conflicts in the agrarian economy, that is large-scale structural social changes in the relations between lords, farmers (yeomen), and peasants in the English countryside. The changes occurred most notably through the processes of wage dependency, leasing, enclosures, dispossession, and depopulation, marking the establishment of capitalist social property relations in a context of politically constituted class strategies of exploitation.

Beyond the classic case of the English transition, Political Marxism is grounded in analyses of conflicts over social property relations to assess the relationship between classes, institutions, and power. It suggests that history, past and present, is nothing but the social (i.e. political, juridical,

[29] These debates recently produced a rich set of discussions between different approaches to historical sociology, such as with proponents of U&CD discussed in Part 1, as well as within Political Marxism, with more structural and 'Brennerite' contributions by Lafrance & Post (2019b) and more 'radically historicist' approaches by Knafo & Teschke (2020). Political Marxists and proponents of the renewal of U&CD in IR since Rosenberg (2013) have taken radically different directions in their conception of and approach to historical sociology. Teschke (2014) laments the neglect of agency and historical specificity for a theoretical framework that claims to explain a priori large-scale historical change, a critique mostly shared by this study for the reasons discussed in Part 1.

and economic) conditions in which all phenomena are grounded and contested. Its first aim is to detach itself from mid- to late-twentieth-century economistic Marxism, moving away from deterministic and structuralist orthodox assumptions. It does so by focusing on the regionally specific resolutions of social conflicts that follow no predetermined scripts. It also reasserts the crucial role of (geo)politics as social power struggles in the overall development and trajectories of social property relations, with a specific focus on explaining and drawing out the wider implications of the separation of the political and economic spheres under capitalism. It thereby reasserts the role of the political as a firm basis to the economic sphere, and hence, to the mode of production. As Wood authoritatively asserts:

> [R]elations of production are, from this theoretical standpoint, presented in their *political* aspect, that aspect in which they are actually *contested*, as relations of domination, as rights of property, as the power to organize and govern production and appropriation. In other words, the object of this theoretical stance is a *practical* one, to illuminate the terrain of struggle by viewing modes of production not as abstract structures but as they actually confront people who must *act* in relation to them.
>
> (1995: 25, original emphasis)

The important problem this raises is the controversial relationship between base and superstructure, to which Wood replies in the following way:

> Political Marxism, then, does not present the relations between base and superstructure as an opposition, a regional separation, between a basic 'objective' economic structure, on the one hand, and social, juridical and political forms, on the other hand, but rather as a continuous structure of social relations and forms with varying degrees of distance from the immediate processes of production and appropriation, beginning with those relations and forms that constitute the system of production itself. The connections between 'base' and 'superstructure' can then be traced without great conceptual leaps because they do not represent two essentially different and discontinuous orders of reality.
>
> (1995: 25–26)

The particularities of this approach are its non-economistic, historicist, and politicised aspects. A first advantage for the present discussion is the emphasis on social contestation, since it translates empirically into spatiotemporally differential and open forms and content of legal activity. In contrast to more 'classical' Marxists, Political Marxism adopts a non-functionalist conception of the interpenetration of social relations between spheres of production and circulation (i.e. capitalism not as an economic but a social relation that is politically constituted). If the juridical is part of this 'continuous structure' Wood identifies, this means that it is not approached as an expression of the commodity form, but rather as a terrain of social conflict.

'Internationalising' Political Marxism – and developing it as an approach in IR and historical sociology – has consisted in using social property relations to explain the emergence of public and private institutions that cut across and shape the domestic–international dichotomy. It is also used to explain various modes of production and international orders. The term has been too quickly identified as internalist and thereby dismissed in recent debates (Anievas & Nişancioğlu, 2015). The concept of social property relations is used by Political Marxists as an alternative to Marx's concept of 'social relations of production' (Wood, 2002a; Dimmock, 2014: 17) or 'relations of class exploitation' (Lafrance & Post, 2019b: 8) by emphasising their 'politically constituted' and 'contested' nature. They can be simply defined as 'nodal points of intersection in which power relations shape social relations' (Teschke, 2010: 47). Brenner defines 'social-property relations' as

> the relations among direct producers, relations among exploiters, and relations between exploiters and direct producers that, taken together, make possible/specify the regular access of individuals and families to the means of production (land, labour, tools) and/or the social product per se.
>
> (2007: 58)

Social property relations are thus a 'three-way dialectical relationship between the direct producers and nature (raw materials, ecology), the "vertical" exploitative social relation between the direct producer and the appropriator of the producer's surplus, and also the "horizontal" social relation within the main classes' (Dimmock, 2017).[30] The horizontal dimension is crucial as it is not constrained by national or territorial

[30] For Lafrance and Post (2019b: 23), the term social property relations 'involves horizontal relationships of competition and collaboration within classes as well as vertical conflicts between classes' which 'are structured by the "rules of reproduction" established by distinct social property relations'. Contra Knafo and Teschke, but following Brenner, they therefore emphasise 'rules of reproduction' as an essential basis to the Political Marxist method of historical analysis. For Lafrance and Post, '[h]uman beings do make their own history, but they do so in a material context that imposes limits to their social action that can only be transcended by exiting an existing mode of production' (2019b: 23). In contrast, Knafo and Teschke (2020) argue for a more historicist approach that

boundaries. Classes can compete and collaborate within or beyond the various political, legal, economic, cultural, and ideological boundaries that may define a mode of production. Therefore, 'the international' is put aside as a criterion for delimiting the field of enquiry, but the trans- or intersocietal remains central to Political Marxist projects. For example, Teschke (2003) developed a geopolitically differentiated narrative of European state formation and international relations from the Middle Ages to the nineteenth century. Many projects have remained concerned with the classic spatiotemporal themes of classic IR – such as early modern and modern European states (Mooers, 1991; Lacher, 2006; Knafo, 2013; Moreno Zacarés, 2018; Lafrance, 2019; McNally, 2020). However, new studies are emerging that are applying the approach outside of those empirically Eurocentric confines, for example to the USA, Canada, Japan, Taiwan, Brazil, China, and the Ottoman Empire (Post, 2011; Turgeon, 2016; Lafrance & Post, 2019a; Salgado, 2019; Duzgun, 2018b).

Social property relations are crucial to this project because they encapsulate the imbrication of legal, political, and economic relations and provide a wider handle on the legal dimension of social relations while emphasising their ever-contested yet interrelated condition. Specifically, the concept implies the identification of, and comparison between, concepts and institutions of property and possession. These are identified through the various actors that participate in the ownership, creation, maintenance, and dispossession of property rights, of the legal principles and customs establishing the individuals and groups entitled to such rights, and the institutions and practices built to uphold or resist them.

Another Political Marxist concept crucial to this project is the one of jurisdictional disputes used by Wood in her early work on France and England (2015 [1991]) and in her later work on the history of political thought (2012: 19–24). The concept implies a search for authority and legitimacy and the possibility of hierarchy beyond private contractual relationships where individuals try to assert themselves or their local

rejects the formalism and structuralism of rules of reproduction determined by the spatiotemporal limits of modes of production. The present project contributes more towards the radical historicist approach, as jurisdictional accumulation is a process that creates and transcends modes of production by emphasising the contest between mercantilism(s) in the Mediterranean through consuls, as well as the continuation of feudal and absolutist processes of jurisdictional accumulation (1) in the Americas through transplants of authority and (2) in continental Europe through the aristocratisation of ambassadors.

interests. Jurisdiction emerges from the Roman distinction between *imperium* and *dominium*, as the tentative elaboration of a public system of law and command distinguished from the concept of property as 'private, exclusive and individual ownership' (2012: 5). Wood traces the relationship between political theory and institutions through the question of whether jurisdiction – and by extension sovereignty – are defined by the social property relations between landlords and tenants, feudal lords and peasants, appropriators and producers, and even local judges (the French *parlementaires*) and state officials. From the present study, we can now extend this to consuls and merchants. These social relations oscillate on a continuum between fragmentation, parcellisation, and centralisation, shaping the categories of the legal, political, and economic; or, more characteristically, the economic and extra-economic in Wood's work on the origins of capitalism.

Thus, the legal parameters of a society are determined by the conditions for the exploitation and appropriation of land and resources, and the distribution of production between appropriators and producers (i.e. social property relations). The contribution of Political Marxism lies in there also being scope to incorporate, in the concept of social property relations, the occurrence of legal relations as determining conditions for appropriation and production. Political Marxism encapsulates the fact that legal relations can take determining forms in various societies. As for example, in medieval Europe and specifically in France through the pressure of local jurisdictions on the monarchy.

Regarding classic narratives of IR, Political Marxism argues that the modern states system, as juridically equal but politically unequal, was only possible *after* the expansion of capitalist relations of production, since only these provided the impetus for the distinction between public sovereignty and private civil society (Rosenberg, 1994). This process is hence sufficiently identifiable only from the nineteenth century. The transition to capitalism was not a temporally and spatially homogeneous, pan-European, and natural progression from the system of sovereign states supposed to rise out of the Peace of Westphalia. Instead, agrarian capitalism in England and continental absolutisms in France and the Holy Roman Empire separately emerged out of feudalism, and through a complex process of contested refraction confirmed the forms through which capital accumulation justified itself politically, that is the separation between the sovereign nation state and transnational capital flows (Teschke, 2003).

Crucially, this means a geopolitical order of multiple territorially defined states emerged as a consequence of conflicts over geopolitical accumulation among premodern and pre-capitalist states and preceded the rise of capitalism (Lacher & Teschke, 2007). If so, this specific historical context renders the 'causal and functional-structuralist triad commodity form/capitalism, bourgeois state/state-system, and legal form/ international law'[31] unable to retrace the more complex co-development between these phenomena. Instead, this study proposes the additional lens of jurisdictional conflicts among differentially developing states and other actors captured in the concept of jurisdictional accumulation.

This study contributes to these narratives by asserting the importance of jurisdictional processes in European absolutisms and cross-Atlantic colonial expansions, and in Mediterranean mercantilisms as a non-capitalist mode of production led by merchant actors with jurisdictional power (i.e. consuls). These processes had differing outcomes shaped by the social property relations of each empire and by each sovereign's strategies of jurisdictional accumulation, which were entangled with capitalist and non-capitalist modes of production. It becomes thus possible to argue that jurisdiction is an essential and historically specific process to the development of early modern imperial expansion, without having to collapse international law, capitalism, and modernity onto the same developmental path.

2.8.2 Retrieving Agency in Political Marxist Approaches to (International) Law

From Comninel (2000) to Dufour (2008) and Mooers (2014), the social property relations approach has paid more *direct* attention to the 'legal' aspect of social relations. However, the legal dimension is theoretically implicit in Political Marxism's original purpose (Dufour, 2008: 77). Generally, there is a presumed tension between the fixed aspects of the law, such as the legal form or property right, and the process or interaction involved in legal content or the property relation. Political Marxism challenges this idea of law as an expression or form of social relations and approaches it from the standpoint of social process. Therefore, this tension between property right (form) and property relation (content) is merely apparent, and the challenge is to explain why an appearance of things takes over the meaning or life of things; in

[31] I am thankful to Benno Teschke for this helpful formulation.

other words, why a particular right prevailed over others in the struggles over content, and thereafter retained that prevailing position of legitimacy beyond the initial struggle that produced it. This is an essential function of modern law, to institutionally preserve the fruits of a social struggle without the burden of winning the struggle anew.

However, recognising this formal function does not justify or automatically lead to negating the continuing social struggles that challenge the formalisation of a right. In other words, if content does not stop in the face of the form, and if the goal is to map out the various challenges to the building of the capitalist state and sovereign states system (so as to understand why it prevailed over other forms and how future challenges might be able to contest it anew), a theory of international law must give up on the primacy of commodity exchange and the domestic analogy between the bourgeois individual and state. It must start instead with historical specificity and the assumption that the international legal form, that is the capitalist state, has to be taken for what it is (i.e. merely the institutional appearance of the legitimacy of dominant class interests). Historical materialism needs to start from the 'real' relations between human beings and things, not their appearances. Crucially, these relations cannot be attributed to states on the basis that throughout modernity, states become abstract institutions in the same way as individuals become abstract bearers of rights. In sum, relations between individuals (i.e. social property relations) must remain the primary basis of analysis for international legal relations.

Building on Political Marxism's historical and theoretical premises, Bachand and Lapointe (2010) introduce an alternative analytical framework of the mechanisms of 'international life'. If international relations and international law are mutually constitutive, international law can nevertheless be broken down into three levels. First, they define the legal form as the values, institutions, and fundamental concepts of the legal order. At this level, the legal is constitutive of the political and vice versa, which excludes a conception of either domain as autonomous. In other words, the values, institutions, and fundamental concepts of the legal order determine the behaviour of political elites, while the power relations between elites in turn shape these attributes of the legal form. Hence, Bachand and Lapointe adopt a much broader definition of the legal form that overlaps with that of the political domain. In short, similar and/or interconnected actors essentially constitute both domains (which begs the question of the history and role of their separation).

The second and third levels consist respectively in the *limitations* and *possibilities* arising out of the legal form. The second level of 'legal constraint' refers to norms and rules generally, while the third level of 'law as argumentative practice and legitimizing discourse' emphasises the transformative potential of discursive practices. This potential is crucial for the latter's capacity to alter the conditions of the legal form. Bachand and Lapointe hereby incorporate agency into the mechanisms of international law. Without such agency, changes in content (i.e. constraints, or rules and norms) could not be anything more than just visible. In other words, they could not substantially affect the values, institutions, and principles of the legal form, which in turn reconstitute the form of relations in the political domain. For example, the authors note that the development of human rights has been disappointing in the face of the structural effects of capitalism, precisely because they have not been accompanied by discursive practices sufficiently critical so as to correspondingly alter the structural dimensions of the legal form.

Building on the previous argument on the need to uncover the social relations behind the apparent tension between form and content, Bachand and Lapointe describe an important aspect of the relations between the state and its citizens. These inform the norm-creation aspect of the legal form, and thus offer the basis to an alternative to Pashukanis's problematic analogy:

> Here the point of analytical interest is the imbalance between the actors involved in the decision-making process and those who will be subjected to the de facto consequences of the legal (and political) repercussions of delinquent state conduct. Concretely the point is to underline the fact that states' decisions are taken in accordance with the existing power relations between the different groups constituting a given society.
>
> (2010: 275)

In schematic terms, dominant groups take or influence decisions that affect the state's population and territory. However, these decisions are assimilated as the 'will' of the state, or the rule of law (*l'état de droit*). They are legitimised through the abstract institutions of the state (themselves sanctioned by the supreme legitimacy of the separation of executive, legislative, and judiciary powers). Hence, this hierarchy a priori annuls or disregards the power relations that structure the decision-making process. This condition is essential to upholding the state's *raison d'être* as a neutral and transhistorical symbol of law and order. In response, social groups engage in different struggles (legal, political, ideological) so as to tamper, counter, or absorb the effects of the dominant classes' influence filtered through the rule of law.

For Marxists, turning the analysis of this process on its head (i.e. starting from the class relations at the origins of decision-making) reveals the dependence of the process of state formation and norm creation on those relations. In this sense, the state as legal form or rule of law, and therefore also the state as only legitimate actor in international law, abstracts or filters the power differentials that operate *within* its legal sphere.[32] Consequently, the point here of Marxist critique is to make these internal power relations reappear to show the real determinants of international legal personality.

Bachand and Lapointe's tripartite analysis and focus on internal social relations is attractive as it provides a heterogeneous and interdependent conception of law, state, and social struggle, opening space theoretically for a more diverse account of international legal relations, that allows for discursive or other forms of social transformation and agency as an alternative to the commodity form theory.

2.8.3 Against English Exceptionalism

The final point in this discussion of Political Marxism is the issue of English exceptionalism that has become associated with it. The 'Brenner debate' and its recent iterations have used significant arguments and evidence relying on legal processes and institutions for the specificity of England in the origin of capitalism. This debate has not sufficiently – if at all – been discussed by international legal scholarship and remains mostly limited to IR and Marxist circles in historical sociology. As a contribution to this limitation, this book argues that a methodology for understanding the legal expansion of early modern empires should focus on jurisdiction and jurisdictional struggles so as to capture the differential, unintended, and agentic dimension of legal relations.

Jurisdiction is a key process that characterises the early modern period and enables a new narrative to understand the processes of the reproduction of certain classes and property rights and the legal institutions and arguments that followed and shaped those ever-contested social property relations. The institutions focused on in this book are those of European embassies and Mediterranean consulates, as well as the more

[32] '[T]he main actor in IR (the state) is, above all, a legal creation' (Bachand & Lapointe, 2010: 274).

explicit processes of colonisation used in the Americas by European empires.

Jurisdiction is not understood here as a 'primitive' process prior to the elaboration of modern territorial sovereignty, rendering England more 'advanced' for its lack of jurisdictional conflicts.[33] Thus, it is not an Anglocentric and stagist or consequentialist approach to history. The contribution here is the tension between jurisdiction and sovereignty at the core of struggles for authority, and at the core of the balance between public and private interests across the early modern period. It therefore contributes to some of the limitations in Wood's work in terms of how to 'integrate the role of *social construction* in the analysis of capitalist transitions' (Moreno Zacarés, 2018: 754), as well as on how to integrate other processes of political constitution in pre-capitalist dynamics.

In other words, this book is not primarily concerned with the origins of capitalism, absolutism, or mercantilism, nor is it primarily concerned with the origins of international law. It is however concerned with the differences between manifestations of these large-scale phenomena, and with the potential to analyse them as separate, as well as explore the ways in which they overlap and may become entangled. Political Marxism's contribution here thus consists more in how it does not assume a priori or theoretically (as the commodity form theory does) the co-constitutive future of capitalism and international law. In other words, it distinguishes the origins and expansion of capitalism from its structural relationship to modern international law. Crucially, the analyses show the limits of these structural concepts in the early modern period. Jurisdictional accumulation is a concept that aims to navigate between these emerging geopolitical orders and to reveal otherwise neglected aspects of legal, political, and economic agency that take these practices in their contested process of becoming, rather than from the perspective of the outcome of their contests.

Shaped by Political Marxism and its social property relations approach, the book nevertheless follows Brenner and Wood's analysis

[33] 'The principal "constitutional" issues [in France] were not between Crown and representative assembly [as in England] but between monarchical power and customary law or traditional rights, and these issues tended to take the form of contests not so much over sovereign legislative power as over questions of jurisdiction' (Wood, 2015 [1992]: 71). Wood contrasts the 'preoccupation of French judicial proceedings with jurisdictional disputes' with the 'English preoccupation with property', noting that the 'French could not make do with a constitutional framework as inchoate as the English' (2015 [1992]: 72).

of the origins of capitalism in England and finds it reinforced by an analysis of the differences of legal relations in Europe. The book also follows work by Neocleous (2012) who laments the neglected role of primitive accumulation – occurring in England – in studies of the construction of international law. He shows how this process was tied to concepts of land improvement and waste constructed by bourgeois political economy and philosophy and how it was shaped by English colonists and reproduced in North American settlements. However, it is crucial to understand that Political Marxism does not assume that the expansion of capitalism thereafter reproduced exclusively the English experience. Instead, if 'similar *basic transformations of social property relations* occurred' in other contexts, 'the processes that led to these transformations were necessarily historically and geographically specific' (Lafrance & Post, 2019b: 26). The notion of exceptionalism is problematic as it sets up a non-exceptional path as the norm and *Sonderweg*, that is an inevitable path of development, whereas Political Marxism is about rejecting any form of consequentialist analysis of socio-economic and political development (Teschke, 2005; Wood, 2016).

Thus, the aim of a Political Marxist approach is not to argue for a stark and definitive *caesura* between the English/British and other early modern empires and their international legal practices, but to open a discussion about these differences and encounters through different instances of jurisdictional accumulation and extraterritoriality according to the social property relations that operate at their core. In effect, this approach leads to a different typology of the role of European empires in international law where England, France, and the Dutch Republic share certain similar practices of transports of authority, and where France and Castile both develop practices that have similar outcomes, albeit different means, in terms of transplanting their sovereign's authority.

2.9 Conclusion

This chapter presented some key debates in historical sociology, Marxism, and law so as to respond to the two objectives set up in Chapter 1. Part 1 responded to problems of Eurocentrism and of linear chronologies of modernity so as to go beyond the narrow and territorially defined concepts of sovereignty and jurisdiction. It discussed the latest waves in historical sociology focused on the problem of how to conceptualise the international and argued against the trend for U&CD and instead for a method of negative and outward internalism driven by methodological humility and specific historical research problems. Part 2 needed to develop a framework that could account for legal agency and the differences between extensions, transports, and transplants of authorities across various modes of production, so as to operationalise the internalism proposed in Part 1. The commodity form theory of law was presented and found to be reproducing the same mistakes as the approaches discussed in Part 1 focused on external similarities and a structural approach to the definitions of capitalism and international law. Moreover, the commodity form theory conflates mercantilism and capitalism, a problem significantly challenged by the jurisdictional aspects of this process discussed in following chapters. Political Marxism was presented in detail as an alternative approach responding to the criteria developed in Part 1 and enhanced by the angle of jurisdictional disputes and jurisdictional accumulation.

This concept is understood as a set of practices in which sub-sovereign actors in the history of international relations and international law were engaged in different means of claiming and establishing authority and defining class struggles and geopolitical dynamics of class reproduction in the early modern period. As the previous chapters argued, the conventional ideas that territoriality ties together jurisdiction and sovereignty, and that jurisdiction is a neutral, apolitical, and transhistorical concept are modern constructs linked to the specific conditions of the sovereign states system. These constructs need to be broken down for the early modern period, before relations between states and sovereigns became fully impersonal, abstract, territorial, and based on the illusory separation between political and economic, public and private spheres. Jurisdiction needs to be deterritorialised and given more independent conceptual value, as it produces legal temporalities redefining the political ordering of space.

Isolating the process of jurisdiction enables us to question to what extent jurisdiction is accumulated, that is whether hegemonic or ruling actors are driven to jurisdictional accumulation by their position in the international order, and what role this process plays in the consolidation of the legal institutions necessary to the rise of the modern international order and transitions to capitalism. In other words, adopting this approach provides conceptual ground for alternative histories of extraterritoriality that emphasise the expansionist drive of certain agents, whether as extension, transport, or transplant of authority.

The various actors, manifestations, and outcomes of these processes remain to be discussed in detail in each chapter. For now, it is important to emphasise that jurisdictional accumulation refers to the accumulation of authority for sovereigns, their representatives, as well as for regional or local lords, princes, or other holders of jurisdictional privileges. It emphasises the agency of sub-sovereign actors that do not fit into classic narratives of modern state formation and of international law. This accumulation of authority is mainly characterised by the accumulation of legal claims, rights, titles, and functions, but it also refers to the income that may be attached to the claims, rights, titles, and functions pursued or established by these actors. To illustrate some important similarities and differences between some of these practices, and dynamically navigate the comparative exercise between the four empires, the following Chapter 3 focuses on extensions of authority mostly understood through the social property relations that shaped each case's varying attempts to assemble their jurisdictional divisions, while Chapters 4 to 7 focus on the differences between transports and transplants of authority in diplomatic and colonial contexts as two major forms of early modern imperial expansion.

3

Social Property Relations

This chapter is a selection of key shifts in European and colonial social property relations through cases of legal agency in the Iberian, French, English, and Dutch empires. Social property relations are the key concept for Political Marxism and the analytical starting point for this study. They reveal cases of extensions of authority and provide the more general conditions enabling other practices of jurisdictional accumulation such as transports and transplants.

Social property relations refer to Marx's concept of social relations of production yet further emphasise the contested imbrication of legal, political, and economic actors and institutions that organise labour, social reproduction, and political representation. They provide a wider handle on the legal dimension of social relations while emphasising their ever-contested yet interrelated condition.

The problem of class and law in Marxist theory is classically framed around the emergence of a bourgeois class in early modern Europe requiring bourgeois rights; the legal class is thereby mapped on the model of the rise of the bourgeoisie, and linked to a commercialisation model of the transition to capitalism in which the bourgeoisie, through bourgeois revolutions, appears more or less naturally and inevitably as the breaker of feudal chains and of backward or slow agrarian and economic development.

This consequentialist or stagist conception of history assumes that the origins of capitalism are waiting to be discovered and unearthed in various contexts rather than understanding their specificity and randomness. However, Political Marxism and revisionist social history forces us to reframe this problem from the perspective of more localised and specific institutional contexts. The approach developed here implies retracing the differential emergence, formation, and impact of legal and jurisdictional actors concerned with the construction of sovereignty in metropolitan and colonial contexts.

The specific practices of jurisdictional accumulation discussed in this chapter refer mostly to metropolitan extensions of authority. However, because of the argument identifying Iberian imperial expansion and diplomatic aspects of French expansion as transplants of authority, analyses of their colonial social property relations are necessary. This is especially the case for Castilian imperialism because of the empire's determination to settle and establish colonies that reproduced Iberian society and incorporated settler and native subjects in that society.[1] In contrast, English and Dutch imperial expansion are better characterised as more commercial and indirect transports of authority through settlements and trade monopolies driven by chartered companies. This chapter will therefore focus on their metropolitan social property relations, rather than their colonial social property relations as this is justified by the analytical angle of the typology chosen for this study.[2]

Another methodological point relates to the significant literature on polycentric and composite monarchies to understand early modern European polities originally developed by Elliott (1992) and Koenigsberger (1986). The concept of composite monarchies highlights sovereigns' attempts to unify, aggregate, or assemble diverse parliamentary, legislative, and juridical entities, through a variety of fiscal, legislative, and collaborative measures privileging or suppressing local ruling elites and emerging classes. The aim of this concept is to highlight the jurisdictional divisions and compromises made by sovereign rulers with ruling classes and with contending actors across the complex early modern patchwork of political and economic authorities. The concept

1 Although the French case is not considered to be best characterised as a transplant in its imperial expansions and is considered instead as defined by transports of authority, this question remains more arguable for this case. Significant juridical aspects of French old regime society were reproduced and lasted longer in some French Caribbean colonies than in France. However, France's settlements were generally demographically smaller, less socially organic, and more concerned by a commercial motive and interest in land than Castilian colonisation, which crucially focused on the incorporation of jurisdictional subjects in the colonies. Important differences therefore remain between the French and Iberian cases justifying the distinction.

2 'Exceptions' to this generalisation of the Dutch and English cases of course exist, especially in terms of legal transplants, and some will be discussed in subsequent chapters. Instead of exceptions, they are best understood as 'overlaps' between these types, such as the Portuguese in Brazil, some Dutch settler colonies in North America, and the English which 'eventually ran the entire gamut of forms' (Rosenberg, 1994: 93). Rosenberg's 'forms' or 'waves' of European expansion in that study loosely correspond to the categories developed here, in terms of the focus on Castilian jurisdictional incorporation of subjects and the French, Dutch, and English focus on territory.

of polycentrism is also usefully deployed by recent political economies of early modern Europe and the empires, emphasising the role of mercantilist networks, particularly relevant to discussions in Chapter 6. These new approaches in economic history focus on networks and often develop the *longue durée* approach of French historian Fernand Braudel (Marzagalli & Marnot, 2006; Roper & Ruymbeke, 2007; Fusaro et al., 2010; Cardim *et al.* 2012; Fusaro, 2012; Amirell & Müller, 2014; Crespo Solano, 2014; Herzog, 2015a; Herero Sanchez & Kaps, 2017; Scarfi, 2017; Cañizares-Esguerra, 2018; Calafat, 2019). This literature also tends to focus on Mediterranean and maritime legal practices, and provides original and promising approaches to the study of jurisdictional practices.

These concepts have obvious connections with the approach and arguments developed in this study and are relied on in various instances. However, the conceptual basis of social property relations developed in this chapter is a crucial addition to this literature, which is not necessarily incompatible but which implies a significant emphasis on class and focus on land, labour, and resources which some of the 'composite monarchies' literature might not be able or willing to adopt.

Specifically, this chapter discusses how the Iberian Empire was shaped by the Castilian legal elite, as well as by the jurisdictional fragmentation between the Iberian kingdoms. This process was to a large extent reproduced in its American colonies with complex and in some cases more open and developed jurisdictional opportunities for settlers and indigenous disputants that also meant incorporating them into the empire and subjugating them to royal authority.

Powerful legal orders evolved in France according to old regime institutions characterised by the process of venality and the rise of the robe nobility, crucial for the monarchy's navigation of jurisdictional divisions through collaboration with elites to maintain and extend its authority.

These jurisdictional divisions and challenges in the Iberian and French case both relate to revisionist debates on their so-called absolutism. As such, both stand in contrast to England's unifying 'Crown in Parliament', sustained by the common law and a powerful legal nomenclature evolving in the context of – and significantly shaping – agrarian capitalism. Moreover, the section on England focuses on the development of private property and the processes of enclosures sustaining this development, generating debates regarding the concept of primitive accumulation, essential to understanding English/British imperialism discussed in subsequent chapters.

Finally, historiography on the Dutch Republic remains a thorny terrain of debate requiring a more theoretical discussion of the transition to Dutch capitalism. Dutch settlement in the Americas was mostly outsourced and of a more limited scale than in other empires. However, jurisdictional questions were essential to the consolidation of the Dutch Republic, and the section asks whether jurisdictional divisions in some regions, the absence of jurisdictional structures in others, and the significant role of magistrates and lawyers help to better understand the specificity of its merchant–industrialist rural–agrarian symbiosis as too constrained by jurisdictional and mercantilist – rather than capitalist – imperatives.

In sum, the chapter expands on Political Marxism's reliance on the juridical aspect of social property relations, while revealing more internalist social aspects of the history of imperial and metropolitan law often ignored in conventional histories and Marxist theories of international law.

3.1 Revisiting Iberian Absolutism

3.1.1 Jurisdictional Fragmentation

Castile was the largest of the Iberian kingdoms known as *reinos* with an estimated population of six and half million people in the sixteenth century (Elliott, 2006: 52) out of an estimated overall population of eight million people. It was therefore naturally at the heart of the unification process which led to Spain.[3] The nobility very largely seized its agrarian property, as 2–3 per cent of the population controlled 97 per cent of the soil (Anderson, 1974: 62). Soil was mostly attributed to sheep farming, which was connected to the textile industry in Flanders. The aristocracy was strong, but it was not part of a fixed or institutionalised estates system.[4] Instead, it developed through 'the rich and formidable military orders … created by the Crusades', still lacked collective authority (Anderson, 1974: 63), and remained 'a relatively minor player in the development of political organization' (Grafe, 2012: 32–33). It did not

[3] 'Spain' is a somewhat misleading term for the early modern period but is nevertheless conventionally used and can therefore appear in this study to refer to the entity that evolved into this political formation. However, the terms Iberian, Hispanic, or Castilian are preferred and used to emphasise respectively the geographical, ethnic, or political–legal dimensions of the empire.

[4] In this study, aristocracy is defined as leading families in the nobility.

constitute as big an adversary to the Crown as elites in France did (Grafe, 2013: 261).

For example, although collaboration between the Castilian nobility and Charles I was essential to unification efforts, members of the elite were expulsed from the governing body of the Cortes (early form of parliament) after 1539 (Marx, 1939[1854]: 23–24). Another element ensuring Castilian political domination was the move of aristocracies from the other *reinos* to Castile to be closer to court and 'focus on the scramble for public office' (for the Catalan case, see Moreno Zacarés, 2018: 567, n. 3).

The Crown of Aragon (the Eastern regions) comprised the *reinos* of Aragon, Catalonia, and Valencia.[5] While all displayed particular structural identities, as a whole they differed politically with Castile.[6] Their commonalities lay in their 'sophisticated and entrenched' estates structure. Each *reinos* had its own Cortes, which decided by unanimity, and institutions with permanent judicial control and economic administration.

The unification of both crowns of Aragon and Castile through the marriage of Ferdinand and Isabella involved a vast programme of administrative reorganisation: military orders were 'decapitated, with their lands and incomes annexed'; baronial castles were demolished; private wars were banned; municipal autonomy was broken by *corregidores* (official administration); royal justice was extended and reinforced; local church revenues were redirected towards the state, so as to be detached from the papacy; the Cortes were 'domesticated' by omission of the clergy and the nobility after 1480 (Anderson, 1974: 65); finally, fiscal yields increased dramatically (from almost 100,000 *reales* in 1471 to 26 million in 1504) (Anderson, 1974: 66).

Three factors characterise early modern Hispanic society. First, elites and specifically the army of *conquistadores* displayed significant medieval

[5] Of these *reinos*, Catalonia was the only principality. In addition, the Balearic Islands had their own separate juridical entity, the Kingdom of Mallorca. Thanks to Javier Moreno Zacarés for these clarifications.

[6] Aragon was the most repressive seigneurial system in the Iberian peninsula. Catalonia was the centre of a mercantile empire with Barcelona, but was ravaged by epidemics, commercial bankruptcies, rebellions from artisans and peasants, and a civil war between the nobility and the monarchy. Valencia, somewhere halfway between Aragon and Catalonia, was based on nobility exploiting Morisco labour and a growing merchant economy (Anderson, 1974: 64). Morisco populations were the Moors left behind in territories taken by the Spaniards during the *Reconquista*.

characteristics, in comparison to the rest of Europe. Culturally, they were motivated by a spirit of chivalry and an imagination captured by stories of monsters and heroic adventures as depicted by the popular corresponding literature, and of which Miguel de Cervantes's *Don Quixote* (1615) is the fascinating illustration (Marx, 1939 [1854]: 24; Weckmann, 1969; Owens, 2005: 240–241).

Second, Iberian politics in this period was symbiotic with religious orders and with military–religious entities that emulated the structures of the Islamic enemy (Anderson (1974: 168–170). As complementary and mutually enhancing, their relationship was accentuated during the fifteenth century, when the Castilian Crown decided to preach religious intolerance to guarantee a stronger state (Hanke, 1974: 5). This marked the motivations behind the *Reconquista* and the takeover of Granada from the Moors, with whom the rest of Iberia had more or less well cohabited and traded until then. Politics and religion were not thought of separately. This translated into the weighty presence of the papacy in Iberian politics, though it developed in favour of the Castilian Crown. Nevertheless, Castilian *raison d'état* consisted first and foremost in being the 'guardian of a universal Christendom', and this had very specific and unique consequences for the relationship between state and non-state actors. For one, it limited Iberian 'absolutism' since it remained in theory accountable to God:

> it was crucial for the Crown to be seen to act on all occasions in strict accordance with Christian ethico-political principles. The task of the theologians and jurists was to establish just what those principles were. This habit of seeking political legitimation ensured the existence of a lively and by no means uncritical enquiry into the behaviour of the state.
>
> (Pagden, 1990: 6)

Third, this form of politico-religious statecraft went hand in hand with a respect for morality and law (Elliott, 1963; Hanke, 1974; Pagden, 1990; Parry, 1990; Owens, 2005; Fernández Castro, 2014; Lesaffer, 2017). The unification of the future Spain meant the implementation of a centralised legal system, or more exactly its attempt. As across Europe, communities lived with concurrent legal systems, such as civil law, canon law, and customs known as *fueros* that granted special liberties. Castile had a civil code, *Siete Partidas*, put in place in 1256–1265, and the civil law prevailed in 1505 with the Laws of Toro. These were assured by the law schools of Iberian universities and by professional lawyers in Roman jurisprudence (Parry, 1990: 192–193). This domination of civil law did not mean that other legislation became void; privileged classes and municipalities still enjoyed special liberties, in Iberia as in the Indies, and all codes of law were in theory valid even if conflicting. Castile also produced large collections of royal decrees such as the *Nueva Recopilación de Leyes de España* (1567), and the corresponding *Recopilación de Leyes de Indias* (1681). The king was the head of powerful and numerous judiciaries as well as being the supreme legislator. This was characteristic of feudal authority and is an important example of the unique character of Iberian absolutism (Parry, 1990: 193; Owens, 2005). Another illustration of the special relationship between authority and legality was the 'school-trained lawyer', as the king's 'most trusted servant' and an 'appropriate and willing agent of centralised authoritarian government' (Parry, 1990: 194).

> judicial procedures do not just provide a frame for the story. In an important respect, they are the story ... many among the political leadership of the Castilian commonwealth had become familiar with ideas developed by jurists about the relationship of rights based in natural law to the proper exercise of monarchical authority. These ideas, therefore, played a significant role in political arenas beyond the courtroom.
>
> (Owens, 2005: 10)

Geopolitically, the new kingdom used legislation to justify its overseas adventures. It did so by requesting donations and bulls from the papacy acknowledging Castile's rights of discovery, while playing its strong military position to influence and pressure other actors such as Portugal in the writing of treaties. Moreover, the organisation of the empire was legally complex, as its 'colonial government heavily relied upon judicial devices and procedures, and on legally trained officials' (Parry, 1990: 192).

At the doctrinal level, the Castilian Crown sought council from theologians and jurists to determine its rights and duties overseas and resolve growing social and political problems arising from the conquests. Next to the influence of Vitoria, the official debate between Las Casas and Sepúlveda, commissioned by the Crown and judged by a board of jurists and theologians, played a significant role (Hanke, 1974). The function of ecclesiastics in the colonies as protectors of the Indians was also crucial for their help in spreading European ideas. Although practices of expansion in the Crusades and Discoveries (or *Reconquista* and *Conquista*), were similar in method and showed signs of continuity in terms of imperial policy, the Castilian Crown, with the full support of the papacy, worked hard to differentiate them legally. The difference in legal classification was crucial, as it was later to become central to the problem of the Native Americans' legal status and the legitimating of war in the Indies. Both types of expeditions are commonly understood as being bathed in Catholic sentiment and ultimately justified by the supreme goal of spreading the Catholic faith. If the aim of Columbus's first expeditions was 'exclusively economic', the project became concerned with evangelisation from Queen Isabella's testament of 1504 (Koskenniemi, 2011: 12–13). However, a significant difference lay in the religious nature of the enemy. Muslims and Moors were referred to as infidels, and the use of force against them was not a subject of dispute as it became concerning the Native Americans (Hanke, 1974). For example, Las Casas, the defender of Indians' rights to be preached and converted peacefully, maintained in contrast the legality of the use of force against non-Christians such as the Turks, asserting that 'the Church may wage war against infidels who maliciously impede the spread of the gospel' (in Hanke, 1974: 91). Infidels were allegedly aware of the Gospel and chose to refuse it; therefore, the use of force was not an abuse of their rights. More importantly in the context of the Reformation, '[o]pposition to the anti-Moslem crusades was considered in Catholic Europe to be a Lutheran error' (Hanke, 1974: 91).[7]

An example of how law shaped the social fabric of the Iberian *reinos* is the struggle for social status fought by thousands of hidalgos in the chancery courts (Crawford, 2014: 1). They enjoyed a range of legal privileges and are usually defined as the lowest rank of the nobility as well as the most numerous group below knights (*caballeros*) and seigneurial aristocrats (*señores* and *títulos*). They faced local resistance to their claims of status which were crucial to obtain tax exemptions. Hidalgos 'filled a liminal social space between the vast majority of the lay population and the small number of titled aristocrats' and constituted from 5 to 10 per cent of the population which equals 108,358 families versus fifty-odd seigneurial families in 1541 (Crawford, 2014: 1). This marks a significant difference with other European societies where 'nobility ranged from less than half a percent to roughly 2 percent' (Crawford, 2014: 1). This mass of legally privileged families has been argued to be a factor of backwardness, leaving the weight of taxation on the peasantry (Crawford, 2014: 2) and leading to indirect taxes and venality. However,

[7] See Chapter 7 for further analysis of doctrinal aspects of Castilian imperialism.

the extraordinary numbers of hidalgos and legal disputes also show that those claiming status only did so precariously, and the few who achieved status did not enjoy the privileges usually ascribed to them. Moreover, the multiplicity of sources for recognising status meant instability, indefinite decisions, and the rhetorical nature of hidalgo status (Crawford, 2014: 3). In other words, the legal system, established by the attempts at a unified state, enabled a vacuum through which aspiring expectations and social struggles were more often disappointed than rewarded, and contributed to a society fragmented jurisdictionally. Another example concerns indigenous or *indio* slaves as litigants in Castile (over 100 lawsuits between 1530 and 1585) who fought to prove their *indio*-ness and who came from Mexico, Peru, South or East Asia (van Deusen, 2015).

The Iberian system of 'donation' was different to the system of French venality – characteristic of so-called absolutist states (Grafe, 2012: 29–30). There were three categories of offices up for 'donation' relating to quill, power, or money. Quill posts (e.g. notaries) were open to sale. The main power posts were not subject to sale (*corregidor*, *intendencias*, judicial posts) and military posts were very rarely sold, which was the main difference with France. But donation was more of an insider game in contrast to the upfront system of venality. Money offices (tax and customs farms) were mostly all sold but against a surety (Grafe, 2012: 31). In America, the sale of office was legal from 1606 and widespread, but it resembled more an agreement between a local, regional, or central authority and an individual investor than the 'classic patrimonial pattern' (Grafe, 2012: 32).

Concerning the economy, privileges were given to the wool cartel, discriminatory measures were taken against cereal farming, such as fixing the retail price, a guild system was put in place to constrict the urban industry, and religious persecution meant the exodus of Jewish capital (Anderson, 1974: 66). When Charles V came to the throne in 1516, the above pattern was accentuated. In reaction, 1520–1521 witnessed the *Comunero* revolt driven by artisan groups in towns and the urban bourgeoisie of north central Castile, at the same time as the Revolt of the Brotherhoods (*Germanías*) in the Crown of Aragon (Valencia and Majorca). This heightened the Crown's chances to secure its goals of unification, and marked the consecration of the golden age of Castilian imperialism. Still, although the country was being centralised, internal and cultural elements made the Iberian state unique and bound to premodernity. The realm of Aragon, for one, remained determined to fight against centralisation, and total unity was never achieved.

Iberia's 'jurisdictional fragmentation' was a hindrance economically and administratively but it also paradoxically provided 'the very strength of a system of governance . . . by negotiation and compromise' (Grafe, 2012: 37). This system 'made sudden tax increases (like those of 1635) or particularly large tax hikes extremely difficult to accomplish without threatening the cooperation between Crown and elites' (Grafe, 2012: 11). The paradox of fragmentation and cooperation occurred on two levels. First, it consisted in a struggle according to status with corporate groups, estates as a social group, guilds, and the church as a sovereign power. Second, it meant a struggle according to location as 'rights and duties could be located in territorial units, historic territories that became part of the emerging nation-states or towns that held sovereign rights' (Grafe, 2012: 26–27). Thus, in addition to the power of these historic territories (*reinos*) in the Eastern regions, towns constituted a 'basic unit of political and fiscal reorganisation' (Grafe, 2012: 34).

3.1.2 Paradoxes of Centralisation and the Impact of the Empire

The most recent literature agrees that Iberian absolutism is more of a myth in the face of its various judicial administrations and the Castilian monarchy's constant need to collaborate and negotiate its claim to a 'royal absolute authority' with 'local notables' and 'territorial aristocrats' (Owens, 2005: 4). Iberia had a relatively late feudalisation, and even though the process slowed down with the Habsburgs, jurisdictional fiefs were still being handed down to local notables up to the War of Succession. The Castilian jurist Castillo de Bobadilla argued in 1597 that 'lords of vassals are the bones and sinews of the state [. . . without them] it would only take a reverse in war or the defeat of an army or the death of a king to bring about its collapse' (Casey, 1999: 91).[8] In other words, the attempt at Iberian absolutism failed to transform the state into a unified fiscal and administrative apparatus. This did not stop Philip II's attempt to assert, in a famous lawsuit analysed in detail by Owens, the right of rulers 'to act according to their own will' (2005: 15). However, such assertion was nullified without the appropriate support and collaboration of the commonwealth. This paradox of Iberian centralisation, that is the way in which its reliance on jurists and on a strong judicial system led to a more restricted, politicised relationship between rulers and law is essential as a more cautious interpretation of Anderson's analyses below.

[8] I am grateful to Javier Moreno Zacarés for this point and reference.

In effect, the defeat of the *Comunero* revolt in the mid-sixteenth century marked, according to Anderson, the consolidation of Iberian absolutism, while also setting it apart from other European absolutisms where 'the primary pattern was the suppression of aristocratic rather than burgher revolts, even where the two were closely mingled' (1974: 68). In contrast, the *Comunero* revolt was conducted by the third estate and was defeated by the royal army with the support of the nobility, who feared any potential radicalism. The absence of a rising bourgeoisie to develop commerce and urban industry, or to take over the administrative state apparatus largely explains for Anderson why Spain was not able to productively benefit from its overseas empire.

This is one of the factors why commercialisation models of the transition argue that Spain did not develop into a capitalist economy, implying that it would have otherwise done so as if its natural path could then unfold through the mere presence of the bourgeoisie. Anderson argues that its overseas empire actually 'slowed down' that process, as the colonies provided a structural substitute for metropolitan provinces:

> The supply of huge quantities of silver from the Americas ... provided Hispanic Absolutism with a plentiful and permanent extraordinary income ... [which] meant that Absolutism in Spain could for a long time dispense with the slow fiscal and administrative unification which was a precondition of Absolutism elsewhere: the stubborn recalcitrance of Aragon was compensated by the limitless compliance of Peru.
>
> (1974: 71)

In the late-sixteenth century, Iberia became the major importer of grain. It included an unusual rural society in New Castile in comparison to the rest of Western Europe (1974: 72), with 60 to 70 per cent of the rural population being agricultural labourers (*jornaleros*), and unemployment remaining high in villages where only one-third of the male population worked in agriculture. However, if this applied to the southern half of Castile and of the Guadalquivir Valley, which comprised the large estates of the aristocracy, agrarian formations were very different elsewhere. Nevertheless, Anderson notes 'a premature and bloated "tertiary sector" ... which prefigured secular stagnation to come' (1974: 73). Manufacturing decreased once the cost of production soared, making the textile industry a victim of Bolivian silver, as the influx of bullion created inflation. In addition, Castile's relationship to the Habsburg Empire became one of interdependent collapse rather than constructive partnership (1974: 74). Finally:

> In the cataclysm of the 1640s, as Spain went down to defeat in the Thirty Years War, and bankruptcy, pestilence, depopulation [from eight and a half million in 1600 to seven million in 1700] and invasion followed, it was inevitable that the patchwork union of dynastic patrimonies should come apart: the secessionist revolts of Portugal, Catalonia and Naples were a judgement on the infirmity of Spanish Absolutism. It had expanded too fast too early, because of its overseas fortune, without ever having completed its metropolitan foundations.
>
> (Anderson, 1974: 81)

Anderson thus concludes on an 'inordinate' Iberian absolutism, which in the end merely consisted in the territorial benefits it acquired from its alliance with the Habsburg dynasty and from the *Conquista*. In other words, Castile's advantage over other European powers was its geopolitical accumulation – its ability to control foreign land through policies of dynastic alliances and war. However, more importantly, its judicial system and model of jurisdictional accumulation and governance never made it possible, bourgeoisie or not, to fully benefit economically from its overseas colonies.

First, the 'direct extraction of resources from the Spanish Americas' is 'easily overestimated' since the highest contribution in the second half of the sixteenth century was an average of 18 per cent of the revenue of the Castilian central treasury with an overwhelming share of revenues spent in the colonies (Grafe, 2012: 21) while large bankers such as Genoese lenders 'demanded their loans to be secured against future colonial receipts' (Grafe, 2012: 22–23).

> Even in the sixteenth and seventeenth centuries, the impact of revenue from the Americas on policymaking in Spain was largely indirect. Spain's expansionist foreign policy during these centuries was not financed through actual income from the Indies but owed to credit.
>
> (Grafe, 2012: 21)

This is also found in Political Marxist analyses (Wood, 2003; Moreno Zacarés, 2018) that reject both commercialisation models and narratives according to which Spain could have become capitalist if the empire had been more profitable, and if capitalists had not been hampered by feudal society and the lack of bourgeois initiative.[9] Instead, for Political Marxism, the factors explaining the specific development of the Iberian

[9] In contrast, world-systems theorists argue that Spain was already immersed in a capitalist world economy, but that the Iberian empires were quickly subjugated into a semi-

reinos are as much internally as externally constituted, since 'the economic hold of the empire was always limited by the capacities of its extra-economic power' (Wood, 2003: 43), that is military conquest, a monopolistic colonial trading system, forms of extra-economic exploitation, and the slave trade, which depended on the social and political organisation of the exploiters and their relation to the Iberian *reinos*, as well as on their relations with producers in the empire.[10]

The question is to what extent was jurisdictional accumulation an internal limitation of Castilian imperialism? If, as this section shows, the role of lawyers and legal institutions in the Iberian *reinos* has not been sufficiently acknowledged in Marxist studies, it remains to be shown how these actors and institutions affected and limited imperial ventures. Chapters 6 and 7 turn to exposing the geopolitical schema and dynamics of this Castilian legalistic empire, and its outward dynamics cross-Atlantic. The empire's continental reach was achieved from the alliance of the Castilian Crown with the Habsburg dynasty, coupled with the expeditions of the *Reconquista* to secure the Iberian peninsula. Meanwhile, maritime expansion was distinguished by two separated but closely linked impulses: the crusades for the North African coasts and Canary Islands, and the *Conquista* – the discovery, appropriation, and colonisation of the new American continent as a transplant of authority. The Castilian Empire therefore moved away from the Mediterranean towards the Atlantic and chose to incorporate colonised subjects into its general drive for jurisdictional unification.

3.1.3 *'New World' Social Property Relations*

Hispanic (and to a lesser extent French) settlements led to the reproduction of legal institutions of metropolitan societies and hybrid regimes of

peripheral position as intermediaries between the industrial–financial centres of north-western Europe and the Americas. Thanks to Javier Moreno Zacarés for this point.

[10] Moreno Zacarés's (2018) analysis of capitalist social property relations in Catalonia is shaped by the way in which this region was independent juridically from other regions in Iberia, and is therefore of significant interest to this project, although Catalonia is not directly significant for the understanding of the Castilian Empire's strategies of jurisdictional accumulation. His work is also an important contribution and step in a new direction for Political Marxism in terms of identifying other pockets of capitalist transition, and how these differed from England and the Dutch case, since he shows through 'a synchronic comparison between Galician and Catalan proto-industrial experiments', how the transition to capitalism was dependent on sociocultural struggles in eighteenth-century Catalonia, rather than, as Brenner had intimated, on its peasantry.

social property relations. Since Castilian colonial expansions not only reproduced but created new social property relations and, crucially, engaged in socially wide transplants of authority, it is necessary to include their discussion in this chapter. However, the following can in no way do justice to the complexity and variety of colonial experiences, and thus mainly points to some key characteristics.

New World Hispanics first consisted of settlers and clergy, then increasingly of a body of officials, lawyers, notaries, and miscellaneous quill-drivers. In the few big towns, one could also find merchants, shopkeepers, and craftsmen (Parry, 1990: 173). The settlers were not an extremely varied social group, as they were divided into *encomenderos* and their followers, ranchers, and mine owners. Generally, they were armed subjects of great privilege and sometimes, great wealth. The clergy was numerous in relation to Hispanics, but not in relation to the Indian population. The clergy served in many ways as mediator between all other social groups, and, alongside proselytising, were given the mission to 'protect' the Indians. The Indian population, who produced grain, vegetables, and poultry, provided the settlers with food and labour. Significant numbers of African slaves were mainly found in the islands and some Caribbean coasts (Parry, 1990: 173). The number of towns and cities created in the 'Spanish Indies' rose from 225 in 1580 to 331 in 1630 with a Hispanic population in 1580 of 150,000 (Elliott, 2006: 41). The eighteenth century also saw significant demographic growth, with total population numbers for the vice-royalty of New Spain increasing from one and a half million in 1650 to two and a half million in 1750 (Elliott, 2006: 261). All these numbers remain estimates of course, but it is certain that the number of Hispanic settlers is significantly higher than those of the other empires, marking a crucial difference between the Castilian enterprise and its contenders.

One of the major problems that emerged from the early stages of the colonisation was the contrast, and consequently conflict, between European and Amerindian ways of living. What seemed to Europeans to be the natives' 'idleness' was the natural consequence of a life sustained by subsistence farming, hunting and fishing. Compulsory labour, accepted in Europe's agrarian societies, meant forced labour or slavery for Indians, a fact which settlers struggled to understand (Parry, 1990: 175). This problem was more largely connected, as Parry shows, to the different conceptions of freedom. The liberty enjoyed by a legally free peasant in Iberia was 'within the context of the whole society to which he belonged, and subject to discharging the appropriate obligations towards that society, as laid down by custom' (1990: 173). In other words, a peasant in Iberia was only free as regards his relationship to the owner of the land on which he lived or for whom he had to pay tribute and services; that legal relationship was personal, and property was conditional, as in any other feudal society. For Indians living on subsistence farming (not all were, as was seen by the discovery of the Aztec and Inca empires), there was no personal and conditional relationship between ruler and ruled, therefore 'instead of laying on Indians a general compulsion to work (which was held to be compatible with liberty) it placed them in permanent personal servitude to individual Spaniards' (Parry, 1990: 176).[11]

Wood sees Castile's American colonies as semi-feudal societies. She explains this ambiguous position as one where, although the model set out at the beginning of the colonisation was feudal (as the 'exchange between monarch and military leaders' was set in terms of 'conditional rights of property and jurisdiction vested in the lord in exchange for military services'), it did not create a European-type feudal aristocracy (2003: 38). Moreover, Hispanic colonisers differed from their English, Dutch, and French followers by their aristocratic rather than commercially or agriculturally productive practices. Wood insists on how this affected property and class relations in the New World, making Castile's conquest and colonisation organic and directed to society as a whole:

> We are told, for instance, that the English and French were interested in commerce and agriculture, and set out to cultivate the land in America, while the Spanish 'had gone to occupy and to benefit, as all good noblemen did, from the labour of others' ... While their imperial rivals were interested in claims to land, the Spanish were at least as concerned with command over people and labour.
>
> (2003: 91)[12]

After Antonio de Montesinos, a Dominican friar, openly attacked the system in 1511, the first general code, the Laws of Burgos, was published

[11] In the case of the Andes, the Hispanics conquered pre-existing agrarian societies with forms of surplus extraction that were already mediated by theocratic domination. Unlike the Portuguese in Brazil, who had to bring slave labour from abroad because they couldn't capture the nomadic Indians living there, the Hispanics, at least here, did find good conditions for a transplant of feudal social relations. The *mita* system of forced labour for mining operations was actually inherited from the Incas. Thanks to Javier Moreno Zacarés for this point.

[12] This distinction is used by various other historians of empire and is further discussed in Chapter 6.

in 1512 governing the status and treatment of the natives: 'Every male Indian was to be required to spend nine months of the year in Spanish employment, and one third of the total labour force was to be employed in gold production' (Parry, 1990: 177). But the code, although seemingly responding to the attacks, did not resolve the problem. Although the concept of Indian liberty was accepted in principle, the code decided 'most Indians were in practice incapable of making use of their liberty' (Parry, 1990: 178). Those who could be free were those who embraced the European way of life (i.e. accepted the conditions of colonisation); this new class of Indians was named *capaces*. 'Accepting' this kind of freedom gave Indians the 'privilege' of being gathered in villages under their own headmen 'supervised' by Hispanic priests and officials (Parry, 1990: 178). Again, this was a conditional and personal relationship of freedom between ruler and ruled. We will see in Chapters 6 and 7 how these new strategies of accumulation were legitimised.

Nevertheless, important new types of legal relations developed in New Spain. For García-Salmones and Eslava (2010: 57), Castile's 'natural/organic view of urban politics' contributed to the founding of colonial cities as cities of God, notably through Phillip II's 1573 Ordinances for the Discovery, New Settlement, and Pacification of the Indies. The role of religion defined the project of expansion in terms of the subjectivities shaped by legal formulae, liturgical ceremonials, urban planning, and a 'transcendental experience' (García-Salmones & Eslava, 2010: 60). This transcendence can even be read in studies that highlight how the Enlightenment, usually ascribed to Europe, was felt more strongly in Hispanic America in 'university lecture halls, laboratories, and especially, courtrooms', and 'was brought to life in the everyday "entanglements and discord" that colonial subjects increasingly placed before royal judges' (Premo, 2017: 2). If 'ordinary and often illiterate litigants in Spanish America, not their legal representatives, were among its most surprising and skilled legal practitioners' (Premo, 2017: 3), colonial courts can be considered more modern than their Iberian counterparts. Chapter 6 explores in more detail the aspects of New Spain's legal institutions that characterise its imperial expansion and thereby tell a different story of Castile's role in the history of international law as a framework for modern and later capitalist international relations. Before going into those more substantial parts of the argument, the next section discusses France in terms of its jurisdictional nature – in its metropolitan and colonial contexts – showing important similarities to the Iberian *reinos*, followed by the more contrasting English and Dutch cases.

3.2 Revisiting French Absolutism

3.2.1 Containing Jurisdictional Spaces

The long reign of Louis XIV (1661–1715), central to the old regime period from the late-sixteenth to the late-eighteenth centuries, is associated with state centralisation, rationalism, and the exuberant display of undivided power, as the overly used metaphor of the 'Sun King' (*le roi-soleil*) exemplifies. However, France's prime period of European hegemony coincided with the preceding decades of 'the still defective and incomplete state structure of Richelieu and Mazarin, marked by institutional anomalies and torn by internal upheavals' (Anderson, 1974: 105).[13] Louis XIV's considerable feat was to contain the multifaceted and dispersed rebellions and divisions provoked by his two regent predecessors. His success can be explained by the various 'micro-conflicts' the regime relentlessly fought so as to eradicate the heterogeneity of the French kingdom (Noiriel, 2018: 105).

Instead of letting the bourgeoisie thrive and the masses breathe from less taxation, the strategy was to glorify the prestige of the monarchy. Louis XIV and his minister Colbert pursued socially suicidal belligerent campaigns and suffocated with aristocratic privileges the entrepreneurial spirit of the technical and commercial classes 'by forcing all these groups back into their appropriate places' (Beik, 2000: 15–16). These 'groups' consisted of the landed nobility (or sword nobility – *noblesse d'épée*); a robe nobility (*noblesse de robe*) including *parlementaires* (local magistrates), and *intendants* (powerful royal commissioners) emerging from the widespread practice of venality; a socially deeply entrenched Catholic church; a diverse group loosely associated as the urban bourgeoisie; and, finally, the lower classes or orders consisting of some craftsmen and labourers, but mostly peasants, who constituted an estimated massive 85 per cent of the population (Beik, 2000: 4–15; Noiriel, 2018: 115).

Half of this peasant population were daily labourers/agricultural workers (*journaliers*), who could use a small parcel of land for their home and subsistence production. The poorest fraction of the peasantry consisted of manual workers (*manouvriers*) who only possessed a few manual tools and would work seasonally where labour was required for

[13] Cardinals Richelieu (1585–1642) and Mazarin (1602–1661) were successive chief ministers during Louis XIV's childhood. Richelieu took office in 1624, and Mazarin continued ruling until 1661, when Louis assumed power.

lords or clergy, and who looked for other menial tasks during the winter. Some minority groups in northern regions such as Île-de-France were more entrepreneurial and cultivated larger parcels or controlled commercial networks. Another elite minority of farmer labourers (*fermiers laboureurs*) combined their own parcels with land cultivated in tenancy from the lord and were influential in local towns and markets (Noiriel, 2018: 133). In sum, the peasantry – and hence social property relations more generally – was diverse in terms of its regimes and activities. However, the variety and heavy burden of taxes meant that productivity stagnated between the fifteenth and eighteenth centuries (Noiriel, 2018: 134). If Malthusian, commercialisation, and tax-based explanations remain dominant in the literature, Political Marxist scholars (Wood, Brenner, Comninel, Miller, Lafrance) have focused on the broader concept of social property relations – as politically constituted and contested social relations of production – to explain the lack of agricultural innovation in the diverse and rich French countryside. The following discussion focuses on the jurisdictional dimensions and divisions of the French kingdom, as an essential part of those social property relations, so as to draw the contours of France's development of jurisdictional accumulation in its diplomatic, mercantilist, and colonial policies.[14]

Louis's reign created a facade of absolutist and insurmountable rule that kept a crumbling society in check. European wars (especially the anti-Spanish struggle) served to forge the new structures of absolutism, even if Louis XIV failed to fulfil his military aims due to strategic and diplomatic errors (Anderson, 1974: 98).[15] Early-seventeenth-century France was an unstable and heterogeneous confederation of corporate bodies (*corps*) loosely coordinated by the central power in Paris. It included approximatively eighteen million people, a population far above other European kingdoms, including Russia's eleven million estimate (Noiriel, 2018: 103). Relations between subjects and the king were based on feudal – personal concepts of direct allegiance – and subjects also

[14] Regarding other key aspects of French social property relations, scholars have emphasised the power of guilds and corporations in defending peasants' and worker's rights against dispossession and market dependence for wages and prices, leading to a system which contrasted with the British agrarian and industrial model of capitalism up until the late-nineteenth century (Lafrance, 2019).

[15] Wars fought by Louis XIV were the War of Devolution (1667–1668), the Dutch War (1672–1678), the Nine Years' War (1688–1697) and the War of the Spanish Succession (1701–1714). The royal army increased from 20,000 men in 1630 to 500,000 in 1715 (Noiriel, 2018: 119).

depended personally on lords and clergy. Borders were not fixed and were conceptualised by elites and subjects depending on the various territorial units and personal relations of dependence defining those units. Borders were therefore not spatially but personally determined by complex and overlapping relations of dependence (Sahlins, 1991; Nordman, 1998).

More specifically, Nordman identifies three conceptions of space and borders defining and evolving to shape French territory from the sixteenth century. The first is a continuous, extended (*étendue*) and indefinite sense (*frontière et continuité*). The second most important notion implies the relation of dependence (*espace et dépendance*) (Nordman, 1998: 511–527). It relates to the personal power tying subjects (or producers) to lords and other holders of jurisdictional power (exploiters) and consists in 'abstract, invisible links, which manifest themselves through relations to lords, to taxes, and especially to jurisdiction' (Nordman, 1998: 517).[16] The third notion is a contiguous form of space which is associated with modern territoriality (*espace et contiguïté*). It appears in the mid-seventeenth century but only gradually conquers the whole of the French space, even the Western European space, in the mid- to late- eighteenth century (Nordman, 1998: 520).

The old regime's relationship to law showcases the kingdom's complexity and heterogeneity, and especially the second crucial notion of jurisdictional space dominant throughout the old regime. The French kingdom was divided up until the mid-sixteenth century according to landowners' domains or governorships. However, these landowners did not constitute a homogeneous class 'of formally equal landed proprietors sharing a common relationship to the state' (Parker, 1996: 154). The state was administratively constituted of *pays d'états* and *pays d'élections*.[17] Sovereign courts were the *parlements, sénéchaussées, baillages*, and *généralités*.[18] Urban centres only accounted for 10–20 per cent of the

[16] 'Ce sont alors plutôt des liens, invisibles, abstraits, qui se manifestent par la relation seigneuriale, par l'impôt, mais surtout par la juridiction' (author's translation).

[17] Under Louis XIV, *pays d'états* (e.g. Languedoc, Provence, Burgundy, Navarre, Brittany, Artois) were provinces with surviving estates (i.e. representative institutions). *Pays d'élections* (the larger group, e.g., Champagne, Ile de France, Lyonnais, Touraine) were provinces with a *généralité* and an *élection* (i.e. major and minor administrative subdivisions and a court where taxes were imposed by an *intendant*, representative of the king).

[18] Most of the North of France (one-third of the whole territory) was under the jurisdiction of the Parlement of Paris. There were in total twelve *parlements* , that is high courts of law whose function was to apply the law but not in theory create it (seven in *pays d'états*: Toulouse, Grenoble, Aix, Dijon, Douai, Rennes, Pau; five in *pays d'élections*: Paris, Rouen, Bordeaux, Besançon, Metz). *Présidiaux, sénéchaussées,* and *baillages* were jurisdictions

population, but cities were central in defining the political and legal authorities for their surrounding populations. The important change to the functioning of these institutions was the increasing sale of offices and the option of their hereditary upgrade with the *paulette* annual fee. This fundraising operation, or venality, provoked the unparalleled rise of the robe nobility.

In historiographical debates, the 'revisionist' turn seeks to uncover the social struggles operating behind the 'grand ideas' (i.e. historical factors analysed by contemporaneous scholars and assumed by later historians to constitute the driving forces behind social change). Although not always explicitly, absolutism, for example, was understood as the basis of the new regime ideology, glorifying and driving the capabilities of the state. Beik identifies two questions that have preoccupied historians, and three traditions of historical analysis: political/institutional, *Annalistes*, and Marxist (1985: 3).[19] Accordingly, the problem with historical studies up to the end of the twentieth century was their separate focus on two distinct questions – the political and economic – that essentially needed to be reunited in a critical analysis by Marxist scholarship.

The first question concerns the role of the state in maintaining absolutism: how effective was Louis XIV's rule? Political and institutional historians see the state and state-building as beneficial and external to society. However, more recent institutionalists have had to drastically temper that claim (Beik, 1985: 13, 17). The second question is the relationship between the state and society, in particular in relation to the sub-question of the transition from feudalism to capitalism. *Annalistes,* or social historians, chose to focus on land, demography, subsistence crises, climate, and disease. Their work, in contrast, suffers from a lack of political dimension. The relation between state and society also preoccupied Marxist historians, but their debates either ignored the seventeenth century by focusing on revolutions and modernity, or mirrored claims made by 'recent institutionalists' (1985: 31).[20] Additionally, they were marred in differentiating feudalism from absolutism and capitalism.

operating below the *parlement* (*sénéchaussées* being the southern equivalent of *baillages*). The lowest judicial institution was the seigneurial court, of which 70,000 were counted in the mid-seventeenth century.

19 The French journal *Les Annales*, founded by Marc Bloch and Lucien Febvre in 1929 became a school of thought later represented by historians such as Fernand Braudel and Emmanuel Le Roy Ladurie.

20 See Shilliam (2009: 30–56) for a review of this literature in the context of early modern France and England.

Building on Anderson's work (1974), Beik applies the condition of extra-economic coercion to the definition of the absolutist regime, and thereby associates absolutism with feudalism. He argues the two questions separately preoccupying strands of historians – the political and economic – need to be intertwined. In effect, Louis XIV's success in ruling France should be seen as directly related to the social relations of absolutism. Beik (2005) argues against the 'grand idea' that Louis XIV's reign was one of coordinated and advancing state-building in the face of the political, social, and institutional remnants of feudal nobility and privileges. His critique focuses on the role and proceedings of regional *parlements* and provincial class relations. He shows that Louis XIV had to collaborate with both the sword and robe nobility to maintain stability across the kingdom. In other words, the nobility did *not* simply acquiesce to Louis XIV's absolute rule, crushed by its overbearing centralising forces. Instead, three separate studies of the estates of Languedoc, of Brittany, Paris, Burgundy, Normandy, and lastly of Artois, 'Walloon' Flanders and Cambrésis (Beik, 2005) reveal that regional elites and the state *collaborated* and mutually gained from their relationship. Moreover, the organisation of the army, so characteristic of eighteenth-century France, had not overcome some of its traditional 'feudal' basic elements (for example, the funding of officers). These studies thus reject 'modernization' theories of the military element of the state (Beik, 2005: 217).

Parker (1989, 1996, 2003) also argues for a reassessment of the 'absolute' character of the old regime as intrinsically feudal. His analysis of property rights under Louis XIV (2003) shows that the king maintained strategies to claim territory or revenue on local landowners' territories (which they then replicated with their own vassals) based on a feudal mode of rentier exploitation. The French regime differed from its English neighbour by developing a stagnating ruling class opposed in principle to the rising bourgeoisie, who was represented as developing the notion of individualism and who was 'constrained by prevailing conceptions of hierarchy, lineage, family and property', in which the robe nobility largely participated (Parker, 1996: 270).

Parker therefore emphasises the assertion of patrimonial interests, deployed in defence of the privileged orders and hierarchical society. If the higher classes chose to stay away from local jurisdictions (i.e. the seigneurial courts over their tenants), this was in defence of the 'patrimonial nature of the legal system'. Either way, the courts were upholding neither the state, nor the higher nobility's interests, and therefore all remained trapped in their own interests. This system continued throughout the eighteenth century, with lords augmenting or maintaining their revenues and properties through the judiciary and elites therefore connected to the monarchy through similar interests (Miller, 2008).

If this dynastic absolutism was marred in a limited cycle of self-reproduction, characterised by personal forms of geopolitical accumulation (Teschke, 2003), how do we understand the innovative diplomatic strategies developed in this period in terms of extraterritorial practices, such as embassies and consulates? This question is pursued in the following chapters, which unpack – from diplomatic actors in Chapters 4 and 5 and from the Westphalia–*droit public de l'Europe* paradigm in Chapter 6 – hidden practices of jurisdictional accumulation. Before doing so, the following presents the legal institutions and actors necessary to understand these particular forms of accumulation.

3.2.2 Containing Legal Orders

Legal uniformity was one of the 'micro-conflicts' fought by the regime against jurisdictional heterogeneity. One strategy was to write down the complex patchwork of rules and customs and the establishment of codes was attempted with the 'Code Louis' referring to the *Ordonnances sur la réformation de la justice civile et criminelle* (1667–1670) and the *Code Noir* (1685) regulating colonial territories.[21] Though the development of the legal profession is one of the main innovations of the old regime, its role is heterogeneous and served to maintain absolutism as much as it tried to resist or contest it. For example, if the Parlement de Paris's role was irreplaceable in helping to establish royal sovereignty, the monarchy nevertheless had growing difficulties in its dealings with *parlementaires* (Krynen, 2009: 63). We saw in the previous paragraphs the complex administrative divisions of the territory associated with France. In the northern regions above the Loire, up until the end of the old regime, one could find sixty-five general customs and three hundred local customs; neither was the south (Midi) a uniform legal space, despite its 'written law' tradition (Krynen, 2009: 56). Moreover, in some areas justice and fief were still in practice tied together under the pressure of patrimonial rights, despite theoretical attempts to separate them. Even when looking

[21] Another key process of uniformisation indirectly led by the king through a plethora of legal actors in the sixteenth century is the writing of customary law through regional *parlements* (Seong-Hak Kim, 2007).

at the differences between northern and southern jurists (the first assumed to be feudalists, and the second more influenced by Roman law), it appears that both 'developed a jurisprudence that reflected the economic interests of the feudal-rentier class to which they – and the monarchy – belonged' (Parker, 2003: 93). Notably, the difference between *pays d'états* and *pays d'élections* is important to understand the power differentials between different seats of *parlements* and local seigneurial courts, as the former maintained 'higher levels of indirect rule' and 'more heterogeneous bargains with central authorities' (Nexon, 2009: 72–73).

An essential difference to note in the making of the legal profession is that between *parlementaires* and advocates or barristers (*avocats*). *Parlementaires* were the judges of the *parlements* and became 'the most prominent robe nobles'. Their influence was felt mostly in three areas. First, they belonged to important families with strong connections in government and finance, thereby affecting the older sword nobility and politics of state. Second, they issued *arrêts* (decrees) for the implementation of laws and the maintenance of public order, thereby competing with other administrative authorities (governor or *intendant*). Lastly, *parlementaires* had the capacity to affect the king's legislation by delaying the registration of edicts or ordinances, or by petitioning the king for changes (Beik, 2000: 8).

Avocats are represented as 'institutional technicians' (Bell, 1994: 8). Events in Dijon in 1627 'highlight the importance of university-educated legal professionals' where *avocats* are 'local *hommes politiques*' (Breen, 2007: 3) and 'recognized experts of France's complex and multifaceted body of law, masters of arcane legal precedents and principles' (Breen, 2007: 3). A symbiosis formed between the *mairie* (town hall) and bar of Dijon. As these advocates or barristers were excluded from royal sovereign courts by the price of offices, they turned to the municipalities.

The rise of the robe nobility and of office venality had advantages and disadvantages for the monarchy. This practice consisted of the private selling of public offices but also the sale of honours and special privileges (taxes, industrial monopolies, trade and rights to a specific profession), at times resulting in the ennoblement of the buyer and his descendants.[22] It affected all functions of the governing apparatus (state, monarchy, administration, army, legal system) thereby constituting a new form of

[22] In total, there existed between three and four thousand offices that conferred nobility, added to thousands of other posts that did not (Beik, 2000: 9).

property. An important exception was ambassadorial posts as is discussed further in the following chapter. Nevertheless, the practice of venality was at the heart of the non-bureaucratic, personalised, patrimonial, and divided characteristics of the old regime (Teschke, 2003: 126, 173–177). Beik notes that if this meant a 'whole new body of individuals whose fundamental interests lay on the side of the state' and the 'tapping of their wealth coming from commerce or finance' (2000: 7), the state nevertheless lost an opportunity to develop productive business. This new group added to the under-taxed privileged elite, 'creating a collegial body of virtually irremovable, powerful figures who might well defend their own interests, even when these clash with royal policies' (Beik, 2000: 7).

Thus, office holders did not become necessarily loyal to the king or to the kingdom's laws through the acquisition of their office. Obtaining an office created the need to defend it, and groups of magistrates (in Bordeaux, then in Périgueux and Agen) led the resistance against tax collection (Noiriel, 2018: 112) in some cases ending in popular revolts against the king.

> The stakes were high, since the dimensions of a jurisdiction determined, in fairly direct measure, the amount of an official's revenue, the value of his office, and even the extent of his honor, measured quite tangibly by his rank in public processions.
>
> (Bell, 1994: 22)

Nevertheless, the case of the *parlementaires* shows strong signs of collaboration between king and judges, in terms of the security and establishment of their status and property (Beik, 2005: 220). These varied dynamics towards the monarchy, alongside those of provincial elites and office-holding nobility, are therefore difficult to homogenise, especially as the short-term royal manoeuvres to control these different groups only created more chaos and uncertainty in the long run.

From the thirteenth century onwards, the king personified legislative sovereignty as the distributor of justice (Krynen, 2009: 17–38). This role represented the potential centralisation of territory, making this function a glorified and pursued agenda by royalists. The realisation of this potential and transition to lawmaker is generally associated with absolutism, but this assumption is now contested by the lack of legal uniformity and the class dynamics of patronage and ensuing clientelism following from office venality (Teschke, 2003: 179–181). From the sixteenth century, if the monarchy had the title of supreme legislator and produced a 'steady stream of ordinances', it was the role of the *parlement* to register the law and give it force. In addition to the role of jurists and jurisprudence, the specificity of the French legal system was its 'peculiar state of equilibrium' between the judiciary, legislature, and legal scholars (Van Caenegem, 1987: 70). Moreover, the king remained hierarchically beneath God and he derived his power and therefore his legislative sovereignty from divine authority (Parker, 1989; Krynen, 2009: 31–38). Thus, next to the practical limits on absolutist rule from diverse social groups, the king was also interpreted by legal and political thought as dependent from the will of God.

Alongside debates between absolutists and constitutionalists on the role of the king and his possession of territory and authority, came the influential movement of Jansenism.[23] For Gerstenberger (2007: 496), it even constituted the most serious challenge to ruling practice. Jansenism was a Catholic movement arising out of the Counter-Reformation causing controversy and condemnation by the Pope but attracting important French theologians and writers such as Blaise Pascal and Jean Racine. Their main influence was St Augustin. Jansenists' opponents were the Jesuits, highlighted the importance of religious divisions on the political scene linked to the Protestant Reformation (Gorski, 2003; Nexon, 2009), and to the rise of an educated anti-nobility class as an essential component of pre-revolutionary social conflicts (Gerstenberger, 2007: 498–500). Jansenism is particularly important in our case as it attracted magistrates and was often defended by the Parlement de Paris:

> magistrates seeking to prevent the Crown and the upper clergy from eradicating the Jansenist current within the church publicized the threat of 'despotism', the monarchy's duty to adhere to 'fundamental laws', and even the concept of national sovereignty.
>
> (Miller, 2008: 5)

[23] Absolutists or royalists were eminently represented by Jean Bodin, whose aim was to transfer 'particularistic, quasi-feudal powers to the monarchy' (Wood, 1983: 295), and to ensure that the 'unity of the state and the "harmonious" balance of its constituent parts were expressed in and maintained by the sovereign power of the king' (Wood, 1983: 292). In opposition to Bodin and his harmonisation of the state–sovereignty–monarch triptych, Huguenot *constitutionalists* formed during the French religious wars of the late-sixteenth century. Also known as *monarchomachs* (those who fight against monarchs) they have been identified as the first Calvinists to transform the concept of religious duty to resist, into a 'modern' political and moral right of resistance (Skinner, 1978a: 240). They were more intent in defending the rights of the people, although they argued these rights should still belong in practice to corporate bodies.

Moreover, Jansenist barristers or *avocats* conceived of France as a 'judicial monarchy' (Bell, 1994: 17). This status was justified by the particular role of *parlements* as organs of royal government (Bell, 1994: 24) and by the legal complexity and ambiguity of the old regime. These ideas therefore contributed, in various rich ways, to produce conditions for practices of jurisdictional accumulation imbued with notions of royal, legal, and religious sovereignty that contested the rays of the Sun King and enabled French society to resist centralising institutions. These also led to more privately driven imperial ventures in the Atlantic, which nevertheless reproduced old regime legal institutions, and to a mercantilist consular policy that fought hard to contain and exploit the expansion of Provençal merchants in the Mediterranean through an elaborate set of legal measures.

Legal categories were also used pragmatically to exclude certain groups politically while benefiting from their entrepreneurship and including them economically in the realm. This was the case for Jews, Protestants, and foreign residents, who 'facilitated the exchange of goods and credit and provided essential services' (Horn, 2015: 168).

Thus, doctrine and practice remained in a constant dialogue with regional and local social struggles. Though intentionally sidelined by the monarchy, the evolving French legal orders kept a link to matters of foreign policy and treaty-making. This manifested itself mainly through the role of the Parlement de Paris in maintaining a presence or an ability to control certain royal acts. However, the role of the Parlement in foreign policy became more and more a matter of debate in the eighteenth century (Belissa, 1998: 117, 184–191; Durchhardt, 2004; Gerstenberger, 2007: 509–510).[24] Foreign policy and the *droit des gens* was increasingly discussed in political literature such as the *Gazette de Leyde*, which included 'reports of the royal family and the court' as well as 'reference to social tensions, to differing views among government officials, and to the mistakes of foreign monarchs' (Gerstenberger, 2007: 504; see also Belissa, 1998: 124).

The *parlementaires* and advocates' role in the French Revolution is an important question, though it cannot be adequately investigated here.[25] For Miller, 'the political body responsible for the transformation of the

[24] If 'the regional or national estates or – in the case of France – the Parisian Parliament were excluded from international relations in the quality of signatories of international treaties', they did not disappear 'completely from the treaties' texts' (Durchardt, 2004: 47).

[25] 'In France, one of the first acts of the first revolutionary assembly was to abolish almost all the legal institutions of the *ancien régime*, including the orders of advocates, to create new decentralized and deprofessionalized system of courts, and to begin the task of simplifying and rewriting the law for the new legal order they had created' (Burrage, 2006: 581).

country between 1789 and 1791 was composed of lawyers and office-holders, not merchants and industrialists' (2008: 4). Ties were also generally found between law schools, the growing bourgeoisie and office holding nobility, resulting in the judiciary playing a strong part in defending and augmenting the revenues of lords. In spite of apparent legal innovations, '[r]oyal institutions and laws anchored the country to its feudal past' (Miller, 2008: 24). The debates and opposite dynamics point to a complex, influential, and overlapping legal system. Furthermore, even if the revolution abolished the old system and has since constituted the dividing line between the history of law (*l'histoire du droit*) and modern, actual law (*le droit*), van Caenegem (2002) argues that post-revolution, the break from the past was not so stark in practice and more difficult to put in place than is commonly assumed. Although the new regime, with its civil codes and rejection of old and patrimonial jurisdictions, contained promises of Enlightenment ideals of justice and popular sovereignty, it also administered and neutralised political and judicial strongholds that would have resisted the new governments.

3.2.3 *Colonial Social Property Relations*

French colonies in North America known as New France (Nouvelle-France) have been privileged by legal histories and are generally used as examples of French settlement and jurisdictional arrangements. However, the role of chartered companies and private entrepreneurs or settlers remained crucial in this case, and more generally, French, English, and Dutch imperial expansions in this period remained largely driven by quasi-private or independent actors, as discussed in more detail in Chapter 6.

In terms of the social property relations developed in these colonial entities, they vary according to the different strategies employed by the French monarchy and the particular prerogatives of the companies put in place to govern. The general policy towards indigenous peoples in North America was to consider them independent, in a certain sense 'free', and able in certain circumstances to remain under the jurisdiction of their own laws and customs (Morin, 2010: 69). Legal regimes varied according to the status and conditions of settlement of the people in question, and there was a large amount of often complex treaties signed between the monarchy and indigenous populations. French law was not imposed on them: for one, because such a thing barely existed in a homogeneous form; but also because this was a safe strategy for the monarchy to keep a hold on the territory in question and its resources (e.g. the fur trade). In other words, the king could not maintain its colonial empire without the help of local warriors and traders. This situation is particular to New France as colonies in Louisiana and in the Caribbean encouraged emigration and thereby territorial settlements. Overall, the old regime's colonial policies permitted fluid, semi-feudal, and innovating legal systems. In contrast, the early-nineteenth century brought a much more categorical and authoritarian system of colonial rule, notably driven by Britain rather than France (Morin, 2010: 70).

Concerning territorial settlements in American colonies such as Louisiana, the private rights of individuals were 'deepened and extended through the increasingly normal practice of granting tenures under free and easy terms' (Keene, 2002: 68), instead of being vested in the state. This led to 'the profusion of divided sovereignty, re-cast in the form of decentralised systems of colonial governance', rather than the consolidation of public authority in the hands of the holders of territorial sovereignty (Keene, 2002: 69). Colonial sovereignty was extremely divided and in effect difficult to localise, that is it was, as in France, more jurisdictional than territorial. In North America, it was distributed between the Crown, proprietary agencies, and settlers' local institutions, while the regime of distribution varied across the country.

The Caribbean also provides significant examples of French settlement, where about five thousand Frenchmen occupied in 1642 around fifteen islands in the 'Petites Antilles' (Noiriel, 2018: 148). Noiriel describes a pattern of feudal settlement put in place ad hoc by aspiring landowners who reproduced relations of vassalage and of 'compagnonnage' (i.e. the recruitment of skilled artisans (*compagnons*) from Normandie to work under the dependence of the settler lower nobility). This voluntary exile dwindled, and settlers either bought slaves to work the land or recruited poor peasants, unemployed artisans, or sailors for three-year contracts (*engagés*). This feudal and quasi-autonomous society of small landowners (*habitants*), often resorting to violent enforcement of hard-working conditions, mostly produced tobacco and food crops, but shifted to sugar in the mid-seventeenth century. In 1664, Colbert founded a new company (Compagnie des Indes Orientales) to look over all American colonies, but these all shifted directly to the Crown a decade later. The colonies reproduced old regime institutions, with an *intendant* and a governor representing the Crown, and a counsel representing the most powerful settlers (Noiriel, 2018: 148–153). On the East African coast, the French took control of La Réunion and Mauritius in 1638, but they remained inhabited until the early-eighteenth century and their subsequent use for the production of coffee (Noiriel, 2018: 154).

Thus, certain French colonies, particularly in the Caribbean, were used by the French monarchy to maintain the particular 'public/private' order of the old regime notably through the *Code Noir* of 1685 regulating French slavery (Nuzzo, 2011; Koskenniemi, 2017: 8). French jurists and lawyers developed views on colonial practices (e.g. Bodin, Jean Bacquet, Pierre Bergeron, Claude Fleury, Cardin Le Bret, Guyot, Charles Loyseau, and Jean Domat) and contested the conventional anthologies discussed by Grewe and Schmitt (Morin, 2010: 12–22). Grotius and other illustrious writers of the law of nations were blacklisted by French lawyers, despite Richelieu's attempts at widely diffusing these works for their legitimating of colonial expansion (Morin, 2010: 4).

Early modern French colonialism was not characterised by the full imposition of state or monarchical sovereignty. Instead, French mercantilism and imperialism diffused a mixed and confused model of domestic rule, which resulted in different forms of jurisdictional accumulation better identified as transports rather than transplants of authority. The plethora of divided and composite colonial sovereignties was taken over more forcefully, militarily and juridically, by nineteenth-century imperialism. In other words, mercantilism can be associated with these processes of jurisdictional accumulation, which exported and imposed different institutional forms but did not lead by themselves to a transformation of the relations of production.

An exhaustive analysis of the establishment of different regimes of colonial social property relations in terms of jurisdictional institutions and relations of dependence in the French, English, and Dutch cases remain beyond the scope of this study. Nevertheless, it is maintained that jurisdictional accumulation as an imperial legal strategy was more about territorial settlement for the French, English, and Dutch empires in the early modern period than it was for Castile. This does not mean that the concept does not apply for these former empires' colonial projects. It means that these empires used jurisdictional strategies differently, that is more for commercial and territorial settlement though the use of chartered settlers and companies (i.e. as indirect and outsourced transports of authority).

3.3 England's Transition to Capitalism, Private Property, and Law

This section and the following one on the Dutch Republic begin with a historiographical debate rather than a descriptive summary of their early modern legal and political context. This contrasts to the previous sections, but is justified in terms of the particular importance of these debates for the argument on jurisdictional accumulation and as frames to the subsequent historical analyses.

3.3.1 Enclosures and Primitive Accumulation

Marx's discussion of 'so-called primitive accumulation', which closes the first volume of *Capital* (1976), is foremost a critique of classical political economy, and specifically of Adam Smith's mythical treatment of the concept of accumulation.[26] Instead, what characterises primitive accumulation for Marx is the coercive process of separating direct producers from their means of production. Transformations in fifteenth- and sixteenth-century England are described as the classic manifestation of primitive accumulation marking the transition to capitalist relations of production (1976: ch. 27). This analysis has generated a longstanding debate on the transition.[27] At the heart of this debate is the process of enclosure in England, coupled with a broader agricultural revolution and the political and legal history of English state formation. If 'the expropriation of the mass of the people from the soil forms the basis of the capitalist mode of production' (1976: ch. 33), this 'fearful and painful' process, this 'prelude to the history of capital' as a social relation, takes the *form* of a transition from a society of slave and serf producers to a society of wage labourers (1976: ch. 32). However, beyond or behind this 'mere change of form' – and thus of legal status from personally bonded and self-sufficient to personally free and waged producer – lies 'the dissolution of private property based on the labour of its owner' (1976: ch. 32).

In other words, under capitalism, private property becomes detached from the labour of those who work and who would thereby own the land. This process is understood as the separation from the means of production. There are 'qualitative' rather than 'quantitative' (Dimmock, 2014: 129) processes through which private property emerges as the defining commodity of private individuals who do not labour on the land. These

[26] The more accurate translation of Marx's concept is 'original accumulation' from the German *ursprünglich*, but as is conventional in Marxist literature, the following retains the translation of 'primitive accumulation'.

[27] See Chapter 2 for a review of this debate in terms of contemporary methodological problems in international law and IR.

legitimise the dissolution of collective or common property and are fundamental legal, political, and economic content that drive the shifts from established or transhistorical legal forms. The analysis of these processes is at the core of this book's critique of the commodity form theory of law, introduced in Chapter 2. This analysis consists in a comparative analysis of English state formation that shows the ability of the English state and ruling class to uphold and defend private property (Wood, 1992[2015]).[28] In contrast, France was concerned with jurisdictional disputes that required the combination and collaboration of various property rights and conceptions of space so as to maintain the kingdom's unity and facade of absolutism, as was seen in the previous section. England's process of state formation was also in stark contrast to Castile, which had to collaborate with regional institutions and find ways to make up for the enduring jurisdictional fragmentation of its kingdoms, a fragmentation which can also be ascribed to the Dutch case albeit with very different consequences and class structures.

The point here is to develop *from* – and not strictly according *to* Marx – a more thorough and historically specific analysis of legal processes central to key transformations in England's social property relations. Moreover, this study cannot do justice to the wide-ranging debates and extensive literature regarding enclosures and, more broadly, early modern English social history, especially the transformations and social relations involved in the Anglo-Scottish union of 1701 (Davidson, 2010) or the colonisation of Ireland in 1649. However, prima facie, these can be understood as extensions rather than transplants or transports of authority. Nor can it do justice to the wider and more contested issues of the role of English colonialism and to its role in imperial and mercantilist rivalry in and outside Europe. The following chapters do include important discussions of some of these processes in the Mediterranean and in North America. However, the broader questions of the role of colonialism and imperialism in England/Britain's transition to capitalism can remain in the background, for now at least, since the aim of the overall study is to focus on some key internal and outward processes of legal expansion (treaties, chartered companies, consulates, colonies) reproduced and experimented by English officials and holders of jurisdictional power. If these are discussed more explicitly in later chapters, the present section focuses on providing a picture of the social relations and legal institutions at the basis of these processes of legal expansion.

[28] See also Wood (2012: 20–23).

England's enclosures are a fundamental legal process of consolidation and expansion of landowners and yeomen's property rights, and thus of forceful exclusion and dispossession of peasants and commoners. Their role in the transition is undisputed, whether one considers England as the birthplace of the capitalist system (Wood, 1992[2015]: 1; Dimmock, 2014), or instead as only one instance determined by various events and contexts in a globally connected history of transition (Wallerstein, 1974, 1997; Anievas & Nişancioğlu, 2015).

Understanding the meaning of the enclosures and raising the issue of their legal importance is essential as a basis to other legal processes of jurisdictional accumulation. Of course, it would be contradictory from a Marxist standpoint, to understand enclosures as jurisdictional rather than primitive accumulation. Marxist legal scholars have already shown the recurring importance of the concept of primitive accumulation for the history of international law (Neocleous, 2012; Chorley, 2018). For Neocleous (2012), the focus on primitive accumulation is speared on by TWAIL's post-colonial emphasis on colonisation and imperialism, an emphasis that, as he regrets, is in denial of the relevancy of Marx's analysis of primitive accumulation. If for Mezzadra the prehistory of capitalism is a permanent feature of its history, for Neocleous this prehistory also manifests itself recurrently as international law.

Nevertheless, as discussed in Chapter 6, Neocleous (2012) shows the specificities of this process tied to English colonists and their reaction to classical political economy. The subsequent chapters focus on extraterritoriality and equivalent processes that have not been considered by the rich and abundant literature on enclosures, primitive accumulation, and their meaning for early modern and contemporary capitalism (Midnight Notes, 1990; Perelman, 2000; Bush *et al.*, 2011; Mezzadra, 2011; Ince, 2014, 2018; Federici, 2017; Pacheco, 2017; Roberts, 2017; Tilley *et al.*, 2017).

Some key aspects of the enclosure process in England are presented so as to introduce the legal dimensions of English state formation and transition to capitalism, point to the jurisdictional elements of these processes, and why they have been problematically conflated with mercantilism, which appears more jurisdictional than capitalist.

Social and economic historians within and beyond Marxist circles agree that the 1600s saw the most significant changes marking England's transformation from an open field to an enclosed country (i.e. the classic transition to capitalism phase). Enclosure was one of the new techniques used by landowners and yeomen in England's early agricultural revolution. It consisted in 'the enclosure of open fields which had been cultivated under regulation by the village community, as well as the enclosure of wasteland and the common land upon which many smallholders and others depended for grazing, wood and other necessities' (Wood & Wood, 1997: 15). By 1700, it is estimated that 70 per cent of cultivable land in England was enclosed, and three-fifths of the English population had primarily become wage labourers (Dimmock, 2014: 139). This needs to be understood in a context where, in 1688, 40 per cent of England's estimated population of 4.5 million people relied on non-agricultural occupations, marking its important divergence from other European societies such as France.

England witnessed various waves and types of enclosures from the late medieval period, and various social conflicts between lords and peasants over these practices, such as in 1381 or 1450. These eventually led to a Commission Inquiry in 1517–1518 and to procedures by the Crown against enclosing. However, this did not stop the larger anti-enclosure rebellions of 1549 as a national conflict between lords, yeomen, and the dispossessed ensemble of peasants and poor commons (Dimmock, 2014: 154). In other words, the history of enclosures needs to account for agricultural and demographic patterns, changes in legal statutes, court proceedings, and social conflicts. What is key from recent debates is the need to differentiate the effects of different types of enclosures depending on their varying social contexts – or, in other words, depending on social property relations.

Based on primary research on enclosure acts in Kent and work by Whittle (2000) and Mate (2006) on other regions in England, Dimmock argues that it was the long fifteenth century (1370s–1530s) – rather than the seventeenth century as is conventionally argued – that produced the most important social changes for the shift to agrarian capitalism. This earlier period produced the structures and logic necessary to the more visible changes that occurred post-1520s (i.e. in the classic transition phase of the seventeenth century). Specifically, the long fifteenth-century's 'new' enclosures, consisting for example of the engrossment of small plots, led to both direct and indirect dispossession and resulted in expropriating peasants at birth by the sixteenth century, following from pressures of depopulation and then population rises post-Black Death (Dimmock, 2014: 133–137). In sum, the fifteenth and sixteenth centuries saw a restructuring of England's social property relations involving cases of forced depopulation on a scale not seen since the Norman conquests of the eleventh century (Dimmock, 2014: 143–144).

Resistance hardened against the system of enclosure in the seventeenth and eighteenth centuries (Thompson, 1975; Holmes, 1997; Wood & Wood, 1997: 15–16). Provoking riots and acts of disobedience famous to this day, landowners sought to tie the right of property to their individual right, through the courts and particularly, through legislation such as the Black Act (1723), which introduced 'fifty new capital offences' without 'serious division' in parliamentary debates (Thompson, 1975: 21). This struggle, alongside many other instances of social unrest during the period of revolutions, provided political thinkers with an unusually fertile ground for debates and ideas.

> 'Enclosure' did not just, or even necessarily, mean closing in or fencing off a piece of land. The real essence of enclosure was the extinction of customary rights – the traditional rights that permitted people to make use in various ways of land held in common or even 'privately' – for example, the right to gather wood or to collect the remnants of harvests. *Enclosure also meant that the community was excluded from the regulation of production.*
>
> (Thompson, 1975: 21 added emphasis)

This emphasis on enclosures as leading to a legal or regulatory shift in the relation of producers to land, and therefore to themselves and to others, is essential. The amount and significance of legal documents and processes – and of the legal battles fought over them to ensure and contest this shift – are often overlooked. This chimes with Dimmock's focus on the less visible structural changes of the long fifteenth century, first because enclosure acts, wills, litigation, and other legal records of holdings and evictions are his main sources. These show the material and ideological support and coercion that the legal system provided in this period to the communities concerned by these transformations. Second, the 'new' enclosures by dispossession and the broader social context that characterised this period (e.g. rise of yeomen and of leasing of demesnes; increase of strategies to dispossess; rise in labour productivity; uneven distribution of new wage workers in pasture-farming, rural cloth and metal industries; rise of workers in industrial occupations) show how the emergence of agrarian capitalism was not simply an economic process exemplified by changing relations of production or agricultural techniques, nor simply 'closing in or fencing off a piece of land', nor pockets of wage labour and control of production by manufacturing merchants such as putting out systems found in various other burgeoning commercial centres, as merchant capital literature argues. Agrarian capitalism was a broader process operating at intersecting levels of social, political, legal, and economic hierarchies and practices (Dimmock, 2014: 146–156).

Specifically, in Dimmock's study of fifteenth-century engrossment and enclosure in Kent, these processes cannot be dissociated from 'conflicts over jurisdiction and custom in the parish' and other key political and territorial changes ('the wider breakdown in government in Kent and its attendant political disorder, the catastrophic loss of English territory in Normandy, and Cade's Rebellion in 1450') (Dimmock, 2014: 273). The complex jurisdictional organisation and independence of the Cinque Port federation determining conflicts in Kent shows 'the high level of politicisation and intimate knowledge of the law that was achieved by a broad range of peasants, petty traders and fishermen in the region in the fifteenth century' (Dimmock, 2014: 265). In other words, in these regions of agrarian production and trade in England, conflicts over the regulation of production were inseparable from the regulation of jurisdiction and territory.

The role of lawyers, judges, and Parliament in the later dispossession made possible by these structural changes, and in Marx's analysis of 'the dissolution of private property based on the labour of its owner', was crucial. A thorough account of these practices is beyond the scope of this chapter. Still, it is clear that in spite of some failed attempts to control and regulate and even prohibit enclosures, these institutions stood for the rights of landowners, interpreted as rightful individuals who acquired such rights because of their propensity to develop agriculture and improve the land. Holding property also gave individuals the right to vote, thereby clinching the circle between the state, property, and the landowning individual.

Jurisdictional efforts to expand, consolidate, or divide authority through new legal techniques and rules are distinctive of the early modern period and part of agrarian capitalism in England. But state formation there also enabled the concentration of efforts by a smaller landholding class.

However, Thompson (1975: 245–269) is also at pains to show the numerous examples where the law and conceptions of rights defended by commoners, rioters, or political thinkers were used, even at times successfully, to uphold their common right to the land or to resistance itself. If Thompson is reluctant to theorise his historical findings, there is nevertheless in his work an emerging argument that law (as institutions and profession) operates *as* a form inevitably fluctuating according to contested social relations. In any case, during the early days of agrarian capitalism, this form was certainly not exclusively tied to private property, and the commodity form theory of law's association of bourgeois rights with private property misses the opportunity to sketch the processes through which legal content oscillated between different conceptions of jurisdiction (i.e. property and ownership), and it especially misses the different processes of dispossession and expropriation they enabled.

> Productive relations themselves are, in part, only meaningful in terms of their definitions at law: the serf; the free labourer; the cottager with common rights, the inhabitant without; the unfree proletarian, the picket conscious of his rights; the landless labourer who may still sue his employer for assault.
>
> (Thompson, 1975: 196)

The question then becomes: why did England witness a stricter association of private property with landowners? Or, in other words, why did England not provide peasants and farmers with the property rights and jurisdictional ambiguities that afforded the French peasantry and the French nobility more leverage to defend their interests against the king's desire to unify and rationalise his hold on the kingdom and economic productivity? Or which provided the jurisdictional structure that pushed Dutch merchants to retreat into public office? The following looks for an answer in the relationship between state formation and the common law.

3.3.2 *English State Formation and the Common Law*

The history of England's state formation begins with the Norman Conquest of Anglo-Saxon England in 1066 and the imposition of Norman feudal rule. From the mid-eleventh century, a 'transnational knightly class' from all regions of Europe and with varied interests and means, expanded north, east, southwest, and southeast (Teschke, 2003: 95–112). The conquest of England resulted in the 'restriction of autonomous noble rule and the generalisation of royal rule' (Gerstenberger, 2007: 63).

> A tenurial revolution steamrollered the country, bringing radical changes to the ownership, size, and constitutional status of lordships. Lords came to hold their estates 'of the king' – hereditarily, but not as private patrimonies. The king remained the supreme landowner of the entire territory.
>
> (Teschke, 2003: 105)

From the twelfth and thirteenth centuries, monarchs were powerful and unavoidable partners of the nobility, rather than contending actors in a fragmented and multifarious patchwork of jurisdictions, codes, and estates, such as in France, Iberia, or the pre-Republic Netherlands. By the early modern period, the English state was the most politically, administratively, and fiscally centralised; it took an estimated 12 per cent of national income in peacetime, in contrast to 11.5 for France, and 10.5 for Castile (Grafe, 2012: 9). This argument about English state centralisation and its larger extraction of revenue from taxes contests neo-institutionalist accounts (North & Weingast, 1989) which argue that absolutist states such as France and Castile were fiscally larger and therefore more inefficient. For Grafe, this shows that so-called absolutist states 'failed' not because of large extractions of revenue but because of 'jurisdictional fragmentation', that is they were 'faced with corporatist power that severely restricted their ability to raise taxes' and with subjects that 'distrusted them and hence evaded and avoided taxation' (2012: 9).[29]

Moreover, ability to control expenditure in Castile and France was limited since 'the French kings (like their Spanish cousins) rarely knew what their disposable resources were or how much they had spent' (Grafe, 2012: 10). McNally has also focused on the specificity of the English Crown in developing state resources through the creation of the Bank of England and money in the seventeenth century. Crucially, McNally focuses on 'a ruling by the English Privy Council, which in 1605 declared that "money inheres in the bones of princes"' (2020: 85–86).[30] This legal judgment begins the process of linking the medieval conception of the king's two bodies (personal and mortal vs. public and immortal) to private markets, followed by the Bank of England set up in 1694 as a creditor to the Crown to fund the war with France. These measures increased the value of the Crown's revenue to finance wars and strengthen its links to the nobility (McNally, 2020: 96).

[29] Although Grafe's study is useful in terms of contesting the neo-institutionalist account, emphasising jurisdictional fragmentation as well as key aspects of early modern European political economy, it maintains a consequentialist historical approach determined by a developmental path to modernity, where so-called absolutist states either failed or succeeded. This *Sonderweg* approach to European history is discussed by Wood (2016).

[30] The Privy Council was an influential advisory body to the sovereign able to issue laws and hear legal disputes in the name of the Crown and was strengthened under Henry VII and Henry VIII as separate from Parliament so as to assist the Crown in the governing of colonies, for example. The legislative function of the Council became increasingly

One of the characteristics of England's institutional framework was to produce, through the work of lawyers, a division 'between those peasants who had access to the legal recourse of the common law [i.e. the royal courts], and those others who were subject to the rule of their lords without any legal protection' (Gerstenberger, 2007: 65). The 'royal-common law' peasants were identified as 'freemen' or *liberi* (freeholders), while those under feudal law were qualified as 'unfree' men or *nativi* (serfs). The common law thus originated simultaneously with the nobility's prerogative of 'fixing the legal status of the villein's unfreedom' (Gerstenberger, 2007: 66). The system of tenure referred to this latter case of peasants under customary law and feudal obligations and is contrasted to the freehold system that applied to peasants on the royal demesne and thus under the jurisdiction of the common law. Both systems emerged from the change in forms of cultivation and the need to formalise 'agricultural relations of production'. However, the way in which tenants or unfree men became necessary and assimilated to the ruling class is distinctive to England and led to the gradual dissipation of the coercive relation between lords and tenants (yeomen) at the basis of the symbiosis that produced agrarian capitalism.

Thus, if the common law did not originally protect the tenants which were to become the 'direct producers and landlords' of agrarian capitalism, it became a shared resource or pool of power for the king and the nobility through the institution of Parliament. Since the characteristic of the common law was its duty to custom and precedent, as enunciated by the royal courts, Parliament developed ways of 'perfecting' it with new legislation; thus both Parliament (representing landlords) and the Crown would struggle to use the common law to their advantage (Parker, 1996: 207–261; Wood & Wood, 1997: 7; Comninel, 2000).

The ongoing process of state formation consolidated these developments, and by '1600, England had become a unified state, with a clear centre of power, a national or "common" law, a national representative body, and even a national Church subordinate to, and sustaining, the

disputed and relinquished to Parliament after Henry VIII's death, but it remained a powerful administrative body significantly developed under Elizabeth I's reign (1558–1603). It was therefore still an important legal body when it issued the above 1605 ruling. For Cavanagh (2017: 459), the Privy Council 'developed a mediatory and investigative jurisdiction over a wide range of "weightie matters of the Realme," both private and public'. It 'often went out of its way to protect English merchant interests at home and abroad', 'was equally prepared to receive petitions concerning foreign interests, and to arbitrate if only to give the appearance of justice' (Cavanagh, 2017: 459).

unified state', encapsulated in the concept of the 'Crown in Parliament' (Wood & Wood, 1997: 5). The seventeenth century was characterised by civil war, popular uprisings, the execution of Charles I, and the consequent institution of the Commonwealth of England with Cromwell as 'Lord Protector' (1649–1658). These decades were then followed by what is termed the Glorious Revolution of 1688. But none of these events eradicated the unity of the state.

It follows that if the common law was a central component to the English unified state and to royal power from the twelfth and thirteenth centuries onwards, lawyers also played a crucial part in early modern English society. For example, before the Reformation they played a key commercial role and occupied a much larger variety of roles than they do today, as 'agents for landowners, foundations of hospitals, wine ordering, land transactions, bankers, possibly also money lenders' (Ives, 1983 in Burrage, 2006: 391).

From the sixteenth century, lawsuits 'became more fashionable than personal violence' for the high nobility and gentry, as well as the lower orders, and 'individual participation in legal proceedings could be remarkable' (Sharpe, 2003: 168).[31] The increase of litigiousness was such that it was considered 'a national problem' (Sharpe, 2003: 169). The demand for legal representation notably increased, with a confusing variety of qualifications and actual corporate bodies (though the role of corporations in England never equalled in kind that of France). Some of the legal orders of the period continue to exist. 'Serjeants' went on to become judges and could be considered at the top of the legal hierarchy, even though a strict hierarchical pyramid did not exist as such. In second came the 'apprentices-at-law' and 'utter-barristers' of the Inns of Court, who later became the modern bar. A third group consisted of the advocates as such, doctorates in civil law and thus specialised for ecclesiastical and admiralty courts. Finally, the largest group was the most varied and less regulated, consisting of attorneys, proctors, solicitors, clerks, and non-qualified practitioners who performed various legal tasks, especially in the provinces (Burrage, 2006: 388–390). The Inns of Court were particularly interesting institutions which distinguished the English legal system. These residences and training grounds for aspiring lawyers, all based in London, also served as educational passages for the gentry and higher echelons of the nobility.

[31] Gentry in this study are generally considered the lowest order of the nobility, though this status was disputed and rising gentry could struggle to obtain this status.

Before the revolution of the 1640s, there was 'no clear and settled principle governing the relationship between the crown and the Inns' (Burrage, 2006: 402). The king, the Privy Council, the judges, and the Parliament all had a legitimate interest in the Inns, but power over them was never defined and they had little respect for their authority especially when these various actors tried to meddle in their affairs (Burrage, 2006: 402). In 1641, on the eve of revolutionary events, the king and Parliament lobbied for the support of the Inns. The latter responded by declaring their support for both authorities. This act symbolised the balance of the parliamentary monarchy and the levelling role played by the common law and its institutions. In contrast, until the late-eighteenth-century revolution and Napoleon's drastic recasting of the legal system, French lawyers and courts were constantly in the middle of political struggles, intrigues, and local–feudal representations. A final specificity of the English case lies in the fact that its revolutionary age (1640s and 1680s) did not, unlike France and the USA, reform the judiciary, since 'parliamentarians appealed to precedent and to the common law whenever they could, and evidently felt themselves to be best justified and more secure when they did so', which 'distinguishes them from other revolutionary leaders' (Burrage, 2006: 430).

In sum, a combination of the centralising evolution of the English state, the independence of its main organising body (Inns of Court), and the structure of legal argument (precedent) enabled a particular arrangement between judges and legal practitioners. All this gave the common law a fundamental albeit background role in English state formation, which maintained and shaped private property as a key tool of landowners' expropriation of England's peasantry. If the sixteenth century saw the emergence of lawyers and legal institutions as balanced institutions, this appearance of neutrality should not be abstracted from the social relations and debates surrounding their active role in the English state.

> Whereas in France magisterial resistance to the claims of royal authority was impeded by the separation of French law into its private and public components, in England the defence of the public authority of Parliament fused with a defence of the rights – particularly the property rights – of the individual.
>
> (Parker, 1996: 247–248)

English law was defined as 'upholding the rights and properties of subjects', a defence of their liberty which came with the price of expensive and delayed judicial proceedings (Holmes, 1997: 288). This in effect meant the protection of the property of the ruling classes. However, if Parker notes the fusion between Parliament, property rights, and the individual, this particular relation was not left unquestioned and took a certain evolution in the arguments of political thinkers before being coherently articulated and exported so as to structure the legal form necessary and manifest in the various expansions and subsequent developments of capitalism in other contexts of social property relations.

England's growing ascendancy in the seventeenth and eighteenth centuries was largely driven by unfettered commercial and colonial expansion in the British Isles, the Caribbean, and North America.[32] This first phase, the 'Atlantic Empire', can be characterised by *Calvin's Case* in 1608, which is discussed in Chapter 7 as key to England's distinctions between *dominium* and *imperium*. The Atlantic phase was followed by a more extensive and widespread phase from the mid-eighteenth to early-twentieth centuries, covering India, South Asia, Australasia, Africa, and the Americas (Armitage, 2000: 1–2). If the first phase exported Britain's agrarian innovations and logic of land improvement (but not necessarily its common law), the second phase displayed a more variegated and compromised pattern between two imperatives of expansion: market extension and political control of territory (Wood, 2003: 110). It also took a turn from its limited and territorial conception of the common law and of jurisdiction and turned extraterritoriality – notably through the Foreign Jurisdiction Act in 1843 – into a process that provided a universal access to common law jurisdiction to all English subjects in any part of the world.

The colonial enterprises of English subjects in the early modern period were commercially and privately driven (private in the sense of led by individuals rather than commissioned and regulated by the Crown). Even when the Crown tried to extend or transport its authority through consuls and regulate their activities, it either used the intermediary of a chartered company or had to bend to the customs and wishes of its locally implanted merchant community, as discussed in Chapter 5. This,

[32] The British Isles started to come under the sovereignty of the English king after Thomas Cromwell and Henry VIII achieved the unification with Wales after 1542, followed by the incorporation of Scotland through the accession of James VI of Scotland to the English throne as James I in 1603, and the conquest of Ireland in 1649. For a comparison of Scotland' different private law, and Ireland's mixture of common law and indigenous law, in contrast to England and Wales's common law, see Houston (2018). These are cases of extensions of authority.

coupled with the distinction between *imperium* and *dominium*, meant that settlement and the establishment of a regime of social property relations and of common law jurisdiction in English colonies were not 'organic' (i.e. concerned with the whole of society, or with people and labour). It was mainly concerned with territory as a strategy of expansion. Any exceptions occurred on a much smaller scale than the Castilian Empire and was not the primary aim of this earlier phase of imperialism.[33]

3.4 The Dutch Republic and the Problem of Transition

Since the Dutch Empire was led by the newly formed Dutch Republic (or United Provinces), it has particular features that significantly set it aside from the other cases. Its analysis is essential to this study, but it nevertheless remains somewhat peripheral for a number of historical as well as methodological reasons. First, it is a new federal state – or confederation of provinces – without a strong central government, in spite of powerful and influential state and substate institutions. It formed in the late-sixteenth century out of intense warfare with Castile as well as against the French and English at various points. The powerful and independent provinces that became the Dutch Republic were known as the Northern Netherlands (or Northern Low Countries) and since the Middle Ages they were ruled, alongside the Southern Netherlands (or Southern Low Countries), by the Burgundian dukes, by the princes of the Holy Roman Empire, and later by the Spanish-Habsburg Empire. The Southern Low Countries (which correspond to today's Belgium) remained under the authority of Habsburg Spain after the Dutch Revolt.

The emergence of the Dutch Republic is therefore tied to these conflicts and to the need to survive and compete militarily with the other empires throughout the remaining early modern period. Its relatively short-lived and difficult institutional history is the first obstacle to being able to compare it with the other cases, which share deeply entrenched institutions and are thus more easily understandable and linked to imperial expansion.

The second major obstacle is the less abundant anglophone literature and the generally divided historiography on the institutional and economic history of the empire. Considering this project is based on

33 These legal aspects of England/Britain's Atlantic and Mediterranean phases of imperialism and their forms of mercantilism are discussed in Chapters 6 and 7.

secondary literature, it remains necessarily limited by existing debates, and specifically by the lack of studies of Dutch legal history. For example, there is a debate on the singularity of the Dutch Republic, which is considered an exception in a Europe of composite monarchies (Fradera, 2018: 2), a forerunner of modernity (Israel, 1989; de Vries & van der Woude, 1997), a 'miracle' (Koskenniemi, 2013: 19; Emmer, 2014: 339), and an 'extreme' case of early modern state formation (Brandon, 2015).

If the history of the Dutch Republic is understood as one of rapid rise and rapid decline, at home and overseas, there is wide disagreement on why and how this phenomenal rise in power, referred to as 'the golden age', was possible considering the conditions of its very small population, its environmental and thus agricultural obstacles, and its institutional fragility. A conventional account of the Netherlands identifies a peak of rapid economic growth attributed to the period from 1580 to 1620, followed by a period of economic stagnation starting in 1670 and lasting two centuries (Emmer, 2014: 345). One explanation relies on how the Dutch accumulated vast amounts of capital, but could not invest it at home, hence the investment in British state bonds in the eighteenth century (Emmer, 2014: 345). Other explanations focus on the fierce competition with the other empires, and others on the specific practices the empire chose or happened to favour.

Presenting the role of its social property relations and potential practices of jurisdictional accumulation contributes to recent analyses that revisit the above general narrative and focus on the economic and institutional specificities of the Dutch case (e.g. Brandon, 2015). Specifically, the analysis of the Dutch Empire in the present book emphasises two neglected aspects of Dutch expansion: first, the role of the jurisdictional structures of the Dutch state and of its means of expansion in shaping imperialism and mercantilism; and, second, the role of neglected actors caught between state and merchant interests (e.g. magistrates and consuls). Another aspect which is mentioned but cannot be further developed is the role of Dutch lawyers and jurists in Europe and the colonies in shaping doctrine as well as mixed systems of law. This last aspect is one that is already significantly discussed by existing literature, especially the role of doctrine through Grotius's influence, and will therefore only be referred to briefly.

Overall, available secondary research reveals that the Dutch Republic is the case for which the concept of jurisdictional accumulation has less purchase and applicability in this particular study. This is considering the unique and conflictual jurisdictional structure of the States General; the outsourcing of warfare and settlement to chartered companies, private entrepreneurs, and other European settlers; the focus in the few Atlantic colonial settlements on coercive forms of labour and the slave trade; and finally the significantly different conditions of jurisdictional encounter and conflict in Asia – the Dutch Empire's main region of expansion – compared to the Atlantic and Mediterranean.

However, considering the dominance of commercial and merchant-driven imperial practices, as well as the role of lawyers in its key cities, a significant area in which the case shares crucial similarities with the other empires is the attempts at and conflicts over jurisdictional accumulation through consular activity in the Mediterranean. This angle can only be briefly introduced in this study as an emerging area of research interest which requires more primary research. However, it points to promising future projects that could add some crucial missing pages for the history of early modern international legal practices. For now, the following presents key aspects of the Dutch Republic's social property relations in terms of its state formation, legal actors, and the debate on agrarian capitalism.

3.4.1 State Formation

The Dutch Revolt against the Spanish-Habsburg Empire began in 1566 and ended in 1648 with the Westphalian treaties, thereby marking the period of the Eighty Years' War. The new Dutch state emerged gradually during the revolt and proclaimed itself as the United Provinces in 1588, but it was only recognised by Habsburg Spain at Westphalia. It was made of seven northern provinces that 'concentrated political and economic power to an extraordinary extent in the hands of a coalition of large-scale international merchants and smaller-scale urban and rural oligarchs' (Brandon, 2015: 30). The end of the struggle with Habsburg Spain was marked by Dutch superiority at sea and their ability to 'transform an essentially defensive "war of liberation" into a war of conquest and empire-building' (Brandon, 2015: 30).

Brandon's work is focused on the Dutch Republic as a brokerage state – and on the explanation of the Dutch Empire's rise and *relative* decline through the organisation of war – to counter explanations focused solely on trade and on a pure model of merchant capitalism. Although it raises many issues in terms of the periodisation and definition of capitalism, it makes an essential argument that speaks to the aims of this study. If brokerage was one of the various options among early modern means of power accumulation, Dutch rulers chose the option that 'reflected structural features of Dutch society', and therefore the analysis throughout Brandon's work unpacks in detail the relations between metropolitan and overseas actors that participated in these complex governance mechanisms and, crucially, in the outsourcing of warfare (Brandon, 2015: 36–37). Merchant warriors and their companies play a key role, as well as the navy, the army, magistrates, financiers, and the various state and semi-state structures that enabled this process of federal brokerage.

Nevertheless, this argument clashes with the approach in this book, since it is based on a much wider definition of capitalism starting from the international context and long-term view of merchant networks and production of commodities in the fifteenth century as key determinants of capitalist activity.[34] It appears to be adopting Banaji's understanding of the coherence (or amalgamation) between merchant and industrial capital, especially as it focuses on putting out systems in its assessment of the emergence of Dutch capitalism.[35] This view stands in contrast to the Political Marxist argument that defines capitalism as characterised by social property relations determined by politically constituted market dependence and market imperatives. The Dutch Empire has been a controversial case among Political Marxists (Brenner, 2001; Post, 2002; Wood, 2002b), let alone the wider Marxist and non-Marxist circles. Here is not the place for me to fully intervene in the debate, but for now it remains important to explain its main lines and to explore how a focus on jurisdictional structures and actors might contribute to the analysis of Dutch transition.

[34] Brandon (2011) concludes his analysis of the Dutch case with a complex and multilayered definition of capitalism that challenges both extremes of the debate (i.e. Wallerstein's commercialisation model and the Political Marxist production-based model). In terms of production, he identifies 'at least three distinct trajectories [that] led to the spread of capitalist relations in agriculture' (140). These trajectories were characterised by an 'urban–agrarian symbiosis' of trade and production which 'depended on the growing division of labour between various regions of Europe expressed in the expansion of international trade' (140). Finally, these conditions required the 'revolutionary transformation of the state-structure' (141). The crucial element of contention in this definition, from a Political Marxist standpoint, is the dependence on international trade. This implies (1) that both producers and appropriators were part of a broader trading network and market and (2) that this network and market were part of a global transition to capitalism defined by the circulation of commodities, rather than by specific transformations in their production and in the social property relations defining the conditions between producers and appropriators.

[35] See Chapter 2 for a discussion of Banaji's concept of merchant capital.

Deep disagreements exist between the Political Marxist view of the transition and Brandon's work (2011), whose analysis of Dutch merchants as capitalists is central to the analysis of the Dutch colonies and a broader view of early modern imperial expansion. These disagreements are discussed in more detail below. Perhaps ironically, though, despite these differences, Brandon's arguments regarding the importance of the Dutch state, the interdependence between local and geopolitical factors of imperial expansion as circulation (though he also emphasises the symbiosis between trade and production), and the emphasis on a variety of economic, political, and legal agents as driving local and imperial competition all share significant parallels to Political Marxism. Points of convergence can be found in the latter's efforts to go beyond economistic readings of imperialism, to focus on the politically constituted structures of capitalism and early modern expansion, and to provide more specific and non-consequentialist narratives of capitalism and of histories of processes of accumulation more broadly.

Moreover, it seems more important, especially in light of these potential parallels or points of agreement, to see past the grand-narrative disagreements and focus on how various analyses of early modern empires, although from different Marxist viewpoints, can contribute to dislodging more influential accounts. If Brandon is more concerned with dislodging new institutionalist economics (NIE), his work can also contribute to critiques concerning jurisdiction and the role of diplomats in the 'epochs of international law' narratives and the cultural histories that downplay the agency of intermediaries, merchants, lawyers, consuls, various other key players, and instigators of practices of imperial plunder, exploitation, and accumulation. In other words, Political Marxists and Brandon may disagree on what to call these key sub-sovereign actors (i.e. whether they should be identified as capitalists or not) but they should not disagree so much on what they were doing. The following therefore begins to explore some of these actors.

3.4.2 Legal Actors

The legal context to the Dutch Republic is similar to the French in terms of regional fragmentation, although the jurisdictional autonomy of its seven provinces constitutes a distinct feature. Nevertheless, pre-Republic sixteenth-century Netherlands under Burgundian–Habsburg sovereignty – including the regions of Holland, Utrecht, Brabant, Zeeland, Flanders, and Friesland – borrowed from French techniques and processes of royal centralisation of judicial authority (de Schepper, 2007).[36] Every region and municipality had its own set of local rules, customs, and a justice system based on 'rural aldermen' and a 'municipal aldermanic bench' (de Schepper, 2007: 188–189). Once the Burgundian–Habsburg prince turned the 'old courts of the pre-Burgundian lords' into 'provincial' and 'supra-territorial councils', legal subjects appeared to prefer monarchic justice by 'going straight to the source of all law' expecting a 'better and speedier ruling' by a 'professional judge' (de Schepper, 2007: 195) and looking for a more 'rational, refined, and uniform' mode of justice (de Schepper, 2007: 205). In civil justice, by 1530, ecclesiastical judges and the Parlement de Paris influenced Dutch jurists exercising justice for the sovereign judge. Jurisdictional conflicts emerged between rural aldermen and courts of royal authority, but aldermen's resistance was 'in vain' (de Schepper, 2007: 194). The 'trade-oriented provinces' were the first to eclipse the local and municipal aldermen and end the 'traditional sovereignty of subaltern judicial systems' while the peripheral provinces continued to contest monarchic jurisdiction (de Schepper, 2007: 198). Overall, 'confidence in lay judicial courts remained in rural provinces' and the communal resistance to centralisation and to the early modern state played a role in the Dutch Revolt (de Schepper, 2007: 205).

This customary law became mixed to a predominant and scholarly Roman tradition which formed the hybrid Roman-Dutch law during the seventeenth century, as written law took over most provinces. The Dutch later adopted a more formal civil law system and drafted the Dutch Civil Code in 1809 based on the French Napoleonic code but the system retained its particular early modern attempt to combine 'the best of Dutch, German, and French law', and was therefore one of the European systems most 'based on the *ius commune* of continental Europe' (Smits, 2003: 556).

Lawyers and merchants dominated the cities of Amsterdam (and Hamburg) and a mercantile background was considered greatly beneficial, if not essential, to be part of the magistracy (Lindemann, 2015: 66). Jurists also had a wider European influence. For example, the literature on legal transplants (Watson, 1995) emphasises the role of Dutch jurists –

[36] The Netherlands were part of the domains of the last Valois Duc of Burgundy Charles the Bold who ruled from 1467 to 1477. From that date, the Netherlands passed into Habsburg hands and became part of the Holy Roman Empire, which in 1516 became governed by the Spanish–Habsburg alliance.

Dionysius Gothofredus's (1549–1622) interpretation of the *Institutes* of Justinian and Ulrich Huber's (1636–1694) *Praelectines Iuris Vivilis et Hodienrni* – in influencing English and American legal systems in terms of the relevant problem of jurisdictional conflicts or conflict of laws. The influence of the seventeenth-century province of Holland is even considered by conventional European legal histories as taking over the 'torch of great legal science' (Wieacker, 1995: 126 in Smits, 2003: 552).[37] Through their colonies, the Dutch exported their 'mixture of Roman law and mainly customary Dutch law' (Smits, 2003: 552), but the most significant part of this exporting occurred in the nineteenth-century phase of empire. Nevertheless, it was based on the '*concordantiebeginsel* (principle of concordance) observed by the Dutch since 1629', which 'ensured uniformity by implying that the law in the colonies would, as much as possible, be the same as that of the mother country' and this principle remains applicable to some of the current Netherland's overseas territories, such as Aruba and the Dutch Antilles (Smits, 2003: 552–553).

Urban magistrates constituted the first local level of political power and 'were chosen from the upper-middle and upper classes by a system of co-optation' (Brandon, 2015: 31). The second level, the Provincial States, was composed of delegations of the urban magistrates (most numerous) and of representatives of the rural nobility (Brandon, 2015: 31). Finally, the States General (*Staten Generaal*) was composed of 'delegations from all seven provinces, each holding a single vote' (Brandon, 2015: 31). This system was characterised by the dominance of urban representation, which therefore meant the dominance of magistrates.

3.4.3 The Debate on the Dutch Transition to Capitalism

Considering the Political Marxist approach adopted in this project and the reliance on the concept of social property relations, it is logical to focus on the debate produced by Brenner's work on the Dutch transition, rather than on explanations focused on international trade. For Brenner,

[37] Classical European legal history lists Italy, Belgium, France, and Germany among other torchbearers, while England, Eastern Europe, Scandinavia, Southern, and South-Eastern Europe are considered 'special cases' (Duvé, 2014b: 34). This classical approach, similar to Grewe's periodisation, is evidently very problematic for its Eurocentric and modernist path dependency and it is contested today by a variety of 'entangled' and contextualist histories (e.g. Duvé, 2014a; Donlan & Heirbaut, 2015).

'the agrarian sectors of the Flemish and Dutch economies' are characterised by

> unusually large urban populations, their extraordinary access to ocean and river transport and the attendant commercial opportunities, the unusual economic flexibility of their populations made possible by their access to the international trade in grain and, finally, their freedom, from early on, from serfdom or the heavy weight of lordship.
>
> (2001: 174)

These conditions are an 'especially demanding test' for Brenner's argument that the 'commercio-industrialism' of early modern towns 'was, on its own, incapable of bringing into being the conditions for self-sustaining economic growth' (i.e. capitalism) (2001: 174). Brenner concludes that in spite of important regional divergences between and inside the Northern and Southern provinces, and in spite of them having attained the status of 'most highly industrialized regions in Europe' (2001: 224), this industrialisation was 'blocked' by 'barriers to the expansion of the domestic market' such as the 'intensification of competition' and the 'saturation of a trans-European, mainly luxury market' that was limited by pre-capitalist social property relations in the rest of Europe (224). In other words, if the Dutch Republic – and especially its Northern maritime provinces – did not become a capitalist economy along the same path as England, this was not due to the Dutch Republic's internal dynamics, which could have led to this development. Instead, the Dutch Republic was 'blocked' by its dependence on external markets.

This argument led to a crucial disagreement between Brenner (2001) and Wood (2002b) which helps to further sharpen analyses of pre-capitalist and capitalist economies. Wood (2002b) argues that Brenner fails to apply his own definition of capitalism consistently and strictly, as developed according to the case of English agrarian capitalism. In particular, he fails to sufficiently distinguish between different types of market dependence, each characterised by opportunities or imperatives. For Wood (2002b), the survival of Dutch producers is conditioned by opportunities on a market driven by exchange or circulation rather than the transformation of production, that is imperatives to improve productivity. Moreover, appropriators are also shown to depend even less on the domestic market and instead on a range of extra-economic factors for their reproduction. Brenner thereby dangerously slips towards a commercialisation model analysis that would tend to assume capitalism is an inevitable and natural expected development of modern societies, since its condition of possibility is in this case distanced from the specific social property relation that requires an imperative dependence on the market for survival, whether through dispossession of land and dependence on wage labour (as in England) or another means through which producers and appropriators would be forced to compete and shape prices according to that competition.

More specifically, Brenner (2001) argues that agricultural producers in the early modern Low Countries or Netherlands experienced an early transition in the 1600s because of their dependence on the market for grain, for which they were 'obliged to produce other commodities for exchange, and, to a substantial degree, to produce them for export' (Wood, 2002b: 52). Wood develops four counterarguments to Brenner's analysis (Moreno Zacarés, 2018: 752–753). These emphasise the maintenance of circulation and of merchant capital as generating profits rather than transforming production; that specialisation and the market in grain were not followed or accompanied by innovations and intensification of production; and that the mid-seventeenth-century stagnation drove investments away from production.

In short, Dutch commercial wealth was generated by its merchant elite and by the freedom of manoeuvre from which its domestic producers benefited, and were thus able to profit from opportunities offered by a more flexible and fragmented market for essential commodities such as grain and dairy farming. These remained economic processes determined by conditions of exchange and circulation of goods in more volatile and luxury-based international markets, rather than by a transformation of the conditions for production, such as access to land and social relations. Crucially for our discussion below, Wood emphasises the ways in which appropriators did not imperatively depend on the market for their survival and reproduction. Instead, they depended on extra-economic means of appropriation, which limit the necessary conditions for a capitalist system of social property relations that requires competition based on price–cost sensitivity and the need for efficiency, access to alternative suppliers, and interdependent relations between producers and their means of production (Wood, 2002b: 68). Though Wood admits that 'we need to know a great deal more' (2002b: 65) especially about the behaviour and conditions of Dutch producers, it is difficult to argue against the extra-economic and politically constituted means of appropriators. These consisted, in terms of international relations, in superiority in shipping and navigation, military might, but more interestingly for our interest in jurisdictional accumulation, in sophisticated methods and instruments of commerce, monopoly privileges and powers, and elaborate commercial networks and trading posts. Domestically, the role of merchant elites and especially urban patriciates also points to opportunities for jurisdictional accumulation in their securing and innovating in terms of access to public office, rentier wealth, commercial ventures, civic status, all generating significant wealth leading them to abandon private activities (2002b: 58–59, 61, 72–73, 80). Although Wood does not mention magistrates, exploring their specific role in this context would enrich the focus on jurisdiction as a means of extra-economic coercion and wealth.

Moreover, Moreno Zacarés makes an important point that speaks to broader critiques of the Brenner and Wood account of capitalism and which focus on the presence of merchant capital in charge of production, on instances of wage labour, and on market dynamics that allow for specialised and 'highly commercial and pluriactive peasantries' (2018: 753). One of the failures or weaknesses of Political Marxism is to not explain the coexistence of capitalist and pre-capitalist pressures in these specific contexts. Moreover, if 'the disembedding of the market' acts as 'a structural precondition for the emergence of capitalist competition' (2018: 753), why should these pre-capitalist dynamics disappear? This is to some extent the point that is made with jurisdictional accumulation for certain practices of England's imperial expansion, and an argument that needs to be further pursued for the Dutch case. For Moreno Zacarés, 'pre-capitalist dynamics will tend to perpetuate themselves out of a certain cultural inertia unless challenged by a new economic culture' leading to 'a clash between old and new subjectivities' and requiring a focus on 'creative agency and subjectivity' (2018: 754). In our present case, this agency is manifested through the enunciation and claiming of jurisdictional rights, titles, and functions, or 'extra-economic coercion' and 'politically constituted means' in Wood's terms. Thus, early modern empires and their agents could be very creative or very limited by the various jurisdictional structures available, and this can be observed in the Dutch case too. Crucially, the coexistence and maintenance of these structures as strategies for proto-capitalists to fall back on remains a significant condition for pre-capitalism to endure.

The discussions of the Dutch case in the following chapters therefore explore other jurisdictional aspects of the Dutch transition debate so as to contribute primarily to the comparative analysis of early modern empires, but also to discuss areas of the debate between Marxist approaches that have been neglected. Brandon (2011) provides a rich and useful critique of the Dutch transition debate that raises a number of questions for the Political Marxist argument. Specifically, he raises the specificities and regional differences shaping the Low Countries in terms of class struggles and alliances, and notably the urban-agrarian symbiosis that in his view led to a transformation in production through the alliance between trade and agriculture – especially in the region of Holland. Peasants were 'increasingly forced ... to combine labour-intensive forms of agriculture with wage-labour in export-oriented fishing, peat-digging and dike-building, proto-industrial activities in rural areas or manufacturing in the towns' (Brandon, 2011: 121). Moreover, Brandon identifies imperatives in the competitive behaviour of Dutch commercial farmers who intensified the turnover rate of land-holding (2011: 133).[38]

At first sight, this could contribute to Wood's argument on the need for identifying clearer market imperatives. However, this symbiosis was generated by 'natural circumstances' (i.e. objective economic forces), and, as Brandon analyses, these urban-rural innovations and this proto-industrialism were not followed by the development of productive capital into an independent force, meaning that merchant–industrialists remained in that condition and did not develop into fully formed industrialists (2011: 133). In other words, Brandon acknowledges how these proto-industrialists 'slowly retreated from productive investment into more secure forms of financial dealing', weakening the 'ties between traders and producers' (2011: 134) and explaining the relative decline of the Dutch Empire with too much capital to invest and nowhere at home to do so. In other words, imperatives disappeared, which begs the question of how imperative and transformative these processes were in the earlier stages he identifies.

Although the following points are merely indicative and point to the need for further research on the jurisdictional conditions and limits on merchants and peasants in the Netherlands, and especially in the key region of Holland, they bring some additional elements to answer the question of market dependence in terms of opportunities and imperatives. During the Middle Ages, peasants in certain maritime provinces such as the Northern Netherlands (e.g. Holland and Utrecht) held significant jurisdictional rights and administrative prerogatives

[38] It is important to recall that if the Dutch case might be extreme, this market-dependent dynamic (intensive peasant farming, commercialisation, semi-proletarianisation, proto-industry) was not uncommon elsewhere in Europe. Eighteenth-century Spain would be another case, as Moreno Zacarés points out.

concerning the management of water, linked to the reclamation process and peat lands that begun in c.900 and lasted until 1500s (de Schepper, 2007; Curtis & Campopiano, 2014). Alongside the phenomenon of small-scale peasant property, this meant that 'feudal lordship, in the sense of lordly surplus extraction by extra-economic compulsion, could barely be said to have existed' (Brenner, 2001: 207), with 'only 5–10% of the total area' belonging to the high nobility (Curtis & Campopiano, 2014: 98).

In effect, the 'lack of exploitative feudal structures or urban jurisdictions' was crucial to the emergence of proto-industrialism in Holland (Curtis & Campopiano, 2014: 104) and thus to the emergence of the rural–agrarian symbiosis identified by Brandon. Moreover, Wood (2002: 74) acknowledges the importance and unique character of this process of land reclamation, whereby in contrast to other agricultural practices in the Netherlands, commercial wealth was invested and 'ploughed into production'. However, this lack of urban jurisdictional structures also shows that, in contrast to England, the 'emergence of a flexible marketing framework for commodities, not dominated by powerful interest groups' (Curtis & Campopiano, 2014: 105) meant that '"outsiders" had freedom and access to this marketing structure, and producers were not forced to sell their goods' (Curtis & Campopiano, 2014: 106). In other words, there was market dependence with various opportunities but no market imperatives.

These distinctions of market dependence in terms of opportunities and imperatives cannot be solved or sufficiently discussed here, but they show interesting avenues for future research. In addition to an emphasis on these distinctions and on international trade, what appears to separate categorically Brandon from the Political Marxist position is his general approach to historical sociology and to the relationship between structure and agency. Brandon hovers between historical specificity and a consequentialist approach to historical development, and the latter cannot be squared with the aims of this project to avoid path-dependencies and fixed *a priori* assumptions. Brandon assumes and looks for 'capitalism' and 'capitalists' before defining and historically tracing what these terms mean, especially since he considers the Dutch case 'as one stage in a fundamentally and *a priori* international process of transformation' (2011: 108). Specifically, the term 'capitalists' is invoked both in his work on the transition (2011) and in his major work (2015) on the military role of the Dutch state, to identify certain merchants without explaining how these agents became capitalists, or what precisely is capitalist about them. Furthermore, we have just seen that he identifies tendencies for certain farmers to specialise and compete because of natural and institutional circumstances, but that they also reverted back to mercantile protectionist measures. If he acknowledges that they failed to produce independent industrial capital, we should therefore be able to distinguish this agency from capitalist agency that did produce industrial capital, but this remains undefined. In other words, the problem with Brandon's critique of Political Marxism is that it conflates agency and structure and wants to argue on both terrains without clarifying the implications of each methodological focus.

Crucially, his assumption of a globally imbricated conception of capitalist development – based on Arrighi's (2002) work and used to contest the Political Marxist and other 'internalist' type arguments – 'consists in a real dialectical unity, in which the stalled fragments of capitalist development in one country formed the elements of its further development in the next' (Brandon, 2011: 142). This appears contradictory to the analysis developed in Brandon's counterarguments to Brenner and Wood. Accordingly, capitalist transformations at the level of production occurred in the Dutch rural–agrarian symbiosis; however, they disappeared and only constituted one element or fragment that needed to be further developed in other countries for capitalism to become dialectically united. This definition of capitalism is difficult to grasp without a fuller analysis that (1) identifies capitalists and how they are determined by the logic of capitalist relations of production and (2) identifies how these fragments or elements in different developmental contexts are determined by the agency of various actors.

Brandon does not engage very critically with Brenner, as their positions are more easily compatible because of Brenner's argument that capitalism did emerge but was blocked and failed to take hold. However, the crucial distinction Brenner makes between the peasants' separation from the means of subsistence (land and dependence on market as essential to the emergence of capitalism) and their separation from the means of production (separation from land *and* tools implying a proletarian condition) (Brenner, 2001: 173) could be a useful way to think more precisely of the specific condition of Holland's proto-industrialists in the rural–agrarian symbiosis identified by Brandon. If their practices did not lead to either a separation of the means of subsistence, nor a separation of the means of production, did it lead to a different separation? These merchant–industrialists were able to invest in other states (e.g. Britain), and to rely on public offices to retain status and privileges (Wood, 2002b: 61, 72; 2012: 112–113). Brandon also acknowledges this as the 'accumulation of political functions' and as a significant source of privileges and revenue (2011: 137–139). If so, their class reproduction was not presupposed on the expropriation of peasants, but on extra-economic means of surplus extraction, and potentially, on means of jurisdictional accumulation through state office and state obligations, as also implied by Wood's analysis summarised above of the extra-economic and politically constituted means of appropriation of Dutch elites.

For Political Marxism, capitalism is a specific set of social property relations, the logic of which is driven by the transformation of production. The payoff of this definition is to understand the ways in which capitalism is not an inevitable and commercially latent process waiting to be liberated from feudal chains at any moment or brought about by a multilayered, transhistorical, and thus more elusive set of global trade relations. Of course, adopting a specific definition implies a methodological choice, and putting social property relations first risks undermining the imbrication of global or international factors. This is then the responsibility of Political Marxists to justify or provide additional analyses that help incorporate or explain the role of other factors than agricultural innovations and market imperatives. This is the aim of the analysis in following chapters. Moreover, if the two approaches discussed above on the Dutch case have to, in my view, accept their incompatible starting points, they can nevertheless agree on the relative importance or detail of certain processes that accompanied or not these major events of expansion and accumulation. In other words, this project turns back to what was jurisdictional about the Dutch Empire, regardless of whether it was capitalist or not. This is explored in the next two chapters in relation to ambassadors and consuls.

3.5 Conclusion

This chapter is concerned with the class dynamics resulting from changes in social property relations relevant to the agency of legal actors and the structuring effects of legal institutions, more specifically what distinguishes the early modern processes of jurisdiction. It discusses the changes and struggles in Western European social property relations identified through the categories of the emergence of agrarian capitalism in England and proto-capitalism in the Dutch Republic and different types of collaborating absolutisms in France and in the Iberian *reinos* from the sixteenth to eighteenth centuries.

The Iberian case established how Castile came to dominate the peninsula but had to navigate a complex dynamic of jurisdictional fragmentation in its various *reinos*. Legal and religious actors were key to the monarchy's efforts to centralise the empire, and Castile's rulers were characterised by a theological form of statecraft. Social property relations in the Iberian peninsula as well as in the colonies reproduced feudal and semi-feudal social relations characterised by innovations in terms of legal subjectivities and institutions. These lay the foundations for understanding the specificity of Castilian jurisdictional accumulation as characterised by colonial transplants of authority. The second section showed how the social property relations of France's various regions and *parlements* – lead by the magistrates of the robe nobility – put pressure on Louis XIV's regime to collaborate with and attempt to co-opt the aristocracy. French absolutism is also revised here in terms of the range of legal actors and mechanisms and the specific focus on jurisdictional conceptions of space and politics. In the case of England, the development of agrarian capitalism relied on the practices of enclosures, but also on the common law and legal profession, linked to the rising gentry. Finally, the legal dimensions of the Dutch process of state formation and colonial expansion are a fascinating case of jurisdictional singularity, emphasising how leading merchants relying on extra-economic coercion during economic decline shows the limits of the proto-industrialism of Dutch cities as pre-capitalist. However, this jurisdictional angle remains to be fully appreciated and integrated in Marxist and non-Marxist studies of the practices of Dutch Empire, especially focusing on the role of magistrates and trading companies.

4

Ambassadors

Having laid out the analytical foundations of this study, the following chapters present analyses of actors and practices identified as jurisdictional accumulation. The first considers ambassadors and asks what role ambassadorial posts played in the class and geopolitical dynamics of European powers between the sixteenth and eighteenth centuries. During the Middle Ages and up until the fifteenth century, diplomatic actors were mostly chosen on the basis of their abilities to exercise their functions (Moeglin & Pequignot, 2017: 374) and consisted mainly of clergy (Moeglin & Pequignot, 2017: 393–398). If secular and lower-order nobles start to become more visible by the thirteenth century (Moeglin & Pequignot, 2017: 399), the high nobility constituted only a small proportion of diplomatic agents up until the seventeenth century.

This chapter is concerned with the rise of an aristocratic diplomatic corps across Europe from the late-seventeenth to late-eighteenth centuries. It discusses explanations for this rise by exploring some of the patterns and ruptures in the social origins of these jurisdictional roles across the early modern period. Examining the dynamics between and among various groups, and the broader institutions and socio-economic conditions through which they interacted – in other words, their social property relations – helps to understand the implications of an aristocratic diplomacy for the history of international law and international relations. In short, a social history of aristocratic diplomacy enriches the study of extraterritoriality in terms of revealing a significant diversity of jurisdictional actors as well as useful patterns of jurisdictional practices that go beyond the classic narratives of diplomatic early modern extraterritoriality and the *droit public de l'Europe*.

According to Bély (2007: 487), in the seventeenth century, one is not born but *becomes* a diplomat.[1] In other words, noble birth does not

[1] Personal translation: 'On ne naît pas diplomate, on le devient'.

provide an automatic entry into diplomatic missions. Moreover, there were infinitely fewer diplomatic posts than noblemen, and only a very small number of noblemen became diplomats. However, recent analyses have shown that the late-seventeenth-century increase of aristocratic ambassadors contributed to forming an amateurish diplomatic corps based on ceremony and protocol. In other words, 'aristocrats clustered around thrones' and contributed to maintaining a court-based old regime Europe throughout the eighteenth century (Scott, 2007; 2016: 222). In this context, was the social structure of the diplomatic corps a jurisdictional – or 'extraterritorial' – strategy for not only gathering information, conducting negotiation, and ensuring adequate representation, but also for class reproduction and a more general expansion of ruling power?

This chapter argues that changes in the recruitment and characteristics of the French, and Castilian, ambassadorial corps can be considered as practices of jurisdictional accumulation, where ambassadors transplanted the authority of their sovereign through their personal status and ceremonial practices to the newly emerging embassies. The rise of the aristocracy, and other variations in diplomatic recruitment reflected the class (geo)politics and needs of European empires. Specifically, the rise of aristocratic diplomacy helped to sustain the rule of French and Iberian aristocrats and dynastic sovereigns over rapidly changing societies and among threatening competing jurisdictions. If aristocratisation was an expression of their established social and political predominance, challenges existed at home and abroad with various legal claims to sovereignty, amplified by the threats from the English and Dutch maritime empires.

In response to these threats, the shift to the aristocratisation of ambassadors is read as a strategy of jurisdictional expansion instead of as part of the territorialisation of sovereignty as found in conventional accounts. This enables a better focus on the class-based and geopolitical dynamics of diplomacy, while providing a more nuanced interpretation of the role of this process in the history of early modern international relations and international law.

This argument emerges from a broad analysis of existing studies in diplomatic and social history that have not yet been systematically or coherently brought together. However, the argument also echoes with a number of existing studies. For example, as a reflection of the need for collaboration between the aristocracies of old regime Europe and dynastic absolutism, Windler (2017a) identifies the tactic of collaboration as a characteristic of mid-seventeenth-century Prussian 'composite diplomacy' (2017a: 261). In addition, though with less focus on diplomatic actors, social historians of France have argued that the maintenance of old regime Europe was made possible by the necessary collaboration between Louis XIV and France's nobilities. This helped to sustain at least a semblance of absolutism and French dominance until Utrecht and the mid-eighteenth-century shift towards British hegemony. This angle has been extended to Europe, characterised by the 'essential inter-connectedness of ruling and aristocratic families' (Geevers & Marini, 2016; Scott, 2016: 218) where 'rulers depended upon co-operation with local social elites in government' (Scott, 2016: 221).[2]

Building on these studies, the chapter reviews existing literature on the social origins of diplomatic actors – and more specifically the rise of aristocratic ambassadors – in France, Castile, England, and the Dutch Republic. It concludes after breaking down the analysis for each case that those of France and Castile can be better understood according to the above-mentioned collaboration theory, but not those of England and the Dutch Republic.

However, first, Section 4.1 introduces early modern diplomacy, focusing on key aspects of representation and immunity relevant to issues of extraterritoriality, such as the use of foreigners, the jurisdictional and personal nature of diplomacy, and the variety of social origins and occupational backgrounds. Section 4.2 presents key scholarship and debates in diplomatic theory and history on the social origins of early modern diplomatic actors. It recalls the debates in early modern diplomatic manuals and treatises, with a gradual move from a general suspicion towards the aristocracy's abilities, to the near exclusion of recruiting ambassadors from any other social origin. It then lays out the historiographical argument for the eighteenth-century 'noble monopoly' and the role of 'internal reasons' and 'social structures' as explanatory factors (Scott, 2007: 74–75).

Finally, Section 4.3 contributes to this argument – and to a more systemic and comparative approach – by presenting each case in turn. In particular, it discusses (1) the importance of landed gentry and Members of Parliament (MPs) in England's diplomatic missions; (2)

[2] In addition, this research puts forward 'the importance of transnational families; the significant role of women within aristocratic lineages; the crucial importance of succession and inheritance and of arrangements to provide for these; and the numerous ways in which aristocratic identity could be represented and, more importantly, manufactured' (Scott, 2016: 226).

the importance of jurisdictional internal conflicts and diplomatic diversity in the Dutch Republic; (3) the rise of diplomatic aristocracy in France under Louis XIV and Colbert; and (4) the rise of an aristocratic Castilian diplomacy in a context of imperial decline.

The chapter concludes that the differences in the social origins of diplomatic actors between England, the Dutch Republic, France, and Castile reflect strongly those polities' changes in social property relations and geopolitical desires. Moreover, some share similar extraterritorial strategies determined by diplomatic social origins. In other words, it is useful to link France and Castile on the one hand as developing diplomatic practices that *transplanted* authority through more territorially innovative, organic, and also personalised or ceremonial forms of embassy. On the other hand, England and the Dutch Republic's diplomatic practices tended to have more limited jurisdictional ambition for their ambassadors, and their diplomatic practices are better characterised as *transports* of authority.

4.1 Personal Representation and Immunity

In an early modern Europe 'riddled with hierarchical ideas about status and precedence' (Keene, 2013: 1082), where ceremonial politics had a variety of meanings and manifestations (Roosen, 1980), representation and rank constituted key factors and strategies for power assertion. Diplomacy was used as a 'way of legitimising regimes and rule, and as a means of advancing such claims when they might be less than watertight' (Dover & Scott, 2015: 666). From the mid-seventeenth century, diplomacy was dominated by France, who played an important role in shaping the *droit public de l'Europe* according to its diplomatic practices. A classic example is Louis XIV's role in shifting the lingua franca of diplomacy from Latin to French, though Latin remained in use (Numelin, 1950: 308).[3] In this context, the following discusses general trends characterising early modern representation and immunity. These cast an additional shadow on analyses in classic diplomatic history and International Relations (IR), which use diplomacy to prove the emergence of territorial sovereignty in the French age without focusing on its jurisdictional aspects.[4]

[3] Before Latin, Babylonian was the diplomatic language across the ancient Orient.

[4] See Chapter 1.

First, the use of foreigners remained important throughout the early modern period and reflected a certain 'cosmopolitanism' in the fifteenth and sixteenth centuries.[5] It gradually disappeared, though the use of Italians and Swiss persisted until the French Revolution (Anderson, 1993: 33). Nevertheless, the use of foreigners was still frequent in the early-eighteenth century (Bély, 2007: 410). Louis XIV, who was brought up by Mazarin – a cardinal in the Catholic Church of Italian origin – continued to use Italians, albeit for secret or unofficial missions (Bély, 2007: 411). More generally across Europe, foreigners were usually chosen for lower-ranking missions and eventually naturalised (Roosen, 1976: 65). For example, Dyson notes the importance of foreign nationals in the early-to-mid-seventeenth-century English diplomatic corps (2013: 31). French diplomats were used in England to serve the king. William III, who did not trust Englishmen, used Dutchmen and refugee French Huguenot Protestants fleeing from the Edit de Nantes or Swiss individuals fleeing poverty (Roosen, 1976: 64–65). A 1701 parliamentary inquiry even accused the king of employing foreigners. Black emphasises the complex politics around the use of foreigners, highlighting the importance of this element even in eighteenth-century British diplomacy (2001: 26–31).

Second, diplomacy 'possessed a jurisdictional quality', which produced a significant amount of 'what we might today call "diplomacy" within, rather than between, states' (Dover & Scott, 2015: 666). As discussed in the previous chapter, European societies were structured by complex regional and transnational bonds of social property relations – patchworks of parcellised sovereignty. Governing institutions and rulers had specific jurisdictional arrangements with local judicial bodies, such as *parlements* in France, or the relation between lords and the commons in England. The Holy Roman Empire, although not discussed in this project, provides perhaps the strongest example of this sort of 'internal diplomacy', and this case is finally becoming better recognised for showing the enduring jurisdictional complexities of the early modern period up until the nineteenth century (Hardy, 2018; Schick, 2018).

These jurisdictional arrangements were often copied or adapted to colonial settings, creating added layers of jurisdictional exchanges and complexities. However, significant differences persisted between the Old and New World regarding the terms of possession. Herzog shows that

[5] See Fusaro (2015) for an analysis of the important diplomatic and commercial links between England and Venice in the fifteenth and sixteenth centuries.

'in contrast to the Americas, in Europe there was no presumption that all territorial incursions were aimed at acquiring rights' (2015a: 139). This led to significantly different conflicts and legal disputes, and different interventions from ambassadors, royal representatives, or local judges, since in Europe 'foreigners could cultivate a piece of land in a territory that was allegedly not their own without suffering opposition unless their activities were understood as indicating the intention of establishing not their private property rights but the rights of their community or kingdom' (Herzog, 2015a: 139–140). Thus, throughout the early modern period (and particularly in the late-eighteenth and early-nineteenth centuries) ambassadors in Spain and Portugal participated in debates and disputes over the establishment of borders and boundaries to delineate property rights between the two Iberian kingdoms (Herzog, 2015a: 154–158).

Moreover, the jurisdictional arrangements between the United Provinces, let alone in the Holy Roman Empire before and after its Spanish-Habsburg phase, were significant sources of disputes and shaped the military and diplomatic international relations of early modern Europe. The composite and jurisdictional nature of early modern politics created transnational bonds between ruling and dynastic families (Scott, 2016) as well as composite forms of diplomacy (Windler, 2017a), rendering territorial and fixed concepts of sovereignty and property relations inappropriate to understand diplomatic representation and immunity even for the post–Westphalian era.

Third, early modern diplomacy across Europe – and particularly in England – remained personal, as in dependent on the person of the sovereign and the person of the diplomat (Dover & Scott, 2015: 670). Personal characteristics were therefore crucial to defining the function of representation. Moreover, too much focus has been placed in previous historical writing on 'training, as opposed to social skills' (Black, 2001: 2). Up until the late-eighteenth century, diplomats were 'royal servants, rather than officials of an impersonal state' (Black, 2001: 24). Thus, if diplomats did not necessarily need to be a national of the country they represented, they also differed significantly in their social origins and occupational backgrounds, as discussed below in detail. In England, for example, merchants as well as members of the clergy were often mobilised to represent the interests of the sovereign or communicate messages (Dover & Scott, 2015: 674–676). If the role of the clergy gradually diminished, that of merchants increased later in the seventeenth century alongside that of parliamentarians (Jettot, 2012). However, by the late-seventeenth century and as is more generally assumed, 'whenever possible, ambassadors were chosen from the ranks of the nobility', mostly because the receiving country would be offended if a lower-ranked diplomat was dispatched; only a noble could 'represent the person of his sovereign and thus his grandeur' (Roosen, 1976: 66). Nevertheless, individual aristocrats presented serious difficulties even in the eighteenth century, as they often refused to serve, did not work very diligently, and could be very expensive for the government (Black, 2001: 39–41). However, the analysis below also reveals that general statements such as Roosen's do not do justice to the various jurisdictional strategies deployed regarding the choice of ambassadors and agents.

One of the main explanations put forward for the shift in the aristocratisation of diplomats in the late-seventeenth century is the rise in importance in the function of representation. Of the three functions of an ambassador – negotiation, information, and representation (Bely, 2007: 3) – representing the monarch is indeed considered to become more fundamental in the latter part of the early modern period with the growing ambitions of European rulers, and the permanence of representation through the increased length of embassies. If representation was performed by diplomats' use of direct communication with the king at least until the late-seventeenth century, in England it became unusual after 1688 (Horn, 1961: 3). In France, however, this practice lasted until the end of the old regime. Callières marks this shift to representation – symbolising Louis XIV's influence – as he puts forward the 'necessity of the diplomat to "bear the person" of his principal' (Napolitano, 2012: 57). Another sign of this shift can be seen when the term 'ambassador' begins to define the term 'embassy' in a French dictionary by Nicot in 1694, reflecting the influence of the notion of representation in the sixteenth and seventeenth centuries (Poumarède, 2007: 11–12). In effect, the ambassador representing the prince or sovereign becomes more important because the person of the ambassador takes precedence over the notion of the embassy, involving specific qualities, prerogatives, and privileges. In the earlier seventeenth century, 'embassy' had a broader variety of meanings, including the content of the mission, what was to be achieved, a group of ambassadors, or even in familiar terms, a simple message (Poumarède, 2007: 10). The embassy made the ambassador, whereas this relation is inversed by the late-seventeenth century, to only eventually become synonymous with a 'defined geographic space established permanently' (Poumarède, 2007: 14).

Across Europe, sovereigns were not the only actors who could be represented by diplomats; semi-sovereigns, princes, cities, and companies also used this prerogative. However, from the end of the seventeenth century, permanent embassies became more widespread and increasingly reserved to certain sovereigns (Anderson 1993: 42). England and other Northern and Eastern kingdoms lagged behind Castile and France, who were the first to copy the Italian city states' practice of continuous diplomatic representation. The first permanent embassies in Europe are dated to the mid-fifteenth century between the Italian city states, with some authors referring to 1455 as the first post, a Venetian delegation established in Genoa.[6]

In terms of ambassadorial immunity and the protection of their representatives, England and the Dutch Republic were at the forefront of legislation. Both provide a legal basis for the enforcement of the privilege of immunity. Elsewhere in Europe protecting ambassadors remained the prerogative of the royal 'absolute authority' (Adair, 1929: 249). One explanation is that French and Castilian diplomats could only count on the authority of their sovereign (Adair, 1929: 247).[7] English diplomats had to operate in a much more unstable institutional climate than their European counterparts (Black, 2001: 9; Jettot, 2012: 16). Adair emphasises this instability when analysing the complexities of the transitions of authority throughout the seventeenth century in terms of the role of various institutions in the enforcement of immunities (the king, the Privy Council, ministers, the council of state) (1929: 231–243). More generally, the instability maintained itself by resting on a particular legal regime – the common law as distinct from royal law or prerogative – to counter the lack of authority of the crown.

As shown in the previous chapter, the legal system and profession were crucial institutions and actors for the colonisation of the Spanish New World, for the entrenchment of agrarian capitalism in England, for Dutch mercantilism or proto-industrialism, and for so-called absolutism in France. Moreover, the common law also came to protect the rights of ambassadors. Prior to the act of Parliament of 1709 (7 Anne, cap. 12),

[6] However, it is important to recall that although Venetians are justifiably branded as major innovators in diplomatic practice, they had training in diplomacy from their contact with the East (Numelin, 1950: 306).

[7] This point was considered of historiographical importance as it is emphasised in reviews by Ronalds (1930: 117) and Stowell (1930: 413). However, its potential significance for separating the English and Dutch cases from the French and Spanish has not yet been sufficiently developed.

enforcement of 'the privileges of an ambassador and his servants was secured by the exercise of royal prerogative, while after 1709 certain of his immunities were protected by statute' (Adair, 1929: 243).

In the case of the Dutch Republic, 'an ambassador's position was not so happy' as in England, because of the conflicts between the provinces and the lack of prerogative power of the central authority regarding diplomatic affairs (Adair, 1929: 243–244). However, the 'Netherlands were the only country in Western Europe where, during the seventeenth century, the privileges of an ambassador and his suite were at all secured by the law of the land', because the recognition of ambassadorial immunity was protected by '"placards" or laws issued by the States General or ordinances of the Estates of Holland' (1929: 245). This was due to the lack of distinction between executive and legislative bodies and the fact that diplomatic negotiations were carried out by self-appointed elected commissioners of the States General. Moreover, the estate of Holland retained more executive power on the matter, as foreign ambassadors mostly resided in The Hague under its jurisdiction and the Court of Holland was mostly responsible for enforcing diplomatic privileges such as immunity (Adair, 1929: 243–246). The court 'was very much inclined to take a strictly patriotic and commercial view of an ambassador's liabilities and to rest him on the exact basis of Dutch law' (Adair, 1929: 244).

In sum, internal and external concepts of sovereignty are far from adequate to describe the patchwork of strategies of representation, negotiation, and information between early modern sovereigns, as well as the evolution of immunities. New diplomatic history, when considering these notions in their more nuanced and cultural dimensions, and by looking at transnational aspects of diplomacy, avoids the presentism and methodological nationalism of much of twentieth-century international history and provides a richer understanding of early modern European geopolitics. However, current historiography still lacks in what Roosen identified several decades ago as 'systems' or 'holistic' approaches (1980: 454), calling for broader temporal and geographical perspectives. In response, Carrió-Invernizzi emphasises the increased focus on agency and networks of ambassadors, surrounded by 'nobles, clergy-men, soldiers, artists, and magistrates' (2014: 607) but also 'merchants' and 'travellers' (2014: 609) who were entrusted with corresponding and reporting back to the state. In addition, the specific and contested social property relations which are mentioned here reveal other dimensions of diplomatic history. The following continues this approach by going deeper into the issue of social origins.

4.2 Debates in Diplomatic Theory and Historiography

The sixteenth and seventeenth centuries are prone to discussions in political and legal theory and in diplomatic treatises and manuals about the desired social origins of diplomatic actors. However, the debates are somewhat detached from practical experience and not particularly useful to get a clear sense of the actual shifts in practices (Picavet, 1923: 388). From a European-wide perspective, Kugeler is worth quoting at length as she neatly summarises the general trends in diplomatic theory regarding social origins, in spite of differences and ambiguities over certain authors' positions:

> Traditionally, the catalogue of virtues contained remarks on the 'external qualities' birth, social status, occupation and, indeed, the financial means of the diplomat. Theorists sought not only to establish the socio-professional background of the 'ideal ambassador', but also to reflect the practices of recruitment. They acknowledged that it was difficult to establish standards in this respect, since the choice of diplomats depended on the sovereign's will, and had to give consideration to the host country and to the subject of the embassy. Theorists listed an 'honnête condition' as an essential requirement for the model diplomat, and aligned his profile to the ruling elites. While earlier treatises had still included the clergy and common-born *érudits*, in the seventeenth century these professions were eclipsed by the advantages noble birth carried on the international stage. Furthermore, theorists agreed that the aristocratic order still provided the best education for diplomacy, including a cosmopolitan outlook and elegant manners. While the 'noblesse d'épée' was regarded as particularly suited for extraordinary and ceremonial embassies, the rise of the 'noblesse de robe' in the state service was also reflected in diplomatic theory, in particular with the increasing importance of the middle and lower ranks.
>
> (2006: 79–80)

Kugeler shares the analysis of a general shift towards aristocratisation in the second half of the seventeenth century, following Roosen, Bély, and Scott's work. Accordingly, 'diplomatic theory followed general trends' of the ruling elites, with the rise of the *noblesse de robe* as 'an academically trained service nobility' (2006: 80), although military backgrounds remained more important than the less respected legal background of the robe nobility. It is not the aim here to engage in a detailed comparative study of the early modern texts and arguments for or against the nobility in diplomatic posts, although such work would be useful. One should thus be particularly careful of drawing any swift comparative conclusions without detailed contextualisation of each author and their works. However, tracing some of these arguments remains instructive to get a sense of the various contexts behind them, and in particular, ask whether we can give more socio-economic and political context to the shift towards the aristocratisation of diplomatic posts.

The most quoted treatise that signifies an upcoming shift and debate about social origins is that written by Abraham de Wicquefort in 1681, considered 'by far the best-known and most influential handbook of the age of Louis XIV', where 'he set his face firmly against sending noblemen' (Scott, 2007: 73). Nobles 'were too fond of war, and too full of their own importance and so given to private initiatives' to follow instructions (73).

However, this was not everyone's view during the seventeenth century. Jean Hotman (1603) warns against an ambassador 'if he be not gentleman or nobilitie', depending on where the ambassador is posted.[8] Dyson refers to the more obscure treatise by Francis Thynne (1652), whose 'work can be said to demonstrate the only particularly English view of diplomacy' (2013: 7) and who emphasises 'that an ambassador be "well born, free, no bonds-man" excluding professions such as "Crafts-man, a Serving-man, a common Citizen, a mean Priest, an Advocate"' (2013: 13).[9]

Scott (2007) notes the opinions of Louis Rousseau de Chamoy (1697) and Jean de La Sarraz du Franquesnay (1731) as reflecting the gradual change towards the diplomatic noble monopoly. Both show that non-nobles clearly played a significant role in this period, while arguing that sovereigns have notable advantages in using noble representatives in terms of financial resources and the 'dignity' required by the function of personal representation. Chamoy's discussion nuances the qualities of a 'distinguished' nobleman against those of an ordinary but instructed and more able man and specifies that the noble distinction is not an 'essential criterion'.[10] Franquesnay notes that the 'shining light of good

[8] Hotman, 1603, *The Ambassador*, p. 8 (in Picavet, 1923: 388 and in Dyson, 2013: 13).

[9] Thynne, *The Perfect Ambassadour*, pp. 143 and 191. Dyson adds that 'Thynne's examples are almost entirely derived from antiquity, showing his lack of diplomatic experience compared with Hotman' (2013: 7).

[10] 'Ainsy l'on peut dire qu'entre deux sujets d'un mérite égal, il paroist juste de préférer celuy qui est d'une qualité distinguée à celui qui est d'une naissance ordinaire mais il n'est pas moins véritable que le bien des affaires demande souvent que, la qualité n'estant pas une condition essentielle à un Ambassadeur, on préfère le plus habile quoyque de moindre naissance au plus noble moins habile' (Rousseau de Chamoy, 1912: 22). Translations by author.

birth' and its 'riches' are additional qualities to those of business ability and common sense, especially for crowned sovereigns.[11]

There are some disagreements in the literature on Callières's (1716) opinions, but one can argue that he epitomises, with Chamoy and Franquesnay, this gradual transition phase by being more ambiguous on the issue. To an extent I argue that this is due to the specificities of France's social elite. Callières was against the use of *parlementaires* (i.e. the *noblesse de robe*) and in favour of 'good birth', as is stated in his 1716 treatise (Picavet, 1923: 393).[12] In a letter from Callières to the marquise d'Hûxelles dated 17 February 1697, Callières complains about the fact that *parlementaires* are too used to acting as judges and are therefore too 'grave' and even perhaps arrogant for diplomatic missions of representation.[13] Similarly, although Antoine Pecquet (1738) is more explicit than Callières, both mark the change towards the rise of the nobility, since both assumed that 'only nobles could head missions, and that the world of diplomacy was dominated by the elite' (Scott, 2007: 73).

However, for Keens-Soper and Schweizer (1994: 29), Callières shares with Wicquefort 'a critical attitude towards the nobility, believing that apart from embassies of ceremony the "real" work of diplomacy was accomplished by envoys of the second order.' Similarly, Davis-Cross summarises Callières's position regarding the perfect ambassador as, inter alia, being 'governed by rationality instead of passion ... of good wealth (so as not to be distracted) ... with courtly manners ... careful of flattery and charm' (2007: 38). This remains ambiguous, as it is difficult to safely attribute all these qualities and criteria to the high nobility.

Picavet's analysis shows that these a priori disagreements between scholars can also be understood as confusions due to the specificities of the French composition of the ruling elites, and its particular distinction between *noblesse de robe* and *noblesse d'épée*. Thus, Callières was critical

[11] 'les têtes Couronnées pour donner plus de relief à leurs Ambassades, ne se contentent pas de les choisir tels qu'on vient de les décrire, ils y joignent souvent le brillant de la naissance & des richesses, etant en effet naturel de les envoïer les plus accomplis et les plus respectables qu'il se peut, pour mieux soûtenir la dignité et les dépenses de ces fortes d'emplois' (de La Sarraz du Franquesnay, 1731: 34). Translations by author.

[12] 'Il est à souhaiter qu'un ambassadeur ait de la naissance, surtout s'il est employé dans les cours principales' (Callières, 1716: 47). Translations by author.

[13] '[Les gens de robe] sont accoutumés à juger des procès et à voir des clients craintifs et soumis par la peine de perdre leurs biens: ils s'accoutument à un air grave, pour ne pas dire orgueilleux, qui n'est nullement propre avec des étrangers indépendants du prince qui les envoie' (in Picavet, 1923: 393). Translations by author.

of a noble rank, the *noblesse de robe*, as Keens-Soper and Schweizer might argue. Nevertheless, he strongly defended the military and court aristocracy and reflected a world dominated by Louis XIV's style of diplomacy, where personal representation required or very strongly advised for representatives of high noble birth, as Scott argues. Moreover, these confusions also reflect the different assessments of various ranks of the diplomatic order. Callières defending the use of nobles for high-profile missions did not mean he was not critical of the nobility's lack of skill and experience for the lower order, which could consist in more important missions.

The final and less controversial marker of a clear shift in the link between birth and essential diplomatic qualities is that made by Pecquet, who represents a significant break from Callières and Wicquefort. He draws a 'lofty' conception of the ideal diplomat and was the first to 'formulate the sense of solidarity among rival diplomats of the old regime' (Keens-Soper & Schweizer, 1994: 38).

Beyond these contemporaneous debates, we can now look at historiography's argument for an eighteenth-century 'noble monopoly' (Scott, 2007: 75). The first point to note is that thanks to the cultural turn in recent decades, biographical details and changes in the socio-economic functions and contributions of individual diplomats have become a more important object of study. Yet the social origins and class dynamics of diplomats remain neglected. For example, these have not yet been considered as a stand-alone subject for a monograph-length study. Thus, research in this area remains in progress as it relies on very few prosopography studies and comments in general and specific works.[14] For now, it is conventionally accepted that in the first part of the early modern period (fifteenth–seventeenth centuries), European diplomacy was still conducted by an often temporary and socially complex patchwork of diplomatic actors. 'Lesser nobles and commoners were far more prominent' as resident ambassadors (Scott, 2007; Dover & Scott, 2015: 676). The ability to negotiate, being in the king's service, in government, engaging

[14] The English/British and French diplomatic services have been the most studied in terms of biographical details of individual diplomats. For general accounts including biographical details or an analysis of diplomats' social origins, see Bittner *et al.*, 1936; Carter, 1966; Roosen, 1976; Bély, 1990, 2007; Scott, 2007. For biographical accounts of English and British diplomatic services, see Horn, 1961; Lachs, 1965; Lee, 1967; Bell, 1990; Black, 2001; Jettot, 2012; Dyson, 2013. For the French services, see Picavet, 1923; Bénazet-Béchu, 1982, 1998; Baillou, 1984; Roosen, 1973; Bély, 2005. For accounts of the Spanish, see Ozanam, 1999.

in courtly matters, or having close ties to the Crown generally determined a diplomatic appointment (Davis-Cross, 2007: 37).

There were a number of reasons why the high and middle-ranked nobility were not interested in taking up or pursuing diplomatic posts: the cost of missions, the danger involved, the lack of financial gain or political opportunities arising from the mission, the risk of estrangement and loss of trust by compatriots when returning home, the problem of missions being hard work if not posted in a special or one of the main embassies, and, last but not least, the problem that diplomatic work was considered beneath the aristocracy and better suited to merchants, clergy, lawyers, and low nobility. As Dyson (2013) recalls, the use of agents rather than ambassadors was also a way of avoiding the need to use the high nobility, which remained in many cases reluctant to serve. Notwithstanding, aristocrats maintained positions in the major embassies (Madrid, Paris, The Hague, London, and Rome for Catholic sovereigns), while middle-ranking nobles were generally sent to other capitals.

However, a shift occurs from the late-seventeenth century, when it became more likely for the larger proportion of diplomats to be chosen from the higher social elite and on the basis of their family connections.[15] By the eighteenth century, 'status became more connected with the skills and reputation of the diplomat himself' (Davis-Cross, 2007: 41), reinforcing the role of the function of representation. Thus, increasingly regular and permanent embassies became occupied by a more socially homogeneous (i.e. aristocratic) and self-conscious diplomatic corps, the 'noble monopoly'. This argument is inter alia based on Bély's analysis of 450 European negotiators from 1697 to 1715, around the signing of the treaties of Utrecht. His analysis reveals that the nobility came to dominate diplomatic missions through two activities: its presence in court and in the army (1990: 301).

This had negative consequences for the development of a professional diplomatic corps, by entrenching leading families in the award of prestige embassies (Scott, 2007: 76), thus mutually reinforcing the function of representation with the phenomenon of aristocratisation. Although this monopoly was tempered by the presence of non-nobles and thus more experienced and skilled diplomats to execute the day-to-day work, it was paralleled with the rise of nobles in government foreign policy posts, a

[15] Roosen, 1976: 66; Anderson, 1993: 80; Dover & Scott, 2015: 685.

model also led by Louis XIV and his ministers. Crucially, the noble monopoly meant a reinforcement of etiquette, ceremonials, and protocol, acquiring new levels of precision and formality (Roosen, 1980; Scott, 2007: 79) but slowing down the process of modernisation of the diplomatic corps. For example, in the 1710s, attempts to open training schools failed because foreign service was considered a one-off opportunity to secure a post at home closer to their sovereign rather than a career (Dover & Scott, 2015: 688). The noble monopoly also meant more 'lavish house decorations or larger parade coaches' (Dover & Scott, 2015: 686), the hosting of luxurious dinner parties – essential during Utrecht to facilitate opportunities for diplomats to impress, negotiate, and influence more privately opponents and partners (Bély, 2007: 510).

However, England and the Dutch Republic are excluded from this aristocratic phenomenon, mainly because of the role of England's parliamentary assemblies in appointing diplomats, and, in the Dutch case, because of the professional and social diversity of diplomats (Bély, 1990: 301). These cases are considered 'an exception' due to their 'distinctive social structures', involving the diplomatic role of the Dutch *regenten* oligarchy (large merchant families distinct from territorial nobility) and the small and thus unreliable number of English peers (Scott, 2007: 74; Dover & Scott, 2015: 685).

Scholars explain the late-seventeenth–early-eighteenth centuries aristocratisation of the diplomatic corps from a variety of factors, but mostly as a consequence of the function of representation and as a 'deliberate political strategy pursued for internal reasons' (Scott, 2007: 75). Among other factors, nobles, who 'still controlled by far the greatest proportion of Europe's wealth', considered diplomatic missions as 'the service which their families had always provided and as opportunities for their own collecting and cultural patronage'; this ensured they would strengthen 'their links with the ruler' (Scott, 2007: 73).[16] This angle emphasises the shared need for – and benefits of – collaboration between ruling dynasties and leading nobilities. In Prussia's 'composite diplomacy', 'the informal practices of local actors offered the local nobility new ways of exerting influence; yet at the same time, they proved

[16] Other factors are the lack of a 'sizeable alternative social group', 'improved travel and communication tools', the 'increased grip of the social elite a hundred years before the Revolution', the decline of clerical diplomats, and an increase in number of posts to fill (Dover & Scott, 2015: 685).

conducive to the monarchy's interest in strengthening the king's control of the newly acquired territory' (Windler, 2017a: 261).

The questions this generates are therefore whether, in Spain – or more exactly Castile – and France, the noble monopoly was 'pursued for internal reasons', and whether the somewhat exceptional cases of England and the Dutch Republic can be explained by their 'social structures'.

4.3 Cases

For diplomatic historians in the lineage of Mattingly's (1955) work, as well as for some proponents of new diplomatic history, the rise of individual diplomats' status is linked to the individual skills of diplomats and the general institutionalisation of international relations post-Westphalia, which remains a driving factor for the late-eighteenth-century territorialisation of diplomacy and the shaping of an 'international society' (Frey & Frey, 1999: 208). According to this narrative, the Westphalian 'assertion of state sovereignty entailed first an extension and then a limitation of ambassadorial privilege' (Frey & Frey, 1999: 216).

However, as reviewed above, a growing literature from various disciplines and approaches is emphasising the social and class dynamics of early modern politics, revealing new factors in the recruitment and social composition of diplomats. Nevertheless, work remains to be done in terms of looking deeper into the 'internal reasons', 'social structures', or 'links with the ruler' explaining the noble monopoly and how this might help to go beyond the narrow Westphalian link between ambassadorial privilege and extraterritoriality. Neglecting these factors is surprising when considering that in some cases, ruling elites were going through radical and revolutionary transformations during this period and constituted a significant element of trans-societal change.

Looking at the English and Dutch cases as possible exceptions is a good entry point to introduce new factors, since they share other points of similarity. However, the following discussion also wants to nuance the notion of exceptionalism concerning diplomatic practices, since by the eighteenth century, Britain, Spain, France, and the Dutch Republic all shared common practices that distinguished them from the rest of Europe, notably because of their extra-European activities (Black, 2001: 16). This dimension will be taken up in the next chapter. Notwithstanding, we discussed in Chapter 1 how the English and

Dutch were at the forefront of tolerating embassy chapels in the seventeenth century, shaping the so-called modern doctrine of extraterritoriality – in Mattingly and Adair's works – by being at the forefront of legislation for ambassadorial immunity and in providing a legal basis for the enforcement of this immunity. Both countries also lagged behind Castile and France in terms of developing permanent embassies.

Since the two states considered a priori as exceptions were at the forefront of capitalist development – albeit the Dutch case more arguably – one could tentatively make a link between the development of aristocratic diplomacy and the development of capitalism in early modern Europe, and how the former evolved as a counter or challenge to the latter contributing to the specific absolutist–capitalist combination of the sovereign states system argued by scholars such as Lacher and Teschke (2007). This chapter cannot do justice to this question. However, opening it up and offering some preliminary directions should be useful for future projects.

The following will thus focus on exploring the potential 'internal reasons' and 'social structures' at the basis of differential diplomatic strategies by linking the discussion to the social property relations in each respective cases of England, the Dutch Republic, France, and the Iberian kingdoms. Although each case presents specificities, the analysis associates on the one hand the English and Dutch cases in terms of how their political particularities pushed them to be more dependent on diverse and aspiring groups of merchants and parliamentarians for diplomatic missions. On the other hand, Castilian and French rulers developed different methods of collaboration with their aristocratic and other noble contingents. Furthermore, if all cases enrich the variety of jurisdictional – or extraterritorial – strategies of accumulation, the similarities inside each grouping help to situate these practices in the book's overall typology of jurisdiction accumulation. Namely, the Castilian and French diplomatic practices are associated with the concept of transplants of authority, while the Dutch and English are associated more easily with transports of authority. These concepts are developed in more detail in Chapter 6, as their main analytical purchase refers to each empire's colonial practices of jurisdictional accumulation. But it is useful to signpost and apply them in this analysis, so as to mark the links between diplomatic and colonial practices as imperial strategies of expansion, and to show nuance and diversity in how these empires navigated jurisdictional opportunities. Specifically, the French case is the most ambiguous, as it developed diplomatic practices that increased the jurisdictional prerogative and impact of ambassadors and especially consuls, significant of transplants of authority, but also held back jurisdictionally in its Northern American colonial practices, which are more suitably identified as transports of authority, notably through the role of trading companies. Before delving more into these distinctions in further chapters, let us return to each case and the social origins of their diplomats.

4.3.1 *England's Gentry and Parliamentarian Diplomats*

Throughout the early modern period, the English peerage was traditionally used for important diplomatic posts (Dover & Scott, 2015: 685).[17] English aristocratic presence in diplomatic missions was actually higher than in France for example pre-1660s. In both cases, though, the percentage of aristocrats was very low in the overall number of diplomatic agents until the fifteenth century (Moeglin & Pequignot, 2017: 393–398). English sovereigns had particular difficulties in 'finding capable diplomats' (Anderson, 1993: 80). Henry VIII used many clerics, in addition to royal servants and courtiers who were carefully selected, prestigious, and entertained a close, personal relationship with the king. However, lords reluctantly accepted missions, which were costly, dangerous, tiresome, and mostly used to assert oneself and gain favour with the sovereign for securing a better post or social position at home (Horn, 1961; Anderson, 1993: 80).

Giry-Deloison's comparative study of French and English diplomatic posts from 1485 to 1520, although selective, nevertheless claims to be representative of diplomatic activity during this period (1987: 208).[18] It shows that of the fifty-seven known English missions to France conducted by fifty-four diplomatic actors, the nobility – 48.15 per cent – was more or less equal to the amount of commoners (*roturiers*) – 46.29 per cent (1987: 213–214).[19] However, the share of the aristocracy or high

[17] Although it is a matter of disagreement among historians, this study follows most of the sources it relies on and considers English gentry as part of the nobility, albeit its lowest possible and in some cases disputed ranks.

[18] In spite of debates over the various ranks and titles of diplomats in the period, Giry-Deloison argues for the use of only two terms for the early-sixteenth century: (1) 'ambassador' (*ambassadeur*), credited with a mission and invested with power to negotiate and (2) 'envoy' (*envoyé*), responsible for letters and messages (1987: 208). His study looks at both.

[19] The remaining 5.56 per cent refer to three diplomats whose biographical origins are unknown.

nobility consisted in only nine individuals (13.89 per cent of the overall nobility), and 16.67 per cent of all agents (1987: 213). The gentry or low and middle-ranked nobility was represented by seventeen individuals: thirteen had the title of knight, three were squires, and one was a gentleman (1987: 214).

In sum, diplomacy in early-sixteenth-century England was open to the low and non-nobility. For Giry-Deloison, the fact that the nobility did not dominate these posts can be mostly explained by two factors: first, the missions did not result in the granting of a title so the use of commoners was not a considerable cost or loss for the Crown; second, English nobility (aristocracy and gentry) was much less numerous than in France so less able to dominate important services to the Crown (1987: 214). In both England and France, the presence of commoners played a significant role in diplomatic missions, even if as secondary agents. Moreover, embassies in this period were more concerned with gathering information rather than ensuring symbolic representation or negotiation, and thus nobles were less necessary.

Bell's survey of diplomatic actors in the service of the English Crown from 1509 to 1688 argues that overseas ambassadors were not 'haphazardly chosen' or a 'randomly prepared lot' as commonly portrayed (1990: 11). Such an assessment can be found for example in Anderson, for whom across Europe, appointments could still be made 'in a remarkably haphazard way on the basis of family connections and sheer luck' up until the late-eighteenth century (1993: 81). British diplomacy was, for Anderson, 'casual and amateurish' and 'happy-go-lucky', constituting an 'interlude' rather than a 'career' (1993: 82). Instead, Bell argues from a more detailed biographical analysis that seventeenth-century diplomats were an 'unusually well-trained and reasonably carefully selected group of royal servants' (1990: 11 12). They were well-educated 'courtiers', with knowledge of historical precedents, the mores of countries, and of legal theory. However, this does not completely negate Anderson's account. Instead, and as Black's (2001) analysis confirms, it should be restricted to the methods of diplomatic recruitment following in the late-seventeenth and eighteenth centuries' period of the European noble monopoly, when rank was increasingly important and diplomacy became more 'amateurish' (Dover & Scott, 2015).

However, for our specific purposes here, Bell does not give any general information regarding the social origins of the representatives he included in his study. His list does not include commoners who might have served as messengers or envoys, those who represented a non-prince, those who were merchants and consuls, nor the military. His survey is therefore concentrated on higher-rank ambassadors, making comparisons between different social groups more difficult to assess.

The early-seventeenth century begins by showing a similar pattern to the sixteenth and entrenches the role of the gentry in English diplomacy (Lachs, 1965: 54; Carter, 1966: 285). Most diplomats of this period 'came from landed families of no great importance' or 'from mercantile backgrounds' and 'connections with the great trading companies' (Lee, 1966–1967: 1264–1265). Thus, 'the majority of the diplomatic corps ... did not hail from a noble background' and was composed of agents who were members of the gentry, 'as a rank which was attained when it was recognised by others ... members of the gentry' (Dyson, 2013: 27). A number came from merchant families and legal families, the legal profession being a good way to maintain and access gentry status (Dyson, 2013: 27).[20]

Crucially, 'these men were not at the forefront of their counties, nor did many ever attend parliament until *after* they had become servants of the Crown' (2013: 30; my emphasis). This point is critical for deepening our understanding of the social conditions of diplomatic appointments. To what extent did the foreign service become a means for members of the aspiring and low gentry to become involved in parliamentary politics? This seems unlikely, given the costs involved, leaving this option to better-off individuals and families. However, if significant, it would suggest that diplomatic or foreign service helped entrench a capitalist landowning class not otherwise particularly involved in foreign or royal politics. Thus, one of the crucial questions this chapter raises – and has to leave open for now – is whether the structural changes of the long fifteenth century in the advent of agrarian capitalism in England were a factor in shaping English diplomacy as less reliant on nobles than its European counterparts. According to Dimmock (2019), the link seems promising, since for the period 1450–1550 'there is a definite movement into government of those from more obscure backgrounds, particularly in the aftermath of the wars of the roses as Henry VII sought to draw the

[20] However, Dyson concludes that from 'the low number of men who had attended the Inns of Courts who were accredited, it would appear that the government did not look specifically for lawyers to send on diplomatic missions' (2013: 38). Diplomatic treatises recommended for legal training to be in Roman civil law rather than common law, reducing the role of the Inns as places for diplomatic education. However, the legal profession 'was an acceptable type of employment for the gentry, as well as a way of becoming a member of the gentry' (Dyson, 2013: 27).

teeth of the aristocracy', and 'the legal profession was critical for this' (personal correspondence). These points remain very tentative, as indeed one could argue that these men, also known as Henry VII's 'new men of legend' were perhaps simply 'less exalted', and therefore mark less of a break with ongoing feudal social property relations than suggested.[21]

Confirming the latter relationship between Parliament and diplomatic agency, Jettot has explored in detail the rise of MPs in the foreign service of England in the period 1660–1702 (2012).[22] MPs were seen as the living symbols of the King-in-Parliament (Jettot, 2012: 537), a cornerstone of the specific development of the English state enabling the class alliances that favoured the development of agrarian capitalism (Wood, 1992).[23] Black also emphasises the importance of Parliament for the conduct of diplomacy (2001: 4–6). In this context, MPs were encouraged to become diplomats rather than consuls. If consuls, they had to vacate their parliamentary seat, and a consul's job was considered beneath them (Horn, 1961: 247).

These trends are confirmed in the early-eighteenth century, though some alignment with the major European powers' practices can be seen in terms of the use of more aristocrats and military men. The English/British network was also expanded from 1689 onwards. The post of diplomatic agent, dominant in the previous period, ended in 1686 (Dyson, 2013: 249) and England's diplomatic history was to follow its politically unstable constitutional evolution (Bély, 1990: 296; Black, 2001). Of thirty-eight English diplomats of all ranks from 1697 to 1715, nearly half belonged to the middle or high nobility, and another significant proportion came from the gentry and other provincial nobility (Bély, 1990: 295). Some had a background in politics, and others came from elite merchant families. By this time, diplomats from humble origins were rare (Bély, 1990: 296). Of the thirty-eight, sixteen were members of the House of Lords, and fifteen were members of the

21 Archival work would need to be explored to fully answer this question, looking at national biographies and parliamentary histories to see whether there are significant links between landholding gentry and access to foreign service posts and to Parliament. I thank Spencer Dimmock and Hamish Scott for discussions on these points.

22 See Pal (2019) for a summary of Jettot's analysis with the development of agrarian capitalism in England as backdrop. Black (2001: 23) also notes in passing that many British diplomats in the early-eighteenth century were parliamentarians. However, this could be simply seen as involving a different branch of public service, alongside the army and navy. Thank you to Hamish Scott for this remark.

23 See Chapter 3 for a discussion of the Crown-in-Parliament.

House of Commons. Thus, the majority of appointments were government-led, from the Houses, political parties, or armies, rather than from the king's entourage (Bély, 1990: 296). This is a shift from the sixteenth and early-seventeenth centuries and from the previous Stuart period examined by Jettot when Charles II used diplomatic envoys to try to secure his rule. These shifting characteristics indeed follow the rise of England's parliamentary politics, but also more tentatively, the rise of its capitalist landowning and merchant class. This picture is in stark contrast to France, where the court was much less 'discreet' in making appointments which coincided with its own interests and with appointing military men.

After 1709, a similar increase in the use of military men as diplomats is observed both in England and France (Roosen, 1976: 67–68), though military men remained relatively less prominent in England (Black, 2001: 44–45). The use of military men is partly explained by the instability of the diplomatic occupation and thus its unattractiveness for aspiring or noble dynasties, exacerbated by the tradition under Queen Anne that a change in the secretary of state or minister meant the dropping of their diplomatic appointees. It is also explained by the need to occupy military men in times of peace (Roosen, 1973), and by their suitability to particular courts (Black, 2001: 44).

An important distinction – though difficult to always clearly trace – existed in eighteenth-century British diplomacy between 'envoys of title' and 'men of business', reflecting the continuous role of diplomats who had risen through the occupation and came from more modest and aspiring backgrounds such as the gentry, in contrast to those who had been nominated because of their peerage or aristocratic courtly qualities (Black, 2001: 46–50).[24] Though Black resists any generalisations in terms of social origins, and fails to focus exclusively on this dimension, he lists various examples where the apparent lack of birth or courtly manners of British envoys was in stark contrast to old regime diplomacy, which led some contemporary observers to describe certain British 'men of business' as 'parvenu' or 'arriviste', lacking 'dignity and decorum', and looking as 'dirty a dog as ever I saw in my life' (Black, 2001: 46).

[24] For Black, mentioning both groups is essential, but '[m]uch of the problem in judging British diplomacy derives from the habit of putting both groups together in order to produce an overall judgement. Although in many cases the differences were readily apparent and sometimes commented upon, there was no rigid divide between the groups' (2001: 49).

In sum, the transition to agrarian capitalism and the successive waves of enclosures in England reveal two processes that are of interest here. They confirm the leading role of a landowning gentry and they entrench the role of the common law in shaping extraterritorial strategies (De Luca, 2008). If, as suggested, the transition also led some of these men into the conduct of foreign service, one could argue that agrarian capitalism constituted one of the decisive 'internal' factors and 'social structures' to explain England's particular culture of diplomacy.

4.3.2 The Dutch Republic and Its Diplomatic Diversity

There is a significant imbalance in the number of studies dedicated to Dutch diplomatic history in comparison to the French and English cases. However, the main characteristics of diplomats of the Dutch Republic appear to be their diversity, in terms of occupational background and social origins, and their propensity for being at the centre of jurisdictional conflicts between the provinces. The length of their missions was also significantly longer than their counterparts, with an average of twenty to over thirty years in certain posts. The United Provinces made good use of the stability of its negotiators, which were entrenched in the politics and society of foreign locations (Bély, 1990: 297; van Meersbergen, 2017: 147).

For extraordinary missions, they sent a deputation of several members (three to sixteen) rather than a single appointee with an entourage. The chartered company of the VOC did its own negotiating and sent deputations. This was a symptom of the identification of interests between the United Provinces and VOC rather than competition for authority (Stern, 2011).

Dutch diplomacy was described as overall 'unspectacular and embarrassingly unimaginative' but spread money in bribes and gifts (Carter, 1966: 282). Carter also describes Dutch diplomats as 'stubborn, obtuse, incapable of calculated compromise, antagonistic, but more successful than Spain, England or France'; the Dutch Republic as a 'nation of fishermen, merchants and carriers (and interlopers, smugglers, colonial squatters and pirates)', 'exceeded all others in its day to day contacts with foreigners' (1966: 281). Accordingly, it was only rivalled by the English in terms of 'complaints arising out of routine economic activity' (281). This analysis is culturally and racially loaded and too general to be very reliable, but interesting in terms of its emphasis on the social diversity of Dutch agents, the economic and mercantile similarities with England,

and the established successes of the Dutch diplomatic missions. Another link with England is made by Anderson (1993: 80–81), who notes the difficulties in both states to find appropriate candidates throughout the seventeenth and eighteenth centuries. From the 1660s, the Dutch resorted to attribute 'run-of-the-mill' expeditions to the highest rank of 'ambassador extraordinary', but even such alluring promotions did not change the fact that Dutch diplomatic posts were either filled by 'second-rate men' or remained unfilled (Anderson, 1993: 80).

In Bély's sample of Dutch negotiators at Utrecht over the 1697–1715 period, 43.5 per cent came from the nobility, which is relatively high considering the role of the aristocracy was in political decline since the beginning of the Republic. Most Dutch diplomats were from the *regenten* oligarchy, while some came from the nobility of landward provinces (Scott, 2007: 74); some diplomats often came from families that governed the cities, and had municipal political functions, the urban magistrates discussed previously (Bély, 1990: 296). Each province had a representative. There were not many military men, except for some military administrators, and some merchants played a modest intermediary role (Bély, 1990: 297). Bély also identifies two lawyers, one doctor, and some diplomats' sons. Finally, one negotiator was director of the VOC. For Bély, the aristocratisation of Dutch diplomats was externally driven, 'as if they had been driven to follow such a model' (1990: 296), and therefore would contrast with other cases.[25] But, eventually, the Dutch also follow the broadly similar social evolution led by France.

4.3.3 *France and the Rise of Aristocratic Diplomacy*

As mentioned above, in the early-sixteenth century, we have similar situations in France and England. From 1485 to 1520, of the seventy-two French diplomatic missions to England, 65.45 per cent or thirty-six envoys were nobles, but only five of those were from the high nobility or aristocracy, thus 9 per cent overall (aristocracy consisted of 13.89 per cent of overall nobility). The remaining 25 per cent of those seventy-two missions were conducted by commoners, mostly from its educated and wealthy strata, whose aspirations can be compared to those of the English lower gentry (Giry-Deloison, 1987: 209–216; Dover & Scott, 2015: 676).

[25] 'Tout se passe comme si, dans un contexte européen où la diplomatie était souvent une affaire d'aristocrates, les Provinces-Unies avaient été conduites à suivre un tel modèle.'

The reign of Louis XIV (1643–1715) led the way for the shift to an aristocratic *corps diplomatique*, focused on etiquette, protocol, and ceremonial practices that maintained the order of the old regime in the European political sphere until at least the end of the eighteenth century (Bénazet-Béchu, 1982, 1998; Bély, 1990). Dover and Scott qualify this new 'European network of resident diplomats' as the 'aggregate of its court societies' (2015: 686), which 'played a central role in diplomacy as the location where ambassadors and envoys could mingle with native aristocrats, ministers of the host government and even members of the ruling dynasty' (Scott, 2007: 78). If this process was led by Louis XIV and his ministers, it was also symptomatic of the fact that 'aristocrats clustered around thrones', as noted in the Introduction (Scott, 2016: 222). In other words, the French leading model of European diplomacy was the result of a collaboration between its social elites.

The high nobility and the military orders were Louis XIV's favourite groups (Picavet, 1923: 390–393). The king kept a close eye on diplomatic nominations, was 'theoretically' free to choose whom he wanted, and chose according to the post's circumstances (Picavet, 1923: 399; Roosen, 1973: 121). If Picavet emphasises the choice of the military order, or *noblesse d'épée*, this is slightly tempered by Roosen (1973) who shows through a close analysis of sixty-six ambassadors and 103 missions, that the role of the 'robe' was of near equal importance to that of the 'sword' in the beginning of the reign. However, he notes that the role of the sword increases and that of the robe decreases towards the end of Louis XIV's reign in the 1710s (1973: 127). The decreasing importance of *parlementaires* and other elite legal professions is subsequently confirmed as less than one-eighth (i.e. forty ambassadors) came from the *noblesse de robe* in the eighteenth century (Scott, 2007: 74). However, I agree with Roosen that it can be misleading to overly focus on the differences between *noblesse de robe* and *noblesse d'épée*, as we saw previously in disagreements over Callières's comments on the nobility. The important fact is that all of Louis XIV's ambassadors were nobles, from either robe or sword predominantly (respectively twenty-four and twenty-eight out of sixty-six), or clergy (eleven out of sixty-six). Three ambassadors did not have an official or public position before taking on a diplomatic role (Roosen, 1973: 123).

Bély's sample of a hundred French diplomats (203 missions) during Utrecht also finds the French group dominated by the '*noblesse de cour*' and '*noblesse illustre*' (1990: 292–294). Thirty-six out of 100 were nobles. Overall, 21 per cent were from *noblesse d'épée* (1990: 292) and 11 per cent from the clergy (1990: 293). The rest was composed of 'commis', 'serviteurs des princes', and embassy secretaries. The *noblesse de robe* produced charismatic diplomats such as the Count d'Avaux,[26] but their role as a social group was more and more criticised and disfavoured. The '*petite noblesse*' and recent nobles were given missions to less important princes (they were envoys and not ambassadors). Finally, a very small number of diplomats came from the bourgeoisie and the literary and artistic world (Bély, 1990: 293).

In sum, the French led the aristocratic trend with a rise of the *noblesse d'épée*, which became more attracted to diplomatic service (Roosen, 1976: 67–68). These men came very predominantly from the army rather than from the navy (Roosen, 1973: 124). One reason for their use was their experience in relation to the duties required, but also because in times of peace, 'unemployed French officers had to find something to do' (Roosen, 1973: 124). As diplomatic posts tended to be put on hold during wartime, their shift back to the army did not pose a problem. From 1648 to 1789, the *noblesse d'épée* constituted one-third of French diplomacy (104 ambassadors out of 350) (Scott, 2007: 74).

Colbert's influence is found to linger close behind Louis's choices, but to what extent Colbert left Louis to decide on ambassadorial appointments, while Colbert focused on developing new secretariats (*secrétaire d'état des affaires étrangères* and the *secrétaire d'état de la marine*), as well as giving more attention to the administration and nomination of consuls, is worth exploring (see next chapter). This might give an indication of the roles these very different diplomatic bodies were expected to play for the expansion of the French commercial empire. Determining the influence of ministers in the appointment of ambassadors is very difficult, since there is very little trace of this process. As an extract from a memoir of Secretary of State de Lionne shows, influence from ministers appears exceptional (Roosen, 1973: 137). However, the influence of Colbert is obviously crucial, such as in the appointment of his brother Charles Colbert de Croissy as ambassador to England as well as for men unrelated to him (137).

In terms of the choice of nominations, the problem of intervention by *courtisans* and princes cannot be ignored (Picavet, 1923: 397–398). But this is tempered somewhat by the fact that Louis XIV kept control and responsibility for the nominations, and that beyond the strict social

[26] See Levillain (2016) and Tischer (2008) for studies of the Count D'Avaux.

origins or occupation of the nominees, considerations of money and personal representation were crucial (Picavet, 1923: 398–399). Roosen maps the destination of the missions sent by Louis XIV to the past occupational background of ambassadors, and the only patterns he can draw are that 'clerics were never sent to non-Catholic states or to the Papacy' and that 'ambassadors to the Papacy were usually military officers' (1973: 128). It is significant that ambassadorial offers of appointment were at times rejected, most often because of financial reasons, but also inexperience, health, or simple unwillingness (Roosen, 1973: 136). This significantly adds to the argument that these appointments were part of a strategy of negotiation and collaboration between the king and nobles rather than either a natural and given evolution or expectation in relation to birth, or an unavoidable consequence of Louis's absolutism.

From these studies alone, it is indeed not clear why the nobility (whether robe or sword) suddenly became the near exclusive choice for ambassadors. The most explicit Roosen gets to answering the question 'why nobles?' is to conclude that the 'restriction of ambassadorial positions to nobles mirrored the seventeenth century's assumption that status and position should be in balance' (1973: 139). This remains rather cryptic, except to say that personal representation of sovereigns was more determined by birth and noble rank than by intellectual capabilities. The problem with the reliance on representation as explanatory factor is that it becomes circular, in the sense that representation and aristocratisation mutually reinforce each other, as discussed in the first section. It thus becomes unclear which process led to the other. As Louis was successful 'in forcing the nobility to gather at his court in order to obtain benefits' (139), it can be suggested that ambassadorial appointments were part of a conscious strategy to manage the nobility. Thus, a more promising line of explanation lies in understanding this process as a jurisdictional strategy for both ruler and social elite, rather than simply one of many 'internal reasons'.

A further point that adds to this line of explanation is the lack of continuity in generations of ambassadors, making it difficult to see the process of aristocratisation as a gradual and long-term change, and helping to see it instead as the result of a more sudden strategy. Seeking ambassadorial positions could not constitute a strategy of class reproduction. In France, ambassadors placed their sons in the military, judicial, or administrative careers, because diplomacy remained too unstable. Diplomatic posts were not venal offices, that is they were not bought and were therefore subject to disappearance (Roosen, 1976: 68).[27] Therefore, one does not find 'diplomatic dynasties', in contrast to in other parts of French administration and government (Roosen, 1973: 139), and contrary to consular positions pre-seventeenth century. A diplomatic career was therefore not a good choice for class reproduction, which as Parker and others argued in the previous chapter, was a characteristic of France's particular dynastic absolutism.

In other words, the French ruling class failed to reproduce itself economically in the accumulative way the English landed gentry was able to. First, because it was stuck in the pursuit of administrative venal offices, and second because peasants and farmers retained important property rights. Instead, the diplomatic corps's relation to power was cemented by a personal link between ambassador and king, which went beyond the mere idea of representation. As seen above, France was the only state to maintain for so long the practice of personal communication between king and ambassador, and it did so until the end of the old regime. Bély (1990: 292) even subtitles his section on French diplomats 'the rays of the sun', implying the reciprocity of each component (i.e. the king and his ambassadors).[28]

To conclude this subsection, French social property relations represented by the powers of the various regions and *parlements* and the legal institutions discussed previously – which put pressure on Louis XIV's regime to collaborate with the aristocracy – can also help explain the shift from the early-sixteenth-century period to the later aristocratic monopoly. These conditions give more social weight to why representation and personal forms of sovereignty and rule, better defined as transports of authority, were crucial to maintain Louis's rule.

The reproduction of this model across Europe ensured the maintenance of an old regime dynastic court society in the capital cities of Europe, in spite of the winds of change blown by more maritime empires such as England and the Dutch Republic, involving more of the gentry, bourgeoisie, or merchants in diplomatic missions. More work is required on these and other European cases, though the literature more or less

[27] Another important exception to the venality of diplomatic posts otherwise found across Europe were the Venetians, who however employed career diplomats (rather than aristocratic favourites or military men) who spent long years on a mission (Roosen, 1976: 68).

[28] 'Les rayons du soleil'. Translation by author.

agrees that 'most European countries' followed from France's lead in this domain.[29] To illustrate one of these followers, we will now look closely at Castile.

4.3.4 Castile's Aristocratic Diplomacy as Collaboration against Decline

Our final case begins from a similar basis as the French and English, as fifteenth- and sixteenth-century Iberian ambassadors were not represented by members of an aristocracy.[30] Iberian diplomats were a 'mixed' group, with no 'great noblemen' or 'grandees', though some 'bore old and distinguished names'; '[o]thers had risen in the Church or the law from among the middle-sized landowners and professional classes of the towns, or from humble and obscure origins' (Mattingly, 1966: 143). Most were Castilians. This is surprising for Mattingly, since the kingdom

[29] The Italians and the Austrian-Habsburgs followed the same pattern of aristocratisation, with the case of Naples as a deliberate and sudden composition of a diplomatic corps made up of powerful nobility. Russia and Prussia took longer to reach the level of other European countries but nevertheless eventually followed the model (Dover & Scott, 2015: 686).

[30] The following discussion excludes an analysis of Portuguese diplomacy for reasons of space and time. Moreover, Portuguese diplomats did not use representation as much as other cases – there were 'no resident diplomats abroad until 1522' even though Portugal 'was involved in diplomatic difficulties pretty much all over Western Europe' (Mattingly, 1966: 173). If Portugal starts to develop residents alongside Castile and France after 1522, this process was interrupted when it was ruled by Castile from 1580 to 1640 (though the latter did not recognise Portuguese independence until 1668). Nevertheless, diplomacy broadly defined was a crucial dimension of Portuguese maritime expansion in the sixteenth century. For an analysis of Portuguese diplomacy in Asia in this period, see Biedermann (2014: 7–32) emphasising 'diversity of interests and strategic inconsistency' as key characteristics (2014: 14), as well as how 'diplomatic activity unfolded in courtly environments congregating cultural and political elites that could understand each other relatively easily' (2014: 20). Biederman makes a cautious estimate of 'a dozen major embassies dispatched from Goa and other points of the *Estado* to Asian and African potentates every single year, and perhaps another dozen coming in' excluding 'envoys of lesser significance who kept going to and fro most of the time' (2014: 23). In terms of their social origins, the most important diplomat was the governor or viceroy who had a complex legal status and range of political prerogatives (2014: 27). The analysis of social origins corresponds with other cases discussed since 'although social status played a role, other aspects had some importance' for obtaining the position of governor (2014: 27): 'Official Portuguese ambassadors were preferably recruited from the middle and upper strata of the nobility, from among *fidalgos* who had already served in courtly environments at home or gained a comparable experience elsewhere. But it is important to take into account the large number of apparently minor agents who, given the general tendency of the apparatus to improvisation, could at times gain considerable importance' (2014: 29).

of Aragon was considered to own more 'cosmopolitan lands' (1966: 144) more prone to producing effective envoys. Instead Mattingly suggests 'that it was easier to pay public servants from the revenues of Castile' (144), and, of course, as discussed previously, Castile was the heart of the monarchy. If all of Ferdinand's ambassadors were Spaniards, 'it would be hard to find any common denominator of birth or education among them', except that they 'had all worked in the royal administration' and had 'some legal training' (144). This confirms analyses in the previous chapter exposing the particular reliance on theologians, legal actors, and legal mechanisms of the Castilian monarchy in its period of imperial expansion, as well as the common 'chivalric, feudal loyalty to the person of the monarch' (144). Castilian renaissance diplomacy was also characterised by the length of its missions. This meant a smaller number of ambassadors overall and the sense of a close community of foreign servants and 'veteran diplomats' who served as advisers after their missions (Mattingly, 1966: 143).

In the period of the late-fifteenth and early-sixteenth centuries, Castile's role in the evolution of European diplomacy is marked by Ferdinand's 'experiments with resident ambassadors', making Castile the only major European power 'ready at once to adopt the diplomatic machinery appropriate to the new phase' (Mattingly, 1966: 138). However, Ferdinand 'neglected his resident ambassadors, sometimes deceived them, starved them of their courier service, and consistently underpaid them', as well as 'distrusted them (unjustly) and set them to spy on one another' (Mattingly, 1966: 141). On their social origins, Mattingly remarks – in another comical but racially loaded comment – that they were 'of the same race as the *conquistadors*', that is a socially mixed group and one characterised by 'flamed tempers . . . who made the subjugation of two continents a mere incident of their civil broils' (1966: 142). However, Ferdinand's approach improved by the end of his reign in the early-sixteenth century turning his foreign service into 'the most impressive diplomatic service in Europe' (142). His successor Charles V, crowned Holy Roman Emperor in 1516, had very different diplomatic challenges, having to integrate the shift of alliances involved in the expansion of the Spanish Crown over the Habsburg Empire. Ambassadorial positions were thereafter filled with a mix of Burgundian, Dutch, and Hispanic nobles, and a Savoyard 'careerist' – the 'ideal public servants for Charles V's polyglot empire' (Mattingly, 1966: 179). The Peace of Vervins concluded in 1598 with France was conducted by a team of Dutch negotiators, directed from Brussels (Bély,

2007: 45). The Spanish-Habsburg diplomacy has even been called a precursor to a Belgium diplomacy (Houssiau, 2000). In any case, after Vervins and during what some call a 'pax hispanica' that lasted until 1635 and the next round of hostilities with France, Castile enjoyed a renewed presence through its ambassadors, relying on its network of informers (Bély, 2007: 119–120) and complex spying operations directed by the office of the '*espia mayor*' (Bély, 2007: 159).

The mixed group of the sixteenth century makes the shift to the eighteenth century, again, particularly intriguing and important to explain. From 1700 to 1808, the Spanish monarchy had the most high-ranking diplomatic corps, with 'one hundred and sixty-seven ambassadors, envoys or "chargés d'affaires"', of which 'thirty were grandees' and the rest were from 'long established and prominent noble families' (Scott, 2007: 75). In the snapshot studied by Bély of thirty-eight Spanish negotiators during the period of Utrecht from 1697 to 1715, thirty-four belonged to the high nobility (1990: 294).[31] Spain continued to use foreign diplomats as well, which tended to come from more diverse social backgrounds (294). Importantly, Spanish diplomats continued to be strongly linked to state offices of high rank by serving in both capacities (Bély, 1990: 295). According to Bély, diplomatic personnel thus reflected the 'avid' nature of the high nobility to maintain its grip on power, eclipsing in negotiations the '*letrados*' – jurists constituting the administrative branch of the state (295). From 1700 to 1759, the aristocracy occupied 76 per cent of diplomatic posts. After Charles VII (Charles III of Spain), this figure rose to 86 per cent (Scott, 2007: 75). The noble character of the Spanish diplomatic corps significantly contributed to the general lack in the process of professionalisation. It contrasted with its 'veteran diplomats' of the sixteenth century, since by the eighteenth century, over 60 per cent of Spanish ambassadors only took on one mission 'with almost half of all posts being held for less than four years' (Scott, 2007: 75).

The role of Castile in the period of the golden age of diplomatic representation, starting from the late-seventeenth century, becomes negligible, as it struggled to fight off imperial decline. In other words, the

[31] From 1700 to 1746, the newly titled kingdom of Spain was ruled by its first Bourbon king, Phillip V, Louis XIV's grandson. Spanish diplomacy during this period was significantly overshadowed and directed by the French, who actually took over in the name of Spain at Utrecht. Spanish diplomacy regained a more prominent and autonomous place after the death of Louis XIV in 1715 (Bély, 1990: 295).

noble monopoly for Castile was not a decisively positive factor in its search for power and jurisdictional accumulation, at least not to the extent it played in its earlier phases of expansion; its seventeenth-century ambassadors did not serve the same function as French diplomats did for France. A short and simple explanation for the shift and aristocratisation of its ambassadorial practices can be based on the hold of France over Iberian politics in the late-seventeenth century. For now, existing research to my knowledge fails to assess the point at which the social origins or occupational backgrounds of Iberian ambassadors during the seventeenth century became more prominent, and whether this was a sudden or gradual shift. However, some elements of explanation can be found in the search for new informal diplomatic strategies linked to reputation and precedence – favouring the use of high nobles – as well as geopolitical and jurisdictional factors at the local, European, and overseas levels.

First, Castile's networks served the Crown well since 'by 1620, [it] maintained residents even with Turks and heretics', who were also the 'strongest prop' of its declining empire (Mattingly, 1966: 211). '*Reputación* (reputation, status, credibility)' had been an important feature of Castilian foreign policy, but precedence took on a more accentuated dimension from the second half of the sixteenth century (Levin, 2002: 234). This translated into an insistence 'on standing or sitting in places of greater honor than their French counterparts' and reflected 'the magnitude of the issues at stake: control of Italy, the balance of power in Europe, and a new understanding of the world geopolitical situation' (Levin, 2002: 235). Castilian diplomats had to deal with the crisis facing the monarchy after the Treaty of the Pyrenees (1659) between Louis XIV and Phillip IV, after which 'new diplomatic strategies' had to be found (Carrió-Invernizzi, 2014: 610). Castilian diplomats' advantages consisted in 'extensive networks of mobility' essential to communication (610).[32] Carrió-Invernizzi argues that they developed a plethora of informal practices such as 'ceremonies, rumours, the exchange of gifts, conspicuous consumption, or the conflicting interests of imperfect diplomacy' and developed 'a greater degree of autonomy' (610). In spite of financial difficulties and lack of state resources, Hispanic ambassadors were able to keep up 'the world of appearances and develop a certain expertise in informal diplomacy', strategies which were more available to – and

[32] This network had been characteristic since the sixteenth century (Mattingly, 1966: 175).

favoured the choice of – a higher nobility. Carrió-Invernizzi emphasises the culture of gift exchange, in which women were particularly important because 'well connected with English members of Parliament' who assisted the Spanish Ambassador in England 'in gathering valuable political information' (2014: 613). This further highlights the role of English MPs in ambassadorial networks, as discussed above.

Second, there are a number of local, regional, and overseas geopolitical factors. In spite of the gradual decline of the empire inside and outside Europe, ambassadors did wield significant influence by laying 'the groundwork which would lead Holland to become Spain's newest ally', showing 'a desacralisation of diplomacy' where 'religious matters had receded into the background' (Carrió-Invernizzi, 2014: 614). The alliance with Holland was important in the face of a dominant France. This does give us some important clues as to the role of diplomats in the social property relations of the Castilian Empire, since 'Olivares had already greatly secularised the practice of the embassies, to propel the alliance with the Huguenots and to deal with a clientele of noble rebels' (614). Considering the importance given to French, English, and Dutch embassy chapels in the development of extraterritoriality, we see here, again, that another power – Castile – was developing very different strategies such as 'desacralisation' to extend their authority, thereby enriching the manifestations of early modern extraterritoriality. This is particularly striking considering the way in which Castilian imperial expansion was shaped by Christian theology and by members of the clergy pre-seventeenth century. In other words, there seems to have been a similar process to France of required collaboration with the nobles by securing them into ambassadorial posts.

The Castilian case also presents unique instances of a monarchy using specific members of its court – and of its politically fragmented society – to advance its geopolitical interests and represent the Crown overseas, again disrupting the factor of 'internal reasons' in this case. Representation and use of second-order nobles and individuals from various social and occupational backgrounds – such as navigators, adventurers, *conquistadores* – played a significant diplomatic role for its imperial expansion during the earlier phase of the sixteenth and seventeenth centuries (Bély, 2007: 345). Cortez presented himself as an envoy of the Castilian king and of the pope (345). By the eighteenth century, according to Herzog, '[m]ilitary men, settlers, administrators, promoters of economic activities, and scientists gradually became major actors on the political and diplomatic scene' of the overseas Iberian Empire

(2015a: 94). They performed the three functions expected of diplomats; representation, information, and negotiation: 'they informed the courts and local authorities about how to proceed, collected information, and negotiated with rival parties' (94). And they also were key at expansion – or jurisdictional accumulation – as these activities, 'including exploring and using the land, were also means by which to press for additional territorial claims' (94).

4.4 Conclusion

To sum up, the last section of this chapter raised (1) the importance of landed gentry and MPs in England's diplomatic missions; (2) the importance of jurisdictional internal conflicts and diplomatic diversity in the Dutch Republic; (3) the rise of diplomatic aristocracy in France as a factor of Louis XIV's necessary collaboration with social elites and maintenance of old regime Europe; and (4) the Castilian rise of diplomatic aristocracy in the context of relative imperial decline and various geopolitical factors requiring collaborating with the nobles.

Some general characteristics associate France and Castile on one side, and England and the Dutch Republic on the other. While the first side displays crucial strategies of collaboration between aristocrats and ruling monarchies, the latter's strategies of ambassadorial recruitment were more driven by the legal peculiarities and ad hoc requirements of their political and economic constellations and class structures. Nevertheless, in all cases, the actors employed by these extraterritorial strategies of representation, negotiation, and information were also actors for expansion. They were more diverse and varied than usually portrayed, and were either key actors of jurisdictional accumulation, or created conditions for these practices. More specifically, considering the typology used in this project to differentiate between different contexts and outcomes of jurisdictional accumulation, Spanish and French aristocratisation is better characterised as transplants of authority, since their model of diplomacy led the way in Europe and gave ambassadors' function of representation and thus jurisdictional standing more emphasis over the previous roles of information gathering.

In contrast, the English and Dutch cases are more easily considered as transports of authority, since they had a more limited long-term impact and relied on a broader variety of actors whose inferior status made them less able to implant their jurisdictional prerogatives and practices. This alternative typology, if necessarily imperfect and generalising, nevertheless contributes to countering the narrow and institutional role of ambassadors in conventional histories of international relations and international law focused on the modernisation and rationalisation of the state system through extraterritoriality as defined by the emergence of permanent embassies.

In conclusion, linking the historiography on the social origins of diplomats to the concept of social property relations helps to reveal essential strategies and opportunities for sovereigns to shape their diplomatic service. It suggests the collaboration between the noble classes and sovereigns at the European level (not just in the French case), as well as the importance of the legal system, jurisdictional divisions, commercial interests, and merchant nobility for England and the Dutch Republic.

In effect, aristocratisation may have slowed down the professionalisation of the diplomatic corps, but perhaps more importantly, it entrenched foreign policy and international negotiation as an aristocratic activity, in spite of the rise of English and Dutch maritime powers. In other words, it was not an inevitable, or particularly capitalist or modern development, but one driven by the general context of jurisdictional accumulation, that is how sovereign rulers found ways to secure their dynastic interests through increasing rights, status, and functions.

Thus, extraterritoriality and other hybrid forms of personal and territorial jurisdiction and sovereignty can be illustrated by shifts in the social origins of diplomats and in the social property relations and legal systems they operated in. Moreover, they resulted in rendering some actors more legitimate than others through different strategies and through establishing – or attempting to establish – the continuing rule of a particular class, in this case European aristocracies. However, this rule was not an inevitable outcome of a general bourgeois revolution or of the slow European march to modernity and capitalism. It was a contested and differentiated process, which emerged as the product of various strategies of elite collaboration and military compromise. Moreover, it cannot be understood separately from the history of consular diplomacy, however much the status of consuls diverged in terms of state administration and legal and political theory compared to ambassadors during the seventeenth century. We will now turn to this neglected history.

5

Consuls

Consuls were most often merchants, sometimes military men, who were elected or commissioned with varying judicial and commercial prerogatives. Their central function was to represent a 'nation' of foreign residents and merchants in crucial trading ports and cities, to protect and in many cases exercise jurisdiction over them. They could also be useful in terms of gathering significant political and commercial information. Consuls were therefore complex types of diplomatic actors. Their status as public ministers was disputed because of their lack of both letters of representation and of immunities, rendering them outside the hierarchies of diplomatic royal agents; a situation exacerbated by their lower social origins and professional backgrounds.

Overseas consuls have been largely excluded from the history of early modern diplomacy and extraterritoriality. In spite of the difficulties in assessing their role – consuls left behind them a large paper trail that constitutes a very rich resource, but it is also painstakingly slow and difficult to research – the neglect remains surprising since consuls have also been considered forerunners of the development and implementation of extraterritorial rights and spaces through commercial practices, treaties, and capitulatory regimes from the late medieval period onwards. In response to this puzzle, Chapter 1 argued that, by narrowly and reductively referring to Grotius, classic diplomatic historians of extraterritoriality exclusively focused on the function and privileges of representation and immunity a priori excluding consuls. As this classic history has been largely adopted by International Relations (IR) scholars, the neglect of consular history has contributed to a confusing array of definitions of extraterritoriality, and to impoverished analyses of the relations between emerging practices of modern international law, mercantilism, and capitalism.

In response, this chapter retraces consuls' different practices of extraterritoriality through four parameters: their jurisdictional functions and privileges, the policies and strategies developed in their name, the implications of their social origins, and their relations to trading communities. These are followed by a case study focused on merchants' relations to the roles of consuls and ambassadors in the French embassy in Istanbul from the 1660s to 1680s. From these analyses, the neglect of consular history becomes even more surprising, as the distinctions drawn between the roles of consuls and ambassadors appear less clear and have important implications for understanding different strategies of expansion in the Mediterranean.[1] Moreover, consuls engaged in complex and varied relations to trading communities and to their sending authorities, enjoyed significant immunities and privileges, and provide a rich terrain of jurisdictional arrangements, divisions, and innovations that shaped various forms of mercantilism in the early modern Mediterranean.

Thus, the chapter fulfils two objectives. First, it provides a rich array of cases and practices that retrace the extraterritorial and diplomatic history of consuls so as to redress their neglect in the domains of IR and international law. Second, through this analysis, the chapter shows that consular jurisdictional spaces and practices contributed to justifying and shaping separate legal spaces for diplomacy and trade between Christian and non-Christian actors in respective Western, Eastern, and Southern parts of the Mediterranean. It argues that these spaces are better understood according to the concept of jurisdictional accumulation shaped in this case by assumptions of social and cultural superiority. The jurisdictional angle helps to avoid the reductive binaries of the political diplomat versus the commercial consul, as well as of personal versus territorial concepts of sovereignty, and provides a new spectrum with which to link and differentiate these actors and their practices. This argument is further pushed in Chapter 7, which joins recent efforts (e.g. Nuzzo, 2017; Windler, 2017b) to expose how early modern consuls played a significant role in shaping crucial distinctions for the nineteenth century international legal order.

Section 5.1 presents a general overview of early modern consular history, followed by the functions and privileges of consuls, namely their extensive jurisdictional prerogatives, their immunities, and how these related to the prohibition on trading. Section 5.2 discusses the policies and strategies for the development of each consular service under review;

[1] This area is chosen over other European cases of consular development, because it brings together and in competition the four empires and provides significant clues to understand legal binaries that developed in later international legal orders relating to extraterritoriality.

the French – as leaders in this domain with the reforms led by Colbert in the mid-seventeenth century – as well as the English and Dutch, which both dominated trade in the Mediterranean in the early-seventeenth century.[2] Section 5.3 discusses the social origins and composition of each service. Merchants largely and unsurprisingly dominate, alongside a proportion of military men and commoners. They were attracted to consulates for the potential of commercial gain but also for the social advancement they could provide. Section 5.4 presents the relation between consuls and trading communities, in terms of their mutual utility, their distrust of each other, and need for collaboration either in support or against their sending authorities.

These first four sections discuss key criteria for how consuls provided opportunities for jurisdictional accumulation as transports of authority, for themselves, their sovereigns, or for a mediating actor such as the English Levant Company, the Dutch Directorate, or the French Chambre de Commerce de Marseille (CCM). These analyses confirm a jurisdictional line separating the non-Christian Eastern and Southern Mediterranean (including the Levant and North African regencies) from the Christian Western coast. This line was shaped through resistance from merchant communities to consuls' jurisdictional powers as well as assumptions of Christian superiority.

Section 5.5 goes deeper into specific examples of disputes and debates over the roles of ambassador and consul by focusing on the case of the unique French embassy and consulate in late-seventeenth-century Istanbul. The clash and overlap between aristocratic ambassadorial functions and consular merchant representation were the source and subject of debates and divergent strategies of diplomatic recruitment based on class divisions. Although this case is unique in many respects, it nevertheless illustrates how the relation between the two roles was more

[2] The Castilian Empire did not have a very significant consular service and could not compete with the French, Dutch, and English on this front, so for reasons of comparative value and space, they have not been included in this chapter. It would have been more interesting from the point of view of consuls to include the Venetian service in this comparison, but this would have required a more thorough analysis of Venice and the Italian states in other parts of the book, which was unfortunately not manageable. Moreover, the Venetian service was quickly losing ground in the face of the other empires in the Mediterranean and is therefore not susceptible to counter the arguments made below. For a comparative analysis of Venetian, French, Dutch, and English early-seventeenth-century consuls, see Steensgaard (1967). For an analysis of English and Venetian diplomatic links, see Fusaro (2015). See Chapter 6 for a brief discussion of Iberian consulates.

complex than is often portrayed and reveals conflicting strategies of aristocratisation and mercantilism. It also shows how merchants and consuls collaborated against aristocratisation to eventually benefit the Crown and its mercantilist policy, adding to the question of merchants' utility to consuls.

Finally, as with the previous chapter, the conclusion draws some distinctions between the cases according to the argument's adopted typology of jurisdictional accumulation as transplants and transports of authority. Considering the points made in the previous chapter for France's ambassadors as transplanting the authority of their sovereign, this can also be argued to be the case for consuls. The distinct model of French consular practices, focused on the deployment of extensive jurisdictional prerogatives with significant implications for the Mediterranean region and, as discussed in Chapter 7, for key legal binaries found in modern international law, provide significant reasons to consider this case as a transplant of authority, whereas the Dutch and English less successful attempts to control their consular services correspond better to transports of authority.

5.1 Functions and Privileges

5.1.1 General Remarks

Although consuls were active in the Mediterranean from the Middle Ages and the period of the crusades under various derivative statuses or titles (Ulbert, 2006: 10–11), the increase of trade and maritime expansion from the fifteenth and sixteenth centuries gave a new impetus to the institution. Consuls became a key factor of French, Dutch, and English foreign policies from the early-seventeenth century. Although consular activity was extremely varied and to a certain extent out of the control of sovereigns, there were nevertheless general patterns and similarities between French, English, Dutch, and to a lesser extent, Italian consuls. These were the most notable merchant communities to develop the practice from the sixteenth and seventeenth centuries in order to benefit from – and potentially overtake each other in – the lucrative trade with the Ottoman Empire and other trading communities. English goods were increasingly exported throughout the seventeenth century, especially for Italian markets, with an equivalent increase in the imports of Italian agricultural products and raw materials (Pagano de Divitiis, 1997: 70). Livorno became England's key trading port for its economic advantages thanks to low customs tariffs as well as its technological advances

(Pagano de Divitiis, 1997: 118). Taking over the Italian market was also a policy pursued by the Dutch (Pagano de Divitiis, 1997: 70). To do this, the English adapted and relied in the Western Mediterranean on several small companies, whereas the Eastern Mediterranean was controlled from the sixteenth century through the monopoly of the Levant Company. Fierce competition with the Dutch and Amsterdam's Levant merchants also defined international relations in this region. Although we cannot explore it here, it is important to recall that jurisdictional and commercial conflicts between the Dutch and English were also critical to their imperial expansions in Asia (Stern, 2011).

In the late-seventeenth century, France eventually took over from both the Dutch and English in the Levant as the dominant trading power, notably through its preferential diplomatic ties with the sultan at the Porte and through its close trade links and consular activities in what was called the Barbary regencies. The Levant consisted of the eastern part of the Ottoman Empire, from Greece to Egypt and Syria, whereas the Barbary regencies were the North African posts of the Ottoman Empire in Algiers, Tunis, and Tripoli in Libya.[3] The Republic of Salé and the kingdom of Morocco with its port of Tangier had a specific status regulated by separate treaties with European powers. The North African regencies were managed by a bey, dey, or pasha with significant autonomy from the sultan. The Castilian Empire had key agents in the Western part of the Mediterranean, through Aragon's and Italian ports and their activity with the regencies, especially Genoa. It was also part of complex corsairing and other military alliances and conflicts with the English and Dutch. However, it gradually became less influential in the region, and did not have a substantial consular service.

Consular representation belonged to port cities or places important for trade, not to capital cities where embassies were developed – with the exception of Istanbul, which was both. Consuls had a wide and complex set of (often conflicting) responsibilities towards the nation they represented, the local authorities, and towards their own ruler. In spite of some general similarities, consular services were better characterised by their differences in terms of appointment, remuneration, privileges, immunities,

[3] According to some historians, the term Barbary was a name given by Europeans to refer to lands inhabited by the Berber people. However, they had important negative connotations of lawlessness and unreliability, and referred to 'a place inhabited by infidels, renegades, barbarians, and pirates' (Heinsen-Roach, 2012: 5–6). I will therefore refrain from using the term where this is not necessary.

and political importance; and by the differences in their relations with ambassadors and other diplomatic posts. Regarding recruitment and appointment, the crucial difference consisted in whether consuls were elected or commissioned. Elected consuls (*electi*) were chosen by their local merchant communities and were often nationals of the trading city (and therefore 'foreign' to the nation they represented). Alternatively, they were chosen from members of the national resident and merchant community. Elected consuls were more the norm in Northern Europe. In contrast, commissioned consuls (*missi*) were sent by the sovereign or state as officials from that country. This model was most developed by the French and put in place in the mid- to late-seventeenth century. It was later adopted and deployed across the Mediterranean by other sovereigns and will therefore be more of a focus than other consular services.

Consuls' functions tend to belong to two broad categories: protection of and jurisdiction over merchants and maritime trade. In modern terms, consuls could be both notaries (or solicitors) and judges (Calafat, 2018a: 143). As notaries, they had to produce documents necessary to trading activities. As judges, consuls had to decide on disputes between individuals of the nation they represented or, though more rarely, between mixed cases involving native disputants. They also had to execute the decisions and, in some cases, sanction offenders. Generally, from the late-sixteenth century onwards, European nations (French, English, Dutch, Italian cities, Iberian, and Scandinavian) obtained from treaties with North African regencies and through capitulations in the Levant that consuls would have complete jurisdiction over cases between their own subjects, and in some cases, involvement in disputes involving one of their subjects (Pennell, 2009). In other words, to borrow Steensgaard's term, consuls were assured 'internal jurisdiction' (1967: 15) and often had a presence, oversight and perhaps right to judge in mixed cases, giving them some form of external jurisdiction.

However, there were also significant discrepancies between custom and treaties, which led to 'confused and vague practices' and a series of disputed cases across the region, eventually prompting the British to draw up the Foreign Jurisdiction Act in 1843 as a codification of existing practices (Pennell, 2009: 236). The confusions between custom and treaties complicating the behaviour of consuls were the result of the 'double function' of being solicitors and judges, with the aims 'to control their subjects as much as to protect them' (Pennell, 2009: 237). We will see in the Section 5.4 on trading communities how this played out in terms of consuls' conflictual relations to merchants and sending authorities.

Consuls were also at times used as information gatherers and more controversially, as diplomatic representatives of the sovereign or nation that commissioned or elected them; and they were in some cases able to negotiate for them (Ulbert, 2006: 14). The French service is looked at in more detail, as it developed more far-reaching privileges and functions than the English and Dutch, especially in its Southern and Eastern Mediterranean consulates.

5.1.2 *Jurisdictional Functions*

Jurisdictional functions are forms of extraterritorial power which contravene local sovereignty and assume a separation or sharing of local jurisdiction, obtained following continuous negotiations in Christian and non-Christian countries. The breadth and application of these functions varies according to disputes between nationals or mixed cases, whether over a civil or criminal matter. Although these powers did not necessarily appear as an encroachment on local power in certain regencies, as capitulations emerged as privileges granted to European powers with practical advantages for the Porte (who according to sharia law could not try non-Muslims), they soon became a way for merchants and consuls to assert themselves and gain significant commercial and diplomatic advantages. The fact that they were contested in North African regencies and ports, and even more so in Christian Mediterranean ports, shows that jurisdictional questions were as political as they were commercial.[4] The following focuses on the adjudicating, policing, and communication of laws constituting consuls' means of jurisdictional accumulation. These means constitute a historically specific relation of power rather than just invoking jurisdiction as a neutral term and empty category, a trap various authors tend to fall into when discussing early modernity.[5]

French consular policy is unique in the number of legal acts it produced to ensure the execution of its reforms. The first important document regulating French consuls' judicial functions is the royal

[4] The situation in Spain and Portugal was an extreme case. The particular jurisdictional regime offered no external jurisdiction possible under these sovereignties: no decision or sentence was possible by a consul or external representative in a contradictory case. However, France did have a privilege of a *juge conservateur* for French interests (Mézin, 1997: 39).

[5] For a discussion of the methodological implications of this for the concept of jurisdiction, see Introduction and Chapter 7.

ordonnance of 1681. Article 12 outlines consuls' civil and criminal jurisdiction, in accordance with the customs and capitulations with local sovereigns (i.e. full civil internal jurisdiction and a limited criminal external jurisdiction).[6] The ordonnance of 28 January 1687 prohibits French subjects from resolving disputes with other French subjects between themselves and commands the use of consuls for resolving any disputes (Mézin, 1997: 37). Judicial functions become further regulated by the royal edict of Versailles of June 1778, according to which consuls should 'render justice' according to 'easily observable rules', in a 'uniform manner' and 'as quickly as is required'. Article 7 of the ordonnance of 3 March 1781 states that consuls will exercise justice 'summarily and without cost'.

In addition to their judicial roles, consuls had important policing functions. Life in the regencies was increasingly regulated from the late-seventeenth century. Consuls were expected to maintain order in their department, including for merchant ships, to prevent disorder and ensure publicity of laws and regulations. Article 15 of title 9 of the ordonnance of 1681 gives consuls the right to expel 'French subjects with a scandalous life and conduct' (Mézin, 1997: 39). French subjects were expected to conduct themselves in an orderly fashion without compromising the tranquillity of the nation or the public order.

The legislation and correspondence of the period emphasises the fear of individuals 'dishonouring' the nation, creating problems with the host country, and with other merchants and nationals residing in foreign lands (Ulbert, forthcoming). Being of good faith, of honourable condition, and with good behaviour and morals were preconditions for being offered posts in the consulates, as well as for being allowed to travel. The Levant was an area particularly considered as a 'space of disorder, intrigues, and debauchery which required cleaning up'.[7]

[6] A consul's competence is general in terms of civil matters (i.e. 'disputes between merchants, navigators and others') and it is forbidden to claim justice from local authorities. Appeals to consular decisions taken in the Levant and North African regencies had to be made to the *parlement* in Aix-en-Provence, and to the *parlement* closest to the decision for other consulates. In principle, for mixed cases in the Levant and North Africa, a local judge was competent with the presence of the consul or a representative. In practice, the general custom was for the consul to be the judge for mixed cases. But decisions were fragile, generating a tendency for consuls to be conciliator or arbitrator rather than judge (Mézin, 1997: 38).

[7] 'foyers de désordres, de cabales et de débauches qu'il fallait assainir' (Farganel, 1996: 4 in Ulbert, forthcoming).

Mézin qualifies certain policing functions as a voluntary jurisdiction of maintaining police regulations, prohibiting meetings 'of any kind whatsoever', as well as visits to local powers. Sailors from merchant ships were forbidden to leave ship without the consul's authorisation and had to remain under the officers' charge. The prohibition on frequenting bars gave consuls permission to run a national ale house near the consulate. Residents and merchants were also prohibited from communicating or sharing any piece of cloth, textiles, or other objects bringing disease, above all plague (Mézin, 1997).

The communication of laws and regulations is an important function that emphasises the jurisdictional power of consuls, in terms of interpreting and policing the laws, but also symbolically in 'speaking' the law. Article 9 of the first title of the ordonnance of 1781 recalls the obligation for consuls to publicise ordonnances and royal decisions transmitted by the *secrétaire d'état de la marine* by reading them to the nation in an assembly (Mézin, 1997: 40).[8] In other words, through adjudicating, policing, and communicating laws, consuls held significant powers over merchants, and had to carefully navigate these relations so as to maintain their authority as much as their loyalty to the king.

As with all consuls, the possible functions of seventeenth-century English consuls were those of judge, solicitor, and spokesperson. Their main function was to determine 'disputes between merchants in the English factory, or between merchants and masters of English ships, or between the masters and their seamen' (Barbour, 1928: 567). However, they also performed a wide array of functions pertaining to the affairs of Englishmen abroad, testament to the versatile and socially experienced skills required, let alone the difficulties of dealing with the English merchant, who was considered by some at least as:

> an expert smuggler, a high-hearted profiteer, an unrepentant dealer in contraband, an exporter of coin and bullion contrary to law, and by no means unversed in the dark arts by which persons who must be squared are squared.
>
> (Barbour, 1928: 568)

[8] There are a range of other functions (certifying and redacting documents, informing and spying, religious duties, and various cultural and hospitality functions due to travellers and visitors to the regencies) which contribute to consuls' broad social and cultural role, but the ones discussed above remain the most important for understanding the jurisdictional importance of consuls.

English consuls under Charles II were also at risk of imprisonment, banishment, and as happened in the case of the consul in Algiers, murder (Barbour, 1928: 569). Consuls in the early-eighteenth century also played significant roles as spies and informants (Black, 2001: 139–140). However, the task of negotiating trade treaties was left to diplomats and envoys (Black, 2001: 151).

In practice, the jurisdictional authority of English consuls in France and Italy went no further than 'informal arbitration' (Barbour, 1928: 576). Horn also shows that English consuls had different jurisdictional roles in the North African regencies, which were also concerned with political matters such as ransoming captives from corsairing, as preconditions to improving trade in the region (1961: 244–245). This is a function they shared with the Dutch, and which was even more pronounced in their case. The Levant Company left the government to deal with these posts, as they were too dangerous (Berridge, 2009: 76). Charles II pushed for their special treatment, and, post-Revolution, Thomas Baker in Algiers was paid £600 a year (£300 equipage in addition to bills for extraordinaries). A similar case occurred in Tripoli. They were the only two consuls to be salaried (Horn, 1961: 245). By 1754, this remuneration policy was applied to all consuls in the North African regencies (Horn, 1961: 246). It was then slowly applied to all consuls by the end of the eighteenth century, but they were still also dependent on fees and perquisites (Horn, 1961: 247).

Dutch jurisdictional functions were similar to the French and English in general terms, but they particularly struggled to apply the terms of the capitulations that benefited them in the North African regencies. Section 5.1 has already discussed the specific difficulties they faced and the attempts by the Republic to remedy these. In the Levant, their functions were less problematic. However, in the Christian ports of the Mediterranean, they faced the same jurisdictional obstacles as their counterparts.

The jurisdictional frameworks and privileges maintained by consuls were linked to their ability to trade. In the Levant, this ability to trade was directly linked to the capitulations. This is where the French were able to develop a stronger authority and legacy of immunity, both from their nation of merchants and from local authorities. French consular immunity in the Levant was recognised by their capitulations in 1601 (Steensgaard, 1967: 18). English consuls were allowed to trade and relied on this to survive financially, have leverage and collect information. Their immunity in the Ottoman Empire was recognised by a capitulation of

1604 (Steensgaard, 1967: 18). The Dutch were not allowed to trade in the Levant, but they faced important remuneration struggles that did little to assert their authority.

5.1.3 French Immunities and the Prohibition on Trading

The French began to restrict the trading function of their consuls in 1618 and the prohibition on trading was firmly established in 1691. This prohibition was linked to French consuls' status as commissaries of the king with some public role of representation. Therefore, their claim to diplomatic immunity – and thus diplomatic status – was stronger than other nations. If they did not, in the eighteenth century, benefit from a full and absolute independence and immunity, this was in principle recognised in practice or officially by some states (Mézin, 1997: 24). Consuls enjoyed personal immunity from local jurisdictions in criminal matters involving them, their residence, and their consulate. Trading could in effect threaten this immunity, further justifying the prohibition.[9]

Prohibition was also justified by the need to open the Mediterranean trade and avoid monopolies by certain merchants or family of merchants. It was also justified so that consuls could focus on their mission to serve the king, on issues that 'interest the government, the military and commercial navy, and the king's subjects', and to 'report back on their conduct, monitor it, and at times reprimand it' (Mézin, 1997). Prohibition was also justified by the fact that French consuls were magistrates, with a 'jurisdiction, a function, and rights', which would clash with the interests of a merchant and make them impartial judges (00).

However, there were numerous exceptions made to French consuls' prohibition on trading with explicit authorisations from the administration (Mézin, 1997: 25–26), or cases where it was implicitly tolerated though not officially granted. However, if a merchant-consul went bankrupt, they had to leave the consular office. In general, the prohibition on trading was not very well respected in the eighteenth century but cases of infraction belonged to second-order posts except for Algiers (though in this case infractions were mostly by chancellors) and for Seyde (where

[9] French consuls could also be exempt from certain impositions and taxes. They also had the benefit of lodging for military men and those in service for national or bourgeois militia. All these prerogatives were necessary for maintaining independence and security (Mézin, 1997: 36).

Mézin suspects bad faith on the part of the nation). But in most important posts, both in Christian and non-Christian ports, consuls tended to get closer and closer to a 'consular ideal' in terms of respecting regulations and exclusively serving the king's missions (Mézin, 1997: 27).

This justifies the understanding of the French consular service as inherently jurisdictional: how it used formal diplomatic rhetoric and legal texts to standardise its institutions according to royal authority, and how it made the most out of its merchants, rather than be driven by them, as in the English and Dutch cases. French mercantilism relied on jurisdictional prerogatives and on consular extraterritoriality. It thus differed from the English merchants' and Dutch Republic's more ad hoc approach dependent on local conditions, which led to separating the Levantine from the rest of the Mediterranean according to either local merchants' interests or those of the Directorate of the Levant Trade and Navigation, in Amsterdam.

5.2 Policies and Strategies

5.2.1 The French Consular Service

The early modern French consular service reached its most mature stage in 1789 with a total of 129 posts, including 82 consuls and 47 vice consuls spread out mostly in the Mediterranean, but also in Europe and North America (Mézin, 2006: 37). Between 1715 and 1792, French consular personnel totalled 650 individuals, including dragomans (translators or interpreters) and chancellors (responsible for the administration and bureaucracy of the consulate's chancery, which authenticated commercial acts). This figure is over the whole period (i.e. not simultaneously). The ratio of French merchants to consuls was approximately six to one, a testament to their role in shaping a relatively dense network of local administrators and representatives across the Mediterranean (Ulbert, forthcoming). The eighteenth century significantly increased the numbers of personnel in comparison to the sixteenth and seventeenth centuries, as the period between 1530 and 1660 accounts for sixty consuls (Poumarède, 2001: 85). However, the seventeenth century is also a crucial period of growth, increasing from twenty consuls in 1643 to seventy-one in 1715 at any one time (Ulbert, 2018: 117) and, over the same period, ninety-two consulate and vice consulate offices are accounted for (Ulbert, 2019: 17). The growth of these numbers linked to the institutional innovations and expansion of French trade and influence in the

Mediterranean during the seventeenth century render the jurisdictional prerogatives attached to these posts particularly relevant. This chapter therefore focuses more on the seventeenth and early-eighteenth centuries as key periods of initial consular growth.

Before the mid-seventeenth-century reforms, French consular posts were venal offices and effectively reserved to leading merchant families and low nobility. They were bought from the king as part of a broader ensemble of 'commercial, patrimonial and social strategies' by which consulate-owners earned revenue and increased their social and career prospects (Poumarède, 2001: 92). They rarely exercised the function of consuls themselves and either sublet or farmed the office to lower-order individuals such as soldiers, sailors, or petty merchants to do the often-difficult overseas job as consuls or vice consuls. Consulates were thus a significant way to improve one's social status (alongside matrimonial alliances and military glory) without much effort.

An impetus of reform begins in France in the 1660s with a series of royal acts and ordonnances spread over two decades and mostly issued from the newly created posts of the *secrétaire d'état des affaires étrangères* and the *secrétaire d'état de la marine* (occupied by Colbert). The general aim was to increase the number of consular posts while strengthening their link to royal authority. The Crown was concerned about losing revenue from increasing trade by merchants from Marseille – and from the South of France more generally. The various reforms were meant to reflect a subtle balance between on the one hand maintaining the thriving exercise of commercial activity by leading merchants and the new trading companies, and on the other making sure those activities were sources of revenue for the Crown and were conducted in the king's interests. This was also a key challenge for the English Crown but one that it managed significantly differently (Stein, 2012: 101).

Stopping this practice was a major objective of Colbert's reforms, alongside capturing revenue generated through the sale of offices to redirect it to the state, and deal with the various complaints and bad reputation of French maritime activity these practices led to. In the Levant, this reputation was particularly bad, as the French organisation of its network of representation, that is the relations between the consul, its sending authority, the local nation, and various principals at home, was 'complicated and weak' (Steensgaard, 1967: 51). In contrast to its European rivals, and especially the English, where the Crown simply and efficiently delegated all consular matters in the region to the Levant Company, the French complex network was primarily a 'safeguard to protect interests unrelated to the duties of the consulates' (Steensgaard, 1967: 53).

The French assumed they had the privilege of precedence over other European powers, and were particularly prone to using prestige, connections and cash to gain advantages (Steensgaard, 1967: 21). Pierre Ariste's 1667[10] treatise also emphasises the importance of ceremonial and dress for the first half of the seventeenth-century consuls.[11] The treatise attempts to explain why French (or more exactly Provençal) trade significantly reduced in the Levant in the 100 years prior to 1667 in spite of the care put in to 'employing only persons with the best possible qualities for the post'.[12] Rather than focusing on issues with consuls' characters or behaviour, Ariste provides a fascinating account of the complex networks and competition between various commodities, linked to the opening of new trade routes by the English and Dutch.

If the French could not physically stop trade advances by the English and Dutch, they could reform their consular services. The main objectives of the reforms were to stop the farming of consulates and ensure that nominated consuls actually took on the post themselves, to reorganise the remuneration and nomination of consuls through the *Marine* state department and the CCM, and to enforce various restrictions and regulations on the behaviour of consuls, merchants, and travellers, not least the consuls' prohibition on trading.

French consuls were gradually forbidden to trade and make profit from any commerce, except for the usual 2 per cent consular tax on transactions, the *consulage*. The process of reforming, codifying, and institutionalising the practice of French consuls began with Colbert, but it was a slow and gradual evolution. Louis Phélipeaux, comte de Pontchartrain, who became the *secrétaire d'état de la marine*, conceived of the royal nomination of consuls and of replacing their remuneration

[10] I deeply thank Jörg Ulbert for bringing Ariste's work to my attention and for his useful notes and transcription of the treatise. Ariste (1617–1697) starts his career with some minor diplomatic missions, before becoming one of the first three 'premier commis des Affaires étrangères' under the Secretary Jean-Louis Brienne. He is then later commissioned by the new Secretary Hugues de Lionne to write memoranda on ambassadors. His treatise on consuls (1667) may be one of those or it may have been commissioned by the chancellor Séguier, in whose archives the treatise was found. The treatise is a thorough analysis of all French consulates in the region pre-1660s and provides a rich analysis of early modern international political economy.

[11] Ariste (1667: ch. 4, point 9).

[12] Ariste (1667: ch. 3).

through customs duties by fixed salaries in 1691, as the salaries were an easier way to control the practices and nominations of consuls (Boulanger, 2006: 128).

A crucial institution to emerge somewhat strengthened from these reforms was the CCM, albeit at the price of accepting the French kingdom's authority over its rebellious and increasingly powerful port city. The CCM was created in 1599 to protect maritime trade in the Mediterranean and counter the competition of corsairing and the threat of piracy from the so-called Barbary Coast. It was composed of leading merchants from Marseille, who had become increasingly rich and powerful and had turned the city into a leading Mediterranean port regularly threatening – throughout the fifteenth and sixteenth centuries – to become more independent and autonomous from the kingdom of France as well as from the regional authority of the Parlement de Provence (situated in the nearby rival city of Aix-en-Provence) (Takeda, 2011).[13]

Thus, through the consular reforms of 1691, the CCM becomes financially responsible for consuls' salaries, in exchange of a new tax, the *tonnelage*, due by every ship entering Marseille from the Levant and North Africa (Boulanger, 2006: 128). However, because the CCM partially funded the payment of the French ambassador in Istanbul, it was relieved of financing French consulates in Spain and Italy (Boulanger, 2006: 128, n. 13). This is an example of the complex compromises made between the French Crown and Marseille's authorities.[14]

Alongside these negotiations with Marseille, France's strategy of jurisdictional accumulation is observed through the consular reforms and the production of legal texts by its emerging state bureaucracy. A memorandum by Maurepas as *secrétaire d'état de la marine* in 1731 illustrates the discrepancy between royal intention and what was happening on the ground (Calafat, 2018a). However, it nevertheless gives us some indication of what the royal council was hoping to establish, or

[13] Aix was also the judicial seat for the admiralty court concerned with strictly maritime matters. It also dealt with appeals in civil cases from consuls' decisions, and with criminal cases involving corporal punishment, for which French consuls did not have jurisdiction (Steensgaard, 1967: 218).

[14] The ruling magistrates of Marseille were also called consuls until 1660, since consuls in the Southern French region of Languedoc and Provence were locally elected magistrates. Their functions were completely separate from those of overseas consuls. After 1660 and Louis XIV's suppression of Marseille's secession from the kingdom, they were called *échevins*.

what it wanted to project was happening in its consular network. The memorandum lists all the various sources for establishing the jurisdictional functions of consuls (royal ordonnances of 1681, 1689, 1719), as well as treaties signed with other European powers such as those concluded in Madrid in 1667 and Utrecht in 1713. The memorandum also refers to imperial decrees and to custom as further legal sources. For Maurepas, the consul is a representative of the king, a 'commercial stimulant' (*adjuvant du commerce*), a factor for growth and economic domination. The consul is a royal agent who contributes to the regulation of foreign trade and must benefit the whole nation. Maurepas distinguishes between a voluntary and a contentious type of jurisdiction held by consuls.

However, actual consular practices do not match these official projections. A crucial difference exists between the jurisdictional functions of consuls in the Ottoman regencies of the Levant and North Africa, versus those exercised in the Christian ports of the Western Mediterranean. In the Levant and North Africa, consuls enjoyed much wider jurisdictional powers, and could be considered public ministers (*ministres publics*) in the sense – required by theorists – of an ambassador or royal representative (Calafat, 2018a: 147).

Such a status was not accepted in Western European ports, where local and French merchants contested the oversight and duties of consuls desired by the king. Late-seventeenth-century merchants in Livorno, for example, argued that as Christians of Italy, Iberia, and of any other non-Ottoman port, they did not require a consul whose powers would curtail their freedom to trade, because, in Christian ports they were not subject to the wills of 'barbarians and infidels', who were seen as bent on extracting money from the public through avania (*avanies*), a practice which required consuls to, according to Maurepas, 'maintain the respectable behaviour of the French' (in Calafat, 2018a: 148).[15]

Thus, merchants considered their trade to be inhibited by the role of consuls, operating as magistrates having to discipline merchants who in their minds were right to contest the system of capitulations. In response, consuls complained that merchants were being selfish and only wanted to increase their personal interests and gains without any interference. Maurepas's memorandum indirectly acknowledges these conflicts by

[15] Avania were a form of collective responsibility, debts incurred by the whole nation of merchants in an Ottoman port or city in which an infringement of the capitulations had occurred (Coller, 2011: 212).

asserting that consuls in the Levant, North Africa, and in the ports of 'Italy, Spain, Portugal and the North have always been and are in true possession of consular jurisdiction, are thus public ministers, without there being any obstacles to these measures from those countries' sovereigns' (in Calafat, 2018a: 153). The memorandum thus aimed to settle the matter for merchants, to remind them of the authority of consuls, even though this authority remained largely ignored in Christian consulates.[16]

Finally, to conclude on French policy and strategy, the previous chapter discussed the emergence of a sphere reserved to inland Europe to protect the *droit public de l'Europe* as an old regime court network of absolutist sovereigns. However, finding adequate sources as evidence to whether policy and practices were actively and intentionally shaped to allow for the development of an aristocratic ambassadorial sphere remains a difficult, if not impossible task. Therefore, it is equally difficult to find a way of proving whether such measures and practices were intended to separate the European aristocratic network from an extra-European consular and mercantile network. This chapter does not claim to be able to fully explore these hypotheses.

However, raising these questions is justified, considering the preceding discussion and archival work explored in the final section. The idea of a French – and eventually European – dual strategy of jurisdictional accumulation consists in an aristocratic ambassadorial strategy mainly in mainland Europe, and a mercantile consular strategy which mainly functioned in the Eastern and Southern Mediterranean. Exploring this hypothesis allows us to test a jurisdictional spectrum that contests the way in which the histories of consular jurisdiction and ambassadorial diplomacy separated in twentieth-century historiography into their parallel yet isolated political and commercial avenues, a critique also raised by Heinsen-Roach (2012).

With these hypotheses in mind concerning the East–West divide and a broader jurisdictional spectrum, the chapter now moves to analyse

[16] Another example of this divide can be seen in the way in which European consuls' prerogatives were curtailed in Western European cities. Colbert pressured Louis XIV to not easily accept foreign consuls on French soil. After the appointment of Colbert, Louis XIV refused to fully recognise Sir David English as consul in Bordeaux in spite of a prior acceptance. He also hindered the development of the Dutch service, by 'trying to force all foreign merchants to use French brokers' (Barbour, 1928: 573). Thus, consular policy was also used as a strategy to counter contending attempts at jurisdictional accumulation by European powers.

English and Dutch policies and strategies, different in many respects but similar in terms of being more merchant-driven.

5.2.2 The English and Dutch Consular Services

The English did not have a clear and unified strategy concerning consular diplomacy that could rival the French model.[17] English/British consular activity and diplomacy was mostly concerned with, and shaped by, merchants and relations with non-European powers, and most consuls operated in the Mediterranean. The Levant Company – originally called the Turkey Company – played a crucial role, albeit only for consuls in the Levantine parts of the Ottoman Empire.[18]

The English consular service was mostly divided between, on the one hand, the Levant, that is the Eastern Mediterranean and the area under Ottoman rule – which came under the authority of the twelve merchants of the Turkey Company from 1581 (Boogert, 2003: 618) – and on the other the Western and Southern Mediterranean, which was originally self-governed but increasingly became the subject of state prerogative as trade in the region increased. The later-seventeenth century saw various attempts by the Crown to establish its authority over its Western and Southern Mediterranean consuls, and to apply its extraterritorial jurisdiction on disputes between merchants. Instead, merchants,

[17] The contemporary texts wholly or with significant sections dedicated to the English and British early modern consular service all rely on pioneering studies by Barbour (1928) and Wood (1935); Horn (1961: 237–258); Steensgaard (1967); Platt (1971: 5–15); Anderson (1989); Pennell (1989, 2009); Saunders (1994); Pagano de Divitiis (1997); Black (2001); Berridge (2009); Mather (2011); Stein (2012); Fusaro (2015); Barbano (2018). There are fewer texts in English on the Dutch consular service: Steensgaard (1967); Israel (1989); Boogert (2003); Heinsen-Roach (2012, 2015); Ebben (2017, 2018); Allain (2018).

[18] The Turkey Company became the Levant Company after a merger with the Venice Company and a new charter in 1592 (Berridge, 2009: 2). Fifty-three men were admitted and another twenty given the option on the condition of a fee, slightly opening a market which remained highly lucrative thanks to the monopoly on Venice currants, wine, and the overland route to the Indies (Brenner, 1972: 370). The Turkey company was founded in 1581 and emerged out of the Russia Company and the split between the Merchant Adventurers and other groups of merchants concerned with the Eastern trades through the Asian continent rather than through maritime and Portuguese-controlled routes. The 'exceptional wealth and influence' of the Turkey Company's original twelve members 'gave them access to the highest circles of national decision-making' (Brenner, 1972: 369). Note that the royal instructions of 29 December 1680 to the new ambassador at the Porte Lord Chandos, for example, still used the original name 'Turkey Company' (in Berridge, 2009: 289, appendix 3).

especially those in Italian cities who were supporting and supported by the local authorities, worked to maintain their autonomy and principles of free trade rather than be governed directly by the state or by a corporation (Stein, 2012: 93–145).

English consular activity was shaped by merchants' interests, which led them to innovate, adapt, and experiment with various jurisdictional practices and institutions (e.g. the various companies in the Western Mediterranean, the Levant Company, or the embassy in Istanbul) (Saunders, 1994). These contributed to shaping different European legal spaces, though the East–West divide remained an issue for all European powers. The French undertook a vast programme of reform aimed at all its consuls, and only managed very gradually and slowly to defeat all resistance from merchants. The English could not overcome the separation between the Levant and the rest of the Mediterranean, in spite of the kingdom's attempts to control consular and merchant activity from above.

All English consuls would also engage in trading, but posts in the Western Mediterranean were also paid by their merchant communities depending on how they determined the amount of *consulage* and how it was raised, bargaining with 'the merchants, masters and factors on the spot' (Barbour, 1928: 563). However, if consuls in the Levant were less subject to the shifts and pressures of royal reforms, they 'had unusually important responsibilities' (Berridge, 2009: 75). They were paid by the Levant Company, which depended on the 2 per cent *consulage* collected by consuls in Levantine ports, as well as on rates or impositions 'levied on its members at home' and 'paid on all goods imported or exported' (Wood, 1935: 209). They took their instructions from the Levant Company through the ambassador in Istanbul. As the royal instructions to Lord Chandos in 1680 state:

> 8. In matters relating to Trade you are to comply and put in execucion such Rules and Directions as you shall from time to time receive from ye Turky Company [Levant Company] and not be wanting in any Thing to perform all good Offices towards Them, to their entire satisfaction.
>
> (in Berridge, 2009: 290)

The consular strategy is more apparent and efficient when left to the Levant Company. The ambassador in Istanbul was responsible for opening and naming the Levantine consulates, but this task was officially removed in 1605 and given to the Levant Company. However, the ambassador's influence and appointment of second-order posts remained (Berridge, 2009: 76). William Harbone, first ambassador at the Porte in 1583, selected the consul for Aleppo in 1580 before even being established himself. Setting up the consular service was therefore a priority for the Crown and the Levant Company's plans in the Eastern Mediterranean (Berridge, 2009: 75). The Levant Company was regulated, as it differed from the model of the joint-stock East India Company. Regulated companies did not trade as legal persons and operated more like a guild and governing structure for their trading members (Pettigrew & Stein, 2017: 342). The Levant Company held the monopoly of Levantine trade from 1581, and operated factories in Aleppo, Istanbul, and Smyrna. In each of those cities it maintained a consul, a treasurer, a chancellor, and native staff at fixed salaries (Anderson, 1989). The situation was different in the case of the ambassador at Istanbul, who was a royal agent but also the consul for that city.

Before 1649, consuls in the Western Mediterranean were selected by their merchant communities, until 'the Council of State of the Commonwealth' and later the protector took over this task (Barbour, 1928: 556). Charles II took advantage of his return to the throne in 1660 to significantly increase the numbers of consuls so as to reward his royalist friends and collect more intelligence and information. This was halted in 1663 by a House of Commons resolution limiting the royal prerogative and giving authority back to merchants' communities to appoint their representatives (Barbour, 1928: 560; Horn, 1961: 237). On the ground, merchants used the assistance of the Crown when it was in their interest, and resisted it when it was not (Stein, 2012: 108–110).[19] In spite of its many attempts to impose itself, the Crown's authority remained very limited. We will return to this question and to the problematic relationships between consuls and merchants in Section 5.3.

The Dutch had the most extensive consular service in the seventeenth century (Barbour, 1928: 574). Their consuls became mostly state appointed by the early-seventeenth century, and between 1616 and 1686, the Dutch Republic created twenty-eight new consulates in North Africa, an exceptionally large number. This followed its first capitulation to the Ottoman Empire in 1612 (Heinsen-Roach, 2015: 71). This wave of appointments also replaced existing consuls in the Levant which had been formerly selected by the local nation. The States General, pressured

[19] For a detailed analysis of these contested relations in the 'Italian states' and of the Plowman Controversy in Livorno as a diplomatic crisis for the Crown, see Stein (2012: 113–145).

by the increasing problem of Dutch subjects captured by corsairing activities in the Southern Mediterranean and by the ambitions of Amsterdam merchants in the Levant (Heinsen-Roach, 2012: 100), started to pursue a clear strategy of state control of their commercial interests through a 'radical change of policies' (Heinsen-Roach, 2015: 70–71). Consular diplomacy became an important vehicle for this enterprise. Since there were no residents or ambassadors in North Africa, consuls in this region combined key political and commercial tasks, mainly ransoming captives (of which Dutch represented a very large share), negotiating with the North African regencies and ports to maintain peace treaties and lobby against Castilian interests in the region, as well as promoting and protecting trade interests (Heinsen-Roach, 2015; 2012: 11). Nevertheless, in spite of the States General's efforts to direct consular policy in North Africa, its consuls had to adapt to the various institutions and practices and were caught between their instructions and local authorities (Heinsen-Roach, 2015: 74). For example, Moroccan and Jewish merchants still managed to trade in Dutch captives, in spite of the consuls' efforts (and of the capitulations) to either stop or monopolise this market (Heinsen-Roach, 2015: 80). Crucially, for Heinsen-Roach, this neglected area of study is an important challenge to classic diplomatic history's reductive separation of early modern ambassadors as political agents on the one hand and consuls as commercial agents on the other. It is also critical for retrieving the role of the early modern Maghreb in driving and shaping diplomatic and consular history (Heinsen-Roach, 2012: 11).

In the Levant, Dutch consuls had more jurisdictional duties, and were established in Aleppo for example from 1612. They were also appointed by the States General, and supposed to be remunerated, especially in the major ports, but issues around payment significantly troubled the early decades of the Dutch service, as their consuls were also prohibited to trade (Steensgaard, 1967: 32; Heinsen-Roach, 2015: 77; 81). The Levantine consuls also depended on the Levant merchants based in Amsterdam, who in 1624 organised as the Directorate.[20] The

[20] The Directorate refers to the 'College of Directors of Levant Trade and the Navigation of the Mediterranean' (i.e. Amsterdam's leading overseas merchants) who 'created a bureaucratic apparatus which supervised the implementation of the States-General's orders' (Boogert, 2003: 619). The States General delegated authority to the Directorate who 'corresponded with the Dutch ambassador in Istanbul, as well as with consuls throughout the Mediterranean' (619). However, they did not have a trade monopoly and could not legislate, so their jurisdictional and commercial powers were not as extensive as those of

Amsterdam merchants' monopoly over consuls in the Levant created disputes with the other cities in the Republic, and conflicts with Rotterdam went on to shape the fate of the service throughout the eighteenth century (Allain, 2018: 00). Amsterdam retained its administrative hold over consuls, but Rotterdam and other cities managed to place their men and fight over crucial appointments (Allain, 2018: 436). However, in contrast to Dutch consuls in North Africa, those in Europe and the Levant worked more to promote trade interests for local merchant communities and especially those at home than to act as political representatives of the Republic (Heinsen-Roach, 2012: 11). The Levantine geopolitical context was particularly difficult, which led to a lack of long-term and unilateral strategy, where actors (merchants and consuls) favoured short-term calculations and spontaneity instead (Allain, 2018: 422).

As with all other cases, Dutch consular practices were therefore divided between the Western and Eastern Mediterranean in terms of resistance from local merchants. Resistance was especially pronounced from Flemish–Dutch merchant communities in Venice and Livorno, who feared 'losing their independence' (Heinsein-Roach, 2012: 102), 'whereas powerful merchants in Amsterdam with large shares in the Mediterranean trade favoured establishing consulates under the supervision of the Dutch state' (102). The States General eventually bowed to this resistance and announced in 1658 'that the state-appointed consul in Italy and France possessed no jurisdiction over merchant communities' and had more the status of a 'commercial envoy whose principal task lay in assisting non-resident merchants and captains in need' (102). Although the States General compromised on jurisdiction, it nevertheless managed to achieve the appointment of consuls.

In sum, like the French, the Dutch consular service depended on two institutions: the States General and the Directorate of Levant merchants in Amsterdam. The French depended on the state department of the *Marine* and the CCM, while the Swedish for example also depended on the king and the Stockholm Company (Bartolomei, 2018b: 394). These three consular services were tied to both the ruling authority of the sovereign or of the Republic on one side, and to a merchant-led company, conglomerate, or regional institution on the other. This differs from the English case, where consular strategies were more determined

the VOC. 'The Directors adjudicated disputes between consuls and merchants abroad, but their verdicts needed to be confirmed by the States General, which also appointed the ambassador in Istanbul and the Dutch consuls' (619).

by the geographical and historical divide between the Western and Eastern Mediterranean shaped by their merchants' practices. On both sides of this divide, the English Crown had to adapt to its merchants to shape consular practices, either through the Levant Company or local nations and smaller companies.

In other words, to conclude on this section, one could identify two extremes in terms of consular policy. At one end of the spectrum, the French model reflects the most state-developed form of mercantilism and jurisdictional accumulation. It directed consular policy and strategy from the king's office as centre of the monarchy and gave instructions to standardise those practices and regulate its merchants across the Mediterranean. It negotiated and, in some cases, compromised with the CCM and local nations to achieve these aims, and results on the ground reflected divisions seen across each service regarding the West–East divide. Yet the intentions of the policy and the means deployed were a clear political and commercial diplomatic strategy of French extraterritorial mercantilism and jurisdictional accumulation that transplanted French authority and jurisdiction in innovative ways.

At the other end, English consular strategy was ad hoc and adapted to the ways in which leading merchants decided to organise themselves. In this sense, it was less jurisdictional for it did not engage in legal practices that aimed at explicitly establishing rights and a consular legal order. However, their jurisdictional strategies were flexible, locally determined, merchant-driven, and they also reproduced a Christian and non-Christian West–East divide. The Dutch consular service appears to sit somewhere in the middle of this jurisdictional spectrum, trying to both govern consuls from the States General in southern and western parts of the Mediterranean and sharing this duty with the Directorate in the Levant. However, both Dutch and English can best be understood as attempts to transport the authority of their rulers and company employers. The following will explore to what extent social origins and composition reflect this spectrum and other aspects of consular strategy.

5.3 Social Origins and Composition of Consular Service

The question of the social origins and composition of the consular service is less problematic and open to varying patterns than in the case of ambassadors discussed in the previous chapter. Most consuls were merchants, though not necessarily so. They also came from the military, local lower gentry, or lower nobility, and could be navigators and sailors.

However, it is still an important angle to emphasise so as to understand the foreign policy rhetoric and jurisdictional challenges of the period. Generally, consuls were of much lower class than other representative diplomatic actors. However, if 'employed in the same area', the tasks of an English 'diplomatist' and those of a consul could overlap in the eighteenth century (Horn, 1961: 190). For some authors, the distinctions between consuls and royal agents are more blurred than not. Consuls could step in as chargés d'affaires or as residents in the absence of the ambassador, as cases for the French ambassador in Istanbul show below, or cases involving British representatives in Venice, Lisbon, and Brussels (Horn, 1961: 161–162). This is especially likely in port cities which were also capitals. Moreover, there were cases of British agents serving as both diplomats and consuls during their careers as is found in St Petersburg, Madrid, and Lisbon (Horn, 1961: 241–243).

Nevertheless, a fundamental line existed, even if only to keep up appearances in some cases, between trade and higher matters of royal business. Commercial connections were considered a 'hindrance' for ambassadorial posts and a bonus for consuls (Horn, 1961: 250). In other words, consuls and ambassadors were very different men. These differences gradually became less stark towards the end of the early modern period, once the professionalisation of both ambassadors and consuls took place in the nineteenth century. For example, British and French consuls in the eighteenth century came from a slightly higher social elite than in the seventeenth century (Horn, 1961: 251). The appointment of consuls probably followed the general trend of aristocratisation and shifts in social elites. However, a large social gap between the positions of ambassador and consul remained.

Concerning French consuls, the only extensive prosopography was directed by Anne Mézin for French consuls from 1715 to 1792. Most consuls in this period came from a merchant background. Detailed information about consuls prior to this date remains patchy and particularly difficult to collect, considering the variety of archival depositaries and biographical sources necessary for exhaustive research. However, Ariste's 1667 treatise claims pre-seventeenth-century consuls were 'chosen among the best families of Marseille' on the basis of their 'moral reputation, discretion, experience, the honour and interests of the community, and their trading connections in the region of the consular post'.[21] Of course, Ariste is not a reliable source here, and the fact that

[21] Ariste (1667 : ch. 1, point 4, pp. 21–22).

it contradicts with the reputation of French consuls tells us something about the desire for this to be hidden and changed. For example, Barbour notes how early-seventeenth-century French consuls were 'at best absentees, and at worst landlubber pirates or maritime robber-baron' (1928: 562), a reputation which Colbert's reforms aimed to improve.

From lists put together by Jörg Ulbert on consuls pre-1715, and following consensus in the literature, consuls were mostly merchants and military men, some perhaps from the lower nobility. However, by the late-eighteenth century, one-third of consuls came from the nobility (Faivre d'Arcier, 2006: 162). Generally, by this point, consuls were essentially representatives of the bourgeois population, with some consuls post-Revolution shortening their names or taking out their *particule* (Faivre d'Arcier, 2006: 184). Family and professional connections were the surest ways to ensure a nomination. There was also a considerable number of military men serving in the Levant (Faivre d'Arcier, 2006: 162), and turnover remained slow.

Merchants provided the main qualities necessary for the post, even though they had in most cases to give up trading. Some posts were always given to merchants.[22] In other cases, there was a gradual acceptance of consuls' need to trade.[23] In some cases, merchants were a requirement: Greece needed merchants to be vice consuls because of the diffusion of French merchants on the territory and the large number of ports. There were also countries where the bad faith of locals forced France to accept local and rich candidates and others where foreigners were necessary because no one else was available (e.g. new consulates in Christian cities). Finally, securing merchants in a post was a way of obtaining influence or loyalty of a particular family such as the Garibaldo family in Savona or the brothers Hansen in Elsinore (Mézin, 1997: 26).

In other words, the reliance on merchants and the need to adapt the reforms show the varying conditions on the ground for selecting and commissioning consuls. The reforms introduced by Colbert and put in place throughout the eighteenth century implied various negotiations and compromises with important merchant families across the Mediterranean, who traded their networks and influence for more personal jurisdictional privileges (securing posts for their descendants or

[22] For example, vice consulate of Rame (Seyde/Saïda), and vice consulate of Alexandrette (brothers Pierre and Xavier-Honoré Reynaud, then cousins Jean and Jean-Baptiste-François Callène, 1744–1776, with a trading house of same dates) (Mézin, 1997: 25).

[23] Porto, Arta in Greece, Saint-Sebastian, Bilbao, Gibraltar in Spain (Mézin, 1997: 25).

family members, annulling the prohibition on trading) in exchange for their loyalty to the king. This collaboration with merchants and push towards increasing the control over – as well as the jurisdictional powers of – consuls shaped Colbert's mercantilism. Merchants and consuls accumulated jurisdiction as a means towards social and commercial capital in the sense of wealth.

Unfortunately, research on the social origins of Dutch consuls is limited. However, their connection to political office and to the lower nobility might be more important than in other cases, though one would expect the *regenten* class to naturally provide merchant expertise and interest in consular positions.[24] Two Levantine consuls in the early-seventeenth century for the important post of Aleppo were patriciates and sons of burgomasters (i.e. chief magistrates), who had some involvement in trade in their early years (Steensgaard, 1967: 31). In the Eastern Mediterranean, consular appointments were mostly merchant men from the *regenten* families of Holland and Zeeland (Israel, 1989: 93–94). However, in European and Christian ports of the Mediterranean, there was a move to appoint Italian and French consuls connected to Batavian commercial interests, (Allain, 2018: 428). This separation between consuls in the Western and Eastern Mediterranean in terms of their nationalities and social origins seems more marked than in other cases. Levantine Dutch consuls were increasingly of Dutch nationality and refused to trade (Allain, 2018: 428). Dutch merchants in the Levant, notably through the Directorate, controlled the appointment of consuls. The States General only confirmed a choice already made, while the ambassador in Istanbul played only a superficial official role (Allain, 2018: 426).

From its growth in the sixteenth and seventeenth centuries, the English consular service consisted of simple merchants who were 'of limited literacy', often 'untrained in the law', 'Scots, and therefore unfamiliar with English law' but with 'working knowledge of law-merchant' (Barbour, 1928: 577). Even 'middle-class men' hesitated to take on these posts (Horn, 1961: 250). As in other cases, the seventeenth century is the crucial period for the growth of the English consular service. The estimated thirty-four posts over the reign of Charles II showed some signs of 'a national and a public character' (Barbour, 1928: 578, 553), but Englishmen considered consular posts 'beneath

[24] See Chapter 3 for a discussion of the importance of this political and jurisdictional office for understanding the Dutch case.

them', according to the resident in Tuscany Sir John Finch in 1668 (Pagano de Divitiis, 1997: 71).[25]

In the eighteenth century, the British consular service did include one or two closely connected members of the peerage, one baronet, and occasional cases of knights, but the title was still considered 'abject' (Horn, 1961: 251). If an MP was appointed as a consul, he had to vacate his seat, but he could be re-elected (Horn: 1961: 167, 247). This would explain the very few numbers of MPs listed as consuls, alongside the fact that MPs were increasingly chosen as ambassadors and residents from the mid- to late-seventeenth century.

In the Western Mediterranean, English consuls were not state officials and were selected by the merchants of their nation. They were 'marginal figures who were highly integrated into the culture of the port where they resided' (Stein, 2012: 105). They were often Catholics and held positions in local institutions, which led to their loyalties being questioned at home. In many cases, especially in Italian ports such as Naples or Civitavecchia, consulates were occupied by foreigners to the authority they represented and especially by Italians (Pagano de Divitiis, 1997: 71).[26] However, English merchants became increasingly interested in these posts as trade in Italy increased from the early-seventeenth century. Some started to offer a price for the consulates, considering the more lucrative *consulage* revenues from the increased passage of ships in the region (Pagano de Divitiis, 1997: 72).

Rejected requests by an Italian widow in Livorno and a Venetian business partner to take over the vacant posts in these locations show nationality becoming a more defined criterion for the selection of consuls (Pagano de Divitiis, 1997: 72). Yet it seemed that being a woman was not necessarily a major problem, even though it remained extremely rare in the eighteenth century (Horn, 1961: 255–256). The nationality criterion

[25] Sir John Finch was English resident in Tuscany from 1665 to 1672, and ambassador in Istanbul from 1672 to 1682 (Pagano de Divitiis, 1997: 13). He was very active and at the centre of the various attempts in this period to establish extraterritorial jurisdiction in the Western Mediterranean, and is thought to have written various memoranda to this effect, as well as against the Levant Company and its corporate form of sovereignty and diplomacy (Stein, 2012: 102, 118). Finch 'thought that merchants were in no position to make effective judgments regarding matters of state and should thus observe the leadership of the Crown's representatives' (Stein, 2012: 133).

[26] In the later period of the eighteenth century, foreigners were still important but mainly for the posts of vice consuls, although this remained an object of controversy (Horn, 1961: 248–249).

became more important because the king wanted to ensure his consul's actions would fall under English jurisdiction, as well as avoid Italian or other interests guiding the consul's decisions (Pagano de Divitiis, 1997: 72–73). However, the king's authority in these matters did not last long.

In the Levant, consuls were often Levantines and Anglo-Levantines. Certain merchant families prevailed such as the 'Werrys, Boddingtons, Calverts and Cumberbatches' (Berridge, 2009: 77), who competed over obtaining the lucrative post at Smyrna. William Prideaux became Smyrna's consul in 1659 after holding ambassadorial positions in Moscow and in China for the East India Company, as well as the famous Ottomanist Paul Rycaut in 1667 (Berridge, 2009: 77). These testify to the significant attractiveness of Smyrna and to the overlaps between ambassadors and consuls in these cases.

If consuls could not compete with ambassadors on most grounds, they did so on the issue of religious representation and privileges. Because a consulate also meant a British colony or group of residents, consuls were also expected to host a chaplain (Horn, 1961: 247; Mézin, 1997). The chaplain could be a problem for English residents with Irish Catholic and Scottish Jacobite chaplains (Horn, 1961: 248). This was emphasised by the particularly strong presence of Scots in the eighteenth-century consular service (Horn, 1961: 249) and earlier under Charles II, aggravating English merchants' resistance to his appeal for authority in establishing consulates.

Overall, in spite of overlaps in functions, and the use of consuls and other third parties by ambassadors and aristocratic travellers wishing to trade, noble Englishmen and royal agents considered the world of trade to be beneath them. This was reflected in correspondence in the eighteenth century by Sir Cyril Wych, who lamented the 'adjusting of differences betwixt merchants, masters of ships and sailors' and considered these 'such disagreeable occupations' that they were not worthy of recollection in his correspondence by fear of 'troubling' the king (in Black, 2001: 149).[27]

This official line of separation between aristocratic royal affairs and mercantile diplomacy was maintained through consular institutions. However, it is important not to collapse this separation into assumptions that the ambassadorial is purely political, while the consular is commercial. To counter this tendency, relations of collaboration and distrust

[27] Wych was an extraordinary envoy, a 'bustling, self-important figure', posted in the Hanse towns from 1713 to 1741 (Black, 2001: 179).

between trading communities and consuls discussed below are useful to illustrate the political implications of consular activities.

5.4 Relations between Consuls and Trading Communities

A recent broad collection of studies on the benefits consuls provided for trade in various European contexts concludes that consuls were overall useful to merchants in a variety of ways (Bartolomei *et al.*, 2018). This depended on, first, whether the consular service was more inclined towards diplomacy or trade, and second, on the territories or spaces where consuls and merchants operated. In other words, consular service was not sufficiently homogeneous or assertive to impose itself on the specific conditions under which it operated. We have already seen some specific examples of this and the major divisions in policy and practices in the Mediterranean. Other examples are the Swedish in the Mediterranean as well as Japanese consuls in general where merchants benefited greatly from consular service. However, there are also cases where consuls were an impediment to merchants' activity; French consuls in Lisbon, Genoese consuls in Cadiz, and more generally Irish and Genoese consuls in Spain. In these cases, consuls' functions were more focused on controlling an informal sector and were at the service of their mercantilist centre. The negative impact of consuls on trade is also explained by technological difficulties and the unreliability of information from consuls (Bartolomei, 2018a: 13).

Aside from these more extreme cases, French consuls became very important for merchant companies in the Levant (Bartolomei, 2018a: 9). They produced juridical certificates and documents which were recognised by Western European courts and jurisdictions. This helped to secure and facilitate commercial exchanges. However, care should be taken when generalising their impact, as important characteristics, linked to the city-centred and fragmented nature of early modern Europe, meant that Dutch, Swedish, and French consuls were more useful to merchants in Amsterdam, Stockholm, and Marseille, than to merchants in Rotterdam, Gothenburg, or Sète (Bartolomei, 2018a: 10). In other words, consuls were part of complex trans-urban networks of interests determined by the different trades, commodities, and jurisdictional divisions operating across Europe and the Mediterranean.

However, analysing the instructions given in French manuals on consular service, Ulbert (2018: 140) concludes that a consul was only expected to help commerce flourish and not to play an active role by opening new markets or trade routes. Consuls were meant to stay focused on providing services and information. This could be read as a way to limit and control the activities of merchants and make sure their profits were redirected to the state, by ensuring that consuls' privileges and abilities would not be used to only profit merchants.

On the Dutch case, scholars have not found any particular correlation proving Dutch consuls' utility to commerce, since generally trade decreased when consul numbers rose. However, this could be read as meaning that consuls were a response to declining trade.[28] Specifically, Rotterdam's wealth grew in importance even though all consular services were at the service of Amsterdam (Bartolomei, 2018b: 401). Merchants played a significant role in North African Dutch consular posts in forcing the consul, as a representative of the Republic, to adapt to local customs (Heinsen-Roach, 2012, 2015). Moreover, information about merchants' activity constituted a crucial part of consuls' correspondence, as well as advice and communication between merchants and consuls implying their function as spies and informants for the Republic or their provinces rather than for Dutch commerce in general (Allain, 2018: 423–424). However, the distinction in the Dutch Republic between commerce and politics is much less defined than in other cases, especially France. Finally, Dutch consuls had also more jurisdictional powers in non-Christian consulates than in Christian consulates, as their European counterparts.

As with French consuls posted in Livorno and other Christian ports (Calafat, 2018b), English merchants were very critical of the consuls' authority. Merchants were considered 'a disputatious lot' (Games, 2008: 169) and reported at the time as 'rebellious' by the new consul posted in Bordeaux, the Scottish Sir David English, who unsuccessfully battled to regain his post as consul for twenty years (Barbour, 1928: 558). Consuls 'complained repeatedly about independent and unmalleable traders' (Games, 2008: 168). Nevertheless, English merchants won their battle against the king and were able to get 'the king's man out and their own man in' (Barbour, 1928: 561) by pressuring the House of Commons to maintain their prerogative and precedence over royal choices. Conflicts on the ground continued in the late-seventeenth century, but gradually the king and his ministers gained more power by having to resolve local disputes. Consuls considered themselves 'the king's men' (Barbour, 1928:

[28] Thanks to Hamish Scott for this point, which would need further exploring.

565), which reassured the state that they could defend its interests against local authorities and merchants' interests. However, as Stein (2012) has forcefully argued, English merchants in Italian cities forced the Crown to abandon its extraterritorial objectives in the Western Mediterranean, in spite of the relentless work of diplomatic residents such as Finch.[29]

Conflicts between merchants and the defence of economic interests became an increasingly important part of all diplomats' tasks, and ambassadors and envoys had to turn to consuls as advisers, since disputes between merchants were 'an irritation to many diplomats' (Black, 2001: 149). In spite of similarities regarding the East–West divide, the way in which English disputes shaped consular policy or strategy marks a significant difference with France. Although the French king and Colbert collaborated and negotiated with merchants, especially those represented by the powerful CCM, the king's authority was carefully crafted through the old regime's 'maquis règlementaire' (Ulbert, forthcoming) so as to gradually ensure, through Colbert's reforms, his hold on the nomination and commercial activities of consuls as well as on the mobility of merchants and travellers.

Overall, two major factors explain consuls' relations to trading communities: the circulation of goods and people on the one hand, and morality and religion on the other. Through these two angles, the development of French trading communities in the Mediterranean was linked to consuls. On the first factor, emigration out of France became highly regulated by Colbert and Louis XIV in 1669, at the same time roughly as consuls became officers of the king. Increasing the financial revenue of the state was the main objective behind the heavy amount of legislation produced in this domain until the Revolution, and for Ulbert (forthcoming), both demographic control ('populationisme') and consular jurisdiction thereby defined Colbert's mercantilism.

This demographic control of mobility outside France included the active participation of the CCM to enforce legislation and was stricter in the Ottoman Empire for reasons of trading interests and feasibility.[30]

[29] For a discussion of the implications of relations between merchants and consuls on extraterritoriality, see Chapter 7.

[30] In 1769, 1,211 French individuals are accounted for in the Ottoman Empire, including 211 individuals working in the consulates, and 350 working for the Compagnie d'Afrique. In comparison, it is estimated that the Spanish town of Cadiz on its own hosted 2,000 French in 1786 (Ulbert, forthcoming: 00).

The policies were justified according to moral and Christian principles and were driven by political–economic objectives of expansion.

Organising the Levant trade was a successful enterprise, since an estimate of France's share in the overall trade with the Ottoman Empire increased from 15 per cent in 1660 to two-thirds in under 100 years (Ulbert, forthcoming). Moreover, Levantine trade as a share of France's commercial activity supposedly increased from 3 per cent in 1716 to 1720 to nearly 10 per cent in 1748 to 1755 (Horn, 2011 in Ulbert, forthcoming).

Behind what we would today call racialising claims marking the superiority of French and Christian peoples – leading consuls to police their nation as well as representing and adjudicating between them – the aim of these policies was also to reduce the number of trading posts and houses. This would increase the power and reach of the few remaining, as well as reduce the number of servants and artisans, judged too high in relation to the volume of trade. By 1743, the *Marine* established quotas of residents for each regency, and travel was authorised on a 'one out, one in' basis. By the end of Louis XV's reign, the CCM delivered thirty-five certificates a year for the sixteen regencies in the Levant, so an average of slightly more than two per regency a year (Ulbert, forthcoming).

The fact that consuls posted in the Ottoman Empire were less and less from Marseille's trading network from the late-seventeenth century helped to secure implementation of the king's legislation, although their presence remains important and Marseille retains a key role in the nomination and regulation of posts at the demand of the Crown (Ulbert, 2019: 26–27). In contrast, in the Christian parts of the Mediterranean, emigration evaded legislation and authorities eventually gave up on strict residency and travel controls (Ulbert, forthcoming). These measures could only help to enforce the increasingly jurisdictional separation between the Western and Eastern Mediterranean.

In terms of the circulation of goods – and as an example of how legislation was used to enforce and shape French consuls' relations to trade – in 1669, Marseille became a 'free port' (*franc port*) and was effectively closed to foreign shipping since 'all goods imported by foreign merchants, those arriving on board non-French vessels, those reaching Marseille via non-French ports, or those destined for ports other than Marseille' had to pay a 20 per cent customs duty (Trivellato, 2009: 116–117). This made it unprofitable for merchants to come to Marseille, a quasi-embargo which mainly affected Livorno, a port which provided '85 percent of the Levantine goods paying the 20 percent tax' in

1686 (Trivellato, 2009: 117). These measures were meant to protect the export of woollen cloth made in Languedoc, but they were subject to 'widespread abuse' (Trivellato, 2009: 117). Livorno was a key trading port for England and was also largely controlled by the Sephardi Jewish community.

The political economy of the Mediterranean was strongly shaped by religious identity, and not only in terms of the Christian and Muslim communities. Across the Mediterranean, specific relations to Jewish trading communities developed showing the importance of religious identity as a means to demarcate jurisdictional lines and thereby secure trading privileges. Diplomats such as Finch used the argument of the Livorno Jewish community to try to develop a similar national and legal identity and self-governing model to unite the English community and its factories in Italy (Stein, 2012: 119). However, Finch wrongly assumed that this applied to all Jewish communities, when in fact the Livorno merchants were the only ones to have this jurisdictional privilege.

Similarly, the religious dimension is evident in the texts of treaties and in determining who were the 'subjects' of jurisdictional 'interactions' (Pennell, 2009: 238–239, 247–248). In the eighteenth and nineteenth centuries, European treaties named their subjects by their nationalities and their counterparts according to racial or ethnic groupings of Turks or Moors. However, in the seventeenth century, when most treaty models were established, the European subjects of jurisdiction were grouped according to religious identity, as the Christians and Jews (e.g. in the Algiers–Netherlands treaty of 1679), while North African local authorities in later treaties in the eighteenth century 'thought in religious terms' but used the ethnic terms of 'Turk or Moor' (Pennell, 2009: 239).

By 1688, some concessions were made to ships sailing through Italian ports, recognising the French dependence on 'the Jews of Livorno to replenish their return cargo' (Trivellato, 2009: 117). The French also offered diplomatic protection to Sephardim in the Ottoman Empire, as a compromise between the CCM's 'staunch opposition to liberalization and toleration and the Crown's commitment to capturing the largest possible share of the market in the southeastern Mediterranean' (Trivellato, 2009: 118). This compromise was possible because 'French consuls for the most part viewed these measures favorably because they gained personally from the trade generated by Sephardim overseas', as Sephardim paid '31 percent of the French customs duties collected in Aleppo' in 1739 to 1741 (Trivellato, 2009: 117–118). Thus, jurisdictional frameworks and privileges maintained by consuls directly helped to secure the leading trading position of France, and consuls and sending authorities used religious divisions to enforce them on, as well as collaborate with, the communities concerned.

To conclude on consuls' relations to trade, this section is evidently barely illustrative of the variety and complexity found across the Mediterranean, and it cannot do justice to the topic. However, it is possible to conclude that overall, European merchants in Western Christian ports were unfavourable to consuls with wide jurisdictional powers, while those in Muslim ports governed by capitulations more or less agreed to them. Moreover, the strength of the consular service was made possible by cooperation with and support from the merchant community, which could take a variety of forms through trading companies, familial and religious trading networks, and positions in local authorities. Crucially, for the French, these relations were shaped by strict and relentless legal reforms and measures limiting the circulation of goods and people. These measures were justified and put in place through religious divisions which created overlapping and autonomous jurisdictional regimes contributing to the East–West divide.

This brings us to our final section, looking at how the French jurisdictional service operated on the ground in Istanbul as an example of the collaboration between merchants and consuls, in accordance with – and to the benefit of – the Crown. In this case, merchants were very vocal in their support for a consul and resident emerging from their ranks. The case thus reflects key class relations crucial to the development of both aristocratic and mercantile diplomatic networks, and how the state managed to control and eventually subsume these dual strategies of expansion.

5.5 Relationship between Ambassadors and Consuls: the Special Case of Istanbul

A significant issue marking the differences between European consuls is the relation between consuls and ambassadors, and specifically whether consuls were considered 'diplomats' by political and legal theorists, in the sense of being public ministers or sovereign representatives of the same order as ambassadors or envoys. For most theorists, consuls were not sovereign representatives since consular agents lacked royal credentials. However, in practice, there were many exceptions and the relations between consuls and ambassadors is murkier and more intertwined than they have often been portrayed by the classic diplomatic theorists.

Lacuna in this domain emerge, inter alia, from the lack of diachronic and comparative work on consuls, especially in anglophone scholarship.

From our discussion above, we have seen that the singularity of French consuls was their prohibition on trading and their increased influence and jurisdictional powers, especially in the Levant and North Africa. These powers and singularities justify differentiating French consuls from the Dutch and English to consider their case as quasi-public ministers. More importantly, however, the analysis justifies considering them able to compete with ambassadors for geopolitical influence. This is not intended to negate the geopolitical role of English and Dutch consuls, but to differentiate it as more ad hoc, controlled by the trading companies, and, in effect, more merchant-driven and therefore less jurisdictional in the sense of being governed more by trade profits than by the establishment of legal rights and duties.

This argument is further emphasised by the conflicts and tensions witnessed in Istanbul over the positions of ambassador, resident, and consul. We will also see that the social origins of consuls are an additional obstacle to being accepted as public ministers. This is shown by the ways in which class relations were invoked in the debates over Istanbul but also how they were used by various actors to assert or defend themselves.

It is useful first to recall the debates in diplomatic theory. Jean Hotman (1603) defended the position that consuls were diplomats in the same sense as ambassadors and envoys. Much later, in the nineteenth century, Johann Jacob Moser and François Borel also agreed that they were public ministers (Ulbert, 2006: 15). However, most other diplomatic theorists did not hold this position, because they argued that consuls were not regulated by principles of the *droit des gens* or of the *droit public de l'Europe* because they did not have the credentials (*lettres de créance, exequatur, lettres patentes, barat* for consuls in the Levant) to represent their sovereign, and therefore were not considered worthy of immunity. Theorists argued that consuls were regulated by bilateral treaties and local communities, especially if elected by them. They therefore most often lacked the immunity reserved to ambassadors and could not be considered public ministers. Wicquefort in 1681 considered that consuls' merchant occupations disqualified them from enjoying 'extraterritorial rights', which Leira and Neumann (2008: 3) interpret here in a narrow and 'ambassadorial immunity' sense. Vattel may have refused to give consuls full diplomatic status but he considered they should enjoy a level of protection as they were recognised by both sending and receiving sovereigns (Horn, 1961: 238; Leira & Neumann, 2008: 3). Mézin (1997:

24) shows that at least for the French case, consuls did enjoy various immunities, weakening the case for a clear distinction and exclusion of consuls as diplomats on this ground. However, Adair (1929: 63) notes that since consuls (especially in Northern Europe) were often natives of the country in which they were serving, issues of immunity were less applicable and also were avoided because they would give consuls exercising as traders an unfair advantage in trade.

For Ulbert (2006: 15), there are many aspects in which consuls are diplomatic agents (relation with sending authority, role as official representative, and procedure and ceremony of their new position), but this status nevertheless rests primarily on the degree of immunity an agent is accorded. Therefore, an in-depth analysis of consuls' immunities across the Western and Eastern divides would be necessary, including other aspects determining diplomatic status, but this task is beyond the scope of this chapter. As an illustration, Callières (1716) did factor in the jurisdictional divide, as he argued that consuls in European posts did not qualify as public ministers, whereas consuls in 'the principal towns of Asia and Africa' did (Horn, 1961: 241; also in Calafat, 2018a: 145), implying that those with wider jurisdictional functions (rather than simply the criterion of protection) gave them full diplomatic status. This line of analysis would give a more accurate sense of the political importance of early modern consuls. Suffice for now to acknowledge that there is evident ambiguity over the definition of extraterritoriality in relation to degrees of immunity, that, if nothing else, should make us question that definition and explore other angles to determining extensions and transports of authority, as this chapter has done. The following section will continue this task in the more specific case of the French embassy-consulate in Istanbul, and show that in contrast to assumptions by Steensgaard (1967: 21) – that French merchants did not have an influence on the appointment of ambassadors – at least in this case they significantly tried and were in line with Colbert's aims in reforming Levantine diplomacy through increasing the powers of consuls.

5.5.1 Ambassadors and Consuls in Late-Seventeenth-Century Istanbul

The French ambassador in Istanbul was the superior of all personnel at the consulate and was in charge of nominating a consul or a dragoman without royal confirmation necessary. This privilege was only revoked in 1756 (Faivre d'Arcier, 2006: 161). The ambassador was therefore the equivalent of the consul in Istanbul. The ambassador's payment was also partially financed by the CCM until 1766 (Boulanger, 2006: 128, n. 13, 138). The first permanent and known French ambassador to the Porte arrived in 1535 and signed the first renewal of a trade treaty of 1526 between France and the Ottoman Empire. There is uncertainty over the first French capitulation, and whether it followed from these negotiations, as a document exists from 1535, but its acknowledgement and application are contested (Steensgaard, 1967: 16). The other date given for the first French capitulation is 1569 (Kaiser & Calafat, 2014: 80). Correspondence of the Istanbul consulate is kept from 1639 (Mézin, 1997: 685), during the beginning of the twenty-one-year residence of ambassador Jean de La Haye, seigneur de Ventelet.

By the eighteenth century, Istanbul became the only regency where the ambassador could properly apply the reforms of ministers Villeneuve and Maurepas. It therefore became, in the heyday of the French consular service, a model for efficient and centrally regulated relations between different representatives of the king necessary for the implementation of the king's Mediterranean mercantile policies. However, in 1660, this was far from the case.

Seventeenth-century ambassadors in Istanbul were associated with 'tyranny' because of their unreasonable financial expenses, their tendency to exact arbitrary taxations, their debts, and the avania incurred by the whole nation because of those debts. Trade stagnated in this regency during the late-seventeenth century. From 1671 to 1675 commodities bought from Istanbul consisted in 8 per cent of all imports from the Levant and Barbary (annual average of half a million livres) (Paris, 1957: 453). The improvements brought by the new 1673 capitulations and the 1660s reforms were felt only by the time of Colbert's death in 1683 (Paris, 1957: 453).

The ambassador Jean de La Haye was forced to leave Istanbul in 1660, opening a five-year period in which a merchant from Aix-en-Provence, Jean-François Roboly, Seigneur de Saint-Martin, took over the ambassador's duties as a resident (Mézin, 1997: 523). Roboly was a key merchant in Istanbul and is considered by Ariste (1667) to have the status of a consul in Istanbul.[31] Born on 23 August 1623, he died in Istanbul on 22 September 1689 (Mézin, 1997: 523). The Roboly family

[31] 'Celuy qui l'exerce presentement [le consulat de Istanbul] se nomme le sieur Robolier. Il reside ordinairement a Constantinople, et a des vice-consulz à Gallipoli, et aux Chasteaux des Dardanelles qui sont de la dependance de son consulat, et ou il fait lever ses droicts' (Ariste, 1667). Transcribed by Jörg Ulbert.

are illustrative of the intergenerational networks that shaped consular services.[32] He had been lending significant sums of money to the ambassador Jean de la Haye, and the first mention of his name by de la Haye in the CCM archives was found in a letter dated to 15 April 1655 (CCM J141). Roboly is also known for being in charge while a fire broke out and a part of the embassy's archives disappeared (Cras, 2016: 61).[33]

Roboly's term as a diplomatic resident was not without other problems of legitimacy. He was charged with unlawfully levying taxes on boats and merchants, but the dispute seems to have been resolved in his favour or without any grave consequences.[34] However, his case is particularly interesting as it illustrates the differences and problems between the roles of ambassador and consul, and how their social origins and occupational backgrounds contributed to these problems.

Of the letters that remain in the archives of the CCM, the first ones sent by Roboly to the CCM claiming his right to the ambassador's pension of 16,000 livres are indicative of his initial clumsiness, while the later ones show a growth of confidence and arrogance, and also a sense of injustice that his work is not being recognised and respected. The first letter is written with an awkward hand, with many mistakes, and lacks authority – the following ones seem to have been copied by someone else and are written in a demanding rather than supplicating tone (J176). The letters also attest to the support of the nation in Istanbul for his passage at the embassy (J176). French merchants also directly defended his residency by regularly writing to the CCM on this matter (J180).

Roboly's passage as resident and its defence by merchants and the CCM was in line with Colbert's aims to reform trade and diplomacy in the Levant. An interesting question is whether it was in line with or thought in conjunction with those to 'aristocratise' diplomacy discussed

32 The Roboly descendants remained important figures in the French consular service as Levantine dragomans and as merchants. Jean-François Roboly's son was Pierre Roboly (*c.* 1680–1743), who was the primary dragoman in Tripoli of Syria, followed by a post in Smyrna. His grandson was Honoré Roboly (1711–1770), who was the secondary dragoman in Smyrna from 1737 to 1770. His great-grandson, Pierre-François Roboly (1739–1783), was dragoman in Seyde and Smyrna from 1768, interim vice consul in Scio in 1779, and dragoman in Salonica in 1781 (Mézin, 1997: 523).

33 This prompted the practice of a 'mobile' chancery, until a separate building was built in 1719 for the purpose of the embassy's archives (Cras, 2016: 61).

34 Roboly apparently wrongly perceived duties and was investigated for this but a letter by the king on the matter appears to clear the issue (CCM J1602). However, some parts of the letter remain unreadable.

in the previous chapter. Colbert wrote a memorandum in 1669 where he asks whether the ambassador Denis de La Haye (son of the former Jean de La Haye) should be replaced by an ambassador or a royal agent.[35] He wrote that ambassadors need to stop taking a personal interest in commerce and work exclusively to protect merchants in the name of the king. Colbert orders an investigation by Arnoul (loyal Marseillais merchant) into the behaviour of the ambassador in Istanbul. The complaints received against the ambassador are confirmed by the investigation (Masson, 1896: 147).

This is followed by various memoranda – in 1670, 1677, and 1685 – arguing for a resident to be in place in Istanbul instead of an ambassador, since merchants are considered better placed for defending French commerce and the interests of the king in this regency.

The memorandum written on 20 January 1670 by deputy d'Arvieux and given to the *secrétaire d'état et des affaires étrangères* Hugue de Lionne and to Colbert, suggests the commissioning of a resident. However, other members of the king's counsel, Louvois and Colbert de Villacerf, argue for an ambassador in the person of M. de Nointel, largely because of his potential links to the Compagnie du Levant (Masson, 1896: 212). In spite of the measures taken by the king to regularise the payment of Nointel's pension and thus avoid his borrowing from merchants, Nointel still committed abuses and is at the centre of complaints in later memoranda.

Nointel liked 'pomp and pageantry', would 'levy extraordinary sums of money', and make 'unnecessary expenses' (Masson, 1896: 147; personal translations). His aristocratic and ambassadorial behaviour pushed the CCM to ask for a resident instead of an ambassador at Istanbul in the 1677 memorandum discussed below. For Masson, this was one of the last echoes of the long-standing conflict between trade and ambassadors in the region (1896: 147–148). However, another instance that produced some conflicts concerned Jean-Baptiste Fabre, a merchant from Marseille, who became resident of Istanbul in lieu of ambassador Guilleragues in 1685 and 1686. His position was disputed by the widow of Guilleragues, who claimed her right to the embassy and felt threatened by Fabre's rich merchant family accordingly trying to secure their interests and the power of Marseille in the regency. Another memorandum from the CCM in defence of a resident merchant thus appeared in 1685.

[35] Masson (1896) refers to Colbert's 1669 memorandum in *Lettres et Instruct., t. VII. supplém.* p. 286.

Since the Roboly case lasted longer and produced more paperwork and dilemmas for administrations in Marseille and Paris, we will focus on this and the 1677 memorandum. Written in August 1677 and addressed to the king, the memorandum, which built on Roboly's case, illustrates the disagreements between merchants and the different roles of ambassador, consul, and resident. It is useful to understand what was at stake and how it became crucial for Colbert to work on this problematic relation in the following years through increased control and regulation of the consular service. The memorandum offers a series of reasons for why the king should replace the ambassador with a resident.[36] It was written by the (*échevins*) merchant deputies (and representatives at the head of the CCM), and according to Masson, more specifically by d'Oppède and Arnoul (1896: 146).[37]

The text argues that a merchant resident is more appropriate for three main reasons. First, the aristocratic character and social manners of ambassadors are considered ill-suited to the post. Ambassadors are accustomed to the air and manners of the court, in other words they can be arrogant, presumptuous, or prejudiced, whereas residents get their intelligence from experience and are therefore better informed of how to negotiate with the Turks. Second, the memorandum argues that the ambassador's function of representation fails to fit with the needs of France and its relation to the Porte. A resident is not a personal representative of the king, so he – since this person is assumed to be a 'he' – is less able to dishonour him. A resident is also wiser and smarter regarding trade matters and is more listened to. The ambassador is too ambitious, he wants to represent the king with bright glory and higher measures, instead of treating matters like a merchant which would seem beneath him and would threaten his dignity or honour.

Finally, the memorandum heavily emphasises the various costs and financial consequences of ambassadors' needs and lack of trading background (debts, fines, avania, costly protection). Ambassadors borrowed without paying back their creditors and spent large sums to try to please the Turks, which caused them to be despised by merchants and brought trouble to trade. Ambassadors cost a lot more money, because they are

36 For now, I have found three copies of this text, two in CCM, J2 (last pieces) and one in CCM B3.

37 I have not seen any other evidence for this, as the various copies of the memorandum I have seen are not signed, except the copy in the CCM deliberations dossier (B3), but I was not able to decipher the names.

expected to show it, whereas residents can get away with not spending so much. It is also cheaper for a resident to travel. The pension accorded to an ambassador is insufficient which leads him to commit bad deeds and injustices; the amount of the pension is more appropriate to a resident.

Underlying these arguments related to the person of the ambassador is the important implication that relations between France and the Ottoman Empire are relations of trade, not dynastic or courtly politics. Istanbul and the relation to Turks is mainly about trade, there are no state affairs or considerable interests, so the resident is more appropriate as he is more supple and useful to trade and can go lower than an ambassador for the greater public good. The memorandum also cites various cases of bad ambassadors (Nointel, Césy) and of 'good merchant' residents since the early-seventeenth century, an agent in 1616 and the resident Roboly, who fulfilled criteria for a good merchant and accordingly made up in two to three years for the failures of previous ambassadors. The criteria are the qualities of being easy-going or practical (*commode*), respectable or honourable, and intelligent. This shows that support for Roboly at the CCM remained in 1677 even after the disputes and issues during his term as resident-ambassador.

With this memorandum, we see a glimpse of the conflicts and power relations between merchants in the Ottoman Empire, many of whom were working to increase the power of Marseille, the CCM, and the 1660s consular reforms.[38] Colbert's aim was to balance the flourishing of trade with expanding the monarchy's control and revenue. The aim of many merchants was, aside from making profit from their commerce, to obtain privileges and payment from the king for consular or similar services.

Was maintaining or surpassing class divisions a strategy for these tensions and challenges? So-called absolutism in France was based on class collaboration and class divisions, implying that social statuses and power hierarchies were used to resolve tensions. This can be seen in the debates by merchants and the CCM who contested the role of ambassador. It can also be seen in the letters by residents claiming revenue and authority from the king using their profits or potential gains as leverage to obtain privileges. Finally, ministers and ambassadors maintained their privilege over lower-class residents and aspiring diplomats by asserting their authority and social status.

[38] The CCM, which also struggled at home against the Parlement de Provence and the *intendant* (i.e. royal agent), acted as mediator between its merchants and the monarchy.

Towards the end of the old regime, in the late-eighteenth century, when a generation or two of consuls had emerged by royal commission and family links remained a sure way to establish oneself in the regencies, the links between consuls and the ambassador at the Porte had improved. For example, we find family links between the ambassador Count of St Priest (1768–1784) and the consul-général in the key post of Aleppo (Faivre d'Arcier, 2006: 16). Moreover, by this time, Marseille's merchants had stopped providing most consuls, and Versailles had won its battle against the contending city (Ulbert, 2019). The 1789 Revolution brought its own challenges for consular policy, but overall, the eighteenth century saw a homogenisation of the posts as royal commissioners who were more or less applying the minister's reforms. The geopolitical influence of French consuls asserted itself in a broader diplomatic framework which relied on the jurisdictional privileges and autonomy of diplomats, as well as, crucially, collaboration with merchants in the Mediterranean. These enabled consuls to play an active role in accumulating jurisdiction for their sovereign, while asserting their position in the old regime's social hierarchies.

5.6 Conclusion

This chapter focuses on the role of consuls, as a neglected object of study in histories of extraterritoriality and empire, a neglect which is especially problematic in light of their consequential and diverse jurisdictional prerogatives. The Mediterranean is revealed as a space where consuls were able to apply vast and diverse jurisdictional powers and strategies, as well as shape legal hierarchies between Christian and non-Christian actors. These powers were not a given or easily obtained through the capitulations. Instead, by looking into the range of jurisdictional functions they exercised, the differential consular policies and strategies by the Dutch, English, and French, as well as the social origins and composition of their services and their relations to trading communities, we can conclude that the French managed to secure significant consular advantages by the eighteenth century. Moreover, new archival research on the relation between French merchant residents and ambassadors in Istanbul reveals an important debate in the late-seventeenth century on the necessary functions of a Levantine consul that shaped Colbert's reforms. In sum, the French consular service provides the most compelling case of jurisdictional accumulation as a result of reforms by Colbert and his followers.

These measures point to an analysis of French expansion that connects the rise of European aristocratic ambassadors as a product of Louis XIV's reign to the rise of extra-European merchant consuls. French consular policies were key and unique to the early modern context and can be considered as uniquely jurisdictional transplants of authority rather than transports, as in the case of the more merchant and company-driven English and Dutch services.

However, these distinctions are porous and there were significant similarities between all consular services. Merchants generally separated between Christian and non-Christian European spaces to first justify different measures and attitudes towards each other's consular services, and second to separate Muslim jurisdictional spaces as inferior. To do this, the Dutch and English significantly relied on their merchant communities, whether locally implanted or through respective trading companies and conglomerates. Moreover, the French consular service made use of its nation of merchants to assert itself in a dense legal landscape and among competing diplomatic strategies of aristocratisation.

The concept of jurisdictional accumulation aims to reveal jurisdiction as a process that accounts for the convergences and divergences between these diplomatic strategies, rather than separating them into political and commercial realms, or as illustrating a shift from personal to territorial sovereignty. These binaries have led to neglecting consuls' key political functions for imperial expansion. Furthermore, this connection – and the jurisdictional spaces it emphasises – bring a new angle to the development of principles and mechanisms of international law appearing in the upcoming nineteenth century based on sovereign and so-called semi-sovereign international legal subjects and on an international legal order defined by Christian standards of civilisation. These aspects, alongside the specific issue of extraterritoriality, will be further discussed in Chapter 7, before presenting the broader picture of the Atlantic colonial practices of jurisdictional accumulation in the following chapter.

6

Colonial Practices of Jurisdictional Accumulation

Jurisdictional accumulation is a device that reveals how certain agents of imperial expansion were extending, transporting, and transplanting the authority of their sovereign, while also, when possible, improving their own social status. This process involved the accumulation of jurisdictional titles, functions, and rights that often led to the accumulation of significant status and commercial capital. This chapter brings together key legal actors, institutions, and practices that most directly constitute colonial practices of jurisdictional accumulation in the four empires under consideration, and which are identified as both transports and transplants of authority.[1]

Section 6.1 emphasises jurisdictional accumulation as transplants of authority in the Americas. The Castilian Crown developed the most explicit and centrally governed strategies of jurisdictional accumulation through a variety of legal actors, practices, and institutions: the *requerimiento*; *encomiendas*; *audiencias*, and, more broadly, colonial Spain's judiciary as a theatre for jurisdictional subjectivities through judicial competition and opportunities for social justice. These practices transplanted Castilian actors and institutions and created hybrid institutions that subjugated people, resources, and land.

Section 6.2 focuses on the more common forms of jurisdictional accumulation as transports of authority, associated with the colonial and mercantile practices of the French, English/British, and Dutch empires in the Atlantic and in the Mediterranean. Transports of authority signify how empires outsourced colonial expansion to individuals and groups of individuals most often organised as chartered or trading companies and settlements. They imply a more indirect form of

[1] Extensions of authority are reserved for geographically contiguous expansions inside or around the metropolitan territory that contributed to the slowly emerging territorialisation of sovereignty in Northern and Western Europe. These practices are discussed in Chapter 3, although they are not the main focus of this project.

expansion, which equated to a jurisdictional distancing between rulers and the territories colonised, and especially between rulers and indigenous peoples, who were either ignored, banished, or forced off their land by treaties. The jurisdiction accumulated in these cases was more subtly constructed – in legal terms – so as to avoid the incorporation problems generated by transplants of authority.

It is important to recall that this typology of jurisdictional accumulation is merely an analytical tool and has many exceptions and nuances. Most importantly, the French case is the most ambiguous and shifts between transplants and transports of authority as it experimented and mixed different approaches to colonisation in North America and the Caribbean, and shifted rather unsuccessfully between royal control and delegation of jurisdiction to companies. However, the following considers that its colonial practices are best characterised overall in terms of transports of authority so as to distinguish its practices from the Castilian. Moreover, aside from excluding key regions of expansion in and around Asia and Africa, the analysis remains necessarily selective in the regional contexts it has chosen. The argument does not preclude that these and other practices of legal expansion were occurring in the American and Mediterranean regions, or in those excluded from this study. For now, however, the argument concentrates on comparing key cases of Atlantic and Mediterranean jurisdictional accumulation.

Another cautionary note concerns the Dutch Republic. To satisfactorily answer the research problem posed in this project regarding the Dutch case, that is the role of a range of imperial agents in transporting Dutch authority through jurisdictional practices, existing historiography remains limited. One would therefore need to engage in significant primary research, a task beyond the possibilities of this project. Existing historiography relating to the Dutch Empire is mostly concerned with Grotius and the VOC, meaning a focus on doctrine, which this project seeks to avoid, and a focus on Asia, which is not the subject of this book. However, the relation to Grotius is crucial to highlight, because it raises similar problems to those raised against Grotius's legacy in narrowly shaping the history of extraterritoriality as a privilege based on the double fiction of territorial sovereignty reserved to ambassadors in Northern Europe. In both cases, modern historians have exaggerated Grotius's influence leading to problematic assumptions and a narrow understanding on both topics of the Dutch Empire and extraterritoriality.

Concerning the book's spatial focus, the Dutch were active in the Atlantic through the Dutch West India Company (WIC) and in the Mediterranean through their consuls and the Directorate. However, their most significant and transformative conquests and areas of legal influence and control occurred in Asia, in sub-Saharan Africa (South Africa and the West Coast), and in the Indian and Pacific oceans through the wide-ranging activities of the VOC. Focusing on their legal colonial practices in these regions would distort the comparative exercise and stand out from the other cases. Notwithstanding, considering their relevance to practices of jurisdictional accumulation, some examples from these cases are mentioned. In spite of these problems, the Dutch Empire's role in practices of jurisdictional accumulation remains important as a comparative marker for the other empires, and through the VOC as a model for the practices of other trading companies.

Leaving aside these limitations, it is now possible, through the analysis in this chapter, to affirm the book's key argument. Early modern empires were characterised by various practices of jurisdictional accumulation (transplants, transports, and extensions of authority) largely determined by the specificities of their own jurisdictional divisions (social property relations) and by the different strategies and sub-sovereign agents (diplomats, magistrates, merchants, lawyers) their ruling elites chose or negotiated with to maintain or elevate themselves among those divisions.

The next chapter digs deeper into the implications of this argument and explores more tentatively the consequences of its jurisdictional focus for the concept of extraterritoriality and for the large-scale and long-term periodisation of international law. For now, the following provides the key examples that substantiate this argument.

6.1 Iberian Transplants of Authority

6.1.1 The 'New World'

Castilian practices of jurisdictional accumulation are mainly characterised as transplants of authority because of their hybrid, organic, and socially wide character, concerned with their relations with people as subjects and labour (i.e. as means of exploitation and surplus extraction through political and juridical means). A set of social property relations, or in other words a structure of jurisdictional relations, was transplanted and grew into a hybrid or new structure of social property relations, which the Crown thereafter sought to control and contain.[2]

Perhaps the best-known legal practice of Iberian conquest and occupation is the *requerimiento*. This refers to 'a Spanish royal proclamation', a legal document drafted by one of the main civil jurists to Castile's court, Juan Lopez de Palacios Rubios. The *requerimiento* then came to be known as the legal ceremony where the proclamation was read and which took place before the appropriation of land by *conquistadores*, 'accompanied by chaplains, missionaries and learned notaries' (Schwarzenberger, 1962: 53). The presence of notaries to make 'sure that due legal form was given to all transactions during such expeditions' (53) powerfully illustrates the intertwined relation between the legal, political, and religious spheres as well as the Hispanics' need to demonstrate their dedication to legitimate colonisation in the eyes of God and European contenders.

> The document had to be read in full by a notary and translated to the Indians. It consisted of a fantastic saga of Papal and Spanish claims to the New World and left the Indians with the alternative of acknowledging the supremacy of the Pope and of the Spanish Crown or enslavement and confiscation of their property. When the ceremony was completed, and the Indians were still proving recalcitrant, the way was free to war or annexation of their territories.
>
> (Schwarzenberger, 1962: 53)

These ceremonies were meant to legally authorise Hispanics either to rule over Native Americans and exploit their labour and land, or to wage a just war against them and claim possession of their labour and land as the victor's right. The war was claimed to be 'just' since the Native Americans were given a choice through the reading of the *requerimiento*. If they refused to acknowledge the Christian faith and Castilian authority, Native Americans were given the same legal status as infidels, and forced conversion became admissible. In either case, the Hispanics established their claim to the ownership of Indian land and labour. The only choice the Indians had was how they would 'give up' something they had in most cases not even conceived as tangible or detachable from their selves or their community. It was first used in 1514 and last used in the 1550s (Dickason, 1989: 190).

[2] For some nuance to the distinction between Iberian colonisation as concerned with labour and people, and the English as concerned with territory, see Herzog (2015b: 79), who argues that 'treaties with natives were mostly concerned with territory'. However, this does not negate their parallel concern with jurisdictional subjection and inclusion into the Castilian Empire and legal order, distinguishing them from the other empires.

Second, the most common practice of settlement was an *encomienda*, that is the 'allocation to leading settlers of groups of natives as labourers or personal servants' (Parry, 1990: 100). *Encomiendas*, similarly to feudal estates, came with duties and privileges. They were an indispensable tool for the Crown to colonise its 'discoveries', but later became a major problem as the settler-elite became more resistant to control and to the extraction of revenue for the Crown.

> The *encomendero* could build a house, maintain a household and continue to feed and arm his personal followers. In return he was required to protect 'his' Indians against other would-be exploiters, appoint and pay parish priests in his villages, and bear his share of the military defense of the province.
>
> (Parry, 1990: 100)

The *encomendero* had no other administrative or judicial duties (i.e. he was not a political agent and was not granted land). Therefore, *encomiendas* were not feudal manors nor slave-worked estates, as agriculture or land was not the major interest. The relationship between the monarchy and *encomenderos* was very similar to what had characterised as European feudalism, but the property relations and privileges in place created something different (Wood, 2003: 39). In some cases, the leading settlers just took the place of Aztec or Inca rulers, appropriating their tributes and services (Parry, 1990: 101). The major role of *encomiendas* was to provide a settled professional army throughout the land to protect the Crown's acquisitions and operate as a 'quasi-feudal militia' (Parry, 1990: 101). This army was also supposed to be transformed into an 'official and permanent organisation for local government' (101), similarly to what existed in Iberia, although the tradition of municipal incorporation was already starting to decay.

Most towns in the Indies were 'thatched huts' (Parry, 1990: 102), but with the essential characteristics of legal incorporation. This meant jurisdiction over the surrounding country, control of Native American labour, a dependence upon their supplies for subsistence, and a geography of Hispanic centres and Native American suburbs. Soldiers became *vecinos*, that is legally enrolled householders of one or other of the incorporated towns from each conquest, but they still lived in the capital city. Finally, legal incorporation meant that the administration of the capital city was responsible for that of the province. The city government, *cabildo*, was composed of twelve *regidores* (councillors) all nominated by the commander of the conquest. The *cabildo* elected from the ensemble of *vecinos* two *alcaldes* (municipal magistrates), whom after a year elected their successors. What is meant here by 'election' is the presenting of a list of names to the commander, who *in fine* decides who is 'elected' (Parry, 1990: 102). In an *encomienda*, each group of Indians (a hundred or several hundreds) was assigned to a Spaniard who could employ their services as he saw fit. This measure was given legislative approval by Ferdinand in a decree of 1509.

In 1542 the New Laws of the Indies were published and represented a 'drastic curtailment' of settlers' privileges. Two articles abolished *encomiendas*, but they remained impossible to execute. The Crown was beginning to lose touch with the new settlements and thus looked increasingly worried of the *encomenderos'* growing power. It was also a response to the mounting criticism in Europe and consisted more of a political move in regard to these rather than a viable policy. In parallel, the 'unity of sovereignty, governance, and religion' in justifications of empire developed after Phillip II's 1573 ordinances establishing the contours of urban planning and the development of jurisdictional subjectivities that 'defined the urban space as Spanish in opposition to an indigenous fringe', where 'the colonial town came to the indigenous' and led to the 'incremental cancellation of the indigenous body and territory' (García-Salmones & Eslava, 2010: 60–61). The founding of *asentamientos*, of these new cities, was drafted in the ordinances through the work of lawyers and theologians so as to merge the secular and theological aspirations of the empire and replaced, on paper, the logic of conquest (García-Salmones & Eslava, 2010: 64).

A third practice of jurisdictional accumulation is the reproduction of powerful legal institutions in Iberian colonies. These led to various outcomes regarding class and social relations in the Americas as well as unexpected problems for the Crown. Intended as a means to control the *conquistadores*, *audiencias* were tribunals with wide judicial, executive, and legislative functions set up across key colonial cities; 'by the early seventeenth century, eleven audiencias operated in the Indies, and by 1687 they contained seventy-six authorized positions' (Burkholder & Chandler, 1977: 1–2).[3] These positions were taken up by metropolitan *letrados* and university-educated nobility who were meant to be the Crown's more impartial judges. They were most often the least 'well-to-do Spaniards', and arrived 'in debt and with no resources', which led

[3] *Audiencias* were created in the sixteenth century in Santo Domingo, New Spain, Panama, Guatemala, Lima, Santa Fe, New Galicia, Charcas, Quito, Chile, and Manila, followed in the eighteenth century by Buenos Aires, Cuzco, and Caracas (Fernández Castro, 2014: 189).

them to 'illegal transactions' and abuses (Burkholder & Chandler, 1977: 7). The rise of a colonial aristocracy – the 'creoles' and 'native sons' attending colonial Spain's new universities – contested Castile's choice of appointments, and complained of abuses, lack of knowledge, and inexperience concerning the communities under the judges' jurisdiction. American-born aristocrats felt discriminated by a 'self-perpetuating' nexus between the *colegio mayor* and the council, that is governing bodies of Castile and its empire (Burkholder & Chandler, 1977: 10).[4] Although their representation did increase during the seventeenth century, this remained low, since '[f]rom 1611 to 1687, natives of the New World totaled at least seventy-nine or one out of five new appointees' (Burkholder & Chandler, 1977: 11).

Concerning the broader legal experience of Hispanic settlers and Native Americans in New Spain, it is evidently not possible here to review and account for the status of judicial activity in all the colonies. Research still remains limited, and previous angles either focused on the technical aspect of legal texts; were split normatively and shaped by assessments of the good or bad legacy of the Castilian Empire; or shared a sense that in spite of the centrality of law for the Castilian Empire, it remained irrelevant to Native Americans' lives or considered primitive in relation to modern and European concepts of the rule of law (Owensby, 2011: 3–5). A few earlier exceptions (Stern, 1982; Borah, 1983) looked at the 'concrete reality alongside derecho indiano's text-driven approach' (Owensby, 2011: 4). However, a new recent impetus focuses on the concrete legal experiences of colonial Hispanics and Native Americans in the broader context of imperial history and geopolitics (Owensby, 2011; Adorno, 2012; Herzog, 2015a; van Deusen, 2015; Duve & Pihlajamäki, 2015; Premo, 2017; Graubart, 2018; Premo & Yanakakis, 2019).[5]

Specifically, it is argued that colonial Mexico was shaped by triangular legal relations between settlers, indigenous groups, and the metropole represented by royal legal institutions. In effect, the Castilian colonial legal system 'became a means to the negotiation of colonial difference' (Owensby, 2011: 1–48). Imperial expansion, and crucially the consolidation of this expansion, became a legal struggle, while colonial Spain

[4] *Colegio mayor* consisted in six Iberian elite residence halls by the late-sixteenth century considered 'bastions of privilege' for the education of the nobility.

[5] There is also a wide literature on native justice and litigation in Spanish American courts. For a review, see Yannakakis (2013).

saw the emergence of overlapping legal concepts and practices on which depended the appropriation of land and resources (Owensby, 2011: 31). This dependence has led some authors to argue for the 'modern' and 'enlightened' nature of legal relations in colonial Spanish American courtrooms, where 'ordinary and often illiterate litigants in Spanish America, not their legal representatives, were among its most surprising and skilled legal practitioners' (Premo, 2017: 3). In effect, eighteenth-century 'colonial women, natives, and slaves sued their social superiors before royal judges in increasing numbers' (3). If I would rather strongly resist adopting the path-dependency consequences of ascribing a modern or enlightened badge to colonial institutions, the hybrid and innovative character of these judicial experiences and practices remain nevertheless essential aspects of Castile's transplanting of authority.

Another example of this triangular relation between the Crown, Native Americans, and settlers is the case of the protection regime and arrangements between the Tlaxcalans and the Castilian Crown (Baber, 2012; Benton & Clulow, 2017: 60). The Tlaxcalans helped Cortés secure the conquest of Tenochtilán, in the Aztec Empire. In spite of ambiguities and different interpretations of the consequences of this alliance, the Crown granted them an exemption from the *encomienda* system, affirming 'their status as free vassals' (Benton & Clulow, 2017: 60). The Tlaxcalans even travelled to Castile to negotiate and avoid the tribute and services other Native Americans were forced to owe Hispanic settlers. This example showcases the interdependence between languages of protection which could grant jurisdictional authority as much as subordination, since the Tlaxcalans used this language to secure some autonomy while the Crown claimed to use it to 'shelter Tlaxcalans from the worst abuses of Spanish colonists' (Benton & Clulow, 2017: 60).

The last, but far from least, aspect of jurisdictional accumulation is the shaping of colonial jurisdictional subjectivities. Studies have emphasised this subjective dimension from a doctrinal or textual perspective, looking at the work of Castile's theologians (García-Salmones & Eslava, 2010; Nuzzo, 2011). Other more practical aspects crucial to these subjectivities is the competition between various authorities such as Spanish colonial judges (*alcalde mayor*), judges of native *cabildos* (*alcaldes*), ecclesiastical officials, missionaries, and superior tribunals such as the Audiencia of New Spain or the viceroy in Mexico City (Premo & Yanakakis, 2019: 53). The competition includes the acknowledgement of 'Indian jurisdiction', which 'refers to a wide-ranging sphere of legal authority based on Spanish recognition of the legal personhood of subjects designated as

"Indians" and the authority of the governing municipal bodies of native pueblos, known collectively as the "Republic of Indians"' (Adorno, 2012; Premo & Yanakakis, 2019: 30). Increasing anthropological and sociological legal research is identifying, through a rich and wide-ranging approach to judicial history, the ways in which Native Americans were recognised as 'semi-sovereign subjects', as litigators as well as judges who 'jockeyed for advantage before various Spanish colonial magistrates' (Premo & Yanakakis, 2019: 33). One might be tempted to see this legal subjectification as an argument against the devastating effects of Castile's jurisdictional accumulation, but this native jurisdictional space – which 'could be housed or mobile', that is 'embodied in persons of authority and in buildings both permanent and temporary', 'in territorial and socio-political units', and in ritualised and ceremonial 'practices and symbols' – was inevitably a legitimising tool for the Crown's sovereign supremacy over the jurisdiction of the natives (Premo & Yanakakis, 2019: 54). In other words, in spite of the potential advantages and opportunities for justice offered by jurisdictional accumulation as transplants of authority, this set of practices remained defined as a strategy for empire-building, as it 'reorganized rather than acknowledged the indigenous world' (Herzog, 2015b: 79).

6.1.2 *Mercantilism and Iberia's Commercial–Legal Institutions*

The question of whether Castile was a mercantilist empire is relevant to help characterise its approach to jurisdictional accumulation, but it remains very much open to debate and cannot be done full justice here. Debates over the boundaries and actors of mercantilism reveal some important legal and social characteristics of jurisdictional accumulation, and these practices contribute to sharpening the understanding of the particularities of Castile and of the future Spain's mercantile basis through key institutions such as *consulados* (i.e. consuls), the House of Trade of Seville, and the Junta de Dependencias de Extranjeros.

The Castilian Empire was multinational, especially concerning its mercantile dimensions. Trading nations (Seville, Lisbon, Antwerp, Genoa) 'lived side by side' and struck commercial partnerships with English, French, and Portuguese merchants, revealing a porous network for the Atlantic circulation of goods and capital (Studnicki-Gizbert, 2007: 28). The role of Portuguese merchants is particularly revealing. The Castilian Crown and Iberian nobility struggled against the Portuguese vision of how to conduct overseas trade and its implications for the boundaries and management of the empire. Portuguese learned merchants, who were considered commoners by the Hispanic aristocracy and therefore to be 'transgressing' their social position (Studnicki-Gizbert, 2007: 161), put forward a more open conception of the 'economy' as more separate from the state than the Hispanic nobility could envisage from their more legalist neo-scholastic doctrine based on a policy of 'retrenchment and closure' (Studnicki-Gizbert, 2007: 12–13). In effect, the Castilian struggles and debates against the Portuguese merchants and diaspora (who constituted a large proportion of settlers in the conquered Americas) contributed to shaping the jurisdictional reach of the Castilian Empire. By failing to take on the Portuguese's more open vision, the outcome of these struggles contributed to entrenching Castile's economic decline (Studnicki-Gizbert, 2007: 133–134).

Generally, studies have focused more on the intellectual history of mercantilism or have argued that Castile was at best a pseudo-mercantilist monarchy (Grafe, 2013: 241–242). Although the basic elements for a mercantilist empire were present, the 'intimate scale, the number, and the geographical spread of merchant houses' created a 'multinational, extensive, and decentralized' empire that escaped the 'state's ambition to fully control its energies' (Studnicki-Gizbert, 2007: 9). Moreover, in spite of the gold and silver exploited from the Americas and the state-led violence involved in that exploitation, Castile 'failed to convert this accumulated mass of precious metals into *capital*' and constitutes a prime example of why the process of primitive accumulation requires 'a class of indigenous capitalists', absent in Iberia (Banaji, 2019). Castilian mercantilism, as it was discussed by its contemporary mercantilist authors, therefore consisted in a 'lament on Spain's failure to develop' and stood in contrast to the other three more commercially orientated mercantilist protagonists, England, France, and the Dutch Republic (Banaji, 2019).

However, literature on the economic history of Spain has been overcrowded by the focus on the Atlantic: the 'regulation of American trades and their role in international competition and in securing metropolitan rents with monopoly and mercantilism' (Grafe, 2013: 246). In contrast, there is much less research on 'the unification of the sources of political power and administrative structures' (246). This point is worth considering because it speaks to this study's central argument on the ongoing need to refute the use of the modern domestic and international dichotomies for the early modern period – and the consequent domestic analogy found in Marxist works such as Miéville (2005) and Anievas and

Nişancioğlu (2015). Instead, and especially for Spain – though this problem also applies to narratives such as Grewe's (2000) that divide a public and political Europe from its mercantilist overseas contexts – the definition of mercantilism should incorporate the 'attempt to transform the constitution of society' (Grafe, 2013: 245). This means situating mercantilism in the structures of metropolitan governance (Grafe, 2013: 246), especially in cases of jurisdictionally fragmented kingdoms such as the Iberian peninsula. In such cases, it is more appropriate according to this project's typology, to identify these practices as extensions of authority.

With this aim in mind, the organisation of military and navy institutions become essential components of not only Castile's jurisdictional accumulation but also its relation to mercantilism. Studies looking at seventeenth-century naval history have emphasised the state of Iberia's forests as the source of raw material for its armadas, the role of seamen, and of broader naval personnel. This later period of naval history, concurrent with the shift from the Mediterranean to the Atlantic, has become a more important topic of research displacing 'the great battles of the sixteenth century' as watershed moments – Lepanto in 1571 and the Armada sent to England in 1588 (Goodman, 1997). Focus on the social property relations enabling outward policies, whether as mercantilism or navy expeditions, shows in both cases the importance of jurisdictional fragmentation and of institutional actors such as naval administrators or clerks whose hierarchy was composed of ten different posts and functioned according to a subordination system where officers switched between positions (Goodman, 1997: 161–163). These administrators came from the lower nobility and municipal elite, or from families of naval administrators or of active military and naval service (Goodman, 1997: 175). Although they did not seem to have jurisdictional duties, their structured and regulated organisation and importance for Castilian imperialism more generally could be compared to the role of consular services for France. They presented 'a mixed image', sharing a 'family hold on offices', accusations of corruption, and a questionable loyalty to other authorities than the king, while also being known for their 'dedication, integrity and efficiency' (Goodman, 1997: 180).

Other institutions were key to Castile's jurisdictional accumulation: consuls and consulates, and more specifically the House of Trade of the Indies (Casa de la Contratación de las Indias) founded in Seville in 1503, the Royal and Supreme Council of the Indies (Real y Supremo Consejo de las Indias) founded in 1524, and the later-eighteenth-century Junta de Dependencias de Extranjeros are important to briefly mention.[6]

The House of Trade of the Indies in Seville became the 'most important official center of the Castilian commerce and Atlantic diffusion' (Fernández Castro, 2014: 190) with a variety of functions, including jurisdiction to enforce the prohibition for 'foreigners' (i.e. non-Castilians), to trade in the Indies (Fernández Castro, 2014: 191) with penalties including 'fines, seizures, or even jail' (Fernández Castro, 2014: 199). This jurisdiction overlapped with that of the merchant guilds and consulates, present in commercial cities such as Barcelona, Valencia, Burgos, and Bilbao (Fernández Castro, 2014: 200). Sevillian traders petitioned the king for a consulate and obtained one in 1543; from this date the House of Trade of Seville was not meant to settle commercial disputes. However, it continued doing so and explaining this according to the usual argument of the period's – and especially Iberia's – 'overlapping of jurisdictions', is limited, argues Fernández Castro. Her analysis of the House's lawsuits highlights the merchants' trust in the House of Trade and its defence of their 'patrimonial rights' (2014: 203–204). Litigants were also able to use a special procedure to recover their debts based on the production of an authentic document – *juicio ejecutivo* – which resolved 60.5 per cent of disputes between 1583 and 1598 and shortened the delays of decisions. This annulled the attractiveness of consulates based on expedience. Moreover, judges of the House of Trade were 'royal officials with special powers to *enforce their judgments*' (Fernández Castro, 2014: 205), and therefore merely applying to the House carried significant authority from the fear provoked by the success of these procedures (Fernández Castro, 2014: 206). The House of Trade was a transnational (in the early modern sense) institution that was possible in the 'jurisdictional culture' of Castile, exemplified by the power of magistrates as 'interpreters of equity able to ponder the adequate instrument of law to formulate a judgment' (Fernández Castro, 2014: 206). They had significant powers and authority over merchants from all over the world and applying the law in a strict way would have been detrimental to the interests of the empire. Therefore, in spite of its more legalist obstacles this royal institution was favoured by merchants over

[6] There is an abundant literature on Iberian consulates, although mostly in Spanish and French (Pradells Nadal, 1992; Ozanam, 1999; Hernández, 2011; Aglietti *et al.*, 2013). For reasons explained in the previous chapter, they are not focused on here, but this does not mean they are not important institutions of the Castilian Empire.

the more ad hoc and self-regulated institution of the consulate relying on arbitration (Fernández Castro, 2014: 207).

The Junta de Dependencias de Extranjeros is interesting to contrast to the House of Trade as it illustrates the shift in the empire's status and strategies. It was 'created in 1714 with the objective of overseeing foreign businesses in Spanish ports' and appointed consuls and other representatives, surveyed foreigners living in or passing through Spain, dealt with 'fiscal affairs related to taxes, as well as the provision of gifts granted by foreign merchants to the Spanish administration at some crucial junctures' (Crespo Solana, 2014: 144–145). As the numbers of foreigners increased after 1716, the Junta became a 'platform for the recovery of privileges that had been granted in the past to the various nations settled on Spanish soil' (Crespo Solana, 2014: 145). The main aim of these laws against foreigners was to 'place under close scrutiny the commercial activities in the Americas of foreign merchants living in Spain' (Crespo Solana, 2014: 144). New laws also led to censuses of the foreign population, similarly to France, but these were incorrect and led to erroneous representations (Crespo Solana, 2006). In other words, this institution illustrates the more protectionist and mistrustful commercial strategy of the eighteenth century.

If some of these commercial institutions were close to other similar European institutions (e.g. the CCM in France), and shared many necessary commercial and juridical links with them through their merchants and consuls, overall the jurisdictional context, goals and impact of Iberian institutions in their colonies differed significantly from the other three empires under consideration, which can be characterised by transports of authority in which sovereigns and states remained indirect designers of imperial expansion.

6.2 English, French, and Dutch Transports of Authority

6.2.1 On Similarities and Differences

Before moving forward with the empirical analyses, some methodological remarks are necessary. The analyses developed below contest histories of international law based on generalising 'external similarities', such as in Grewe (2000) and Miéville (2005). The key argument is to think of jurisdictional accumulation as a process that captures the different boundaries and orders that shaped the early modern world, and in particular the jurisdictional divisions and actors that shaped empires in their metropolitan as well as colonial contexts. As Cavanagh shows through his work on trading companies and jurisdictional conflicts, 'the politics of jurisdiction in the history of early modern imperialism were just as significant in the Old World as they were in the New World' (2017: 455).

This emphasis highlights the inadequacy of the internal–external and public–private binaries linked to state formation that characterise classic and critical approaches mentioned previously. Jurisdictional agencies – or the 'politics of jurisdiction' – are different in each case but they transgress modern binaries. Old regime France was jurisdictional in terms of its extensions of authority for the French kingdom's estate to counter regional fragmentation as well as unregulated and untaxed mobility and trade. Jurisdictional agency was also fundamental overseas through the use of different types of diplomatic and commercial actors, including a vast but less effective number of trading companies. The Dutch Republic developed practices of jurisdictional consolidation and extension through its emergence as a new confederation of jurisdictionally autonomous provinces closely linked to its leading merchants and magistrates and transported the authority of these provinces and merchants beyond those borders through trading companies and consular agents. Finally, the English Crown did not share similar jurisdictional divisions or institutions in its royal domain. However, it also transported its authority – through concepts of the common law, agricultural improvement, trading companies, and consuls – and faced jurisdictional debates about the legal boundaries of the royal domain and its overseas dominions.

If France, the Dutch Republic, and England/Britain developed specific practices of jurisdictional accumulation, with various similarities and differences, they nevertheless all differed from the Castile-led Iberian peninsula in a significant way. They lacked its mix of secular, religious, and socially organic imperial design concerned with the jurisdictional incorporation of subjects. Instead, the other empires engaged in more commercial and outsourced practices of jurisdictional accumulation concerned with territorial occupation. They copied each other, especially regarding trading companies, even though they each had different aims and contexts, making each case important to assess for its specificities and impact on concepts of jurisdiction and sovereignty. Nevertheless, these empires are considered together in this section, for reasons of clarity and because they involved more third parties, or private individuals, than the state directly (e.g. semi- or quasi-sovereign trading companies, settlers, colonists, conglomerates of merchants, free ports) thereby justifying the concept of transport of authority.

Various authors separate the Castilian from the other three. For Fitzmaurice (2014: 8), 'the English, French and Dutch were more disingenuous than the Spanish in their understanding of what constituted legitimate expansion', that is they called conquest 'something altogether different' by relying on the concepts of occupation and requirements of land improvement. Put differently, only the Castilian were expressly concerned with justifying their colonial or imperial expeditions through arguments of natural law or *jus gentium* (Koskenniemi, 2017: 8–9). Moreover, for Tomlins (2010: 132–134), only the Castilian were expressly concerned with controlling labour and people rather than simply territory, a point also made by Wood (2003), Seed (2001), and earlier historians of early modern empires such as Pagden (1990, 1995) discussed in Chapter 3.

However, there are other key differences which would lead to regrouping these four empires differently. For example, the common-law system in England and its colonies stands in contrast to the 'nonspecialized mercantile law in the Spanish, Dutch, and French empires', a key distinction required to make sense of early modern jurisdictional conflicts for Benton (2010: 145). For García-Salmones and Eslava (2010: 77), although the Castilian and British empires differ significantly in terms of their approaches to colonisation, they share an important similarity regarding the need for conversion of new subjects and the use of religion as either a 'legitimising or delegitimising factor', shaping the jurisdictional according to theological (for the Castilian) or civil (for the British) subjectivities. Other important differences are noted between Iberian and French versus English and Dutch colonisation, where the former placed proprietorships 'directly under royal authority', and the latter used 'additional links between the metropolis and the fringe' (Roper & Ruymbeke, 2007: 7). Moreover, the 'availability of land actually reinforced manorial structures in Spanish America and New France, and, thus, gave these crowns additional opportunities to create *encomiendas* and seigneuries (Roper & Ruymbeke, 2007: 17).

The concept of 'proprietary ventures' (Roper & Ruymbeke, 2007) is used to emphasise the similarities between all early modern empires. These ventures encompass the variety of colonising initiatives in the early modern period and refer to chartered companies, individuals or 'non-incorporated groups' who 'received charters from central governments that granted them powers to recruit settlers, exercise governmental functions in colonies, and own land overseas' (2007: 2), for example 'joint-stock companies, encomiendas, seigneuries, captaincies, patroonships, and individuals who served as agents of empire in conjunction with their personal interests' (2007: 10). All these empires relied on '"private" individuals and entities overseas well into the eighteenth century' and on the 'privatization of colonizing efforts' (2007: 4). Early modern monarchies were composite, and prolonged feudal remnants of their societies in their colonies (Roper & Ruymbeke, 2007: 7). For England, the 'defense of remote American boundaries, the cultivation of local government, and the need to recruit migrants required the devolution of substantial powers'. These authors note similar situations for Castile's *encomenderos*, Dutch 'patroons in New Netherland, Brazilian donatary captains, and various seigneurs and companies in the French empire' who exercised authority 'just as aristocrats and lower landholding orders did in Western Europe' (Roper & Ruymbeke, 2007: 7). This concept is useful and, in many ways, relates to the concept of jurisdictional accumulation. However, it also brushes over crucial differences between the empires' practices, and thus remains limited for our purposes.

A final methodological point is necessary. This study has developed a significant nuance to the more commercially driven and 'disingenuous' group of empires. If, in general, extra-European activities by the French, English, and Dutch empires were left to elite merchant or lower-class individuals and companies, the previous chapters' analyses of diplomatic actors (i.e. ambassadors and especially consuls), showed that special legal regimes were developed and used by sovereigns, although not always successfully, to extend, transport, and even, in the French case, transplant European sovereignty to the shores of the Mediterranean and beyond. This history has been neglected by both histories of empire and histories of international law. This leads us to the further comparative implications which slightly complicate the division between the Castilian Empire and the others and focus on the need for narratives of intertwined political and commercial aspects of jurisdictional accumulation.

In effect, diplomatic aspects of France's imperial expansion should be considered as jurisdictional practices similar to Castile's in terms of being more directly driven and regulated by royal institutions. Louis XIV's aristocratisation of ambassadors and grand-scale development of commissioned and highly regulated consular representation were an explicit effort to centralise and govern imperial expansion and were driven by clear jurisdictional concerns and outcomes. They are therefore considered as transplants of authority. In contrast, the more modest and unsuccessful English and the Dutch attempts to engage in such practices in the Mediterranean are better characterised as transports of authority. However, the most significant aspects of colonial and imperial expansion by the Dutch and English/British empires, and in many cases also the French, relied on individual merchants, settlers, companies, or corporations in the Atlantic and Asian contexts.

To close this study and present in more detail the emergence of these more commercially driven and indirect practices of jurisdictional accumulation, the remainder discusses the case of French mercantilism and the practice of corsairing in the Mediterranean, the mostly Dutch and English trading companies, and finally, the differences in settlement practices and the jurisdictional conditions between these three empires.

6.2.1 *The Classic Case of French Mercantilism*

Much of the focus on mercantilism in IR studies has been on the Atlantic competition between the main European empires. The aim of this subsection is to highlight certain aspects of mercantilism that tend to be neglected (e.g. their Mediterranean context), and which reveal the importance of the jurisdictional make-up of these early modern empires to understand how they transported authority, using the classic case of France as illustrative of the need to develop more analyses of the varieties of mercantilism in the early modern period.

The case of France is often considered the archetypal case of mercantilism as protectionism – or Colbertism. However, preceding discussions emphasise the multiplicity and variation of political and legal debates and France's complex, powerful and collaborating set of regional and royal institutions (Chapter 3). Even though a key outcome of the king's strategies was to distance foreign affairs from those of the realm – and how this manifested itself powerfully through ambassadorial aristocratisation and consular policies (Chapters 4 and 5) as well as through the vast system of trading companies and networks (Marzagalli, 2014; Horn, 2015) – doing so was always a contested and continuous struggle, and various actors maintained functions and held aspirations to trade, organise, and travel outside and inside the kingdom beyond their ascribed jurisdictions. In other words, the so-called protectionist boundaries of the state were much more porous than is often assumed or was wished by the king.

However, some aspects of French mercantilism as regulation get neglected by conventional definitions, such as demographic control or '*populationisme*' (Ulbert, forthcoming). The idea that populations constitute a valuable resource emerged in the late-sixteenth century, as a basis to increase tax revenue, join the army, and to develop agriculture and industries. Richelieu and Mazarin thereafter begin to develop measures such as financial privileges for marriage and reproduction, combating the clergy's celibacy, and controlling emigration and immigration, with specific artisans and professions requested and allowed to emigrate and immigrate, whereas others were strictly forbidden.[7] Mercantilism was deeply embedded as the regional and micro-control of populations, even before effective means of collecting information or of mapping territory were used (Branch, 2013). In France, it was not strictly concerned with merchants but with broader sections of the population, which became increasingly defined in terms of their value as a resource. These measures also show how personal relations of sovereignty were maintained through mercantilism's demographic control, as well as new techniques of census-taking in the Ottoman Empire and the control of travel through specific passports and certificates.[8]

Certain mercantilist practices became instances of jurisdictional accumulation beyond the control of the French state, such as those involving trading companies and instances of collaboration with local rulers. However, overseas mercantilism in the Mediterranean, embodied by a unique consular model, brought commercial and diplomatic successes to the monarchy, and helped to dislodge English and Dutch competition in trading with the Ottoman Empire. Thus, simply by looking at the French case, mercantilism cannot be homogeneously invoked to define the universalisation of international law in this era à la Miéville and according to Marxist histories of international law. Doing so ignores the different practices of jurisdictional accumulation that shaped and enabled imperial competition in the Mediterranean and the ways in which diplomatic practices contributed to legitimising legal distinctions based on early modern concepts of Christian and

[7] Immigration to France was actively promoted for the recruitment of Flemish, Dutch, and Italian technicians, who worked in sectors of tar and tin, as well as lace, mirrors, and tapestries (Ulbert, forthcoming).

[8] Controls were particularly important and stricter in the Ottoman parts of the Mediterranean, the main reasons being the region's crucial commercial interests and the smaller and thus more manageable numbers of merchants and travellers in the region, making census taking more reliable and effective (Ulbert, forthcoming).

non-Christian spaces.[9] Crucially, these practices had nothing or little to do with capitalist social property relations.

Moreover, the types of mercantilism observed in the Mediterranean differ significantly from types developed for the Atlantic and Asian spaces of imperial expansion (Games, 2008: 47–79; Stein, 2012: 8). By characterising empires as polycentric systems with a 'multijurisdictional nature' (Herrero Sanchez & Kaps, 2017b: 13–14), analyses of mercantilisms in Europe and the Mediterranean incorporate consuls, maritime consulates, and other commercial–legal or corporate institutions such as 'merchant guilds or fraternities' that emphasise the importance of 'legal norms', 'mercantilist regulation, the acquisition of citizenship' (Herrero Sanchez & Kaps, 2017b: 11) as essential conditions that help identify practices of jurisdictional accumulation. These studies also emphasise the dynastic element of early modern Europe, and more specifically the importance of 'kinship and family' for merchant and jurisdictional networks (Herrero Sanchez & Kaps, 2017b: 6), as well as the 'circulation of elites across polycentric empires' (Herrero Sanchez & Kaps, 2017b: 17). Similar arguments regarding familial networks and patrimonial power (particularly relevant to the Dutch case) can also be found in the work of Adams (2007). This literature will need to be further discussed in relation to jurisdictional accumulation and social property relations, but for now it provides useful introductions to alternative focuses on the legal aspects of mercantilism, particularly neglected in Marxist historiography.

6.2.3 Corsairing

An important manifestation of mercantilisms in the Mediterranean region is corsairing (or privateering). This practice consisted in 'raids on the coast, capturing people and the seizure of ships at sea' (Kaiser & Calafat, 2014: 73). In this context, sovereignty meant 'the power to define what was legitimate corsairing and what was criminal piracy' or 'to keep this difference unclear' (Kaiser & Calafat, 2014: 73). Istanbul was a key port where European powers competed to secure trade and protection, especially in response to corsairing.

Corsairing 'shaped the commercial and diplomatic relations between Southern Europe, the Ottoman Empire and its dependent territories in North Africa' and was crucial to Braudel's account, who defined it as 'a

[9] See Chapter 7.

secondary form of war' (Kaiser & Calafat, 2014: 74). It even became more 'profitable than the traditional slave trade' (Kaiser & Calafat, 2014: 76). Corsairing has generated a rich array of studies (e.g. Colás, 2016) which cannot be reviewed or done justice to here, but it is important to keep in mind as a 'trading platform that crossed religious, legal and normative boundaries' (Kaiser & Calafat, 2014: 76) and therefore greatly contributed to jurisdictional disputes and to opportunities for jurisdictional accumulation as a component of Mediterranean mercantilisms. It is not considered here a practice of jurisdictional accumulation per se, since its primary aim and outcome was commercial and did not consist in the enunciation of rights, titles, and functions for corsairs, even though it led and relied on these, especially treaties and capitulations with the Ottoman Empire and specifically with the North African regencies (Calafat, 2018c). Corsairs made the most of existing jurisdictional arrangements, but they did not pursue them, in contrast to companies, consuls, and other diplomats.

Nevertheless, corsairing relations became a 'laboratory for the evolution of the law of the sea and the law of nations' (Kaiser & Calafat, 2014: 76). They were crucial for the law of nations or 'juridical Europeanisation', and led to a 'sea of paper': safe conducts, trade licences, passports, lists of passengers, cargo, bills of lading (*police de chargement*), 'Turkish passports' for Denmark and Sweden (sold by French consuls), and 'certificates delivered by French consuls to the corsairs of Algiers and Tunis, attesting their quality and role in legitimate warfare' (Kaiser & Calafat, 2014: 82).

According to these authors, corsairing cannot be simply understood as 'extraterritorial violence' à la Thomson (1994), since the Mediterranean situation is too complex in terms of overlapping and contested jurisdictional regimes, based on personal, maritime (e.g. *dominium maris*) and territorial principles (Kaiser & Calafat, 2014: 70). In other words, corsairing is another example of how narrow definitions of extraterritoriality and jurisdiction cannot capture the early modern context and require different concepts that can incorporate the various ways in which actors of different geographical and institutional provenances set the context for, or even tried to accumulate jurisdiction for themselves, for their sovereigns, or for their employers. In other words, the varieties of mercantilism, enabling different practices of wealth creation through the circulation of commodities and titles, created an array of conditions for agents of jurisdictional accumulation, two of which are discussed below: trading companies and settlers.

6.2.4 *Trading Companies: the Dutch and English*

Classic analyses, found in Grewe (2000) for example, assume a clear separation by contemporaneous actors of the European and overseas spheres of mercantilism and legal expansion. According to Grewe, trading companies took a 'semi-State, semi-private intermediate position', making it 'possible to avoid a complete transfer to the overseas colonial sphere of the European concept of State' (2000: 298). This marked the development of a 'separate, flexible system of a colonial law of nations' that 'required different standards' (298). Grewe emphasises the fact that by the eighteenth century the concept of 'state' was established, since the companies' 'very function was to prevent the transfer of the concept of "State" to the non-European world' (2000: 302). This resulted, accordingly, in making the colonies only able to enter the future international society of nations as half-admitted members, with duties but no rights (Bowden, 2005).

Grewe assumes that this 'semi-State, semi-private' condition was not a direct import from Europe, but a *half-import* of the modern attributes Europe was by that time to have produced (i.e. legislative sovereignty, nationality, and fixed territoriality). Grewe interprets this as an intentional strategy of the European states to differentiate themselves from the rest of the world, but this ignores the difference and struggles between ruling classes, monarchs, and urban bourgeoisies in the state apparatus, and, crucially, how these differences and struggles were also played out geopolitically through trading companies, for example. On the simplest level, since early modern European monarchies did not possess attributes of exclusive and abstract state sovereignty, trading companies could not be attributed a portion of European sovereignty.

Instead, European dynastic monarchies were faced with the complexity of their own systems when trying to export them and resorted to inter-dynastic practices of 'privately' isolating the European 'public' space. The more complex and self-sustaining early modern world of jurisdictional layers resists any facile transitional or global analysis of international politics based on these so-called external similarities. Absolutist states and trading companies were linked as an alliance between European monarchies and 'their privileged merchants-manufacturers' (Teschke, 2003: 203) and mercantilism 'extended the pre-modern logic of absolutist territorial organization into the non-European world' (Teschke, 2003: 204). This analysis retrieves the links between metropole and colony obscured by Grewe. However, it fails to differentiate the different jurisdictional contexts and outcomes – often shaped by trading companies – of how empires reorganised the non-European world.

Analyses of trading companies has recently significantly developed, and these actors are best understood as public–private partnerships developed on the basis of the VOC (Koskenniemi, 2014: 20–21). The most influential analysis of trading companies as corporate sovereignty or 'company state' is developed by Stern (2011), who mostly compares the EIC and VOC. His work has been developed by various scholars concerned with their role in international law, notably the analysis by Weststeijn (2015: 33), for whom the VOC 'obtained as a private entity the rights and duties of a sovereign actor in the international legal constellation'. The VOC ensured that the Dutch Empire became the classic case of 'empire by treaty' (2015: 19). If the treaty relations it developed implied some form of indigenous and peaceful consent, this consent was only achieved by the threat of force and the 'warlike enforcement of the obligation that followed from it' (Weststeijn, 2015: 41). Similarly, for Cavanagh, the EIC 'was a company with sovereignty and subjects' who 'made war and peace', held 'courts, tax systems and a complex governmentality'; in other words, the outsourcing and transporting of authority to trading companies insured that they 'did the dirty work of empire' (2014: 103).

This recent trend emerging out of the historical turn in international law, largely shaped by a global legal pluralist approach (Benton, 2018), is helpful in that it focuses on trading companies as developing original and specific regimes, depending on various factors and sources of legal conflict, and on disputes over the legitimate holders of – and the best means of transporting – authority. However, the discussion here wants to add analytical counterweight to this trend by identifying the role of companies in transporting authority as a practice of jurisdictional accumulation instead of as a doctrinal 'paradox' (Weststeijn, 2015: 40–41). Moreover, companies have been loosely associated with the history of early modern extraterritoriality (e.g. Miles, 2019) but their extraterritorial condition has not been sufficiently explored or compared.

It makes most sense to start with the Dutch case, as it led the way in this domain. The focus here is on the role of companies in accumulating jurisdiction and engaging in jurisdictional disputes. However, some cautionary words about the Dutch Empire and the VOC are necessary. If the study of the Dutch Empire in international legal history has been more limited than in the case of the other empires, the studies dedicated to the Dutch have either been concerned with the VOC (and in some exceptions, the WIC), or have largely related their analysis of the empire to Grotius.[10] This is problematic, since Grotius's influence on the Dutch Empire remains of questionable impact. Even his work for the VOC, which is stated in every study but is rarely reflected on more thoroughly, remains limited since *Mare Liberum* (1609) is the only chapter of *De Indis* published in his lifetime.[11] Unsurprisingly, it is considered as the most (though probably only) influential text for the VOC. Grotius's main work *De Juri Belli ac Pacis* (1625) was not fully integrated into the doctrine of international law and acknowledged by practitioners until the nineteenth century (van Ittersum, 2016).

Therefore, we have a temporal distortion and a problem of presentism when trying to understand the practices of Dutch legal imperialism, questioning how the early modern Dutch Empire was shaped or influenced by Grotius's writings.[12] If the reverse remains certain, that Grotius's writings were influenced by the Dutch Empire, his posthumous influence on international law means that his principles and support of the VOC, similarly to the principles of the Salamanca School, were used to justify 'the emergence of centralised states, a global economic system based upon private property, and continual warfare to uphold the principles of that system', as well as the 'understanding of informal empire' (Koskenniemi, 2011; Fitzmaurice, 2014: 50). Yet his work, like that of many classic authors, was used (retroactively) to justify reductive narratives of imperial expansion according to a Eurocentric modern teleology (Keene, 2002), as the important work on reception in the nineteenth century is increasingly showing (Vergerio, 2018). Therefore, it is not as reliable as always assumed to use Grotius to understand the Dutch

[10] This is the case in the most recent critical volume on empire and international law (Koskenniemi *et al.*, 2017). Although the contributions by Weststeijn (2017) and Barreto (2017) provide essential critical angles to the study of Grotius, they leave the volume without a study of the Dutch Empire that disaggregates it from Grotius. Another example of this limitation is found in a recent volume on imperial languages and regimes of protection (Benton *et al.* Attwood, 2017). Although the volume provides a neglected aspect of extraterritorial history that escapes the usual state- and ambassador-centric assumptions and is careful not to use the term 'extraterritoriality' for the early modern period, it nevertheless limits its discussion of the Dutch Empire to remarks on the VOC.

[11] Grotius's *De Indis* and *De jure praedae* (Commentary on the Law of Prize and Booty), which was written for the VOC, were published in 1898 soon after being found in Grotius's family papers (Fitzmaurice, 2014: 91). The thorough study of this is by van Ittersum (2006).

[12] See d'Aspremont (2019: 101) for a summary of the critiques of Grotius in the historical turn in international law.

Empire; or at the very least, other sources and analytical angles need to be explored.

The main theoretical achievement of Grotius's work on the VOC is to give 'legal authority to the Dutch commercial expansion in the Indies and elsewhere', 'by liberating Dutch merchants to seek wealth wherever they could find it' (Koskenniemi, 2011: 9). However, it is safe to assume that the Dutch (and others) would have done so regardless. Grotius's justification was just a cherry on the cake – or more exactly, booty. His work confirms the commercial and coercive determination of Dutch expansion in a maritime context in which empires claimed monopolies and where the actions of the Dutch required some form of legitimation, but not to an extent comparable to Castile's relation to legitimation. In Wetsteijn's words, 'his theories could be used as a resource for claiming colonial authority on the basis of obligation by consent' (2015: 40) and contribute to the role of treaties as a key means of Dutch expansion.

Coming back to our focus on jurisdictional conflicts, Chapter 5 has already noted the importance of disputes between the conglomerates of merchants in leading commercial cities (e.g. relations between Amsterdam's Directorate and the VOC) and between agents of different commercial cities (Rotterdam and Amsterdam). The focus on the VOC as an actor of jurisdictional accumulation is important since the Dutch Empire gave the VOC the authority to be a sovereign entity and have jurisdiction over the territories it colonised, settled on, and traded in (Koskenniemi, 2014: 20). In spite of significant differences between the VOC and WIC, Wetsteijn (2015: 38) argues that they developed similar strategies. However, if we focus on the Atlantic, it is not clear whether the WIC exercised that jurisdiction in any other significant way than to enforce its authority over trading operations and back up any coercive measures needed to protect those operations. In other words, there does not seem to have been any jurisdictional accumulation as transplants of authority from the WIC, in the sense of profiting from the offer or imposition of jurisdictional subjectivities or spaces for Native Americans or for settlers, since the Dutch American colonies mainly used or traded in slaves and the transport of settlers. Crucially, if the States General acknowledged the jurisdiction of the companies, they did not look to transplant their own jurisdiction through them, and therefore were mostly outsourcing and transporting their authority to companies in exchange for profit, since the relation between the Dutch Republic and trading companies consisted in 'brokerage', that is 'the outsourcing, wholesale or in part, of warring tasks to independent or semi-independent entrepreneurs who executed these tasks with the aim of making a profit' (Brandon & Fatah-Black, 2015: 86).

The VOC was left to its own devices and developed strategies of accumulation that were not directly, if even indirectly, governed by the States General. Another indication of how the Dutch Empire relied heavily on its 'men on the ground' is shown by the way in which, through the VOC, it tolerated a very mixed set of pass regimes for its imperial agents. This lasted until it set up the *pascedullen* system in 1641, when all passes for shipping had to be acquired at the port of Melaka. Before this, the cases of the Banda Islands, Batavia, and the Taiwan straits had very different systems because these often emerged from the actions and petitions of merchants rather than being directed from the imperial centre (Benton & Clulow, 2017: 54).

Turning to the EIC and other leading English companies, a significant part of their practices were dedicated to competing with each other over regional monopolies or certain commodities. The conflicts between the Levant Company and EIC in London, which eventually merged in terms of their common interests against the rise of the colonial companies (Brenner, 1972: 384), can be linked to debates over how to conduct overseas trade. One major debate concerned the defence of corporate or free trade, based on the differing prerogatives of chartered companies as well as of those of consuls and ambassadors, which led to different attempts to impose sovereignty beyond the territorial borders of the English Crown (Stein, 2012). For Brenner (1972), the shifts in influence and range of disputes between London merchants was a political process linked to parliamentarians and the process of the Crown-in-Parliament. There were differences in the use and in the structure of trading companies, which show different conceptions of how and why to apply jurisdiction overseas. Moreover, as discussed in Chapter 5 and in the concluding chapter, these often depended on the Christian or non-Christian identity of the merchants and how they used these arguments when it suited their economic interests and their assumptions about other legal regimes.

Developing different trading companies and jurisdictional regimes was an unavoidable strategy, considering the heterogeneity of law and jurisdictions in European regimes and the presence of indigenous communities in North America, in spite of the many efforts to ignore and extinguish this presence. Moreover, the shift in influence from the companies engaged in establishing trading monopolies with the East – Levant Company and EIC – to the colonial companies was based on the latter's increase of jurisdictional reach in North America, on the commercial innovations of their merchants, and on their concern with Dutch competition (Brenner, 1972: 378–384). Crucially, these were different men with different trades and practices, ready to replace the old merchant elite focused on carrying commodities to the East).

The Virginia Company, chartered in 1606, is often presented as the classic case of England's expansion of authority over the New World. It was granted extensive rights which presumed 'the inseparability of property and personal jurisdiction' (Koskenniemi, 2017b: 374). However as Cavanagh shows through the study of specific jurisdictional conflicts between companies, or between companies and conglomerates of merchants and settlers, the reality of disputes reveals a 'confusing legal context' in which private law aspects are emphasised, and in particular concerning the Virginia Company, the extent of the 'London entity's corporate privileges and responsibilities' (2017: 455). Moreover, the Virginia Company also reflected on this preferred indirect mode of a transport of authority. The company, in 'a conciliatory debate of the Council in 1607–1608', distinguished its actions from those of Castile, which it considered to be only able to achieve 'a Magistracy, and Empiry' and 'no title, of Dominions or Property' by the nefarious actions of 'fryars', 'men of all learning', 'men of discourse', 'Civilians', 'Canonists,' and 'Devines' (García-Salmones & Eslava, 2010: 63–64).

Another important jurisdictional aspect of these companies was the issue of protection. These companies' 'right of just war in protection of an ally as a monarch or republic' illustrates and influenced Grotius's theory of the law of nations and freedom of the seas, according to which sovereignty was 'divisible and embedded within a pluralistic and overlapping political system, parcelled out among monarchs, republics and corporations alike' (Stern, 2017: 121). In other words, 'monarchs, republics, and corporations' should be understood as agents with different jurisdictional prerogatives, instead of anachronistically trying to understand companies in relation to modern conceptions of the state. However, corporations also 'required protection to provide protection' (Stern, 2017: 121), meaning these jurisdictional agents could never be completely independent or autonomous. The way in which jurisdictional authority was distributed and linked – transported – between these entities was politically determined and ad hoc. Chartered companies such as the VOC and EIC were able to 'internalise the costs of protection' that 'allowed them to outpace their European rivals' as well as transform 'the spatial and economic geography of the maritime Indian Ocean trade' (Stern, 2017: 120). This was linked to the companies' 'fusion of public and private functions of protection' as a central means of colonial expansion.

Finally and very briefly, in France, the significant rise of trading companies during the reign of Louis XIV – when thirty-nine new companies emerged – did not yield the profits and interests desired in light of the significant investments made by the monarchy and leading nobles (Horn, 2015: 96–131). The other significant actors and institutions in this period to emerge are the merchants and magistrates involved in the designation of free ports and the practice of factories and entrepôts. This adds to the argument in the previous subsections on the shaping of French mercantilism beyond the conventional assumptions of its state-controlled protectionist model. It shows the importance of the privilege of liberty and the failure of the principle of the 'exclusive system' prohibiting trade with foreign merchants. This policy's efficacy and application is disputed by approaches that focus more on the negotiated and ad hoc understandings of early modern empires, whose nearly perpetual state of warfare and trading difficulties rendered the conception of the links between metropolitan and colonial markets as pipelines with significant and intentional 'leaks' (Marzagalli, 2016).

6.2.5 *Jurisdictional Differences regarding Settlement*

Recent historical research focusing on the development of international law and colonialism highlights the specificity and variegated nature of colonial sovereignty, instituting at times a semi-feudal regime and institutions exported from the Iberian kingdoms or old regime France, and at others experimenting with legal innovations and negotiations otherwise fettered by these imperial centres. It is not possible to look in detail here at the many forms of colonial settlement or settler colonialism; rather, the point is to stress the heterogeneity of processes of jurisdictional accumulation, and the generally indirect and commercially driven characteristic of the French, English/British, and Dutch practices of settlement. The following discusses some French, English, and Dutch practices in turn to illustrate this shared similarity.

The social property relations of the French colonial regimes reveal a mixed pattern of experiments in sovereignty based in struggles between local and mercantilist interests. These practices can be seen to resemble Iberian overseas endeavours, and reinforce the ambiguity of the French case as being interpreted as developing both transplants and transports of authority. During the seventeenth and eighteenth centuries, disputants in

French colonies disposed of more locally based judicial opportunities to settle disputes – not only because the French reproduced autonomous and 'identical' juridical institutions in the colonies – but also because these institutions kept very close links to the struggles over offices and their privileges found in the metropolitan context: 'New France became a new judicial battleground where old legal conflicts over long-held privileges and customs in France could be fought – albeit with new stakes and conditions' (Dewar, 2013: 50).

However, focusing more on the 'negotiation of jurisdiction by indigenous leaders and company men', instead of Dewar's focus on the relationship between 'company men and officials in France', Cavanagh (2014: 103) finds that French companies in New France were outsourced corporate entities with only a 'vague endorsement' from the Crown and, at the beginning of colonisation, no endorsement from indigenous communities and therefore no recognition of their property rights (Cavanagh, 2014: 98). New France pre-1663 was colonised by *seigneurs* and *censitaires* (i.e. farming tenants), who dispossessed on the basis of a reversed 'logic of *vacuum domicilium* or "empty lands"' led by companies, and according to which, if 'no treaties of purchases were made, therefore, no one was there' (Cavanagh, 2014: 124–125). After 1663 and following the reign of Louis XIV and his efforts to bring colonisation into state control,[13] the Crown replaced the companies, but the logic remained and was later replicated by the British Crown (Cavanagh, 2014: 124–125). In other words, the logic of transport would seem to prevail over transplant as incorporation of subjects.

Concerning the judicial authority over disputes in the colonies, some legal differences existed between French and British colonisation:

> There appears to have been a striking contrast between the metropolitan legal jurisdictions involved in English overseas disputes and French ones. Whereas parties in the latter frequently came before local admiralty courts, the English admiralty's jurisdiction did not extend – in theory at least – to colonies but was limited to the sea itself. Contemporary disputes that I have examined seem to uphold this fact: factional conflicts within the Virginia Company, for example, drove disputants to the king and the Privy Council. In addition to metropolitan appeals, companies in the American colonies had their own general courts, a practice not seen in French America.
>
> (Dewar, 2013: 78)

[13] See Chapter 3 for examples of settlement in the Caribbean.

This difference between French reliance on local admiralty courts for disputes at sea and in the colonies, and the English restriction of the Admiralty Court jurisdiction to disputes at sea emphasises that French colonisation remained more ambiguous whereas England distanced its imperial agents jurisdictionally from its settlements. The English restriction and reliance on its own jurisdictional bodies (either in the metropole or as developed by the companies) rather than on local colonial ones can be partly explained by conflicts between common lawyers and civilian lawyers in England over territorial and maritime jurisdiction. In the seventeenth century, common-law courts took over from admiralty courts issues of commercial law and 'authority over nontidal waters and maritime disputes arising on land' (Benton, 2010: 145–146). Admiralty courts retained criminal jurisdiction (piracy, prize cases) and jurisdiction for disputes arising on the high seas (Benton, 2010: 146). In other words, commercial courts in England failed to retain their prerogatives as the Admiralty Court disappeared in the nineteenth century by being absorbed by the High Court (Cutler, 2003: 173).

English merchant disputes were increasingly settled through the common-law courts, even though merchants continued to pursue private means such as arbitration (Cutler, 2003: 174) and the common-law courts were reluctant to recognise their authority (Cutler, 2003: 175). In contrast, France's commercial courts and jurisdictions retained their independence from regular courts with 'special rules of procedure' and 'merchant judges' 'elected by merchants and by business corporations' (Cutler, 2003: 175).

Generally, English colonisation is associated with the development of 'rational jurisdictions' and the influence of the common law (García-Salmones & Eslava, 2010). However, as discussed by Koskenniemi (2017b), the reality is more complex in terms of jurisdictional conflicts between two conceptions of the law of nations; one based on the royal prerogative and the work of civil lawyers supporting the king, and the other concerned with the 'expansion of English private and public interests across the world' and 'defending the rights of property of Englishmen' (Koskenniemi, 2017b: 357–358). In addition to this pluralism, the English/British lacked a 'uniform imperial design or public policy' and used a 'mixture of legal traditions' and a 'selection of British rights and liberties that suited' colonists (García-Salmones & Eslava, 2010: 64–65). In contrast to the Hispanics, English colonists were 'entitled to a local legal forum' and 'the British did not aim to create a legal geographical space' (García-Salmones & Eslava, 2010: 66).

Throughout the eighteenth century, however, they used the competition and overlapping authorities of various legal institutions (e.g. Privy Council, colonial courts, the Royal Commission) to reject and annul indigenous property rights and decisions in their favour (García-Salmones & Eslava, 2010: 66).

In other words, 'in English America, the distance between rulers and ruled, the availability of arable land in North America, coupled with the natural delegation of responsibility by proprietors to their colonists, furthered localist tendencies that early modern English people had cultivated in the "Old World"' (Roper & Ruymbeke, 2007: 17). There were a variety of 'designs' possible for the shaping of jurisdiction: 'crown licensed adventures and conquests', 'chartered corporate enterprises', 'direct Crown rule', and 'delegated seigneurial privilege' (Tomlins, 2010: 7). Law became the 'principal technology' for English imperialism to make 'jurisdictional and substantive claims' upon landmass and over a varied population of natives, English and European settlers and migrants, enslaved Africans and indentured servants (Tomlins, 2010: 68, 28–30).

This 'technology', understood here instead as a set of practices, used the Crown's letters patents or charters, agreements and treaties, as well as imported practices such as tenures and deeds. These practices therefore mixed feudal, modern, and contractual forms of law (Tomlins, 2010: 68). They consisted in 'new complex jurisdictional and governmental structures' with the various legal statuses of (1) freemen and (2) of those dependent on households or on the land as owners and settlers; or as landless, wanderers, vagrants, runaways, and slaves (2010: 70).

These statuses had different consequences for jurisdictional claims regarding subjecthood, citizenship, and sojourn. In 1606, the Virginia Patent authorised the departure of eight people including, following his petition, Richard Hakluyt (the younger), who became a famous promoter of English colonisation.[14] The patent also authorised 'all who should willingly accompany them for America' (Tomlins, 2010: 73). However, the Crown retained its 'right to licence departure' throughout the seventeenth century, in spite of promoting colonising (Tomlins, 2010: 73). In the early-eighteenth century, restrictions were still imposed on the migration of skilled workers and later on artisans.

[14] Hakluyt's cousin and guardian, the lawyer also named Richard Hakluyt (the elder), wrote a 1585 *Pamphlet for the Virginia Enterprise*, which is used as a key reference for legal discourses and practices of colonising (Tomlins, 2010: 5).

Following historians on this point since the pioneering work of Pagden (1990), Tomlins (2010: 132–134) reiterates the crucial difference that sets English (in particular, but also French and Dutch) colonisation apart from the Castilian model of jurisdictional accumulation. In its indirect and jurisdictionally divided transports of authority, more limited than the Castilian transplants, England favoured colonising as the possession of territory and the 'exclusion of its inhabitants', since Native Americans were a 'hindrance' and 'passive objects' (Tomlins, 2010: 132). English settlement occurred among a narrative of colonising that

> progressively banishes existing inhabitants to the margins of its consciousness by denying their civil capacity, their sociability. In the English narrative the indigenous become brutes, in whose place the colonizer first desires, then actively imagines, an empty landscape to populate anew.
>
> (Tomlins, 2010: 132)

Finally, a significant argument that shows the indirect dimension of English jurisdictional accumulation is the role given to governors in the American colonies, a 'cadre of men' who 'resembled' consuls and ambassadors posted in the Mediterranean and in the East (Games, 2008: 147). Games (2008) provides a rare account of the links between these men and colonial spaces from outside the diplomatic literature and which emphasises their role as imperial agents. She attributes to them a wide range of functions and privileges, recalling the analyses in Chapters 4 and 5 and the particular roles of Mediterranean consuls. These men had significant powers and, similarly to French consuls, could have jurisdictional functions of enunciating the law and Crown policies (Games, 2008: 160). However, they represented a 'weak sovereign', adapted to 'varied constraints', and instead of being deployed and regulated with clear instructions and controls, they instead 'could influence English policies on matters ranging from likely places for settlement or trade to diplomacy with foreign rulers' (Games, 2008: 178–179). Although Games uses the term 'transplants' (2008: 175) as a subsection title for some of the practices developed by these actors, she qualifies this loosely as 'transmission of useful and relevant experience from place to place' (2008: 175), and as the 'transporting' of people and experience, emphasising the 'ingenuity and adaptability of governors, consuls, and ambassadors' (176). Moreover, focusing significantly on Thomas Roe, Games notes 'the merging of private, state, and commercial interests' (2008: 177) in these men, which speaks to the outsourcing of sovereign duties to them as agents with significant independence and autonomy from the Crown, especially in the case of settlements.[15] If the need to represent the sovereign remained important symbolically with 'visible signs of English office' sent by employers and the Crown (Games, 2008: 174), and struggles to maintain their status for which they needed support from their home authorities (2008: 157), these men had 'to improvise and adapt, to know when to dispense with rules and policies from England in favour of the necessities dictated by circumstances on the ground' (178).

In the Atlantic, the Dutch Republic's first phase of expansion was characterised by rapid and impressive manoeuvres between 1580 and 1650, conquering Pernambuco in the New World (large sugar plantation in Brazil), a sizable part of North America (New Netherland), and some islands of the Caribbean. However, after this period, they lost their two largest colonies (Brazil and Suriname), and their share of Atlantic trade and shipping dropped to less than 10 per cent because of 'increasing trade barriers due to the protectionist legislation of its commercial rivals' (Emmer, 2014: 340). This was significantly less than their trade with Europe and Asia.

Emmer favours external factors to explain this decline, although internal factors have been stressed by the historiography and remain essential (decline of competitiveness of Dutch shipping, low return on Dutch investments, a relatively small population and lack of settlement opportunities and intention, leading to lack of transatlantic market opportunities for Dutch services and goods) (Emmer, 2014: 340). External factors tend to focus on the 'military, naval, and demographic superiority' of its rivals (Castilian exclusion policies, English Navigation Acts, French protectionist legislation) (Emmer, 2014: 341). Over the long term, Dutch merchants and their governments were not interested in transplanting to the New World. Instead, they brought German settlers to British colonies (Emmer, 2014: 343), while the presence of Scottish, German, French, British, and Jewish settlers in the colony of Suriname governed by the WIC (and later the Suriname Company), as well as the presence of British settlers in the 'neighbouring Dutch colonies of Berbice, Demerara and Essequibo', show the Dutch Empire's 'outward-

[15] Roe became ambassador in Istanbul in 1621 for the Levant Company after being the first ambassador to the EIC in 1614 in Surat at the court of the Mughal emperor, and following various positions in the Virginia Company and missions across the Atlantic (Games, 2008: 154–157).

looking nature' (Alston, 2018: 19). Moreover, 'these colonies reflected the large role of federal and private bodies in the structure of the Dutch state at home' and 'the execution of colonial rule rested on the same private-state cooperation that underlay the entire Dutch overseas empire' (Brandon & Fatah-Black, 2015: 101).

Comparing the Dutch and British expansions, Emmer suggests that 'the English mercantile community had a better eye for long term economic growth' than the Dutch because they invested more in migration and naval power than in ventures yielding higher profits (Emmer, 2014: 343). High among these ventures was the slave trade, in which the Dutch were 'only second to Portugal until 1675' and was originally led by private entrepreneurs from Amsterdam (Brandon & Fatah-Black, 2015: 96).

> Dutch slave ships, until 1734 under the monopoly of the WIC and then along with free traders, subsequently brought almost a quarter of a million enslaved Africans to the Dutch Guianas – 16,000 to Essequibo; 11,000 to Demerara; 15,000 to Berbice; and 200,000 to Suriname. Between 1750 and the early 1780s large amounts of money were invested in Suriname, including in the purchase of these enslaved Africans, and the colony became notorious for the extravagant lifestyle of its planters.
>
> (Alston, 2018: 19)

The alliance between the Dutch and British between 1674 and 1780 shows the connections between these two empires and their practices of commercial expansion (Morgan, 2014). Moreover, the Dutch Empire in the Atlantic was characterised by 'boundary crossers and middlemen' – a term developed by Games (2014: 363) – who shared 'a willingness to assimilate others', and 'forged regional economic ties across boundaries of nation, language, religion and culture' (Alston, 2018: 20).

Thus, prima facie, the overall lack of interest in settlement and developing jurisdictional authority through settlers to focus instead on high-profit ventures in the Atlantic limits our opportunities for analysing the Dutch in comparison to the British, French, and Castilian cases of transplants and transports of authority in the Americas, and renders their case less relevant to this particular practice. Although Brandon and Fatah-Black (2015: 85) make a strong case for why, contra Emmer, 'state power and territorial control' remained significant factors for Dutch Atlantic expansion, by 'creating the operating bases for the slave-trade on the West-African coast and in the Caribbean, by setting the geographic perimeters of the Dutch slave production system, or by creating the physical boundaries between bondage and escape', these practices did not aim to transplant but merely to transport Dutch jurisdictional authority and were therefore more mercantilist than jurisdictional. Crucially, the primary aim of the accumulation was not the acquisition of rights, titles, or functions, but wealth. Moreover, this wealth or merchant capital did not result from that authority but from the buying, selling, and transport of commodities and people.

However, in the Mediterranean, as discussed in Chapter 5, the Dutch were heavily involved in commercial diplomacy and developed a significant consular service, especially in the North African ports and in the Levant. This is illustrated by the sums spent by the Amsterdam Navy Board to sustain the decades of 'long low-intensity warfare against the North-African privateering states of Sale (Morocco) and Algiers' (Brandon & Fatah-Black, 2015: 99). This is a more fruitful area of research for colonial jurisdictional conflicts, as was discussed in the previous chapter, and will hopefully be developed further in the future.

6.3 Conclusion

This chapter traced European empires' colonial practices of jurisdictional accumulation. The first section turned to imperial expansion as a form of accumulating jurisdiction through *transplants* of authority. Transplants consist in not only the conquest of people as subjects and as labour, as well as of resources and land, but also the transformation of the social property relations in those colonised spaces as hybrids of the colonising power. These forms of jurisdictional accumulation were set up by Iberian military and feudal institutions in the Americas and led to the transplanting of Iberian social property relations in the 'New World' through legal innovations and institutions linked to principles of the law of nations. The chapter discussed the *requerimiento*, *encomiendas*, *asentamientos*, *audiencias*, and various jurisdictional processes and arrangements between the Crown, settlers, and Native Americans. Crucially, transplants involved the incorporation, control, and containment of jurisdictional subjectivities for settlers and natives. Moreover, the section discussed the role of the House of Trade of the Indies in Seville, favoured over consulates, and how mercantilism in Spain should be analysed in terms of Iberian jurisdictional fragmentation.

The second section focused on *transports* of authority as the other empires' more commercial, private, and indirect jurisdictional practices concerned with territory rather than people, which involved trading or chartered companies and various types of settlement arrangements. These practices and institutions used lawyers and merchants to transport, rather than transplant, their sovereigns' authority and make use of this authority in a way that profited most to these imperial agents (i.e. agents with either more jurisdictional or mercantilist aims). This transport of authority resulted in a jurisdictional distancing between rulers and the peoples colonised, which had significant advantages for these empires in terms of focusing on land improvement and using legal mechanisms such as treaties and jurisdictional disputes to ignore and erase indigenous property rights.

This analysis thus contributes to debates on varieties of mercantilism, by looking at the classic case of France in the Mediterranean. It questions the general use of mercantilism as an external similarity that is conflated with capitalism to explain the role of international law in shaping the states' sovereign system. In contrast, this chapter shows the variety of jurisdictional practices Dutch, French, and English merchants were engaged in that fuelled competition between empires and shaped early modern international legal orders according to the jurisdictional divisions of their metropolitan and colonial contexts. This analysis opens the way for the concluding chapter to recap on the key contributions and implications of the concept of jurisdictional accumulation for the histories of international law and international relations.

7

Analytical Crossroads

Dominium, *Consuls, and Extraterritoriality*

This chapter concludes this project by bringing together its most important elements and exploring two key implications of the concept of jurisdictional accumulation. First, the importance of different definitions of early modern jurisdiction is illustrated by doctrinal and case-based examples in the Iberian and English contexts, which further justify the distinction between transplants and transports of authority. Second, the role of consular practices, understood as practices of jurisdictional accumulation, is highlighted in shaping key disciplinary divides and international legal binaries showing how the economic study of mercantilism needs to be intertwined with geopolitical dynastic diplomatic strategies. Before delving into these concluding arguments, the following summarises the book's methodological contributions in relation to disciplinary boundaries and influential approaches in classic and critical histories of international law.

The study has focused mainly on two influential approaches in the history of international law. The first classic narrative is best illustrated by Grewe (2000) and Schmitt's (2003) work, which has known various critiques in the last decades, especially in terms of the specific empirics of their arguments. However, there has not been any radically new large-scale and long-term narrative of the construction of modern international law that has replaced their accessible but highly problematic epochal divisions.[1] These epochs are built on the assumption of the gradual hatching, throughout the early modern period, of modern principles such as an abstract, territorial, and rational state, the international–domestic dichotomy, and the distinction between the European sphere as political and the overseas as economic. The second critical narrative is the commodity form theory of law developed by Miéville (2005) as a leading Marxist theory of international law. This focuses on external similarities between early modern empires – thus leaning on

[1] See Chapter 2 for discussions of other examples.

Grewe – and on a conflation between mercantilism and capitalism as defining structures of the international legal form.

Both narratives adopt a consequentialist or stagist approach to history, that is a history that is mainly concerned with the way in which international law managed to shed its feudal, dynastic, and absolutist skins, to emerge as a modern or capitalist system. In contrast to both these approaches, this project has produced a narrative that traces jurisdictional practices of accumulation without being guided by the need to find a linear causal link to modernity or capitalism. Moreover, it finds overlaps between these practices and those associated with mercantilism, notably in terms of instances when actors are accumulating certain rights, titles, and functions – and thus acquiring jurisdiction – so as to accumulate commercial capital – or buy and sell more.

Concerning its contribution to international legal history and the history of empires more generally, the book's argument contests analyses structured by the external and internal distinction by emphasising the need for methodological choice and humility and a better understanding of the logics of internalism. It retrieves the (structural) role of social property relations (as internally outward) in shaping empires' jurisdictional and mercantilist practices. It thus provides a broader and more socio-economic conception of jurisdiction that develops the practice turn in international legal history found in the general approach of global legal pluralism (Benton, 2010; Wallenius, 2019).

In sum, practices of jurisdictional accumulation constitute transplants, transports, and extensions of authority, often determined by the need for ruling elites to maintain a particular class in check or at their service, as well as by the aspirations and expectations of intermediary classes to profit and gain status from new trading routes and imperial ventures. Legal actors and mechanisms are thus situated in a political and class-based context that is based on the specificities of each empire's social make-up and entanglements, or, in other words, their social property relations.

This argument also concerns the disciplinary field of historical sociology in IR as it moves away from an elitist angle on early modern politics. It integrates the political economy underlying strategies of jurisdictional expansion focused on the agency of sub-sovereign actors considered outside the classic political and legal spheres and belonging to intermediary classes, such as consuls, magistrates, and merchants, and their impact on changing the social structures maintaining and threatening political elites.

Specifically, conventional analyses defining extraterritoriality as ambassadorial immunity share a narrow and elitist approach that ignores consuls as key agents of jurisdictional expansion (i.e. as agents with both political and economic prerogatives and implications for shaping key fictions of the transport of authority). In other words, the history of jurisdictional accumulation is a history of some of the men (and though more rarely, women) whom we have forgotten about in the history of legal expansion and who tend to have worked for – or aspired to be closer to – the ruling elite through their jurisdictional practices.

This is not a story of resistance, or a history 'from below', but it is a history of the shadows of empire, of the people who contributed to European imperialisms. These need to be better situated into histories where dynastic rulers and aristocrats are considered the only or main actors responsible for the building of modern state sovereignty and the international legal order, and for the structural inequalities these principles entrenched for the centuries to come.[2]

Revisiting the social history behind the doctrine of extraterritoriality through a focus on its practices – a doctrine otherwise narrowly defined by IR and diplomatic scholarship as emerging out of the shift from the personal to the territorial – provides a new critique of how that doctrine allows sovereignty to be divided, extended, and imposed over and above existing indigenous jurisdictional practices. The doctrinal shift from the personality of the king to the territoriality of the state, when conventionally understood, hides the myriad practices of jurisdictional accumulation which occurred 'in between' those processes, and which, in their most extreme form, took authority and common ownership away from colonised peoples and replaced them with European models of jurisdiction in more subtle ways than often described.

Ignoring these processes reproduces historical narratives according to which the division, extension, and imposition of sovereign rights is part of a progressive and inevitable process for the development of a professional diplomacy, balance of power, and a system of formally equal sovereign states, *sine qua non* elements of an international society. This

[2] These men and their transnational networks also bring up the contexts in which they interacted, such as port cities, which have been neglected because of an exaggerated emphasis on the cities that only later became the capitals of nation-states. Of course, these port cities are also witness to a large underclass of workers and sailors, who remain even more ignored in histories of international law and international relations. For recent contributions on colonial port cities in the Atlantic, see Rediker (2019) and Brandon (2019).

critique of conventional approaches to international history is far from new and has known various iterations. Since the critical historical turn of the 1990s in international law, one might think it not necessary to reiterate these arguments. Unfortunately, nostalgia for empire in Europe remains at the fore of government policy, especially regarding transnational legal institutions and conceptions of sovereignty. Digging out forgotten passages of imperial expansion through new jurisdictional angles helps to explain how legal actors were intrinsic to empires' more coercive, exploitative, and exterminatory practices, and how jurisdiction was a contested process in metropolitan areas of royal extensions of authority as well as in colonial transports and transplants of authority. This history aims to provide an analysis of early modern jurisdictions *sui generis*, yet it also hopes to better contextualise discussions about jurisdictional actors today and their role in shaping authority.

Simultaneously, as an intervention into critical histories, understanding the specificities and complexities of these actors according to various class strategies of reproduction and accumulation of wealth and status, is more useful and representative than assuming they operate blindly according to an empirically homogeneous and structurally uniform transition from pre-modern or pre-capitalist legal forms to the commodity legal form of capitalism. In sum, going back to the social origins of jurisdictional practices of accumulation in the early modern context contributes to the history of European expansion as well as to contemporary debates in historiography.

Although they are meant to conclude this project, the following sections are written in the spirit of opening debates rather than closing remarks. They discuss two key contributions of the book – the definitions of jurisdiction and the role of consuls – and offer these as potential future research directions. Section 7.1 consists in a more thorough discussion of the different meanings of jurisdiction which are better understood through the early modern concepts of *dominium* and *imperium*. Only the Iberian and English cases are used here as examples and key cases of transplants and transports of authority. Section 7.2 moves to the question of consular activities in the Mediterranean and the significance of their neglect for histories of early modern and modern extraterritoriality, focusing on the shaping of the political–economic and Christian–non-Christian legal binaries.

7.1 *Dominium* and Jurisdictional Accumulation

Early modern European empires are jurisdictional empires. There is nothing controversial in this claim since early modern historians rarely fail to mention this jurisdictional condition or use the adjective to qualify aspects of political organisation. The problem is not with the lack of historiographical attention to the early modern world as composed of 'several types of distinct jurisdictions'; the problem is the fact that these distinct jurisdictions have been studied 'separately, often ignoring the ways by which they dynamically interacted' (Herzog, 2015a: 3).

There have been a number of recent works that push the study of jurisdictional practices in the early modern period and this project builds on these studies.[3] However, there is also a lack of 'macrostructural' histories of law (Tomlins, 2010: 69), as too few of these studies take a large-scale and long-term perspective. Moreover, many resort to a neutral and transhistorical use of the term jurisdiction. Historiography generally makes the mistake of assuming that these practices are always a function of other more important assemblages of rights (e.g. territorial sovereignty, personal sovereignty, suzerainty, *imperium*, judicial authority, vassalage) and that the terms jurisdiction or jurisdictional conflicts can be used transhistorically and universally without contextualisation.

Generally, jurisdiction is assumed to be a neutral and transhistorical term used to denote the executive power to enforce laws over a set area and/or people. This technical definition is the most commonly used and most simply refers to the 'right to exercise justice' (Kaiser & Calafat, 2014: 70). This judicial *dominium* (*dominium jurisdictionis*) is contrasted to *imperium* (as the sovereign right to govern). However, the concept of *dominium* is not restricted to judicial jurisdiction and is also composed of an element referring to property or ownership (*dominium proprietatis)* (Koskenniemi, 2014: 9). In other words, early modern jurisdiction, when referred to by the concept of *dominium*, is composed of two elements, the exercise of justice and the ownership of things.

The problem is that most uses of the term jurisdiction reproduce its modern technical definition which focuses on the exercise of justice separated from the other element of *dominium* implying property or ownership.[4] What is missing, and which is crucial to better understand the early modern period, is the way in which judicial rights and practices are mixed with rights and practices of ownership, as signalled with the two elements of *dominium*. For example, Tomlins summarises the twin

[3] See introductory chapter.

[4] Some studies focus on possession rather than ownership (Tomlins, 2010; Benton, 2011). For example, Tomlins (2010: 5) defines *dominium* as 'possession or rule', referring to both notions of ownership and judicial authority.

and wide-ranging processes of 'designing *dominium* and establishing jurisdiction', in the case of English colonisation, as

> procedures for the occupation of territory, the marginalization of its inhabitants, and the organization and government of new settler populations.
>
> (2010: 220)

In other words, it is important to reintegrate the notions of *proprietary* and *judicial* rights and practices as defining early modern jurisdiction. For example, when looking at Iberian practices of jurisdictional accumulation, these referred to both ownership and judicial authority. The following shows in more detail how Castilian strategies of expansion – transplants of authority – consisted in practices of jurisdictional accumulation but also in doctrines that developed the twofold definition of jurisdiction and resulted in restricting *jus gentium* – the medieval law of nations – into colonial concepts of ownership and judicial jurisdiction (i.e. colonial forms of *dominium*). In England, practices of jurisdictional accumulation – transports of authority – reflected, in its first imperial conquests, the important distinctions between *dominium* and *imperium* in relation to the jurisdiction of the common-law courts versus the imperial sovereignty of the Crown.

7.1.1 Ownership and Rule over People: Iberian Transplants of Authority

Spain's overall influence in the history of international law consists primarily in developing rights to wars of discovery, occupation, and reconstructing European-type property rights and jurisdictional subjectivities for colonised Native Americans and Hispanic settlers. How and why did Castile develop such explicit and direct practices of jurisdictional accumulation between the Crown and its colonised subjects? Although this book moves away from doctrinal accounts, it is not possible to answer this question without reference to certain key doctrinal elements and their relation to Castilian geopolitics.

As discussed in Chapter 6, the Castilian Empire was distinct by its efforts at legitimising imperial expansion and its explicit approach to the conquest of peoples through jurisdictional practices rather than occupation of territory through indirect commercial practices.

> Technologically the colonization of the Americas was a relatively simple matter ... But the very simplicity of their collective enterprise, and the

> almost bewildering rapidity with which it advanced, posed for the Castilian crown serious problems of legitimation. From these early beginnings until Independence, the crown remained . . . overwhelmingly concerned with the need to defend its claims to sovereignty (*imperium*) and property rights (*dominium*) in America before an increasingly hostile world.
>
> (Pagden, 1990: 13–14)

The reliance on legal mechanisms and recourse to legitimation is not simply linked to medieval legal doctrine. It needs to be explained by other factors.[5] A significant factor is the context of the Reformation. Castilian doctrine was radically opposed to the Northern waves of Protestant political thought. Vitoria's work on natural law was in defence of the Catholic order and was 'far less concerned with the particulars of the American case than . . . with the opportunities it provided for a refutation of Lutheran and later Calvinist theories of sovereignty' (Pagden, 1990: 18). This context is often forgotten in discussions of the Salamanca School, and it places the analysis of this doctrine in a more local and Christian-governed context than when considered as the 'primitive origins' of modern international law. This context is also illustrated by how the 'rhetoric of the *Reconquista*' was used to justify expansion in Europe as well as the Americas by asserting 'the Pope's lordship over all the world' – 'a new Rome' according to the Italian lawyer Mercurio Gattinara, Chancellor to Charles V – as well as in the 1513 memorandum by Juan Manuel Palacios Rubios linked to Vitoria's 1539 *Relectio de Indis* (Koskenniemi, 2017: 7).[6]

The Castilian doctrine of the law of nations is contrasted to later Northern Protestantism attributed to the later 'fathers' of international law, Hugo Grotius and Samuel von Pufendorf. These scholars have been attributed the task of restricting the term *dominium* to the notion of private property (Pagden, 1990: 16). However, this is disputed to a certain extent by Koskenniemi, who argues that the Salamanca School's contribution to the relation between empire and international law was to

[5] Some authors have focused on highlighting the paradox of why and how Castile's highly 'legalised' and 'legalising' imperial power was not a product of medieval legal doctrine. For example, although doctrinal and theological work on *jus gentium* was extensive and sophisticated from the twelfth century onwards – by trying to resolve the problems posed by the legal status of non-Christian peoples – Castile's legal elite departed from this tradition to become politically highly instrumentalised (Dickason, 1989: 143–173).

[6] For a reading of Rubios as an unduly neglected architect of Spain's legacy for modern international law, see Birr (2018).

develop a vocabulary which focused around three notions, '*dominium*, *ius gentium*, and the *belllum iustum*' (2011: 11), and shaped the 'emergence of a global economic system based on private ownership and the search for profit' (2011: 12). The notion of *dominium* from the Castilian to Grotius embedded the distinction between private and public law, and Grotius only translated (through the work of Suárez) the more restricted sense of *dominium* to private property, which effaced the element of judicial jurisdiction.

Castilian natural law scholars started with a much wider definition of *dominium* (Pagden, 1990: 16) 'covering use and non-use, trading and exchange as well as throwing away of the object' (Koskenniemi, 2011: 27). Vitoria included *dominium* 'in both of its senses as "jurisdiction" and "ownership"' (Koskenniemi, 2011: 15), but the discussions evolved to widen the private ownership element. Through the discussion of *dominium*, the Salamanca School 'grounded an extensive right for human beings to appropriate, use, transfer, or abandon things in accordance with their choice' (Koskenniemi, 2011: 16). Specifically, they extended the theory of *dominium* to a 'subjective (but non-arbitrary) theory of the "just price"' (Koskenniemi, 2011: 20) according to which money 'had value in itself so that it could also be understood to accumulate for investment purposes and be exchanged for profit (interest)' (Koskenniemi, 2011: 22–23). This universal right of *dominium* was 'applicable all over the world' (Koskenniemi, 2011: 26) and could 'reveal an international system of commerce, based on the free use of their *dominium* by private merchants and bankers, which princes were not entitled to impede' (2011: 26–27).

Restricting princes' right to intervene limited the (judicial) jurisdiction element of *dominium*, since the Salamancans extended the theory of dominium to 'commutative and not distributive justice', that is to 'relationships among subjects themselves', which excluded 'ideas about the intervention of public power' (Koskenniemi, 2011: 28). Nevertheless, in spite of this 'empire of private rights', the authority of the prince was insured through the theory of just war (28). War 'was allowed only so as to enforce the public-law jurisdiction of the sovereign prince, which might have been violated by the enemy, or when the private *dominium* that individuals had over their freedom and their property had been violated' (Koskenniemi, 2011: 29). However, if the jurisdictional authority of the prince needs to be restored to the theory of *dominium*, Suárez does so through developing a significant distinction in *ius gentium* between 'public international law as law among those who hold *dominium* in terms of jurisdiction over territory and the universal laws governing inter-individual relations of contract and ownership', which has come to structure modern international law into its public and private domains (Koskenniemi, 2011: 31).

Finally, Koskenniemi links Grotius to this evolution of the theory of *dominium*, and argues that both the Salamanca School and Grotius were reacting to capitalism as 'the expansion of trade and commerce' and produced 'a legal and political vocabulary that takes expansion as largely natural and articulates the social world created through it as a universal network of inter-individual relations' (Koskenniemi, 2011: 35). This is a definition of capitalism he takes from Arrighi (2002), like other commercialisation models discussed previously.

This argument is worth quoting and presenting at length, because it appears to pose serious challenges to some of the arguments developed in this book regarding the differences between the Castilian and other empires according to jurisdiction or *dominium*. In effect, Koskenniemi recentres the contribution of the neo-scholastics in terms of their 'texts discussing *dominium* as the subjective right of property that is valid universally under the *ius gentium*, and that can be, together with the derivative rights of travel and trade, enforced by just war' (2011: 32). Since the neo-scholastics started the process of making war and *dominium* (as jurisdiction over territory) conditional to the subjective notions of *dominium* (as private ownership) this means that jurisdictional accumulation, as *doctrine*, would in fact be a justification for capital or primitive accumulation. Therefore, the distinctions I have presented throughout this book in terms of practices of jurisdictional accumulation as transplants (in the Castilian case) and transports of authority (in the other cases) – as counter-arguments to Miéville and assumptions of mercantilism as capitalism – would lose significant purchase.

However, it is crucial not to conflate doctrine and practices here. First, there are problems with the definition of capitalism from a commercialisation approach, which do not need to be rehearsed here again (see Chapters 2 and 3); the most important problem being its consequentialist and path-dependency approach to history. Second, this definition appears to be invoked because it facilitates assimilations of concepts of private property between scholars of different contexts (and whose influence differed greatly on the practices of imperial agents and sovereigns). Capitalism is therefore a secondary conceptual device in this argument because its main purpose is to provide the missing thread through which Koskenniemi can dislodge a conventional discourse and particular reception of the Salamanca School, and thus of the Castilian doctrinal contribution to empire and international law, which has obscured the links between them and Grotius. In other words, the designation of this era as capitalist is secondary to the actual links between these authors, which hold regardless. When reflecting on this very issue of the importance of the transition debate, Koskenniemi clarifies that being aware of 'changes in patterns of economic activity is sufficient for understanding the need of legal innovation during early modernity' (2014: 23).

Reinserting the context of the trade and ownership of things into sixteenth- and seventeenth-century legal doctrine is an essential contribution to understanding jurisdictional accumulation.[7] However, the distance between doctrine and practice remains considerable, even in the Castilian case. The fact that, as Koskenniemi notes, the practices of Dutch, English, and to some extent French imperialism reflected 'the imperialism of free trade, carried out by private companies through private transactions and private war' (2011: 36), remains in stark contrast to the 'conquest and settlement, administration, and mercantilist policies' of Spain (2011: 35), regardless of what the Salamanca School had developed conceptually.

In other words, the practices discussed in Chapter 6 and developed by Iberian rulers and settlers imbued with royal authority consisted in *dominium* in terms of jurisdiction over people and territorial resources, as judicial authority *and* as ownership of things in the broader sense of people/subjects/bodies and their resources. These differences were driven by jurisdictional and mercantilist interests and concerns shaped by theological transplants of jurisdictional subjectivities and 'eschatological narratives of Catholicism' (García-Salmones & Eslava, 2010: 56). These differ from practices of transforming means of production characterising capitalism as it developed in the classic phase of England's enclosures, of the development of private property related to land improvement, and its unified Crown-in-Parliament balanced by the common law. In contrast, in the colonies, the English balanced between *imperium* and *dominium* so as to merely transport authority and retain jurisdictional distance.

[7] See Shilliam (2012) for an interesting analysis of thingification in the context of English conceptions of law and commerce necessary for imperial expansion, and Kochi (2017) for an alternative genealogy of the construction of international law according to the mutually reinforcing relation between peace and commerce and the role of hegemonic empires such as the Dutch, British, and US.

7.1.2 Ownership as Private Property: English Transports of Authority

A significant literature has now appeared on the first phase of the English/British Empire as an 'empire of law' (e.g. Bilder, 2004; Hulsebosch, 2005; MacMillan, 2006; Games, 2008; Tomlins, 2010; Fitzmaurice, 2014). For Fitzmaurice (2014: 85), the 'first English colonizers of America' reversed the Castilian theologians' argument of occupation through which they attributed rights of property to Native Americans by adopting an extended conception of *dominium*. The English thus restricted the notion of *dominium* before applying it to the colonies and conceived 'of occupation in terms of different stages of society' (Fitzmaurice, 2014: 85). If Koskenniemi shows that concepts of private rights of ownership were developed by the Salamanca School, Castilian jurisdictional practices nevertheless maintained the twofold definition of *dominium* as jurisdiction and ownership. They used this to their advantage to give rights and jurisdictional subjectivities to Native Americans as it suited their needs to control settlers. In contrast, English colonisers used concepts of land improvement constructed by political philosophers and colonists to justify their rights, claiming that the land of Native Americans should be stripped from them because their use of it was considered wasteful (Neocleous, 2012; Koskenniemi, 2017b: 380).

Among the many dimensions of this legal empire, the most relevant here is the effort to determine the application of the common law outside of England, notably since *Calvin's Case* (1608) and its distinction between the Crown's *imperium* and the common-law's *dominium*.[8] This case and subsequent debates have been highlighted as key moments in the first phase of English/British imperialism and are also one of the rare early modern markers of extraterritoriality found in the literature (e.g. De Luca, 2008; Stein, 2012) that contrasts with the focus on ambassadorial privileges.

The judgment in *Calvin's Case* – ruling on 'whether one born in Scotland after the accession of James I could take up an inheritance in England' – defined 'who was an alien', 'who was a subject', and the relationship between king and subject (Brett, 2017: 97). The judgment also stated the difference between the Crown's sovereignty, which extended across its empire and the British Isles, and the Parliament and common-law's jurisdiction, which did not extend to those territories. The common law and its institutions were conceived as applying to a

[8] *Calvin's Case* 7 Coke Report 1a, 77 English Reports, 377, 1608.

strict domestic and English jurisdictional domain and represented the Crown's power of *dominium*. In contrast, the Crown's sovereignty over its subjects and land beyond England was represented by its power of *imperium* (MacMillan, 2006: 31–37). In other words, England's jurisdictional limits were defined by the common law and they were separated from England's imperial expansion of sovereignty. The implications and specificities of this approach for the history of international law and imperial expansion imply a significantly different understanding of jurisdictional accumulation for early modern England and Britain.

In effect, Tomlins analyses a wide range of practices (discussed in the previous chapter) through which 'law was the conceptual structure, the organizational discourse, by which their [English settlers] moves were enabled, the bridge that bore them across the ocean and planted them on the other side' (2010: 69). It may have 'planted' settlers, but it did not transplant their king's authority directly over them or over natives. In effect, the range and jurisdictional complexity of practices of settlement and subjectivities showed elaborate and diverse mechanisms and concepts – what Koskenniemi (2017b) refers to as the pluralism of the English legal order – but English practices of jurisdictional accumulation were predicated on the separation between the jurisdiction of the common law and the imperial sovereignty of the Crown. This produced two concepts of the law of nations, the first developed by civil lawyers for the royal prerogative, and the second developed by civil and common lawyers for expansion overseas (Koskenniemi, 2017b: 380).

Since the mobility of English subjects was based on sovereign prerogative, jurists such as Hale in the 1650s made a jurisdictional distinction between processes of sovereign, that is imperial acquisition (charters, royal letters patent) and domestic English law (Tomlins, 2010: 91). For Tomlins, *Calvin's Case* is a manifestation of an 'extraterritorial' fiction that designates sovereignty 'out of this land' (2010: 88) and illustrates this distinction between *dominium* and *imperium* since it

> underlined that English law as such was available to all natural subjects and free denizens, wherever within the king's dominions they might be born or domiciled, only in England. Guaranteed the status of natural subjects, migrants and their offspring would enjoy those rights on their return. When domiciled overseas and answerable to a local jurisdiction, however, subjects did not gain access to English law per se, but to such law that had been formulated according to the limits specified, and through the jurisdictional structures described, in the charters granting permission to proceed with settlements.
>
> (89)

Later colonists and historians have used this case (and specifically Coke's arguments in the case) to establish the type of extraterritoriality that emerged in the nineteenth century: that 'subjects of the English monarchy anywhere in the royal dominions had access to the benefits of English law' but this was not the question nor the conclusion of *Calvin's Case* (Tomlins, 2010: 85). This illustrates the tendency to conflate the different meanings and practices of extraterritoriality and *dominium*, as well as the importance of resituating this term in each case and context.

In England, the struggle for rights and property in its early capitalist era shows how important the early processes of primitive accumulation, and more generally social property relations, were for founding theories of sovereignty alongside the problem of the common law as theoretical arbiter between contending social factions. In effect, the conflicts between royal sovereignty and individual property rights ultimately reflect the ways in which these concepts and practices were intertwined (Koskenniemi, 2017b). As shown in Chapter 3, the relation between the common law, state formation, and primitive accumulation produced a specific nexus between the individual, private property, and state. This contributed to a sort of 'isolation' of Britain from European dynastic geopolitics which led to a practical focus on private property regardless of earlier doctrinal debates.

England's social property relations were marked by the balance between the Crown, the Parliament, and the judges and lawyers of the common law and this balance was expressed in legal terms in relation to legal subjectivity in *Calvin's Case.* This explains a crucial part of the specific trajectory of Britain's influence on international legal practices. In terms of legal and political thought, this can be linked to the shift after Locke and eighteenth- to nineteenth-century utilitarianism (e.g. Smith, Bentham) to a new conception of *terra nullius*, or vacant land. This period developed two new rights essential to British-led international relations: the right to the *use* of vacant lands, and the right to punish those transgressing the law of nature (Pagden, 2003: 181). However, the first and most important of these two rights, that regarding land improvement, was predicated on practices and debates specific to English state formation (i.e. enclosures as a strategy of primitive accumulation). Yet these practices were also specific to mercantilism and practices of settlement which developed as jurisdictional accumulation discussed in the previous chapters: chartered companies, colonial settlements, and attempts at consular representation, even if they were also determined by land improvement and were developed commercially and territorially rather than militarily and personally as in New Spain.

The 'exclude or exterminate' logic of primitive accumulation is bound with a restricted form of jurisdictional accumulation. Crucially, Tomlins shows how this narrative is not the product of isolated and obscure scholars with little influence or connection to the colonising process, although he does note the influence of Grotius on Winthrop. More importantly, the narrative is found in lawyers, settlers, and diplomatic agents' documents, court cases and practices from the late-sixteenth century onwards, showing 'the influence of contemporary English enclosure debates and practices', which anticipate legal theory and are confirmed by legal institutions (MacMillan, 2006: 205; Tomlins, 2010: 150). In other words, there was an indirect (rather than informal) relation of empire involving an additional party or document that put the Crown at a jurisdictional distance from people overseas (i.e. as transport rather than transplant).

A final important implication of this discussion is the way in which processes of jurisdictional accumulation are considered different to capitalist processes. This is the result of various factors and cases and remains to be further explored – in other words, the following opens rather than closes the debate on the relationship between jurisdictional, primitive, and capitalist accumulation.

As an entry into this debate, however, one reason proposed to differentiate these practices is that the exploitation and commercial capital engendered by jurisdictional accumulation was determined by jurisdictional goals and practices: that is, practices driven by the aim to exercise and enunciate jurisdictional rights, titles, and functions (some including notions of judicial authority and ownership of things and subjects, and others using more restricted notions). Some of these practices may have been essential in exporting forms of law that also later helped to structure and justify capitalist social property relations (e.g. jurisdictional subjectivities and procedures according to Roman and civil law, techniques of land improvement, *dominium* as private property rights, relationship between concepts of political freedom and principle of private property transported from early modern England to North America). However, most of these jurisdictional practices were primarily aimed in the early modern period at exercising and enunciating a legal relation (and acquiring rights, titles, and functions) that was exploitative to the benefit of the sovereign and to executing parties (corsairs, consuls, chartered settlers, companies) by extracting surplus through political and juridical means, or surplus from exchange (as buying and selling). In other words, jurisdictional accumulation was not capitalist because it did not originate from a direct aim to transform social property relations through economic means: it did not aim for the transformation of labour through market imperatives so as to produce surplus value from those relations.

Jurisdictional accumulation established jurisdictional rights and privileges, which could tangentially and only potentially also lead to significant commercial capital (e.g. mainly profit from trade of goods – buying and selling – but also *consulage* tax, imports on trade and passage, port customs, revenue from passes, revenue from settlements and plantations). In the cases I have found, it did not lead to capital as a capitalist social relation that transforms the producers' personal relation to lords and land or to merchants and crafts manufacturing (in feudalism and mercantilism) into a relation of legal and political freedom, which needs to be predicated on economic subjection and the commodification of labour. Under capitalism, in contrast, this subjection is due to the lack of means of production and to the politically constituted and imperative dependence on the market. One of the practices through which this is clearly seen is consular activity, which generated and regulated merchant capital, but was framed by jurisdictional goals and outcomes. Moreover, the following shows that by shaping key legal binaries usually associated with later-nineteenth-century practices of extraterritoriality, the history of mercantilism and jurisdictional accumulation in the Mediterranean are closely intertwined and shaped the international legal order in different ways than those developed by England and its processes of primitive accumulation.[9]

7.2 Consular Diplomacy and the Historiographical Neglect of Consuls

One of the key contributions of the project is to reconsider the importance of early modern consular jurisdiction as a practice of jurisdictional accumulation. By discussing this contribution in relation to the concept of extraterritoriality, this chapter is therefore able to return to the book's

[9] This can perhaps resolve a tension and impasse between proponents of mercantile capitalism and Political Marxism. Developing Political Marxism's argument regarding colonial practices of expansion and consular forms of mercantilism acknowledges the importance of these practices. As discussed in relation to Brandon's (2011) work on the Dutch transition in Chapter 3, scholars can be seen to agree on the actual practices occurring, but disagree strongly on the typologies used and some of their causal sequencing.

initial problematique regarding the confused narratives and definitions of early modern extraterritoriality.

Early modern historiography tends to separate mercantilism in the Mediterranean – and the jurisdictional importance of consuls and merchants – from the ambassadorial politics of European diplomacy – the 'Westphalian', dynastic, and old regime heritage of modern IR and the sovereign state. In continuation from Chapter 5, the following argues instead that these histories are intertwined and need to be understood in terms of dialectics and praxis. This is one of the crucial implications of a social history of jurisdiction.

Since extraterritoriality was retroactively linked to ambassadorial immunity by twentieth-century historians, who tied its legacy to Grotius's definition, consuls have consequently not been considered very important to understand the origins and development of modern extraterritoriality, in spite of the recognition of their role in applying and shaping the various capitulatory regimes and other 'extraterritorial' assertions of jurisdiction and authority. In other words, their legacy is recognised by certain authors but 'cut off' from the genealogy of modern international relations and international law. Although consuls had the most jurisdictional powers in the early modern diplomatic landscape – and were on the front line of implementing and interpreting questions of extraterritorial privileges – this role has been subtly disconnected from the story of extraterritoriality, European state formation, and international legal orders.[10]

Moreover, consuls sit uncomfortably in the general typology and historical narratives of modern sovereignty and diplomacy, interchangeably as aberrations and as necessary exceptions to modern forms of territorial sovereignty. Similar issues are found in the study of extraterritoriality. In other words, consuls and extraterritoriality refer to jurisdictional practices which either escape completely or are considered useful counterexamples to the formal territorial order of states and their ambassadors developing in the eighteenth and nineteenth centuries. As Leira and Neumann have described them, they remain diplomatic 'sidekicks' as their largely maritime and more hidden history has remained marginal to the grand narratives of the modern states system.

A key implication or consequence of how consuls are a challenge for diplomatic historians is that they oscillate between or belong to both

[10] See Chapter 1 for a more detailed analysis of this neglect.

(what we now define as) private and public as well as economic and political spheres. This is linked to the separation which occurred in historiography – but also through the jurisdictional practices of empires – between the noble monopoly of old regime European court diplomacy on the one hand, and merchants' consular diplomacy in the Mediterranean on the other.

Revisiting the jurisdictional practices of consuls, through their relations to trade and ambassadors, reveals consuls' roles as imperial agents who shaped early manifestations of what became key legal divides – and also illusions – for the nineteenth century. These divides or fictions are, first, the separation between political and economic spheres, and second, the categories of Christian and non-Christian legal spaces. The questions of social origins and social property relations have been discussed in Chapters 4 and 5. The following therefore applies the constitutive and broad definition of jurisdiction adopted in this project by looking at the other fictions – beyond that of extraterritorial ambassadorial privileges – that were shaped by early modern jurisdictional accumulation. It explores how key legal binaries were produced by the empires' jurisdictional practices.

7.2.1 The Separation between the Political and Economic Spheres

One of the innovations of the French 1781 collection of consular reforms – which summarised efforts since the late-seventeenth century to regulate consuls as commissioned and salaried royal agents – 'was to graduate the juridical boundaries of French subjects into cultural boundaries of European practice' (Coller, 2011: 214). Although Coller fails to sufficiently substantiate this argument, he is correct to emphasise that consular reforms had wide ramifications that have not been sufficiently acknowledged. Research in previous chapters explored some of these potential ramifications, and proposed that consular activity illustrates and contributed to an institutional separation, engineered by Louis XIV's regime, between an increasingly aristocratic, dynastic, and court diplomacy on the one hand; and the salaried, royal official, set in a more jurisdictional and locally administered regime of consular mercantilism in the Mediterranean on the other. However, instead of critically analysing this development, historiography has tended to accept it at face value and emphasised it by studying separately ambassadors as political agents and consuls as economic agents.

Other factors contributed to this separation. For example, English/British diplomatic relations with non-Europeans was mostly driven by merchants. This meant a particular jurisdictional division of diplomatic labour according to political and economic manifestations of power, as well as occupational background and class. This division also contributed to separating European and non-European diplomacy and international relations according to political and economic determinants.

The increasingly structural difference between political and economic diplomatic actors can also be seen in the class hierarchy between nobles and merchants, which was replicated in the foreign service as consul positions were considered degrading and well beneath the aristocracy, an assumption reproduced in the behaviour of the new aristocratic diplomacy of the eighteenth century.

The separation between increasingly aristocratic ambassadorial posts in mainland Europe[11] and a merchant-based extra-European consular network, contributed to building a history of extraterritoriality defined by ambassadorial privileges and excluding the role of consuls. Failing to reconnect them – and thus building a history of extraterritoriality based exclusively on ambassadorial immunity – is a significant problem, because the role of commerce and mercantilism in the evolution of diplomatic posts and practices is indicative of the ways in which capitalism, empires, and states developed in Europe. It also reveals new class dynamics and enables an alternative focus on the aristocratisation of ambassadors as a strategy of jurisdictional accumulation, which is better understood in tandem with efforts to control the Mediterranean trade and develop two diplomatic 'extraterritorial' fronts. The clash of these two fronts – and the need to understand them simultaneously – is illustrated by the case of the French embassy in Istanbul, where local merchants, the Chambre de Commerce de Marseille, as well as Colbert, Louis XIV's first minister, petitioned – mostly unsuccessfully at first – for a merchant resident to replace the aristocratic and thus inappropriate ambassador. This case also shows that the two fronts coexisted, and that the separation remains an illusory, fictive one, that has been reified by historiography.

A central argument made by Marxists, and especially by Wood (1982/1995), is the role of the fiction of the separation of the political and economic in shaping assumptions about first, the structure of state societies (with a public political space and an economic private space),

[11] This process was led by France and eventually emulated by all European powers by the end of the eighteenth century, in spite of English/British and Dutch specificities in this aspect of diplomatic social composition (see Chapter 4).

and, second, the structure of the capitalist international legal order (based on the distinction between a system of fixed independent sovereign states and a system of free-flowing private economic exchanges). This argument is a useful template through which to work through these diplomatic state strategies and how they have been reified. It also contributes to Wood's analysis, by adding that the political and economic division of diplomatic labour and its concurrent class hierarchies shaped the international order before capitalism had become the motor of imperialist expansion and was able to shape the system of sovereign states. To further historicise this proposition, the following looks at another key separation that can be identified in the practices of Mediterranean consuls.

7.2.2 The Separation between Christian and Non-Christian Legal Spaces

Another effect of consular diplomacy in this rapidly changing imperial environment was to contribute to the shaping of distinct legal and political spaces for relations between Christian and non-Christian peoples. Since the latter were to be gradually removed from the parameters of modern diplomacy by the nineteenth century, in spite of being forerunners of these practices for millennia, this legal ordering is of paramount importance.[12]

The Christian–non-Christian division is illustrated by the distinction between the significant reach and breadth of consuls' jurisdictional powers in ports of the Ottoman Empire vs. their more limited and contested roles in the Christian parts of the Mediterranean. The rise of jurisdictional duties was a means to dominate the Ottoman Empire and starts with – or was significantly advanced by – seventeenth-century consuls in the North African regencies.

This separation participated in entrenching the legal divisions between Western, Christian, so-called civilised, sovereign states on the one hand; and 'semi-sovereign', 'semi-civilised', non-Western, and non-Christian polities on the other. These divisions and categories shaped the system of international law that emerged in the late-nineteenth century, notably

[12] For studies that replace the role of Eastern and Asian kingdoms in the pre-modern history of diplomacy, albeit grounded in modernising and consequentialist assumptions, see Alexandrowicz (1967).

though the institutions of the classical phase of extraterritoriality (i.e. unequal treaties and extraterritorial courts).

The growing legal divide between Christian and non-Christian jurisdictional spheres was made possible by the capitulations signed with the Ottoman Empire as the legal arrangements on which the existence of consuls depended. (In terms of jurisdictional conceptions of expansion and space, capitulations illustrate the contrast between the territorialisation occurring in France under Louis XIV and the 'islands of sovereignty' pursued in the Ottoman Empire (Coller, 2011).) Similarly to colonial ventures in the Atlantic, capitulations created an opportunity for the aristocracy and aspiring bourgeois to act differently than they would at home or to use privileges they were losing in their metropolitan spaces, which links back to the separation between political and economic spheres.

> In the Echelles [regencies], unlike in France, nobles were permitted to engage in trade without forfeiting their aristocratic status. Indeed, as was the case in Britain, the 'Turkey trade' conferred a particular social prestige, even upon its richer bourgeois practitioners. Unlike the simple extraterritorial sovereignty of a consular space such as a modern embassy, the Echelles were also socially, economically and politically exceptional in relation to their complex fabric of dual sovereignty.
>
> (Coller, 2011: 212)

In other words, there is a fundamental difference between the 'simple extraterritoriality of modern consular space' and the consular spaces tolerated by the early modern capitulations accorded by the Ottoman sultan. It is therefore legitimate to understand early modern consular spaces as more complex and uncertain jurisdictional opportunities, as potential laboratories for later mechanisms of international law and divided concepts of sovereignty and territory which became more restricted and limited by Northern European conceptions of international law and diplomacy.

For example, in the 1740 French capitulations, the sultan agreed to a clause whereby subjects of states without representatives wishing to place themselves under the jurisdiction of the French king would be considered Frenchmen, thus placing foreigners 'under the wing' of the French Crown (Trivellato, 2009: 115). However, a similar clause was found in the English capitulation of 1661 (Trivellato, 2009: 317, n. 63). Subjects without representatives such as Sephardic traders 'often took advantage of rivalries between European powers to negotiate advantageous conditions for themselves' (Trivellato, 2009: 115). For various reasons such as the exclusion of Jews from the English Levant Company's monopoly, and the influence of Marseille as a trading centre, these traders preferred to be sponsored by the French. This provided them with jurisdictional advantages such as being tried by the French consul for criminal matters or making use of French consular authorities' issuing of certificates to contest abusive charges (Trivellato, 2009: 116).

However, these foreign communities also suffered from being financially abused by French consuls, who made them pay for their avania (collective fines owed to the sultan) in exchange for being exempt or charged with lower customs duties (Trivellato, 2009: 115). French consuls were supposed to pay their avania through their fixed salary or their special revenues, that is *avaries*, a small tax they were allowed to impose on ships sailing under a French flag after being prohibited to trade from 1681 (Trivellato, 2009: 317–319).

These ambiguities and complex circuits of commercial capital depending on jurisdictional arrangements contrast with later territorial restrictions of the concept of jurisdiction, and render assessments of who the capitulations were serving best, and to whom they were most profitable, particularly difficult for historians. This helps to explain why the political economy and diplomatic legacy of capitulations, alongside that of consuls, and their links to nineteenth-century extraterritoriality, has not been sufficiently or adequately explored. Regardless of why, the jurisdictional impact of consuls and their neglect in narratives of international law is considerable. If this impact shows the historical inadequacy of modern notions and separations of the personal–territorial, public–private, and political–economic binaries to categorise early modern practices, it also shows the ways in which legal spaces were shaped according to consular agency, and how (as with Spain in the Atlantic context) Christendom and Christian subjectivity remained powerful means of legitimation and othering of diplomatic activity.

In effect, the capitulations and the consular spaces they created differed from consular activity in areas of the Mediterranean not governed by the capitulations; the Eastern and North African Mediterranean governed by the Ottoman Empire on one side and the Christian Western European Mediterranean on the other. Here is not the place to explore the genesis and development of these spaces, how they came to be justified and the various actors involved in that process. However, it is possible to signal the ways in which Mediterranean merchants, consuls, and in some instances, their rulers, justified these different spaces, and how they predominantly seemed to invoke the Christian and non-Christian divide to do so, regardless of whether the interests driving them were more commercial or diplomatic than of a religious nature. This aspect of the history of consular jurisdiction is one that is potentially more fruitful for its links to the nineteenth-century history of extraterritoriality and is discussed in what follows in terms of this connection.

English consular practices provide important aspects of the history of extraterritoriality, which have been neglected because of the focus on absolute ambassadorial immunity. The establishment of more English consulates from the early-seventeenth century is evidence of a shift to a more 'direct responsibility' between merchants' activities and the king's jurisdiction through the increased need for merchants to be protected by the king, after the decline of companies and factories in Western Europe (Barbour, 1928: 555). This meaning of extraterritoriality as protection legitimised the foreign practices of merchants and helped to establish imperial expansion, mercantile privileges, and their nefarious consequences in terms of creating conflicts and exploiting weaker competitors as a natural and central part of European expansion.[13] As seen below, the commercial arguments for only having consuls in non-Christian spaces were cloaked in other assumptions based on political rather than religious unity.

The English and Dutch – considered the 'two greatest commercial nations' of the period – 'maintained no consuls in each other's ports'; the agents they used as emergency or extraordinary missions 'had no official status or recognition' (Barbour, 1928: 574).

> The merchants of Amsterdam in a memorial to the burgomasters and council declared that the privilege of establishing consuls in England would be of slight value by reason of the Navigation Acts; that the *propinquity of the two lands* made consuls unnecessary; that foreigners received as good and as prompt justice in the ordinary courts as did natives, and that it would be a stigma upon those courts to withdraw foreigners from their jurisdiction; that there were really no services which consuls could render masters of ships to earn their fees; that these fees, once allowed, would surely be increased by the consuls at the first opportunity, to the injury of trade.
>
> (Barbour, 1928: 575; emphasis added)

[13] On the relation between protection and empire, see Benton *et al.* (2017) and specifically for English political thought and the role of corporations, chapters by Brett (2017) and Stern (2017) respectively.

We find here a very useful summary of opinions concerning consuls in Northern and Western Europe, and another illustration of the potential conflicts between merchants and consuls discussed in Chapter 5, especially in those regions. The recognition of similar institutions and interests, coupled with the fear of being surveyed or spied on and a scepticism towards the integrity of consuls, provide solid arguments against the establishment of consulates. In other words, the memorial argues, there is no need for formal extraterritorial privileges among similar Christian trading powers. For Barbour, the main reason for this objection to consular representation among seventeenth-century Western and Northern Europe's traders was the fear of 'judicial extraterritoriality for the foreign factories' (i.e. their existence as separate from their home judicial institutions).[14]

However, objections illustrated in the memorial quoted above were not so common. One reason why this extraterritoriality was not raised as a problem even if merchants were against it in principle was that extraterritoriality 'for the courts or factories of foreign mercantile associations or companies, such as the Steelyard in London' was commonly accepted at the time, though it was also in the process of being 'withdrawn' (Barbour, 1928: 576). Another potentially more important reason raised for not commonly objecting to judicial extraterritoriality was that national ordinary jurisdictions were an option preferred by foreigners. Barbour cites a case from Bordeaux, where an English merchant in 1664 praises the local jurisdictions (though she warns that such opinions would be assumed to change following the later belligerence of Louis XIV's reign against foreign traders). This use of local jurisdictions is also observed for foreign merchants in Iberia, and more generally, by the fact that the residence of French subjects in Christian countries was not regulated or limited, leading to a tendency by residents to go to local courts (Mézin, 1997). In mixed cases, it was therefore difficult for France or other European nations to protect their subjects. Moreover, the Christian vs. non-Christian argument was used at length to contest the presence of consuls in Italian ports of the Mediterranean (Calafat, 2018b).

[14] Barbour uses the term 'extraterritoriality' across the early modern and modern periods. This underlines her lament that extraterritoriality was not raised more explicitly as a central objection in the seventeenth century. Her sleight-of-hand comment against the problematic development of extraterritoriality in the early-twentieth-century Near East in terms of a government failure links the processes in the different periods, but without any further explanation or context (1928: 575).

There is a paradox in the sets of reasons and objections to consular jurisdiction among Western Mediterranean realms. On the one hand, it is argued that consular jurisdiction is not required between similar trading and Christian nations (even if they are regularly at war with each other) because there is an equivalence of values and processes, a sense that all Christian merchants are brothers of trade and can share each other's institutions.

On the other hand, Western European institutions were quite explicitly and openly discussed as encroachments of privilege and as opportunities for the self-interested behaviour of consuls in the Western Mediterranean. In other words, behind claims of the 'propinquity of the two lands' lurked an inherent distrust in merchants, and thereby, in consular jurisdiction.

In contrast, in the Eastern Mediterranean, consular jurisdiction was considered to operate for the defence of merchants' interests and merchant consuls were argued to be the champions of those interests. This was shown in the various memoranda in defence of merchant Jean-François Roboly to replace, as resident consul, the French ambassador in Istanbul (see Chapter 5).

Generally, for Mézin, jurisdictional prerogatives are fewer in Christian states because the 'structure of the nation is weaker than in Muslim countries' (1997). Similarly, Stein (2012: 95) explains the lack of English jurisdictional functions in Italy by the existence of older customs of merchants in those cities and growing principles of territorial sovereignty asserted by the local authorities. Moreover, colonial and consular jurisdictional spaces in the Ottoman regencies developed according to different processes than European processes of state formation, and were often more advantageous and progressive to foreign merchants than their original context:

> in the Echelles the idea of the nation as an autonomous collectivity was a non-territorial one. It represented a degree of democracy and political liberty independent of the territorial concept of the modern nation state. In France, by contrast, the development of the spatial and temporal axes of the territorial state continued unabated, without any real movement toward the idea of deliberative participation, until the eve of the Revolution itself.
>
> (Coller, 2011: 212)

In sum, although consular jurisdiction was contested and limited in Western and Southern Europe, it was defended and used for its commercial advantages in the Ottoman-governed Eastern Mediterranean.

This contributed to a crucial jurisdictional division. On one side, in Christian Europe and parts of the Mediterranean, merchants admitted their mutual distrust for each other while considering themselves superior to non-Christians and in no need of consular protection. On the other side, we find an extra-Christian space where Christian merchants either favoured the advantages of their consuls' prerogatives as a means to assert and defend their privileges, or accepted what they otherwise saw as an illusion in Christian spaces: that consular jurisdiction could prevail above the self-interested nature of merchants and the so-called barbarism of non-Christian others.

A final point adding to the alternative narrative of the links between spaces for jurisdictional accumulation and later forms of extraterritoriality, is the jurisdictional fluidity and diversity of Southern Mediterranean ports – culturally, religiously, and socially (Pennell, 2009: 247). Recalling the opening anecdote on consular ale houses, these ports provide numerous cases and examples of 'extraterritorial fictions' that go far beyond the classic Northern European cases of embassy chapels and the transition from personal to territorial forms of sovereignty.

For example, in terms of classic international law instruments, treaties between North African regencies and Morocco on the one hand, and Western European and North American nations on the other, show the development of a 'customary diplomatic law' from the mid-seventeenth century (Pennell, 2009). This is argued to constitute at first a challenge to European extraterritoriality and imperialism. Europeans did not enjoy extraterritorial privileges in the North African context until the nineteenth century, because in spite of the treaties aimed to assert these privileges, they faced consular practices and disputes that made any simple unilateral imposition of power impossible. This argument makes sense of the jurisdictional complexity and diversity of early modern consular and mercantile practices.

Finally, to end this section on consuls, two important recent studies have explored their role and importance for constructing the institutions of international law. Windler (2017b) and Nuzzo (2017) provide promising avenues to continue incorporating further analyses of the socio-economic agencies of these legal and diplomatic actors. Nuzzo (2017: 266) confirms the link between the early modern construction of international law and Christianity, and more specifically analyses how consular law became a key tool and model for how relations between the West and non-West – considered less civilized by early international lawyers – were shaped in the nineteenth century (Nuzzo, 2017: 271). Windler

(2017b) provides more nuance to this picture by looking at the North African regencies, and how the plurality of jurisdictions operating in these port cities of the Mediterranean created significant practical and theoretical problems concerning the sovereignty and legal personality of the regencies in the international legal order. If consuls tended to respect the sovereignty of their hosts, reflecting the links between local elites and European traders, this was often and increasingly disputed by their rulers (2017b: 206–207). The jurisdictional plurality was also contested by the evolving law of nations in the eighteenth century and even more so in the nineteenth. Civilizing missions became more prominent and took over from decisions based on the 'consul's comparative overview, which asked for respect of treaty and customary law' (Windler, 2017b: 218). What distinguishes these two studies is their links back to the early modern period, calling for the need for further studies to clarify how we historicise links between the seventeenth and eighteenth centuries in terms of this rich, neglected, and jurisdictionally challenging consular history.

Epilogue

Rethinking early modern extraterritoriality from a social, entangled, and trans-imperial perspective, to see if it could reveal more practices than that of ambassadorial immunity, led us to a wider variety of practices of jurisdictional expansion. The angle chosen emphasised social property relations as a basis to understanding key structural changes in conceptions and practices of jurisdiction, territory, and sovereignty. This approach to historical sociology is shaped by a Political Marxist methodology focusing on the structural (political and legal) specificities of early modern social property relations, and a radically historicist, processual, and non-consequentialist conception of historical development.

In other words, the project has explored a variety of practices and actors used to expand the authority of early modern imperial rulers. If these practices constitute a break from previous concurring strategies of dynastic or geopolitical accumulation, this does not mean they are the first steps of the modern or capitalist system of international law. Instead, these different modes coexisted in various local and geopolitical contexts.

This contrasts with doctrinal approaches to the history of international law that reify distinct and chronologically progressive hegemonic orders or epochs that obscure many overlapping and contested trajectories of social relations. The hidden history of jurisdictional expansion accounts for contested processes of extraterritoriality that have been neglected by the dominant Westphalian and *droit public de l'Europe* accounts of seventeenth–eighteenth-century Europe. These favour an explanation of the process of extraterritoriality defined as ambassadorial privileges and found in the rise of Northern European permanent embassies.

This narrative omits the jurisdictional complexity of a key set of early modern diplomatic actors – consuls in the Mediterranean – as well as the strategic and social origins of the aristocratisation of ambassadors led by Louis XIV. These actors helped to forge the separation between political and economic spheres, as well as the separation between Christian and non-Christian legal spaces. These fictive divisions became further entrenched through the diverging narratives of the Westphalian history of public international law on the one hand, and the maritime history of private international law on the other.

This project also contrasts with recent Marxist and institutionalist attempts to broaden the definition of capitalism to the early modern period, following commercialisation models that conflate mercantilism with capitalism. Instead, jurisdictional accumulation marks some of the specificities of the early modern period that break up this conflation. It permits us to draw a more spatially and temporally heterogeneous picture of legal strategies of expansion while reconnecting neglected social relations to the construction of modern international law and histories of extraterritoriality. Jurisdictional accumulation can be used to discuss the universalisation of the institutions concomitant to commodity exchange or commodity capitalism; or, in other words, the universalisation of the 'legal form' implied by the commodity form theory of law. Although problematic from a methodological and historical perspective, Miéville's powerful theory forces Political Marxism to reassess the role of legal strategies in the expansion of territorial sovereignty.

This reassessment is necessary because existing concepts of accumulation fail to account for the specificity and agency of juridical expansion. They do not allow for specific juridical processes that have political and economic consequences and which are driven by actors juggling with absolutist and mercantilist interests. During the long process of imperial political expansion from the sixteenth to the late eighteenth centuries, these processes played a crucial role; one that has not been sufficiently acknowledged. If geopolitical accumulation has been used to refer to Iberian and French legal strategies of expansion, this book argues that this concept misses the constitutive role of jurisdiction for state formation, and thus the enduring role of jurisdictional conditions of accumulation for social and political processes.

The project defines early modern jurisdiction as a practice constitutive of territorial sovereignty and of other legal forms of power. The concept of jurisdictional disputes helps to focus on the practices that make individual actors, groups, and institutions participate and struggle in the concrete realisation of forms of public and private property and sovereignty. Jurisdictional conflicts form one of the bases of Political Marxism's apparatus to understand the multiplicity, overlap, and contests between and among Western European political and legal institutions. This concept has also been enriched by the turn to critical histories of empire in international law. By bringing together these contributions, the concept of jurisdictional accumulation emphasises, first, the focus on trans-societal contestation, legal pluralism, and entanglement; and, second, the more privilege-based and personal social property relations specific to early modernity and concerned with accumulating or preserving jurisdictional rights, titles, and functions, and the merchant capital potentially generated by these rights, titles, and functions.

In effect, jurisdictional accumulation enables important differentiations between the practices of the Iberian, Dutch, French, and English/British empires. The Iberian expansion was focused on militarily controlling peoples, on transplanting authority through a variety of jurisdictional actors directly representing the Crown, and through institutions establishing jurisdictional subjectivities to incorporate and subjugate existing legal cultures. The more indirect and commercial Dutch, French, and English/British empires relied more on trading and chartered companies, settlers, and treaties with indigenous populations which often resulted in their complete evacuation, extermination, and dispossession, and consisted in a varied set of transports and extensions of authority in the Atlantic and European contexts. Moreover, these empires also developed practices of jurisdictional accumulation in the Mediterranean through consular activity and competition over diplomatic privileges accorded by the Ottoman Empire.

This analysis reveals the types of practices early modern extraterritoriality – or, better, jurisdictional accumulation – covers as concrete processes as well as how some historians have ignored these processes so as to construct the history of public international law as a series of reified orders or epochs of international relations. Instead, a historical materialist approach to international law constructs a history of international legal orders as one of *struggle* over contested practices of jurisdictional expansion. Mapping these practices and historiographical omissions – from a comparative and selective research method – provides a more complex and socially rich narrative of extraterritoriality that emphasises specificity first and similarity second.

In fine, the book has explored the links between law, empires, and capital, and the importance of these links for constructing arguments in the disciplines of international relations and international law concerning the emergence of modernity, sovereignty, and territoriality. Therefore, the book is first and foremost a social history and political economy of so-called early modern extraterritoriality. The importance of this phenomenon – and the processes that have been excluded from it – is resituated in the history of international relations and international law and reframed as jurisdictional accumulation.

Understanding colonial and diplomatic practices of expansion in terms of social property relations and jurisdictional accumulation reveals new aspects of these early modern empires and provides a clearer picture of the different extraterritorial practices developing in this period. This narrative goes beyond the classic focus on embassy chapels in Northern Europe – as the invention of the 'extraordinary fiction' of sovereign territoriality and extraterritoriality – and shows the inadequacy of narratives of the emergence of the sovereign state based on the shift from the personal to the territorial as defining the modern international legal order.

The early modern period was jurisdictional, not only because of the plurality and overlapping of jurisdictional regimes; it was also jurisdictional because of the use of jurisdictional rights, titles, and functions (institutions and subjectivities) as a means of imperial ownership and rule over indigenous groups and against competing empires. The early modern period was not jurisdictional because this condition naturally explains the emergence of territorial sovereignty. The early modern period was jurisdictional because a variety of actors used jurisdictional devices and arguments that shaped imperial expansion in ways defined here as extensions, transplants, and transports of authority. Jurisdictional accumulation thus contrasts with mercantilism and capitalism, and constitutes a significant mode of expansion that brings consuls, merchants, and lawyers out of the shadows of empire and onto the main stage of the construction of modern international relations and international law.

BIBLIOGRAPHY

Adair E. R. 1929, *The Exterritoriality of Ambassadors in the Sixteenth and Seventeenth Centuries*, New York: Longmans, Green and Co.

Adorno, R. 2012, 'Court and Chronicle: A Native Andean's Engagement with Spanish Colonial Law', in S. Belmessous (ed.), *Native Claims: Indigenous Law against Empire 1500–1920*, Oxford: Oxford University Press, 63–84

Adams, J. 2007, *The Familial State: Ruling Families and Merchant Capitalism in Early Modern Europe*, Ithaca, NY: Cornell University Press

Adams, R. & Cox, R. (eds.) 2011, *Diplomacy and Early Modern Culture*, Basingstoke: Palgrave

Aglietti, M., Herrero Sanchez, M., & Zamora Rodriguez, F. (eds.) 2013, *Los cónsules de extranjeros en la Edad Moderna y a principios de la Edad Contemporánea*, Madrid: Ediciones Doce Calles

Alexandrowicz, C. H. 1967, *An Introduction to the History of the Law of Nations in the East Indies (16th, 17th and 18th Centuries)*, Oxford: Clarendon Press

Allain, T. 2018, 'Relations de pouvoir et enjeux marchands autour du réseau consulaire néerlandais en Méditerranée (XVII–XVIIIe siècles)', in A. Bartolomei, G. Calafat, M. Grenet, & J. Ulbert (eds.), *De l'utilité commerciale des consuls: L'institution consulaire et les marchands dans le monde méditerranéen (XVIIe–XXe siècle)*, Rome: Publications de l'École française de Rome, 421–438

Alston, D. 2018, 'Scottish Slave Owners in Suriname 1651–1863' *Northern Scotland*, 9, 17–43

Amir, M. & Sela, R. 2016, *Extraterritorialities in Occupied Worlds*, Puctum Books

Amirell, S. E. & Müller, L. (eds.) 2014, *Persistent Piracy: Maritime Violence and State-Formation in Global Historical Perspective*, New York: Palgrave

Anderson, M. S. 1993, *The Rise of Modern Diplomacy 1450–1919*, New York: Longmans

Anderson, P. 1974, *Lineages of the Absolutist State*, London: NLB

Anderson, S. P. 1989, *An English Consul in Turkey: Paul Rycaut at Smyrna, 1667–1678*, Oxford: Oxford University Press

Anghie, A. 1999, 'Finding the Peripheries: Sovereignty and Colonialism in 19th Century International Law', *Harvard International Law Journal*, 40(1), 1–80

2005, *Imperialism, Sovereignty and the Making of International Law*, Cambridge: Cambridge University Press

Anievas, A. (ed.) 2010, *Marxism and World Politics: Contesting Global Capitalism*, London: Routledge

Anievas, A. & Matin, K. (eds.) 2016, *Historical Sociology and World History: Uneven and Combined Development over the Longue Durée*, Lanham, MD: Rowman & Littlefield

Anievas, A. & Nişancioğlu, K. 2015, *How the West Came to Rule: The Geopolitical Origins of Capitalism*, London: Pluto

Ariste, P. 1667, *Traicté des consulz de la nation françoise aux paÿs estrangers*

Armitage, D. 2000, *The Ideological Origins of the British Empire*, Cambridge: Cambridge University Press

Aron, R. 1986, *History, Truth and Liberty: Selected Writings*, Chicago: University of Chicago Press

Armitage, D. & Pitts, J. (eds.) 2016, *C. H. Alexandrowicz, The Law of Nations in Global History*, Oxford: Oxford University Press

Armstrong, D., Farell, T., & Lambert, H. 2007, *International Law and International Relations*, Cambridge: Cambridge University Press

Arrighi, G. 2002 [1994] *The Long Twentieth Century: Money, Power, and the Origins of Our Time*, London: Verso

d'Aspremont, J. 2019, 'Critical Histories of International Law and the Repression of Disciplinary Imagination', *London Review of International Law*, 7(1), 89–115

Aston, T. H. & Philpin, C. H. E. (eds.) 1985, *The Brenner Debate: Agrarian Class Structure and Economic Development in Pre-Industrial Europe*, Cambridge: Cambridge University press

Baars, G. 2019, *The Corporation, Law and Capitalism: A Radical Perspective on the Role of Law in the Global Political Economy*, Leiden: Brill

Baber, R. J. 2012, 'Law, Land and Legal Rhetoric in Colonial New Spain: A Look at the Changing Rhetoric of Indigenous Americans in the Sixteenth Century', in S. Belmessous (ed.), *Native Claims: Indigenous Law against Empire 1500–1920*, Oxford: Oxford University Press, 41–62

Bachand, R. & Lapointe, T. 2010 'Beyond Presentism: Rethinking the Enduring Co-Constitutive Relationships between International Law and International Relations', *International Political Sociology*, 4, 271–286

Baillou, J. (ed.) 1984, *Les affaires étrangères et le corps diplomatique français, I: de l'Ancien Régime au Second Empire*, Paris: Editions du CNRS

Banaji, J. 2007, 'Islam, the Mediterranean and the Rise of Capitalism', *Historical Materialism*, 15(1), 47–74

2011, *Theory as History: Essays on Modes of Production and Exploitation*, Leiden: Brill

2018, 'Globalising the History of Capital: Ways Forward', *Historical Materialism*, 26(3), 143–166

2019, 'State and Capital in the Era of Primitive Accumulation', keynote lecture for conference 'IISG towards a Global History of Primitive Accumulation', Amsterdam, 6 May 2019, unpublished paper, www.academia.edu/39761764/State_and_Capital_in_the_Era_of_Primitive_Accumulation [accessed 28 October 2019]

forthcoming, 'Merchant Capitalism', in S. R. Farris, B. Skeggs, & A. Toscano (eds.), *The SAGE Handbook of Marxism*

Barbano, M. 2018, '"*A Lucrative, Dangerous Business*" Le consulat anglais à Alger, Tunis et Tripoli dans la deuxième moitié du XVIIe siècle', in A. Bartolomei, G. Calafat, M. Grenet, & J. Ulbert (eds.), *De l'utilité commerciale des consuls: L'institution consulaire et les marchands dans le monde méditerranéen (XVIIe–XXe siècle)*, Rome: Publications de l'École française de Rome, 253–263

Barbour, V. 1928 'Consular Service in the Reign of Charles II', *American Historical Review*, 33, 553–578.

Barreto, M. J. 2017, '*Jus Gentium* and the Transformation of Latin American Nature: One More Reading of Vitoria?', in M. Koskenniemi, W. Rech, & M. Jimenez Fonseca (eds.), *International Law and Empire: Historical Explorations*, Oxford: Oxford University Press, 123–148

Bartelson, J. 1995, *A Genealogy of Sovereignty*, Cambridge: Cambridge University Press

Bartolomei, A. 2018a, 'Introduction', in A. Bartolomei, G. Calafat, M. Grenet, & J. Ulbert (eds.), *De l'utilité commerciale des consuls: L'institution consulaire et les marchands dans le monde méditerranéen (XVIIe–XXe siècle)*, Rome: Publications de l'École française de Rome, 1–16

2018b, 'Entre l'état, les intérêts marchands et l'intérêt personnel, l'*agence* des consuls. Introduction', in A. Bartolomei, G. Calafat, M. Grenet, & J. Ulbert (eds.), *De l'utilité commerciale des consuls: L'institution consulaire et les marchands dans le monde méditerranéen (XVIIe–XXe siècle)*, Rome: Publications de l'École française de Rome, 391–402

Bartolomei, A., Calafat, G., Grenet, M., & Ulbert, J. (eds.) 2018, *De l'utilité commerciale des consuls: L'institution consulaire et les marchands dans le monde méditerranéen (XVIIe–XXe siècle)*, Rome: Publications de l'École française de Rome

Beaulac, S. 2004, *The Power of Language in the Making of International Law*, Leiden: Brill

Beik, W. 1985, *Absolutism and Society in Seventeenth-Century France: State Power and Provincial Aristocracy in Languedoc*, Cambridge: Cambridge University Press

2000, *Louis XIV and Absolutism: A Brief Study with Documents*, Boston, MA: Bedford/St Martin's

2005, 'Review Article: The Absolutism of Louis XIV as Social Collaboration', *Past and Present*, 188 (August), 195–224

2009, *A Social and Cultural History of Early Modern France*, Cambridge: Cambridge University Press

Belissa, M. 1998, *Fraternité Universelle et Intérêt National (1713–1795): Les cosmopolitiques du droit des gens*, Paris: Éditions Kimé

Bell, G. M. 1990, *A Handlist of British Diplomatic Representatives 1509–1688*, London: Royal Historical Society

Bell, D. A. 1994, *Lawyers and Citizens: The Making of a Political Elite in Old Regime France*, Oxford: Oxford University Press

Belmessous, S. (ed.) 2012, *Native Claims: Indigenous Law against Empire 1500–1920*, Oxford: Oxford University Press

2015, *Empire by Treaty: Negotiation European Expansion 1600–1900*, Oxford: Oxford University Press

Bély, L. 1990, *Espions et ambassadeurs au temps de Louis XIV*, Paris: Fayard

2005, 'Les temps modernes (1515–1789)', in F. Autrand et al. (eds.), *Histoire de la diplomatie française I. Du Moyen Age à l'Empire*, Paris: Perrin, 181–460

2007, *L'art de la paix en Europe: Naissance de la diplomatie moderne, XVIe–XVIIIe siècle*, Paris: Presses Universitaires de France

Bénazet, C. 1982, *Ambassadeurs et Ministres de France de 1748 à 1791. Étude institutionnelle et sociale*, Thèse de l'École des Chartes

Bénazet-Béchu, C. 1998, 'Les ambassadeurs français au XVIIIe siècle', in L. Bély & I. Richefort (eds.), *L'invention de la diplomatie*, Paris: Presses Universitaires de France

Benton, L. 2002, *Law and Colonial Cultures: Legal Regimes in World History, 1400–1900*, Cambridge: Cambridge University Press

2006, 'Constitutions and Empire: A Review', *Law and Social Enquiry*, 177–198

2010, *A Search for Sovereignty: Law and Geography in European Empires 1400–1900*, Cambridge: Cambridge University Press

2011, 'Possessing Empire: Iberian Claims and Interpolity Law', in S. Belmessous (ed.), *Native Claims: Indigenous Law against Empire 1500–1920*, Oxford: Oxford University Press, 19–40

2018, 'Afterward: The Space of Political Community and the Space of Authority', *Global Intellectual History*, 3(2), 254–265

2019, 'Beyond Anachronism: Histories of International Law and Global Legal Politics', *Journal of the History of International Law/Revue d'histoire du droit international*, 21(1), 7–40

Benton, L. & Clulow, A. 2017, 'Webs of Protection and Interpolity Zones in the Early Modern World', in L. Benton, A. Clulow, & B. Attwood (eds.),

Protection and Empire: A Global History, Cambridge: Cambridge University Press, 49–71

Benton, L., Clulow, A., & Attwood, B. (eds.), 2017, *Protection and Empire: A Global History*, Cambridge: Cambridge University Press

Benton, L. & Ford, L. 2016 *Rage for Order: The British Empire and the Origins of International Law, 1800–1850*, Cambridge, MA: Harvard University Press

Benton, L. & Ross, R. J. (eds.) 2013, *Legal Pluralism and Empires, 1500–1850*, New York: New York University Press

Berman, H. J. 1983, *Law and Revolution*, Cambridge, MA: Harvard University

Berridge, G. R., 2009, *British Diplomacy in Turkey, 1583 to the Present*, Leiden: Martinus Nijhoff

Besson, S. 2012, 'The Extraterritoriality of the European Convention on Human Rights: Why Human Rights Depend on Jurisdiction and What Jurisdiction Amounts to', *Leiden Journal of International Law*, 24(4), 857–884

Bhambra, G. 2007, *Rethinking Modernity: Postcolonialism and the Sociological Imagination*, Houndmills, UK: Palgrave Macmillan

2010, 'Historical Sociology, Modernity, and Postcolonial Critique', *American Historical Review*, 116(3), 653–662

Biedermann, Z. 2014, *The Portuguese in Sri Lanka and South India: Studies in the History of Diplomacy, Empire and Trade, 1500–1650*. Wiesbaden: Harrassowitz Verlag

Bilder, M. S. 2004, *The Transatlantic Constitution: Colonial Legal Culture and the Empire*, Cambridge, MA: Harvard University Press

Bilgin, P. 2016, 'How to Remedy Eurocentrism in IR? A Complement and a Challenge for *The Global Transformation*', *International Theory*, 8(3), 492–501

Binns, P. 1980, 'Law and Marxism', *Capital and Class*, 4, 100–113

Birr, C. 2018, '*Dominium* in the Indies. Juan López de Palacios Rubios' *Libellus de insulis oceanis quas vulgus indias appelat* (1512–1516)', *Rechtgeschichte*, 26, 264–283

Bittner, L., Gross, L., & Santifaller, L. (eds.) 1936–1965, *Repertorium der diplomatischen Vertreter aller Länder* (3 vols.), Zurich: Fretz & Wasmuth

Black, J. 2001, *British Diplomats and Diplomacy 1688–1800*, Exeter: University of Exeter Press

Boogert, van der M. H. 2003, 'Consular Jurisdiction in the Ottoman Legal System in the Eighteenth Century', *Oriente Moderno*, 22(3), 613–634

Borah, W. 1983, *Justice by Insurance: The General Indian Court of Colonial Mexico and the Legal Aides of the Half-Real*, Berkeley: University of California Press

Boulanger, P. 2006, 'Les appointements des consuls de France à Alger au XVIIIe siècle', in J. Ulbert & G. Le Bouëdec (eds.), *La fonction consulaire à l'époque moderne: L'affirmation d'une institution économique et politique (1500–1800)*, Rennes: Presses Universitaires de Rennes, 123–146

Bowden, B. 2005, 'The Colonial Origins of International Law. European Expansion and the Classical Standard of Civilization', *Journal of the History of International Law*, 7, 1–23

Bowring, B. 2008, *The Degradation of the International Legal Order? The Rehabilitation of Law and the Possibility of Politics*, London: Routledge

Bozeman, A. 1960 *Politics and Culture in International History: From the Ancient Near East to the Opening of the Modern Age*, Princeton, NJ: Princeton University Press

Brabazon, H. (ed.) 2016, *Neoliberal Legality: Understanding the Role of Law in the Neoliberal Project*, Abingdon, UK: Routledge

Branch, J. 2013, *The Cartographic State: Maps, Territory, and the Origins of Sovereignty*, Cambridge: Cambridge University Press

Brandon, P. 2011, 'Marxism and the "Dutch Miracle": The Dutch Republic and the Transition Debate', *Historical Materialism*, 19(3), 106–146

2015, *War, Capital, and the Dutch State (1588–1795)*, Leiden: Brill

2019, 'Between the Plantation and the Port: Racialization and Social Control in Eighteenth-Century Paramaribo', *International Review of Social History*, 64

Brandon, P. & Fatah-Black, K. 2015, '"For the Reputation and Respectability of the State": Trade, the Imperial State, Unfree Labor, and Empire in the Dutch Atlantic', in John Donoghue & Evelyn P. Jennings (eds.), *Building the Atlantic Empires: Unfree Labor and Imperial States in the Political Economy of Capitalism, ca. 1500–1914*, Leiden: Brill, 84–108

Breen, M. P. 2007, *Law, City and King: Legal Culture, Municipal Politics, and State Formation in Early Modern Dijon*, Rochester, NY: University of Rochester Press

Brenner, R. 1972, 'The Social Basis of English Commercial Expansion 1550–1650', in S. Subrahmanyam (ed.), *Merchant Networks in the Early Modern World, 1450–1800*, London: Routledge, 1996, 280–302 [orig. pub. in *Journal of Economic History* [1972] 32(1), 361–384]

1976, 'Agrarian Class Structure and Economic Development in Pre-Industrial Europe', *Past and Present*, 70

1977, 'The Origins of Capitalist Development: A Critique of Neo-Smithian Marxism', in *New Left Review*, 104, 25–92

1997, 'Property Relations and the Growth of Agricultural Productivity in Late Medieval and Early Modern Europe', in A. Bhaduri & R. Skarstein (eds.), *Economic Development and Agricultural Productivity*, London: Edward Elgar, 9–44

2001, 'The Low Countries in the Transition to Capitalism', in Peter Hoppenbrouwers & Jan Luiten van Zanden (eds.), *Peasants into Farmers?: The Transformation of Rural Economy and Society in the Low Countries (Middle Ages–19th Century) in Light of the Brenner Debate*, Turnhout: Brepols, 275–338

2003, *Merchants and Revolution: Commercial Change, Political Conflict, and London's Overseas Traders, 1550–1653*, London: Verso

2007a, 'Property and Progress: Where Adam Smith Went Wrong', in Chris Wickham (ed), *Marxist History-writing for the Twenty First Century*, Oxford: Oxford University Press, 49–111

2007b, 'Structure versus Conjuncture', *New Left Review*, II(43) (Jan.–Feb.), 33–59

Brett, A. 2011, *Changes of State: Nature and the Limits of the City in Early Modern Natural Law*, Princeton, NJ: Princeton University Press

2017, 'Protection as a Political Concept in English Political Thought, 1603–1651', in L. Benton, A. Clulow, & B. Attwood (eds.), *Protection and Empire: A Global History*, Cambridge: Cambridge University Press, 93–113

Brophy, S. 2017, 'An Uneven and Combined Theory of Law: Initiation', *Law Critique*, 28: 167

Buckley, M. 1966, 'Origins of Diplomatic Immunity in England', *University of Miami Law Review*, 21, 349–365

Bull, H. 1977, *The Anarchical Society: A Study of Order in World Politics*, London: Macmillan

Bull, H. & Watson, A. (eds.) 1984, *The Expansion of International Society*, Oxford: Oxford University Press

Burkholder, M. A. & Chandler, D. S. 1977, *From Impotence to Authority: The Spanish Crown and the American Audiencias, 1687–1808* Columbia: University of Missouri Press

Burrage, M. 2006, *Revolution and the Making of the Contemporary Legal Profession: England, France and the United States*, Oxford: Oxford University Press

Bush, R., Bujra, J., & Littlejohn, G. 2011, 'The Accumulation of Dispossession', *Review of African Political Economy*, 38(128), 187–192

Butler, G. & Maccoby, S. 1928, *The Development of International Law*, London: Longmans

Butterfield, H. & Wight, M. (eds.) 1966, *Diplomatic Investigations*, London: Allen & Unwin

Buzan, B. & Lawson, G. 2014, 'Rethinking Benchmark Dates in International Relations', *European Journal of International Relations* 20(2), 437–462

2015 *The Global Transformation: History, Modernity and the Making of International Relations*, Cambridge: Cambridge University Press

van Caenegem, R. C. 1987 *Judges, Legislators and Professors: Chapters in European Legal History*, Cambridge: Cambridge University Press

2002, *European Law in the Past and the Future: Unity and Diversity over Two Millennia*, Cambridge: Cambridge University Press

Calafat, G. 2018a, 'Les juridictions du consul: une institution au service des marchands et du commerce? Introduction', in A. Bartolomei, G. Calafat, M.

Grenet, & J. Ulbert (eds.), *De l'utilité commerciale des consuls: L'institution consulaire et les marchands dans le monde méditerranéen (XVIIe–XXe siècle)*, Rome: Publications de l'École française de Rome, 143–153

2018b, 'La juridiction des consuls français en Méditerranée; litiges marchands, arbitrages et circulations des procès', in A. Bartolomei, G. Calafat, M. Grenet, & J. Ulbert (eds.), *De l'utilité commerciale des consuls: L'institution consulaire et les marchands dans le monde méditerranéen (XVIIe–XXe siècle)*, Rome: Publications de l'École française de Rome, 155–172

2018c, 'A "Nest of Pirates"? Consuls and Diplomatic Intermediaries in Algiers during the 1670s', *Studi e Materiali di Storia delle Religioni*, 84(2), 529–547

2019, *Une mer jalousée. Contribution à l'histoire de la souveraineté (Méditerranée, XVIIe siècle)*, Paris: Éditions du Seuil

Calafat, G. & Monnet, E. 2017, 'The Return of Economic History?', *Books & Ideas* (30 Jan.), https://booksandideas.net/The-Return-of-Economic-History.html [accessed 27 October 2019]

Callières, François de. 1716, *De la manière de négocier avec les souverains : de l'utilité des négociations, du choix des ambassadeurs et des envoyez, et des qualitez necessaires pour réussir dans ces emplois.* Amsterdam: La Compagnie

Calvin's Case 7 Coke Report 1a, 77 English Reports, 377, 1608

Cammack, P. 2017, 'How The West Came to Rule Reviewed', *Progress in Political Economy Blog*, http://ppesydney.net/west-came-rule-reviewed [accessed 27 October 2019]

Cañizares-Esguerra, J. (ed.) 2018 *Entangled Empires: Anglo-Iberian Atlantic Worlds 1500–1830; the Atlantic in Global History, 1500–2000*, Philadelphia: University of Pennsylvania Press

Cardim, P., Herzog, T., Ibanez, & Sabatini, G. (eds.) 2012, *Polycentric Monarchies: How Did Early Modern Spain and Portugal Achieve and Maintain a Global Hegemony?* Brighton, UK: Sussex Academic Press

Carrió-Invernizzi, D. 2014, 'A New Diplomatic History and the Networks of Spanish Diplomacy in the Baroque Era', *International History Review*, 36(4), 603–618

Carter, C. H. 1966, 'The Ambassadors of Early Modern Europe: Patterns of Diplomatic Representation in the Early 17th Century', in C. H. Carter (ed.), *From the Renaissance to the Counter Reformation: Essays in Honour of Garrett Mattingly*, London: Jonathan Cape

Cassel, P. K. 2012, *Grounds of Judgment: Extraterritoriality and Imperial Power in Nineteenth-Century China and Japan*, Oxford: Oxford University Press

de Carvalho B., Leira, H., & Hobson, J. M. 2011, 'The Big Bangs of IR: The Myths that Your Teachers Still Tell You about 1948 and 1919', *Millennium*, 39(3): 735–758.

Casey, J. 1999, *Early Modern Spain: A Social History*, London: Routledge

Cavallar, G. 2008, 'Vitoria, Grotius, Pufendorf, Wolff and Vattel: Accomplices of European Colonialism and Exploitation or True Cosmopolitans?', *Journal of the History of International Law*, 10, 181–209

Cavanagh, E. 2014, 'Possession and Dispossession in Corporate New France, 1600–1663: Debunking a "Juridical History" and Revisiting *Terra Nullius*', *Law and History Review*, 32, 97–125

2017, 'The Atlantic Prehistory of Private International Law: Trading Companies of the New World and the Pursuit of Restitution in England and France, 1613–1643', *Itinerario*, 41(3), 452–483

Chambre de Commerce de Marseille Archives J141, J1602, J176, J180, J2, B3

Chimni, B. S. 1993, *International Law and World Order: A Critique of Contemporary Approaches*, New Delhi: Sage

1999, 'Marxism and International Law: A Contemporary Analysis', *Political and Economic Weekly*, 337–349

2007, 'The Past, Present and Future of International Law: A Critical Third World Approach', *Melbourne Journal of International Law* 8(2), 499

2008, 'An Outline of a Marxist Course on Public International Law', in Susan Marks (ed.), *International Law on the Left: Re-examining Marxist Legacies*, Cambridge: Cambridge University Press, 53–91

Chorley, J. 2018, 'Law and Primitive Accumulation: Canadian Settler Colonialism', *Legal Form Blog* (6 Jan.), https://legalform.blog/2018/01/06/law-and-primitive-accumulation-canadian-settler-colonialism-jasmine-chorley [accessed 27 October 2019]

Colás, A. 2016, 'Barbary Coast in the Expansion of International Society: Piracy and Corsairing as Primary Institutions', *Review of International Studies*, 42 (5), 840–857

Coller, I. 2011, 'Cosmopolitanism and Extraterritoriality: Regulating Europeans in 18th Century Turkey', in Barbara Schmidt-Haberkamp (ed.), *Europa und die Türkei im 18. Jahrhundert/Europe and Turkey in the Eighteenth Century.* Grenzüberschreitungen in kosmopolitischer Zeit, Bonn: V&R Unipress, 205–218

Comninel, G. 1987, *Rethinking the French Revolution: Marxism and the Revisionist Challenge*, London: Verso

2000, 'English Feudalism and the Origins of Capitalism', *Journal of Peasant Studies*, 27(4), 1–53

Cooper, L. 2017, '*The Global Transformation: Critical Reflections on the Historical Sociology of the Long Nineteenth Century* [review]', *Journal of Historical Sociology*, 31: 78– 91

Corrigan, P. & Sayer, D. 1981, 'How the Law Rules: Variations on Some Themes in Karl Marx', in B. Fryer *et al.* (eds.), *Law, State and Society*, London: Croom Helm, 21–51

Craig, G. A. 1979, 'On the Nature of Diplomatic History: The Relevance of Some Old Books', in P. Gordon Lauren (ed.), *Diplomacy: New Approaches in History, Theory and Policy*, New York: Free Press, 21–42.

Cras, J. 2006, 'Une approche archivistique des consulats de la Nation française: Les actes de chancellerie consulaire sous l'Ancien Régime', in J. Ulbert & G. Le Bouëdec (eds.), *La fonction consulaire à l'époque moderne: L'affirmation d'une institution économique et politique (1500–1800)*, Rennes: Presses Universitaires de Rennes, 51–84

Crawford, M. J., 2014, *The Fight for Status and Privilege in Late Medieval and Early Modern Castile, 1465–1598*, Philadelphia: University of Pennsylvania Press

Crespo Solano, A. 2006, 'Merchants under Close Scrutiny: Spanish Monopoly with America and Laws against Foreigners' Illegal Commerce', in Lars Nilson CD-ROM Stads-och (ed.), *Urban Europe in Comparative Perspective*, Kommun: Historika. Institutet

2014 'A Network-Based Merchant Empire: Dutch Trade in the Spanish Atlantic 1680–1740', in G. Oostindie & J. V. Roitman (eds.), *Dutch Atlantic Connections 1600–1800: Linking Empires, Bridging Borders*, Leiden: Brill, 139–158

Curtis, D. R. & Campopiano, M. 2014, 'Medieval Land Reclamation and the Creation of New Societies: Comparing Holland and the Po Valley, *c.* 800–1500', *Journal of Historical Geography*, 44, 93–108

Cutler, A. C. 1997, 'Artifice, Ideology and Paradox: The Public/Private Distinction in International Law', *Review of International Political Economy*, 4(2), 261–285

2001, 'Critical Reflections on the Westphalian Assumptions of International Law and Organizations: A Crisis of Legitimacy', *Review of International Studies*, 27, 133–150

2002, 'Historical Materialism, Globalization, and Law: Competing Conceptions of Property', in M. Rupert & H. Smith (eds.), *Historical Materialism and Globalization*, London: Routledge, 230–256

2003, *Private Power and Global Authority: Transnational Merchant Law in the Global Political Economy*, Cambridge: Cambridge University Press

2008, 'Toward a Radical Political Economy Critique of Transnational Economic Law', in Susan Marks (ed.), *International Law on the Left: Re-examining Marxist Legacies*, Cambridge: Cambridge University Press, 199–219

2014, 'New Constitutionalism and the Commodity Form of Global Capitalism', in S. Gill & A. C. Cutler (eds.), *New Constitutionalism and World Order*, Cambridge: Cambridge University Press, 45–62

Cutler, A. C. & Gill, S. (eds.) 2015, *New Constitutionalism and World Order*, Cambridge: Cambridge University Press

Cutler, A. C., Haufler, V., & Porter, T. (eds.) 1999, *Private Authority and International Affairs*, Albany, NY: State University of New York Press

Davidson, N. 2010, 'Scotland: Birthplace of Passive Revolution?' *Capital and Class*, 34(3), 343–359

Davis-Cross, M. 2007, *The European Diplomatic Corps: Diplomats and International Cooperation from Westphalia to Maastricht*, New York: Palgrave

De Luca, K. A. 2008, 'Beyond the Sea: Extraterritorial Jurisdiction and English Law, c. 1575–c. 1640' (DPhil. dissertation, University of Columbia)

van Deusen, N. E. 2015, *Global Indios: The Indigenous Struggle for Justice in Sixteenth-Century Spain*, Durham, NC: Duke University Press

Dewar, H. 2011, 'Souveraineté dans les colonies, souveraineté en métropole: le rôle de la Nouvelle-France dans la consolidation de l'autorité maritime en France, 1620–1628', *Revue d'histoire de l'Amérique française*, 64(3–4), 63–92

2012, 'Y establir nostre auctorité': Assertions of Imperial Sovereignty through Proprietorships and Chartered Companies in New France, 1598–1663 (PhD thesis, University of Toronto)

2013, 'Litigating Empire: The Role of French Courts in Establishing Colonial Sovereignties', in L. Benton & R. J. Ross (eds.), *Legal Pluralism and Empires, 1500–1850*, New York: New York University Press, 49–79

Dhondt, F. 2016, 'Recent Research in the History of International Law', *Tijdschrift voor Rechtsgeschiedenis/Revue d'histoire du droit/Legal History Review*, 84 (1–2), 313–334

Dickason, O. P. 1989, 'Concepts of Sovereignty at the Time of the First Contacts', in L. C. Green & O. P. Dickason, *The Law of Nations in the New World*, Alberta: University of Alberta Press, 141–295

Dimmock, S. 2014, *The Origin of Capitalism in England 1400–1600*, Leiden: Brill

2017, 'The Eastern Origins of Capitalism?', *Historical Materialism Blog*, www.historicalmaterialism.org/book-review/eastern-origins-capitalism [accessed 27 October 2019]

2019, 'Expropriation and the Political Origins of Agrarian Capitalism in England', in X. Lafrance & C. Post (eds.), *Case Studies in the Origins of Capitalism*, London: Palgrave, 39–62

Donlan, S. P. & Heirbaut, D. eds., 2015, *The Law's Many Bodies: Studies in Legal Hybridity and Jurisdictional Complexity, c. 1600–1900*, Berlin: Duncker & Humblot

Dorsett, S. & McVeigh, S. 2012, *Jurisdiction*, New York: Routledge

Dover, P. & Scott, H. 2015, 'The Growth of Diplomacy, c. 1450–1815', in Hamish M. Scott (ed.) *The Oxford Handbook of Early Modern European History, 1350–1750, Volume II: Cultures and Power*, Oxford: Oxford University Press

Dufour, F. G. 2008, 'Le retour du juridique comme dimension constitutive des théories critiques des relations internationales ?', *Études internationales*, 39(1), 63–81

Dupuy, P., & Chetail, V. (eds.) 2013, *The Roots of International Law/Les fondements du droit international*, Leiden: Brill/Nijhoff

Durchardt, H. 2004, 'Peace Treaties from Westphalia to the Revolutionary Era', in R. Lesaffer (ed.), *Peace Treaties and International Law in European History: From the Late Middle Ages to World War One*, Cambridge: Cambridge University Press, 45–58

Duroselle, J. B. 1953, *Histoire diplomatique de 1919 à nos jours* Paris: Dalloz

Duvé, T. (ed.) 2014a, *Entanglements in Legal History: Conceptual Approaches, Global Perspectives on Legal History*, Frankfurt am Main: Max Planck Institute for European Legal History, Open Access Publication

Duvé, T. 2014b, 'Introduction', in T. Duvé (ed.), *Entanglements in Legal History: Conceptual Approaches, Global Perspectives on Legal History*, Frankfurt am Main: Max Planck Institute for European Legal History, Open Access Publication, 3–25

Duvé, T. & Pihlajamäki, H. (eds.) 2015, *New Horizons in Spanish Colonial Law Contributions to Transnational Early Modern Legal History*, Frankfurt am Main: Max Planck Institute for European Legal History, Open Access Publication

Duzgun, E. 2020, 'Against Eurocentric Anti-Eurocentrism: International Relations, Historical Sociology and Political Marxism', *Journal of International Relations and Development*, 23(2), 285–307

2018b, 'The International Relations of "Bourgeois Revolutions": Disputing the Turkish Revolution', *European Journal of International Relations*, 24(2), 414–439.

Dyson, T. 2013, 'English Diplomatic Agents 1603–1688' (PhD thesis, Oxford University)

Ebben, M. A. 2017, 'Lodewijck Huygens' Spanish Journal, 1660–1661: Perceptions of Spain and Confirmation of the Identity of the Dutch Republic', *Dutch Crossing: Journal of Low Countries Studies*, 42(2), 118–134

Ebben, M.2018, 'Cross-Confessional and Diplomatic Incidents: Dutch Ambassadors in Madrid, 1648–72', in Jorge Fernández-Santos and José Luis Colomer (eds.), *Ambassadors in Golden-Age Madrid: The Court of Philip IV 'The Planet King' through Foreign Eyes*, Madrid: CEEH, 247–272

Elliott, J. H. 1963, *Imperial Spain 1469–1716*, London: Edward Arnold

1983, 'A Question of Reputation? Spanish Foreign Policy in the Seventeenth Century', *Journal of Modern History*, 55(3), 475–483

1992, 'A Europe of Composite Monarchies', *Past & Present*, 137, 48–71

2006, *Empires of the Atlantic World: Britain and Spain in America, 1492–1830*, London: Yale University Press

2012, *History in the Making*, New Haven, CT: Yale University Press

Emmer, P. C. 2014, 'The Rise and Decline of the Dutch Atlantic, 1600–1800', in G. Oostindie & J. V. Roitman (eds.), *Dutch Atlantic Connections 1600–1800: Linking Empires, Bridging Borders*, Leiden: Brill, 339–356

Eslava, L. 2019, 'TWAIL Coordinates', *Critical Legal Thinking Blog*, http://criticallegalthinking.com/2019/04/02/twail-coordinates [accessed 27 October 2019]

Eslava, L., Nesiah, V. and Fakhri, M. (eds.) 2016, *Bandung, Global History and International Law: Critical Pasts and Pending Futures*, Cambridge: Cambridge University Press

Ewald, W. 1995, 'Comparative Jurisprudence (II): The Logic of Legal Transplants', *American Journal of Comparative Law* 43, 489–510

Faivre d'Arcier, A. 2006, 'Le service consulaire au Levant à la fin du XVIIIe siècle et son évolution sous la Révolution', in J. Ulbert & G. Le Bouëdec (eds.), *La fonction consulaire à l'époque moderne: L'affirmation d'une institution économique et politique (1500–1800)*, Rennes: Presses Universitaires de Rennes, 161–188

Farganel, J. P. 1996, 'Négociants marseillais au Levant et dirigisme commercial: l'émergence d'une contestation nouvelle de l'autorité monarchique (1685–1789)', *Provence Historique*, 183, 3–25

Fedele, D. 2016, 'The Renewal of Early-Modern Scholarship on the Ambassador: Pierre Ayrault on Diplomatic Immunity', *Journal of the History of International Law/Revue d'histoire du droit international* 18, 4, 449–468

2017, *Naissance de la diplomatie moderne (XIIIe–XVIIe siècles) L'ambassadeur au croisement du droit, de l'éthique et de la politique*, Baden-Baden: Nomos Verlagsgesellschaft

Federici, S. 2014, *Caliban and the Witch: Women, the Body and Primitive Accumulation*, 2nd rev. ed., New York: Autonomedia

Fernández Castro, A. 2014, 'A Transnational Empire Built on Law: The Case of the Commercial Jurisprudence of the House of Trade of Seville (1583–1598)', in T. Duvé (ed.), *Entanglements in Legal History: Conceptual Approaches*, Frankfurt am Main: Max Planck Institute for European Legal History, 187–212

Fernández Chavez, M. & Gamero Rojas, M. 2017, 'Nations? What Nations? Business in the Shaping of International Trade Networks', in M. Herrero Sanchez & K. Kaps (eds.), *Merchants and Trade Networks in the Atlantic and the Mediterranean 1550–1800*, Abingdon, UK: Routledge, 145–168

Fine, B. 2002 [1984], *Democracy and the Rule of Law: Marx's Critique of the Legal Form*, Caldwell, NJ: Blackburn Press

Fine, B., Kinsey, R., Lea, J., Picciotto, S., & Young, J. (eds.) 1979, *Capitalism and the Rule of Law: From Deviancy Theory to Marxism*, London: Hutchinson

Fitzmaurice, A. *Humanism and America: Intellectual History of English Colonisation 1500–1625*, Cambridge: Cambridge University Press

2014, *Sovereignty, Property and Empire, 1500–2000*, Cambridge: Cambridge University Press

Ford, L. 2010, *Settler Sovereignty: Jurisdiction and Indigenous People in America and Australia, 1788–1836*, Cambridge, MA: Harvard University Press

Ford, L. & Rowse, T. (eds.), 2013, *Between Indigenous and Settler Governance*, Abingdon, UK: Routledge

Ford, R. T. 1999, 'Law's Territory (A History of Jurisdiction)', *Michigan Law Review*, 97, 843–93

Fradera, J. M. 2018, *The Imperial Nation: Citizens and Subjects in the British, French, Spanish, and American Empires*, trans. Ruth MacKay, Princeton, NJ: Princeton University Press

Frey, L. S. & Frey, M. L. 1999, *The History of Diplomatic Immunity*, Columbus: Ohio State University Press

Frigo, D. (ed.) 2000, *Politics and Diplomacy in Early Modern Italy: Structure of Diplomatic Practice 1450–1800*, Cambridge: Cambridge University Press

Fryer, B., Hunt, A., McBarnet, D., & Moorhouse, B. 1981, 'Law, State and Society', in B. Fryer *et al.* (eds.), *Law, State and Society*, London: Croom Helm, 9–20

Fusaro M. 2010, 'After Braudel: A Reassessment of Mediterranean History between the Northern Invasion and the Caravane Maritime', in M. Fusaro, C. J. Heywood, & M.-S. Omri (eds.), *Trade and Cultural Exchange in the Early Modern Mediterranean. Braudel's Maritime Legacy*, London: I.B. Tauris, 1–22

2012, 'Cooperating Mercantile Networks in the Early Modern Mediterranean', *Economic History Review*, 65(2), 701–718

2015, *Political Economies of Empire in the Early Modern Mediterranean the Decline of Venice and the Rise of England 1450–1700*, Cambridge: Cambridge University Press

Games, A. 2008, *The Web of Empire: English Cosmopolitans in an Age of Expansion, 1560–1660*, Oxford: Oxford University Press

2014, 'A Dutch Moment in Atlantic Historiography', in G. Oostindie & J. V. Roitman (eds.), *Dutch Atlantic Connections 1600–1800: Linking Empires, Bridging Borders*, Leiden: Brill, 363–

Garcia-Salmones, M. 2017, 'The Disorder of Economy? The first *Relectio de Indis* in a Theological Perspective', in S. Kadelbach, T. Kleinlein, & D. Roth-Isigkeit (eds.), *System, Order and International Law: The Early History of International Legal Thought from Machiavelli to Hegel*, Oxford: Oxford University Press, 443–463

Garcia-Salmones, M. & Eslava, L. 2010, 'Jurisdictional Colonisation in the Spanish and British Empires: Some Reflections on a Global Public Order and the Sacred', in H. Ruiz Fabri, R. Wolfrum, & J. Gogolin (eds.), *Select Proceedings of the European Society of International Law*, vol. II, London: Bloomsbury, 53–81

Gathii, J. 2000, 'Neoliberalism, Colonialism and International Governance: Decentering the International Law of Governmental Legitimacy', *Michigan Law Review*, 98, 1996–2065

Geevers, L. & Marini, M. 2016, *Dynastic Identity in Early Modern Europe: Rulers, Aristocrats and the Formation of Identities*, Abingdon, UK: Routledge

Gerstenberger, H. 2007, *Impersonal Power: History and Theory of the Bourgeois State*, trans. D. Fernbach, Leiden: Brill

Giry-Deloison, C. 1987, 'Le personnel diplomatique au début du XVIe siècle. L'exemple des relations franco-anglaises de l'avènement d'Henry VII au camp du Drap d'or (1485–1520)', *Journal des Savants*, 3, 205–253

Go, J. 2013, 'For a Postcolonial Sociology', *Theory and Society*, 42(1), 25–55

Go, J. & Lawson, G. 2017, 'For a Global Historical Sociology', in Julian Go and George Lawson (eds.), *Global Historical Sociology*, Cambridge: Cambridge University Press, 1–34

Gong, G. W. 1984, *The Standard of 'Civilization' in International Society*, Oxford: Oxford University Press

Goodman, D. C., 1997, *Spanish Naval Power, 1589–1665: Reconstruction and Defeat*, Cambridge: Cambridge University Press

Goodrich, P. 2008, 'Visive Powers: Colours, Trees and Genres of Jurisdiction', *Law and Humanities*, 2, 213

Gorski, P. S. 2003, *The Disciplinary Revolution: Calvinism and the Rise of the State in Early Modern Europe*, London: University of Chicago Press

Grafe, R. 2012, *Distant Tyranny: Markets, Power, and Backwardness in Spain, 1650–1800*, Princeton, NJ: Princeton University Press

2013, 'Polycentric States: The Spanish Reigns and the "Failures" of Mercantilism', in P. Stern & C. Wennerlind (eds.), *Mercantilism Reimagined: Political Economy in Early Modern Britain and Its Empire*, Oxford: Oxford University Press, 241–262

Grafton Wilson, G. 1930, '*The Exterritoriality of Ambassadors in the Sixteenth and Seventeenth Centuries* by E. R. Adair [review]', *American Historical Review*, 35(3), 592–593

Graubart, K. B. 2018, 'Containing Law within the Walls: The Protection of Customary Law in Santiago del Cercado, Peru', in L. Benton, A. Clulow, & B. Attwood (eds.), *Protection and Empire: A Global History*, Cambridge: Cambridge University Press, 29–46

Green, L. C. & Dickason, O. P. 1989, *The Law of Nations in the New World*, Alberta: University of Alberta Press

Grenier, B. 2004, '"Nulle terre sans seigneur?": Une étude comparative de la présence seigneuriale (France–Canada), XVIIe–XIXe siècle', *French Colonial History*, 5, 7–24

Grewe, W. G. 2000, *The Epochs of International Law*, Berlin: Walter de Gruyter

Grisel, E. 1976, 'The Beginnings of International Law and General Public Law Doctrine: Francisco de Vitoria's De Indis Prior', in F. Chiapelli (ed.), *First Images of America, Volume I The Impact of the New World on the Old*, Berkeley: University of California Press, 305–325

Grotius, H. 1901, *Rights to War and Peace Including the Law of Nature and of Nations*. Translation of *De jure belli et pacis* by A. C. Campbell, Washington, DC: M. Walter Dunne

1925, *The Law of War and Peace in Three Books (1625) [De Jure Belli ac Pacis Libris Tres]*, trans. Francis W. Kelsey, Oxford: Clarendon Press

2005, *The Rights of War and Peace*, edited with introduction by Richard Tuck, from the edition by Jean Barbeyrac, Indianapolis: Liberty Fund (3 vols.)

Grovogui, N. S. 2009, 'Counterpoints and the Imaginaries behind Them: Thinking beyond North American and European Traditions', *International Political Sociology*, 3(3), 327–331

Gulsah Capan, Z. 2017, 'Decolonising International Relations?', *Third World Quarterly*, 38(1), 1–15

Halperin, J. L. 2009, 'The Concept of Law: A Western Transplant?' *Theoretical Inquiries in Law*, 10(2), 333–354

Hamilton, B. 1963, *Political Thought in Sixteenth-Century Spain: A Study of the Political Ideas of Vitoria, De Soto, Suarez, and Molina*, Oxford: Clarendon Press

Hampton, T. 2009, *Fictions of Embassy: Literature and Diplomacy in Early Modern Europe*, Ithaca, NY: Cornell University Press

Hanke, L. 1974, *All Mankind Is One: A Study of the Disputation between Bartolomé de Las Casa and Juan Ginès de Sepúlveda on the Religious and Intellectual Capacity of the American Indian*, Dekalb, IL: Northern Illinois University Press

Hardy, D. 2018, *Associative Political Culture in the Holy Roman Empire: Upper Germany, 1346–1521*, Oxford: Oxford University Press

Hart, H. L. A. 1958, 'Positivism and the Separation of Law and Morals', *Harvard Law Review*, 71(4), 593–629

Haskell, J. 2019, 'Ways of Doing Extraterritoriality in Scholarship', in D. S. Margolies, U. Özsu, M. Pal, & N. Tzouvala (eds.), *The Extraterritoriality of Law: History, Theory, Politics*, Abingdon, UK: Routledge, 13–29

Hébié M. 2015, *Souveraineté territoriale par traité: Une étude des accords entre puissances coloniales et entités politiques locales*, Paris: Presses Universitaires de France

Heine, C. & Teschke, B. 1996, 'Sleeping Beauty and the Dialectical Awakening: On the Potential of Dialectic for International Relations', *Millennium – Journal of International Studies*, 35, 399–423

Heinsen-Roach, E. 2012, 'Consuls, Corsairs, and Captives: the creation of Dutch diplomacy in the early Modern Mediterranean, 1596–1699' (DPhil. dissertation, University of Miami)

2015, 'Consuls-of-State and the Redemption of Slaves: The Dutch Republic and the Western Mediterranean, 1616–1651', *Itinerario*, 39(1), 69–90

Hennings, J. 2016, *Russia and Courtly Europe: Ritual and the Culture of Diplomacy, 1648–1725*, Cambridge: Cambridge University Press

Herrero Sanchez, M. & Kaps, K. (eds.) 2017a, *Merchants and Trade Networks in the Atlantic and the Mediterranean 1550–1800*, Abingdon, UK: Routledge

2017b, 'Connectors, Networks, and Commercial Systems: Approaches to the Study of Early Modern Maritime Trade History', in M. Herrero Sanchez & K. Kaps (eds.), *Merchants and Trade Networks in the Atlantic and the Mediterranean 1550–1800*, Abingdon, UK: Routledge, 1– 36

Hernández, J. 2011, 'Chapter Ten. A History of the Spanish Consular Service: An Institution in Its Own Right', in *Consular Affairs and Diplomacy* (vol. VII), Leiden: Brill, 225–246

Herzog, T. 2015a, *Frontiers of Possession: Spain and Portugal in Europe and the Americas*, Cambridge, MA: Harvard University Press

2015b, 'Struggling over Indians: Territorial Conflict and Alliance Making in the Heartland of South America (Seventeenth to Eighteenth Centuries)', in Saliha Belmessous (ed.), *Empire by Treaty. Negotiation European Expansion 1600–1900*, Oxford: Oxford University Press, 78–101

Hill, C. 1991, *The World Turned Upside Down: Radical Ideas during the English Revolution*, London: Penguin

Hobsbawm, E. 1994, *The Age of Extremes: The Short Twentieth Century, 1914–1991*, London: Penguin

Hobson, J. M. (1998), 'The "Second Wave" of Weberian Historical Sociology - The Historical Sociology of the State and the State of Historical Sociology in International Relations. *Review of International Political Economy*, 5:2, 284–320

2002, 'What's at Stake in "Bringing Historical Sociology Back into International Relations'? Transcending "Chronofetisism" and "Tempocentrism" in International Relations', in John M. Hobson & Stephen Hobden (eds.), *Historical Sociology of International Relations*, Cambridge: Cambridge University Press, 3–41

2012, *The Eurocentric Conception of World Politics, Western International Theory, 1760–2010*, Cambridge: Cambridge University Press

Hobson, J. H. & Hobden, S. (eds.) 2002, *Historical Sociology of International Relations*, Cambridge: Cambridge University Press

Hobson, J. H. & Sajed, A. 2017, 'Navigating beyond the Eurofetishist Frontier of Critical IR Theory: Exploring the Complex Landscapes of Non-Western Agency', *International Studies Review*, 19(4), 547–572

Hobson, J. M. Lawson, G. & Rosenberg, J. 2010, 'Historical Sociology', in Denemark, Robert A. (ed.), *The International Studies Encyclopaedia*, Wiley-Blackwell; International Studies Association, UK

Holdsworth, S. 1945, *A History of English Law*, London: Methuen

Holmes, C. 1997, 'The Legal Instruments of Power and the State in Early Modern England', in A. Padoa-Schioppa (ed.), *Legislation and Justice*, Oxford: Clarendon Press, 269–289

Horowitz, R. S. 2004, 'International Law and State Transformation in China, Siam, and the Ottoman Empire during the Nineteenth Century', *Journal of World History*, 15(4), 445–486

Horn, D. B. 1961, *The British Diplomatic Service 1689–1789*, Oxford: Oxford University Press

Horn, J. 2011, 'Marseille et la question du mercantilisme: Privilège, liberté et économie politique en France, 1650–1750', *Histoire, économie & société*, 2 (30e), 95–111

2015, *Economic Development in Early Modern France: The Privilege of Liberty, 1650–1820*, Cambridge: Cambridge University Press

Hotman, J. 1603, *L'ambassadeur*, London

Houssiau, J. 2000, 'Les ambassadeurs des Pays-Bas à Vervins: prémices d'une diplomatie "belge"?', in J. F. Labourdette, Jean-Pierre Poussou and Marie-Catherine Vignal (eds.), *Le Traité de Vervins* Paris: Presses de l'Université de Paris-Sorbonne, 267–282

Houston, R. A. 2018, 'The Composition and Distribution of the Legal Profession, and the Use of Law in Britain and Ireland, *c.* 1500–*c.* 1850', *Tijdschrift voor Rechtsgeschiedenis/Revue d'histoire du droit/Legal History Review*, 86(1–2), 123–156

Hueck, I. J. 2001, 'The Discipline of the History of International Law', *Journal of the History of International Law/Revue d'histoire du droit international*, 3(2), 194–217

Hulsebosch, D. 2005, *Constituting Empire: New York and the Transformation of Constitutionalism in the Atlantic World, 1664–1830*, Chapel Hill, NC: University of North Carolina Press

Ince, O. U. 2014, 'Primitive Accumulation, New Enclosures, and Global Land Grabs: A Theoretical Intervention', *Rural Sociology* 79(1), 104–131

2018, 'Between Equal Rights: Primitive Accumulation and Capital's Violence', *Political Theory*, 46(6), 885–914

Israel, J. 1989, *Dutch Primacy in World Trade 1585–1740*, Oxford: Clarendon Press

van Ittersum, M. J. 2006, *Profit and Principle: Hugo Grotius, Natural Rights Theories and the Rise of Dutch Power in the East Indies, 1595–1615*, Leiden: Brill

2016, 'Hugo Grotius: The Making of a Founding Father of International Law', in Anne Orford & Florian Hoffmann (eds.), *The Oxford Handbook of the Theory of International Law*, Oxford: Oxford University Press, 82–100

Ives, E. W. 1983, *The Common Lawyers of Pre-Reformation England*, Cambridge: Cambridge University Press

Jacobsen, H. 2011, *Luxury and Power: The Material World of the Stuart Diplomat, 1660–1714*, Oxford: Oxford University Press

Jahn, B. 2000, *The Cultural Construction of International Relations*, Basingstoke, UK: Palgrave

2006, *Classical Theory in International Relations*, Cambridge: Cambridge University Press

Jettot, S. 2012, *Représenter le Roi ou la Nation? Parlementaires dans la diplomatie anglaise 1660–1702*, Paris: Presses de l'Université de Paris-Sorbonne

Kadelbach, S., Kleinlein, T., & Roth-Isigkeit, D. (eds.) 2017, *System, Order, and International Law: The Early History of International Legal Thought from Machiavelli to Hegel*, Oxford: Oxford University Press

Kaiser, W. & Calafat, G. 2014, 'Violence, Protection and Commerce: Corsairing and *ars piratica* in the Early Modern Mediterranean', in S. E. Amirell & L. Müller (eds.), *Persistent Piracy: Maritime Violence and State-Formation in Global Historical Perspective*, London: Palgrave, 69–92

Kaplan, B. J. 2002, 'Diplomacy and Domestic Devotion: Embassy Chapels and the Toleration of Religious Dissent in Early Modern Europe', *Journal of Early Modern History*, 6(4), 341–361

Kassan, S. 1935, 'Extraterritorial Jurisdiction in the Ancient World', *American Journal of International Law*, 29, 237

Kayaoglu, T. 2010, *Legal Imperialism: Sovereignty and Extraterritoriality in Japan, the Ottoman Empire, and China*, Cambridge: Cambridge University Press

Keene, E. 2002, *Beyond the Anarchical Society: Grotius, Colonialism and Order in World Politics*, Cambridge: Cambridge University Press

2013, 'International Hierarchy and the Origins of the Modern Practice of Intervention', *Review of International Studies*, 39, 1077–1090

2017, 'International Intellectual History and International Relations: Contexts, Canons and Mediocrities', *International Relations* 31(3), 341–356

Keens-Soper, H. M. A. & Schweizer, K. W. (eds.) 1994, *François de Callières, The Art of Diplomacy*, Lanham, MD: Rowman & Littlefield

Knafla, L. A. & Binnie, S. W. S. (eds.) 1995, *Law, Society and the State: Essays in Modern Legal History*, London: University of Toronto Press

Knafo, S. 2007, 'Political Marxism and Value Theory: Bridging the Gap between Theory and History', *Historical Materialism*, 15, 75–104

2010, 'Critical Approaches and the Legacy of the Agent/Structure Debate in International Relations', *Cambridge Review of International Affairs*, 23(3), 493–516

2013, *The Making of Modern Finance: Liberal Governance and the Gold Standard*. London: Routledge

2017, 'A Methodological Turn Long Overdue: Or, Why It Is Time for Critical Scholars to Cut Their Losses', in Jan Selby, Synne L. Dyvik, & Rorden Wilkinson (eds.), *What's the Point of International Relations?* London: Routledge, 242–252

Knafo, S. & Teschke, B. 2020, 'The Rules of Reproduction of Capitalism: A Historicist Critique', *Historical Materialism*, 28(3)

Knox, R. 2009, 'Marxism, International Law, Political Strategy', *Leiden Journal of International Law*, 22, 413–436

2010, 'Strategy and Tactics', *Finnish Yearbook of International Law*, 21, 193–229

2016a, 'Valuing Race? Stretched Marxism and the Logic of Imperialism', *London Review of International Law*', 4(1), 81–126

2016b, 'Marxist Theories of International Law', *The Oxford Handbook of the Theory of International Law*, Oxford: Oxford University Press, 306–326

2018, 'Marxist Approaches to International Law', *Oxford Bibliographies Online*, www.oxfordbibliographies.com/view/document/obo-9780199796953/obo-9780199796953-0163.xml [accessed 27 October 2019]

Kochi, T. 2017, 'Dreams and Nightmares of Liberal International Law: Capitalist Accumulation, Natural Rights and State Hegemony', *Law Critique*, 28, 23–41

Koenigsberger, H. G. 1986, *Politicians and Virtuosi: Essays in Early Modern History*, London: Hambledon Press

Koskenniemi, M. 1992, 'Introduction', in Martti Koskenniemi (ed.), *International Law*, Dartmouth: Aldershot, xi–xxxii

2000, 'Carl Schmitt, Hans Morgenthau, and the Image of Law in International Relations', in M. Byers (ed.), *The Role of Law in International Politics*, Oxford: Oxford University Press

2001, *The Gentle Civilizer of Nations: The Rise and Fall of International Law 1870–1960*, Cambridge: Cambridge University Press

2004, 'The History of International Law Today', *Rechtsgeschichte*

2005, *From Apology to Utopia: The Structure of International Legal Argument*, Cambridge: Cambridge University Press

2008, 'What should international lawyers learn from Karl Marx?', in Susan Marks (ed.), *International Law on the Left: Re-examining Marxist Legacies*, Cambridge: Cambridge University Press, 30–52

2011, 'International Law and Empire: The Real Spanish Contribution', *University of Toronto Law Journal*, 61, 1–36

2014, 'International and the Emergence of Mercantile Capitalism: From Grotius to Smith', in P. Dupuy & V. Chetail (eds.), *The Roots of International Law/Les fondements du droit international*, Leiden: Brill/Nijhoff, 3–38

2016, 'Expanding Histories of International Law', *American Journal of Legal History*, 56, 104–112

2017a, 'Introduction', in M. Koskenniemi, W. Rech, & M. Jimenez Fonseca (eds.), *International Law and Empire: Historical Explorations*, Oxford: Oxford University Press, 1–18

2017b, 'Sovereignty, Property and Empire: Early Modern English Contexts', *Theoretical Inquiries in Law* 18, 355–389

Koskenniemi, M., Rech, W., & Jimenez Fonseca, M. (eds.) 2017, *International Law and Empire: Historical Explorations*, Oxford: Oxford University Press

Krasner, S. 1993, 'Westphalia and All That', in Judith Goldstein and Robert O. Keohane (eds.), *Ideas and Foreign Policy: Beliefs, Institutions, and Political Change*, Ithaca, NY: Cornell University Press, 235–65

Krever, T. 2018, 'The Rule of Law and the Rise of Capitalism', in Christopher May and Adam Winchester (eds.), *Handbook on the Rule of Law*, London: Edward Elgar, 184–200

Krynen, J. 2009, *L'État de justice France, XIIIe–XXe siècle. Tome I: L'Idéologie de la magistrature ancienne*, Paris: Gallimard

Kugeler, H. 2006, 'Le *Parfait Ambassadeur*: The Theory and Practice of Diplomacy in the Century Following the Peace of Westphalia' (DPhil. thesis, University of Oxford)

Kuru, D. 2016, 'Historicising Eurocentrism and Anti-Eurocentrism in IR: A Revisionist Account of Disciplinary Self-Reflexivity', *Review of International Studies*, 42, 351–376

Lacher, H. 2006, *Beyond Globalisation: Capitalism, Territoriality and the International Relations of Modernity*, London: Routledge

Lachmann, R. 2018, 'What Empires Can and Can't Do', *Comparative Studies in Society and History*, 60(4), 1127–1142

Lachs, P. S. 1965, *The Diplomatic Corps under Charles II and James II*, New Brunswick, NJ: Rutgers University Press

Lafrance, X. 2019, *The Making of Capitalism in France*, Leiden: Brill

Lafrance, X. & Post, C. (eds.) 2019a, *Case Studies in the Origins of Capitalism*, London: Palgrave

Lafrance, X. & Post, C. 2019b, 'Introduction', in Xavier Lafrance & Charles Post (eds.), *Case Studies in the Origins of Capitalism*, London: Palgrave, 1–38

Lapid, Y. 1989, 'The Third Debate: On the Prospects of International Theory in a Post-Positivist Era', *International Studies Quarterly*, 33, 235–254

Lapointe T. & Dufour, G. 2012, 'Assessing the Historical Turn in IR: An Anatomy of Second Wave Historical Sociology', *Cambridge Review of International Affairs*, 25(1), 97–121

Lee, M. Jr, 1966–1967, 'The Jacobean Diplomatic Service', *American Historical Review*, 72, 1276–1280

Legrand, P. 1997, 'The Impossibility of "Legal Transplants"', *Maastricht Journal of European & Comparative Law*, 4, 111–124

Leira, H. & Neumann, I. B. 2008, 'Consular Representation in an Emerging State: The Case of Norway', *The Hague Journal of Diplomacy* 3, 1–19

2012, 'Consular Diplomacy', in Pauline Kerr & Geoffrey Wiseman (eds.), *Diplomacy in a Globalizing World: Theories and Practices*, New York: Oxford University Press, 160–175

Lesaffer, R. 2002, 'The Grotian Tradition Revisited; Change and Continuity in the History of International Law', in James Crawford and Vaughan Lowe (eds.), *British Yearbook of International Law*, vol. 73, Oxford: Oxford University Press, 103–139

2017, 'Between Faith and Empire: The justification of the Spanish Intervention in the French Wars of Religion in the 1590s', in M. Koskenniemi, W. Rech,

& M. Jimenez Fonseca (eds.), *International Law and Empire: Historical Explorations*, Oxford: Oxford University Press, 101–122

Levillain, C.-E. 2016, 'French Diplomacy and the Run-up to the Glorious Revolution (1688): A Critical Reading of Jean-Antoine d'Avaux's Correspondence as Ambassador to the States General', *Journal of Modern History*, 88(1), 130–150

Levin, M. J. 2002, 'A New World Order: The Spanish Campaign for Precedence in Early Modern Europe', *Journal of Early Modern History*, 6(3), 233–264

Lindemann, M., 2015, *The Merchant Republics: Amsterdam, Antwerp, and Hamburg, 1648–1790*, New York: Cambridge University Press

Little, R. 2000, 'The English School's Contribution to the Study of International Relations', *European Journal of International Relations*, 6(3), 395–422

Liu, S. S. 1925, *Extraterritoriality: Its Rise and Decline*, New York: Columbia University Press

McDougal, M. S. & Lasswell, H. D. 1996 [1959], 'The Identification and Appraisal of Diverse Systems of Public Order', in R. Beck, A. Clark Arend, & R. D. Vander Lugt (eds.), *International Rules: Approaches from International Law and International Relations*, New York: Oxford University Press, 113–143

McNally, D. 2012, *Monsters of the Market: Zombies, Vampires and Global Capitalism*, Leiden: Brill

2020, *Blood and Money: War, Slavery, and the State*, Chicago: Haymarket

Macmillan, K. 2006, *Sovereignty and Possession in English New World*, Cambridge: Cambridge University Press

Mann, M. 1986, *The Sources of Social Power Vol. 1*. Cambridge: Cambridge University Press

Margolies, D. S., Özsu, U., Pal, M., & Tzouvala, N. (eds.) 2019, *The Extraterritoriality of Law: History, Theory, Politics*, Abingdon, UK: Routledge

Marks, S. 1997, 'The End of History? Reflections on some International Legal Theses', *European Journal of International Law*, 3, 449–477

2007, 'International Judicial Activism and the Commodity Form Theory of International Law', *European Journal of International Law*, 18(1), 199–211

2008, 'Introduction', in Susan Marks (ed.) *International Law on the Left: Re-examining Marxist Legacies*, Cambridge: Cambridge University Press, 1–29

Marx, K. 1959, *Capital: A Critique of Political Economy, Vol. 3*, London: Lawrence & Wishart

1971, *A Contribution to the Critique of Political Economy*, London: Lawrence & Wishart

1976, *Capital: A Critique of Political Economy Vol. 1*, trans. Ben Fowkes, London: Penguin

Marx, K. & Engels, F., 1939 [1854]. *Revolution in Spain*, London: Lawrence & Wishart

Marzagalli, S. 2014, 'The French Atlantic and the Dutch, Late Seventeenth-Late Eighteenth', in G. Oostindie & J. V. Roitman (eds.), *Dutch Atlantic Connections 1600–1800: Linking Empires, Bridging Borders*, Leiden: Brill, 103–118

2016, 'Was Warfare Necessary for the Functioning of Eighteenth-Century Colonial Systems? Some Reflections on the Necessity of Cross-Imperial and Foreign Trade in the French Case', in C. Antunes & A. Polónia (eds.), *Beyond Empires: Global, Self-Organizing, Cross-Imperial Networks, 1500–1800*, Leiden: Brill, 253–277

Marzagalli, S. & Marnot, B. (eds.) 2006, *Guerre et économie dans l'espace atlantique du XVIe au XXe siècles*, Bordeaux: Presses Universitaires de Bordeaux

Masson, P. 1896, *Histoire du commerce français dans le Levant au 18e siècle. Thèse*, Paris: Librairie Hachette

Mate, M. E. 2006, *Trade and Economic Developments, 1450–1550: The Experience of Kent, Surrey and Sussex*, Woodbridge, UK: Boydell Press

Mather, J. 2011, *Pashas, Traders and Travellers in the Islamic World*, London: Yale University Press

Mattingly, G. 1955/1966, *Renaissance Diplomacy*, London: Penguin

van Meersbergen, G. 2017, 'The Dutch Merchant–Diplomat in Comparative Perspective: Embassies in the Court of Aurangzeb 1660–1666', in T. A. Sowerby & J. Hennings (eds.), *Practices of Diplomacy in the Early Modern World c. 1410–1800*, Abingdon, UK: Routledge, 147–165

Meguro, M. 2019, 'Backlash Against International Law by the East? How the Concept of "Transplantation" Helps Us to Better Understand Reception Processes of International Law', *Völkerrechtsblog* (11 Jan.) https://voelkerrechtsblog.org/backlash-against-international-law-by-the-east [accessed 27 October 2019]

Mézin, A., 1997, *Les consuls de France au siècle des Lumières (1715–1792)*, Paris: La Documentation Française

2006, 'La fonction consulaire dans la France d'Ancien Régime: origine, principes, prérogatives', in J. Ulbert & G. Le Bouëdec (eds.), *La fonction consulaire à l'époque modern: L'affirmation d'une institution économique et politique (1500–1800)*, Rennes: Presses Universitaires de Rennes, 37–49

Mezzadra, S. 2011, 'The Topicality of Prehistory: A New Reading of Marx's Analysis of "So-called Primitive Accumulation"', *Rethinking Marxism: A Journal of Economics, Culture & Society*, 23(3), 302–321

Midnight Notes, 1990, *New Enclosures*, Jamaica Plain, MA: Midnight Notes

Miéville, C. 2005, *Between Equal Rights: A Marxist Theory of International Law*, Leiden: Brill

2008, 'The Commodity-Form Theory of International Law', in Susan Marks (ed.), *International Law on the Left: Re-examining Marxist Legacies*, Cambridge: Cambridge University Press, 92–132

Milanovic, M. 2011, *Extraterritorial Application of Human Rights Treaties*, Oxford: Oxford University Press

Miles, K. 2019, '"Uneven Empires": Extraterritoriality and the Early Trading Companies', in D. S. Margolies, U. Özsu, M. Pal, & N. Tzouvala (eds.), *The Extraterritoriality of Law: History, Theory, Politics*, Abingdon, UK: Routledge, 87–104

Miller, S. 2008, *State and Society in Eighteenth-Century France: A Study of Political Power and Social Revolution in Languedoc*, Washington, DC: Catholic University of America Press

Moeglin, J.-M. & Pèquignot, S. 2017, *Diplomatie et relations internationales au moyen-âge (IXe–XVe siècle)*, Paris: Presses Universitaires de France

Mooers, C. 1991, *The Making of Bourgeois Europe: Absolutism, Revolution and the Rise of Capitalism in England, France and Germany*, London: Verso

2014, *Imperial Subjects: Citizenship in an Age of Crisis and Empire*, New York: Bloomsbury

Moore, B. 1967, *Social Origins of Dictatorship and Development: Lord and Peasant in the Making of the Modern World*, New York: Beacon

Moreno Zacarés, J. 2018, 'Beyond Market Dependence: The Origins of Capitalism in Catalonia', *Journal of Agrarian Change*, 18, 749–767

Morgan, K. 2014, 'Anglo-Dutch Economic Relations in the Atlantic World 1688–1783', in G. Oostindie & J. V. Roitman (eds.), *Dutch Atlantic Connections 1600–1800: Linking Empires, Bridging Borders*, Leiden: Brill, 119–138

Morgenthau, H. J. 1967, *Politics Among Nations: The Struggle for Power and Peace*, 4th ed. (rev. Kenneth W. Thompson) New York: Knopf

Morin, M. 2010, 'Des nations libres sans territoire? Les Autochtones et la colonisation de l'Amérique française du XVIe au XVIIIe siècle', *Journal of the History of International Law*, 12, 1–70

Moyn, S. & Sartori, A. (eds.) 2015, *Global Intellectual History*, New York: Columbia University Press

Napolitano, E. C. 2012, 'Prospects of Statecraft: Diplomacy, Territoriality, and the Vision of French Nationhood in Rome, 1660–1700' (PhD thesis, University of Toronto)

Neff, S. C. 2006, 'A Short History of International Law', in M. D. Evans (ed.), *International Law*, Oxford: Oxford University Press, 29–55

2014, *Justice among Nations: A History of International Law*, Cambridge, MA: Harvard University Press

Neocleous, M. 2012, 'International Law as Primitive Accumulation; or, the Secret of Systematic Colonization', *European Journal of International Law*, 23–4, 941–962

Nexon, D. H. 2009, *The Struggle for Power in Early Modern Europe: Religious Conflict, Dynastic Empires and International Change*, Princeton, NJ: Princeton University Press

Noiriel, G. 2018, *Une histoire populaire de la France: De la guerre de cent ans à nos jours*, Agone

Nordman, D. 1998, *Frontières de France: De l'espace au territoire, XVIe–XIXe siècle* Paris: Gallimard

North, D. & Weingast, B. 1989, 'Constitutions and Commitment: The Evolution of Institutions Governing Public Choice in Seventeenth-Century England', *Journal of Economic History*, 49(4), 803–832

Nys, E., 1894. *Les origines du droit international*, Brussels: A. Castaigne

Numelin, R. J. 1950, *The Beginnings of Diplomacy: A Sociological Study of Intertribal and International Relations*, Oxford: Oxford University Press

Nussbaum, A. 1954, *A Concise History of the Law of Nations*, New York: Macmillan

Nuzzo, L. 2011, 'Colonial Law', *European History Online (EGO)*, Leibniz Institute of European History (IEG), Mainz, www.ieg-ego.eu/nuzzol-2011-en [accessed 28 October 2019]

2017, 'Territory, Sovereignty, and the Construction of the Colonial Space', in M. Koskenniemi, W. Rech, & M. Jimenez Fonseca (eds.), *International Law and Empire: Historical Explorations*, Oxford: Oxford University Press, 263–292

O'Connell, P. 2017, *Masking Barbarism: Human Rights in the Contemporary Global Order*, London: Hart

2018, 'Law, Marxism and Method', *tripleC*, 16(2), 647–655

O'Connell, P. & Öszu, U. (eds.) forthcoming, *Handbook of Law and Marxism*, London: Edward Elgar

Odysseos, L. & Pal, M. 2017, 'Towards Critical Pedagogies of the International? Student Resistance, Self-formation and Other-regardedness in the Neoliberal University', *International Studies Perspectives*, 19(1), 1–26

Orford, A. 2009, 'Jurisdiction without Territory: From the Holy Roman Empire to the Responsibility to Protect', *Michigan Journal of International Law*, 30, 981–1015

2017, 'International Law and the Limits of History', in W. Werner, M. De Hoon, & A. Galán (eds.), *The Law of International Lawyers: Reading Martti Koskenniemi*, Cambridge: Cambridge University Press, 297–320

Osiander, A. 2001, 'Sovereignty, International Relations, and the Westphalian Myth', *International Organization*, 55, 251–287

Owens, J. B. 2005, *'By My Absolute Royal Authority' Justice and the Castilian Commonwealth at the Beginning of the First Global Age*, Rochester, NY: University of Rochester Press

Owensby B. P. 2011, *Empire of Law and Indian Justice in Colonial Mexico*, California: Stanford University Press

Ozanam, D. 1999, *Les diplomates espagnols du XVIIIe siècle: introduction et répertoire biographique, 1700–1808*, Madrid: Casa de Velázquez

Özsu, U. 2012, 'Ottoman Empire', in Bardo Fassbender & Anne Peters (eds.), *The Oxford Handbook of the History of International Law*, Oxford: Oxford University Press, 429–448

2014, *Formalizing Displacement: International Law and Population Transfers*, Oxford: Oxford University Press

2019, 'Grabbing Land Legally: A Marxist Analysis', *Leiden Journal of International Law*, 32, 215–233

Pacheco, A. J. C. 2017, 'Primitive Accumulation in Indigenous Mexico', *City*, 21(3–4), 503–519

Pagano de Divitiis, G. 1997, *English Merchants in Seventeenth-Century Italy*, Cambridge: Cambridge University Press

Pagden, A. (ed.) 1987, *The Languages of Political Theory in Early-Modern Europe*, Cambridge: Cambridge University Press

1990, *Spanish Imperialism and the Political Imagination: Studies in European and Spanish-American Social Political Theory 1513–1830*, London: Yale University Press

1995, *Lords of All the World: Ideologies of Empire in Spain, Britain and France, c. 1500–c. 1800*, New Haven, CT: Yale University Press

2003, 'Human Rights, Natural Rights, and Europe's Imperial Legacy', *Political Theory*, 31(2), 171–199

Pahuja, S. 2011, *Decolonizing International Law: Development, Economic Growth and the Politics of Universality*, Cambridge: Cambridge University Press

2013, 'Laws of Encounter: A Jurisdictional Account of International Law', *London Review of International Law*, 1(1), 63–98

Pal, M. 2018 'My Capitalism Is Bigger than Yours! Against Combining "How the West Came to Rule" with "the Origins of Capitalism"', *Historical Materialism*, 26(3), 99–124

2019, 'Early Modern Extraterritoriality, Diplomacy and the Transition to Capitalism', in D. S. Margolies, U. Özsu, M. Pal, & N. Tzouvala (eds.), *The Extraterritoriality of Law: History, Theory, Politics*, Abingdon, UK: Routledge, 69–86

forthcoming, 'Historical Sociology in IR', in Keene Bukovansky & Reus-Smit Spanu (eds.), *The Oxford Handbook of History and International Relations*, Oxford: Oxford University Press

forthcoming, 'On the Methodological Limits of the Commodity Form Theory of Law in *The Corporation, Law and Capitalism*', *London Review of International Law*

Parfitt, R. 2019, *The Process of International Legal Reproduction: Inequality, Historiography, Resistance*, Cambridge: Cambridge University

Paris, R. 1957, *Histoire du commerce de Marseille, tome V: De 1660 à 1789. Le Levant*, Paris: Plon

Parker, D. 1989, 'Sovereignty, Absolutism, and the Function of the Law in Seventeenth Century France', *Past and Present*, 122 (Feb.), 30–74

1996, *Class and State in Ancien Régime France: The Road to Modernity?* London: Routledge

2003, 'Absolutism, Feudalism and Property Rights in the France of Louis XIV', *Past and Present*, 179 (May), 60–96

Parry, J. H. 1990 [1966], *The Spanish Seaborne Empire*, Berkeley: University of California Press

Pashukanis, E. 1978, *Law and Marxism: A General Theory*, London: Ink Links

2005, 'International Law' [entry in *Encyclopedia of State and Law*, 1925, Communist Academy] in C. Miéville, *Between Equal Rights: A Marxist Theory of International Law*, Leiden: Brill, 2005, 321–335

Pecquet, A. 1738, *De l'art de negocier avec les souverains*, Paris

Pennell, C. R. (ed.) 1989, *Piracy and Diplomacy in Seventeenth Century North Africa: The Journal of Thomas Baker. English Consul in Tripoli 1677–1685*, Rutherford, NJ: Fairleigh Dickinson University Press

2009, 'Treaty Law: The Extent of Consular Jurisdiction in North Africa from the Middle of the Seventeenth to the Middle of the Nineteenth Century', *Journal of North African Studies*, 14:2, 235–256

2010, 'The Origins of the Foreign Jurisdiction Act and the Extension of British Sovereignty', *Historical Research*, 83(221), 465–485

Péquignot, S. & Belissa, M. 2016, 'Thémis en diplomatie: regards croisés en guise de conclusion', in N. Drocourt & E. Schnakenbourg (eds.), *Thémis en diplomatie. Droits et arguments juridiques dans les relations internationales de l'Antiquité tardive à la fin du XVIIIe siècle*, Rennes: Presses Universitaires de Rennes, 303–313

Perelman, M. 2000, *The Invention of Capitalism: Political Economy and the Secret History of Primitive Accumulation*, Durham, NC: Duke University Press

Pettigrew, W. A. & Stein, T. 2017, 'The Public Rivalry between Regulated and Joint Stock Corporations and the Development of Seventeenth-Century Corporate Constitutions', *Historical Research*, 90(248), 341–362

Picavet, C. G. 1923, 'La carrière diplomatique en France au temps de Louis XIV (1661–1715)', *Revue d'histoire économique et sociale*, 11(3), 383–408

Pitts, J. 2017, 'International Relations and the Critical History of International Law', *International Relations*, 31(3), 282–298

2018, *Boundaries of the International: Law and Empire*, Cambridge, MA: Harvard University Press

Platt, D. C. M. 1971, *The Cinderella Service: British Consuls Since 1825*, London: Longmans

Post, C. 2002, 'Comments on the Brenner–Wood Exchange on the Low Countries', *Journal of Agrarian Change*, 2(1), 88–95

2011, *The American Road to Capitalism: Studies in Class Structure, Economic Development and Political Conflict 1620–1877*, Leiden: Brill

2015, 'The Separation of the "Economic" and the "Political" under Capitalism: "Capital-centric Marxism" and the Capitalist State', *Verso Books Blog*, www.versobooks.com/blogs/2345-charles-post-the-separation-of-the-economic-and-the-political-under-capitalism-capital-centric-marxism-and-the-capitalist-state [accessed 18 July 2020]

Poumarède, G. 2001, 'Naissance d'une institution royale: les consuls de la nation française en Levant et en Barbarie aux XVIe et XVIIe siècles', *Annuaire-bulletin de la société de l'histoire de France*, 65–128

2007, '"Ambassade" et "Ambassadeur" dans les dictionnaires français et italiens (XVIe–XIXe siècle)', *Mélanges de l'Ecole française de Rome. Italie et Méditerranée*, 119(1), 7–16

Pradells Nadal, J. 1992, *Diplomacía y comercio: La expansión consular española en el siglo XVIII*, Alicante: Universidad de Alicante

Premo, B. 2017, *The Enlightenment on Trial: Ordinary Litigants and Colonialism in the Spanish Empire*, New York: Oxford University Press

Premo, B. & Yanakakis, Y. 2019, 'A Court of Sticks and Branches: Indian Jurisdiction in Colonial Mexico and Beyond', *American Historical Review*, 124(1), 28–55

Putnam, T. 2016, *Courts without Borders: Law, Politics and U.S. Extraterritoriality*, Cambridge: Cambridge University Press

Rasulov, A. 2018, 'A Marxism for International Law: A New Agenda', *European Journal of International Law*, 29(2), 631–655

Raustiala, K. 2009, *Does the Constitution Follow the Flag? The Evolution of Territoriality in American Law*, Oxford: Oxford University Press

Rediker, M. 2019, 'Afterword: Reflections on the Motley Crew as Port City Proletariat', *International Review of Social History*, 64(27), 255–262

Renouvin, P. 1954, *Histoire des relations internationales* (4 vols.), Paris: Librairie Hachette

Reus-Smit, C. 2016, 'Theory, History, and Great Transformations', *International Theory*, 8(3), 422–435

Reynolds, J. 2017, *Empire, Emergency and International Law*, Cambridge: Cambridge University Press

Roberts, W. C. 2017, 'What Was Primitive Accumulation? Reconstructing the Origin of a Critical Concept', *European Journal of Political Theory*, https://journals.sagepub.com/doi/abs/10.1177/1474885117735961?journalCode=epta#articleCitationDownloadContainer [accessed 21 July 2020]

Ronalds, F. S. 1930, '*The Exterritoriality of Ambassadors in the Sixteenth and Seventeenth Centuries* by E. R. Adair [review]', *Journal of Modern History*, 2(1), 116–117

Roosen, W. 1973, 'The True Ambassador: Occupational and Personal Characteristics of French Ambassadors under Louis XIV', *European History Quarterly*, 3(2), 121–139

1976, *The Age of Louis XIV: The Rise of Modern Diplomacy*, Cambridge, MA: Schenkman

1980, 'Early Modern Diplomatic Ceremonial: A Systems Approach', *Journal of Modern History*, 52(3), 452–476

Roper, L. H. & Ruymbeke, B. V. (eds.) 2007, *Constructing Early Modern Empires: Proprietary Ventures in the Atlantic World, 1500–1750*, Leiden: Brill

Rosenberg, J. 1994, *The Empire of Civil Society: A Critique of the Realist Theory of International Relations*, London: Verso

2006, 'Why Is There No International Historical Sociology?' *European Journal of International Relations*, 2(3), 307–340

2013, 'The "Philosophical Premises" of Uneven and Combined Development', *Review of International Studies*, 39(3), 569–597

2016a, 'International Relations in the Prison of Political Science', *International Relations*, 30(2), 127–153

2016b, 'Uneven and Combined Development: "The International" in Theory and History', in A. Anievas & K. Matin (eds.), *Historical Sociology and World History: Uneven and Combined Development over the Longue Durée*, Lanham, MD: Rowman & Littlefield, 17–30

Rousseau de Chamoy, L. de 1697, *L'Idée du parfait ambassadeur*, ed. L. Delavaud, Paris, 1912

Ruggie, J. G. 1983, 'Continuity and Transformation in the World Polity: Toward a Neorealist Synthesis', *World Politics*, 35(2), 261–285

1993, 'Territoriality and Beyond: Problematizing Modernity in International Relations', *International Organization*, 47(1), 139–174

Rush, P. 1997, 'An Altered Jurisdiction: Corporeal Traces of Law', *Griffith Law Review*, 6, 144

Ruskola, T. 2013, *Legal Orientalism: China, the United States, and Modern Law*, Cambridge, MA: Harvard University Press

Ryngaert, C. 2015, *Jurisdiction in International Law*, 2nd ed., Oxford: Oxford University Press

Sabaratnam, M. 2011, 'IR in Dialogue ... But Can We Change the Subjects? A Typology of Decolonising Strategies for the Study of World Politics', *Millennium: Journal of International Studies*, 39(3) 781–803

Sahlins, P. 1991, *Boundaries: The Making of France and Spain in the Pyrenees* Berkeley: University of California Press

Salgado, P. 2020, 'Agency and Geopolitics: Brazilian Formal Independence and the Problem of Eurocentrism in International Historical Sociology', *Cambridge Review of International Affairs*, 33(3), 432–451

Sarraz du Franquesnay, J. de la, 1731, *Le Ministre Public dans les cours étrangères: Ses fonctions et ses prérogatives*, Paris: Etienne Ganeau

Saunders, L. 1994, 'The Motives, Pattern and Form of Anglo-Ottoman Diplomatic Relations, c. 1580–1661' (PhD thesis, University of Oxford)

Scarfi, J. P. 2017, *Hidden History of International Law in the Americas*, Oxford: Oxford University Press

Schick, S. 2018, *Des liaisons avantageuses: Ministres, liens de dépendance et diplomatie dans le saint-empire romain germanique*, Paris: Editions Sorbonne

de Schepper, H. 2007, 'The Individual on Trial in 16th Century Netherlands', in C. H. Parker & J. H. Bentley (eds.), *Between the Middles Ages and Modernity: Individual and Community in the Early-Modern World*, Lanham, MD: Rowman & Littlefield, 187–209

Schmidt, S. 2011, 'To Order the Minds of Scholars: The Discourse of the Peace of Westphalia in International Relations Literature', *International Studies Quarterly*, 55, 601–623

Schmitt, C. 2003, *The Nomos of the Earth in the International Law of the Jus Publicum Europaeum*, trans. G. L. Ulmen, New York: Telos Publishing Press

Schwarzenberger, G. 1962, *The Frontiers of International Law*, London: Stevens & Sons

Schweizer, K. W. & Schumann, M. J. 2008, 'The Revitalization of Diplomatic History: Renewed Reflections', *Diplomacy and Statecraft*, 19, 149–186

Schwöbel-Patel, C. 2012, 'Whither the Private in Global Governance?', *International Journal of Constitutional Law*, 10(4), 1106–1133

Scott, H. 2007, 'Diplomatic Culture in Old Regime Europe', in Scott, H. and Simms, B. (eds.), *Cultures of Power in Europe during the Long Eighteenth Century 1680s–1815*, Cambridge: Cambridge University Press, 58–85

2016, '"The Line of Descent of Nobles Is from the Blood of Kings": Reflections on Dynastic Identity', in L. Geevers & M. Marini (eds.), *Dynastic Identity in Early Modern Europe: Rulers, Aristocrats and the Formation of Identities*, London: Routledge, 217–241

Scully, E. P. 2001, *Bargaining with the State from Afar: American Treaty Citizenship in Treaty Port China, 1844–1942*, New York: Columbia University Press

Seed, P. 2001, *American Pentimiento: The Invention of Indians and the Pursuit of Riches*, Minneapolis: University of Minnesota Press

Seong-Hak Kim, M. 2007, 'Custom, Community, and the Crown: Lawyers and the Reordering of French Customary Law', in C. H. Parker & J. H. Bentley (eds.), *Between the Middles Ages and Modernity: Individual and Community in the Early-Modern World*, Lanham, MD: Rowman & Littlefield, 169–186

Sharpe, J. A. 2003 [1983], '"Such Disagreement betwyx Neighbours": Litigation and Human Relations in Early Modern England', in J. Bossy (ed.), *Disputes and Settlements: Law and Human Relations in the West*, Cambridge: Cambridge University Press, 167–188

Shaw, M. N. 2008, *International Law*, Cambridge: Cambridge University Press

Shilliam, R. 2009, *German Thought and International Relations: The Rise and Fall of a Liberal Project*, New York: Palgrave

2012, 'Forget English Freedom, Remember Atlantic Slavery: Common Law, Commercial Law, and the Significance of Slavery for Classical Political Economy', *New Political Economy*, 17(5), 591–609

Simpson, G. 2001, 'Two Liberalisms', *European Journal of International Law*, 12(3), 537–571

2004, *Great Powers and Outlaw States: Unequal Sovereigns in the International Legal Order*, Cambridge: Cambridge University Press

Skinner, Q. 1969, 'Meaning and Understanding in the History of Ideas', *History and Theory*, 8(1), 3–53

1978a, *The Foundations of Modern Political Thought, Vol. I: The Renaissance*, Cambridge: Cambridge University Press

1978b, *The Foundations of Modern Political Thought, Vol. II: The Age of Reformation*, Cambridge: Cambridge University Press

Skocpol, T. 1979, *States and Social Revolutions*, Cambridge: Cambridge University Press

Skocpol, T. (ed.) 1984, *Vision and Method in Historical Sociology*, Cambridge: Cambridge University Press

Smith, D. 1991, *The Rise of Historical Sociology*, Cambridge: Polity

Smits, J. M. 2003, 'Import and Export of Legal Models: The Dutch Experience', *Transnational Law Contemporary Problems*, 13(2), 551–574

Sowerby, T. A. & Hennings, J., 2017, *Practices of Diplomacy in the Early Modern World c. 1410–1800*, Abingdon, UK: Routledge

Stammers, N. 2009, *Human Rights and Social Movements*, London: Pluto

Steensgaard, N. 1967, 'Consuls and Nations in the Levant from 1570 to 1650', *Scandinavian Economic History Review*, 15(1–2), 13–55

1996, 'Consuls and Nations in the Levant from 1570 to 1650', in S. Subrahmanyam (ed.), *Merchant Networks in the Early Modern World, 1450–1800*, London: Routledge, 179–221

Stein, T. 2012, 'The Mediterranean in the English Empire of Trade, 1660–1748' (PhD thesis, Harvard University)

Stern, P. J. 2011, *The Company-State: Corporate Sovereignty and the Early Modern Foundations of the British Empire in India*, Oxford: Oxford University Press

2017, 'Limited Liabilities: The Corporation and the Political Economy of Protection in the British Empire', in L. Benton, A. Clulow, & B. Attwood (eds.), *Protection and Empire: A Global History*, Cambridge: Cambridge University Press, 93–113

Stern, S. J. 1982, *Peru's Indian Peoples and the Challenge of Spanish Conquest: Huamanga to 1640*, Madison, WI: University of Wisconsin Press

Stowell, E. C. 1930, '*The Exterritoriality of Ambassadors in the Sixteenth and Seventeenth Centuries* by E. R. Adair [review]', *American Journal of International Law*, 24(2), 413–414

Studnicki-Gizbert, D. 2007, *A Nation upon the Ocean Sea: Portugal's Atlantic Diaspora and the Crisis of the Spanish Empire, 1492–1640*, Oxford: Oxford University Press

Sugarman, D. (ed.) 1983, *Legality, Ideology and the State*, London: Academic Press

Sylvest, C. 2005, 'Continuity and Change in British Liberal Internationalism, c. 1900–1930', *Review of International Studies*, 31, 263–283

Szigeti, P. 2019, 'In the Middle of Nowhere: The Futile Quest to Distinguish Territoriality from Extraterritoriality', in D. S. Margolies, U. Özsu, M. Pal, & N. Tzouvala (eds.), *The Extraterritoriality of Law: History, Theory, Politics*, Abingdon, UK: Routledge, 30–48

Tait Slys, M. 2014, *Exporting Legality: The Rise and Fall of Extraterritorial Jurisdiction in the Ottoman Empire and China*, new ed. [online], Geneva: Graduate Institute Publications (generated 11 Sept. 2014), http://books.openedition.org/iheid/788 [accessed 28 October 2019]

Takeda, J. T. 2011, *Between Crown and Commerce: Marseille and the Early Modern Mediterranean*, Baltimore: John Hopkins University Press

Tallon, A. 2017, *La France et le concile de Trente (1518–1563)*, 2nd ed., Rome: Bibliothèque des Écoles française d'Athènes et de Rome

Taylor, O. 2019, *International Law and Revolution*, Abingdon, UK: Routledge

Teschke, B. 2003, *The Myth of 1648: Class, Geopolitics, and the Making of Modern International Relations*, London: Verso

2005, 'Bourgeois Revolution, State-Formation and the Absence of the International', *Historical Materialism*, 13(2), 3–26

2010, 'Revisiting the "War-Makes-States" Thesis: War, Taxation and Social Property Relations in Early Modern Europe', in Olaf Asbach and Peter Schroeder (eds.), *War, the State and International Law in Seventeenth Century Europe*, Aldershot: Ashgate, 35–62

2011a, 'Fatal Attraction: A critique of Carl Schmitt's international political and legal theory', *International Theory*, 3(2), 179–227

2011b, 'Decisions and Indecisions: Political and Intellectual Receptions of Carl Schmitt', *New Left Review*, 67 (Jan.–Feb.), 61–95

2017, 'IR Theory, Historical Materialism, and the False Promise of International Historical Sociology', *Spectrum: Journal of Global Studies*, 6(1), pp. 1–66

forthcoming, 'Reinterpreting the Peace of Utrecht and the Origins of the Balance of Power: A Historical Sociology of International Politics'

Teschke, B. & Lacher, H. 2007, 'The Many "Logics" of Capitalist Competition', *Cambridge Review of International Affairs*, 20(4), 565–80.

Tilley, L. Kumar, A. & Cowan, T. 2017, 'Introduction: Enclosures and discontents', *City*, 21(3–4), 420–427

Tilly, C. 1990, *Coercion, Capital, and European States, AD 990–1990*, Cambridge, MA: Blackwell

1993, *European Revolutions, 1492–1992*, Cambridge, MA: Blackwell

Tischer, A. 2008, 'Claude de Mesmes, Count d'Avaux (1595–1650): The Perfect Ambassador of the Early 17th Century', *International Negotiation*, 13(2), 197–209

Thompson, E. P. 1975, *Whigs and Hunters: The Origin of the Black Act*, New York: Pantheon

1978, *The Poverty of Theory, and Other Essays*, London: Merlin

Thomson, J. E. 1994, *Mercenaries, Pirates, and Sovereigns: State-Building and Extraterritorial Violence in Early Modern Europe*, Princeton, NJ: Princeton University Press

Thynne, F. 1652, *The perfect ambassadour treating of the antiquitie, priveledges, and behaviour of men belonging to that function* (London)

Tomlins, C. 2010, *Freedom Bound: Law, Labor and Civic Identity in colonizing English America 1580–1865*, Cambridge: Cambridge University Press

'Historicism and Materiality in Legal Theory', In Maksymilian Del Mar & Michael Lobban (eds.), *Law, Theory and History: New Essays on a Neglected Dialogue*, Oxford Hart Publishing, 57–83

Traverso, E. 2016, *Left-Wing Melancholia: Marxism, History, and Memory*, New York: Columbia University Press

Trivellato, F. 2009, *The Familiarity of Strangers: The Sephardic Diaspora, Livorno, and Cross-Cultural Trade in Early Modern Period*, New Haven, CT: Yale University Press

Tuck, R. 1999, *The Rights of War and Peace. Political Thought and the International Legal Order from Grotius to Kant*, Oxford: Oxford University Press

Turgeon, N. 2016, 'Revisiting Imperial China's Trajectory in the Context of the "Rise of the West". The Eurocentric Legacy in Historical Sociology' (PhD thesis, University of Sussex)

Tzouvala, N. 2020, *Capitalism as Civilisation: A History of International Law*, Cambridge: Cambridge University Press

Ulbert, J. 2006, 'Introduction: La fonction consulaire a l'epoque modern définition, état des connaissances et perspectives de recherche', in J. Ulbert & G. Le Bouëdec (eds.), *La fonction consulaire à l'époque moderne: L'affirmation d'une institution économique et politique (1500–1800)*, Rennes: Presses Universitaires de Rennes, 9–20

2016, 'L'histoire de la fonction consulaire jusqu'au début de la première guerre mondiale: une bibliographie', *Cahiers de la Méditerranée*, 93

2018, 'Les manuels consulaires français d'avant 1914 comme source des études consulaires', in A. Bartolomei, G. Calafat, M. Grenet, & J. Ulbert (eds.), *De l'utilité commerciale des consuls: L'institution consulaire et les marchands dans le monde méditerranéen (XVIIe–XXe siècle)*, Rome: Publications de l'École française de Rome, 117–140

2019, 'L'origine géographique des consuls français sous Louis XIV', *Cahiers de la Méditerranée*, 98, 11–27

forthcoming, 'Identifier pour contrôler. La monarchie française et ses ressortissants expatriés (XVIIe–XVIIIe siècle)', *Mélanges de la Casa de Velásquez*

Ulbert, J. & Le Bouëdec, G. (eds.) 2006, *La fonction consulaire à l'époque moderne: L'affirmation d'une institution économique et politique (1500–1800)*, Rennes: Presses Universitaires de Rennes

Vergerio, C. 2018, 'Context, Reception, and the Study of Great Thinkers in International Relations', *International Theory*, 11(1), 110–137

2019, 'System, Order, and International Law: The Early History of International Legal Thought from Machiavelli to Hegel, ed. Stefan Kadelbach, Thomas Kleinlein, & David Roth-Isigkeit', *Journal of the History of International Law/Revue d'histoire du droit international*, 21(2), 331–335

Vitalis, R. 2015, *White World Order, Black Power Politics*, Ithaca, NY: Cornell University Press

Vries, Jan de & van der Woude, A. 1997, *The First Modern Economy: Success, Failure, and Perseverance of the Dutch Economy, 1500–1815*, Cambridge: Cambridge University Press

Wallenius, T. 2019, 'The Case for a History of Global Legal Practices', *European Journal of International Relations*, 25(1), 108–130

Wallerstein, I. 1974, *The Modern World-System I: Capitalist Agriculture and the Origins of the European World-Economy in the Sixteenth Century*, New York: Academic Press

1997, 'Eurocentrism and Its Avatars: The Dilemmas of Social Science', *New Left Review*, I(226), 93–107

Warrington, R. 1983, 'Pashukanis and the Commodity Form Theory', in D. Sugarman (ed.), *Legality, Ideology and the State*, London: Academic Press, 43–67

Watkins, J. 2008, 'Toward a New Diplomatic History of Medieval and Early Modern Europe', *Journal of Medieval and Early Modern Studies*, 38(1), 1–14

Watson, A. 1982, *Diplomacy: The Dialogue between States*, London: Methuen

1995, 'From Legal Transplants to Legal Formants', *American Journal of Comparative Law*, 43(3), 469–476

Weber, M. 1949, *Methodology of the Social Sciences*, Glencoe, IL: Free Press

Weckmann, L. 1969, 'The Middle Ages in the Conquest of America', in Lewis Hanke (ed.), *History of Latin American Civilization, Volume 1 – The Colonial Experience*, London: Methuen

Werner, M. & Zimmermann, B. 2006, 'Beyond Comparison: *Histoire Croisée* and the Challenge of Reflexivity', *History and Theory*, 45(1), 30–50

Weststeijn, A. 2015, "Love Alone Is Not Enough': Treaties in Seventeenth-Century Dutch Colonial Expansion', in Saliha Belmessous (ed.) *Native Claims: Indigenous Law against Empire 1500–1920*, Oxford: Oxford University Press, 19–44

2017, 'Provincializing Grotius: International Law and Empire in a Seventeenth Century Malay Mirror', in M. Koskenniemi, W. Rech, & M. Jimenez Fonseca (eds.), *International Law and Empire: Historical Explorations*, Oxford: Oxford University Press, 21–56

Whittle, J. 2000, *The Development of Agrarian Capitalism: Land and Labour in Norfolk 1440–1580*, Oxford: Clarendon Press

Wicquefort, Abraham de 1681, *L'ambassadeur et ses fonctions*. The Hague: Chez Jean & Daniel Steucker

Wieacker, F. 1995, *A History of Private Law in Europe*, Oxford: Clarendon Press

Wight, M. 1977, *Systems of States*, Leicester: Leicester University Press

Windler, C. 2017a 'Afterword: From social status to sovereignty – practices of foreign relations from the Renaissance to the *Sattelzeit*', in T. A. Sowerby & J. Hennings (eds.), *Practices of Diplomacy in the Early Modern World c. 1410–1800*, Abingdon, UK: Routledge, 254–265

2017b, 'Towards the Empire of a "Civilizing Nation": The French Revolution and Its Impact on relations with the Ottoman Regencies in the Maghreb', in M. Koskenniemi, W. Rech, & M. Jimenez Fonseca (eds.), *International Law and Empire: Historical Explorations*, Oxford: Oxford University Press, 202–223

Wood, A. C. 1935, *A History of the Levant Company*, Oxford University Press

Wood, E. M. 1981, 'The Separation of the Economic and the Political in Capitalism', *New Left Review*, 127

1983, 'The State and Popular Sovereignty in French Political Thought: A Genealogy of Rousseau's "General Will"', *History of Political Thought*, 4(2), 281–315

1992 [2015], *A Pristine Culture of Capitalism*, London: Verso

1995, *Democracy against Capitalism: Renewing Historical Materialism*, Cambridge: Cambridge University Press

2001, 'Eurocentric Anti-Eurocentrism', *Against the Current*, 92 (May–June), https://solidarity-us.org/atc/92/p993 [accessed 28 October 2019]

2002a, *The Origin of Capitalism: A Longer View*, London: Verso

2002b, 'The Question of Market Dependence', *Journal of Agrarian Change*, 2(1), 50–87

2003, *Empire of Capital*, London: Verso

2008, *Citizens to Lords: A Social History of Western Political Thought from Antiquity to the Middle Ages*, London: Verso

2012, *Liberty and Property: A Social History of Western Political Thought from Renaissance to Enlightenment*, London: Verso

2016, 'Britain versus France: How Many *Sonderwegs*?', *Historical Materialism*, 24(1), 11–29

Wood, E. M. & Wood, N. 1997, *A Trumpet of Sedition: Political Theory and the Rise of Capitalism 1509–1688*, London: Pluto Press

Wright Mills, C. 1959, *The Sociological Imagination*, Oxford: Oxford University Press

Yannakakis, Y. 2013, 'Indigenous People and Legal Culture in Spanish America', *History Compass* 11(11), 931–947

Zourek, J. 1957, 'Histoire des relations consulaires', *Revue de droit international pour le Moyen-Orient*, 6, 194

INDEX

Note: for reasons of clarity and ease of reference, terms relating to Castile, Iberia, Hispanics, etc. are indexed under 'Spain' or 'Spanish' accordingly.

CPSIA information can be obtained
at www.ICGtesting.com
Printed in the USA
LVHW081154281120
672906LV00007B/148

9 781108 497206